D0907268

Democracy under Blair

"Democracy under Blair"

A Democratic Audit of the United Kingdom

WITHDRAWN

Written and edited by

David Beetham, Iain Byrne, Pauline Ngan and Stuart Weir

With

Anthony Barker, Steven Barnett, Sarah Bracking, Ruth Brander, Tufyal Choudhury, Robin Clarke, Darren Darcey, Judith De Bueno Mesquita, Alison Gerry, Brigid Hadfield, Graham Hobbs, Ben Jackson, Iain Kearton, Christopher Lord, Joni Lovenduski, Helen Margetts, Colin Mellors, Gay Moon, Anisa Niaz, Richard Norton-Taylor, Ellie Palmer, Roisin Pillay, Madeleine Shaw, Chris Skelcher, Robin Wilson and Mitchell Woolf

Politico's
PUBLISHING

In assocation with Democratic Audit, Human Rights Centre, University of Essex

MAY   2003   DELTA COLLEGE LIBRARY

JN 231 .D45 2002

Democracy under Blair

First published in Great Britain 2002
by Politico's Publishing
8 Artillery Row
London
SW1P 1RZ
www.politicos.co.uk/publishing

Coypright © Democratic Audit 2002

Cover design by Tony Garrett

A catalogue record of this book is available from the British Library

ISBN 1 84275 011 9

WITHDRAWN

All rights reserved. No part of this publication may be reproduced or transmitted in any form or by any means, electronic or mechanical including photocopying, recording, or any information storage or retrieval system, without the prior permission in writing from the publishers.

This book is sold subject to the condition that it shall not by way of trade or otherwise be lent, resold, hired out, or otherwise circulated without the publisher's prior consent in writing in any form of binding or cover other than that in which it is published and without a similar condition including this condition being imposed on the subsequent publisher.

Contents

Section 1. Citizenship, law and rights

Section 2. Representative and accountable government

Acknowledgements

As we say in the introduction, this Democratic Audit of the United Kingdom is very much a collaborative affair. We have researched and written most of this book, but we could not have carried out the whole audit without the important contributions that various people have made, writing and often revising first drafts of sections or answers to particular criteria; giving advice; and reading and checking sections. We have ourselves however revised and edited every draft and it is we, not the contributors we list below, who should be held responsible for the finished product. But their initial drafts are vital to the overall quality we have sought to achieve in the Audit.

Contributors who wrote drafts are as follows:

Nationhood	Nationhood, citizenship and cultural difference – *Gay Moon and Anisa Niaz;* Constitutional arrangements – *Brigid Hadfield*
Rule of law	*Ruth Brander and Roisin Pillay*
Civil and political rights	*Alison Gerry and Mitchell Woolf*
Economic and social rights	Statistical data on poverty and benefits – *Graham Hobbs*
	Judicial review – *Ellie Palmer*
Free and fair elections	Electoral process and choice – *Helen Margetts*
	Voting procedures and turnout – *Ben Jackson*
	Composition of the House of Commons – *Colin Mellors and Darren Darcey*
Political parties	*Ben Jackson*
The police and security forces	*Richard Norton-Taylor*
The media	*Steven Barnett*
Political participation	Statistical information – *Iain Kearton*
Responsive government	Official consultation – *Robin Clarke*
	Public inquiries and general – *Tony Barker*
Decentralisation	Local government – *Chris Skelcher*
	English Regions – *Stephen Marks*
The international dimension	*Sarah Bracking*
	Asylum – *Madeleine Shaw*

We must also thank Christopher Lord and Tufyal Choudhury for outstanding contributions that have been integrated into the text over several sections. Christopher Lord wrote an analysis of the accountability of links between the European Union and the UK. Tufyal Choudhury provided an overall essay on racial equality, discrimination and anti-discrimination laws.

We have also benefited a great deal from advice on sections in the draft stage. Tony Barker has cast a scrupulous eye over most of the audit (as well as making a direct contribution to Section 12). Joni Lovenduski advised us on Sections 5 and 6 as well as on gender issues. Andrew Puddephatt advised us on Sections 1 to 4. Ann Dummett commented on citizenship issues; Paul Hunt and Judith De Bueno Mesquita checked out Section 4; Robin Wilson responded to endless queries on devolution and policing in Northern Ireland; Brigid Hadfield read Section 13 with great care and Jo Dungey steered us through the intricacies of the government's local government reforms. Rosie Campbell, Ben Jackson and Iain Kearton took on specific research tasks.

We have benefited greatly from co-operation with JUSTICE on issues of citizenship, the rule of law and asylum. We owe special thanks to Jonathan Cooper, the assistant director, for organising the contributions of JUSTICE staff (who are all directly acknowledged above). We should also thank Professor Paul Hunt, director of the Human Rights Centre, University of Essex, our parent organisation, for his continued support and encouragement; the Trustees of the Joseph Rowntree Charitable Trust, for their past sponsorship that allowed the Democratic Audit to grow; the staff of the Centre for Democratisation Studies, University of Leeds, and of International IDEA, Stockholm, for their work in expanding the democratic framework on which this audit is based; and Hazel Atherton and Anne Slowgrove, who made this book and much more possible.

Acronyms and abbreviations

AEEU – Amalgamated Engineering and Electrical Union

AMS – Additional Member System (a proportional electoral system)

AV – Alternative Vote (a disproportional electoral system)

BBC – The British Broadcasting Corporation

BNP – British National Party

BSC – Broadcasting Standards Commission

CAB – Citizen's Advice Bureau

CBI – Confederation of British Industry

CDU – Christian Democratic Party (Germany)

CERD – UN Convention for the Elimination of Racial Discrimination

CEDAW – UN Convention for the Elimination of Discrimination Against Women

CFSP – EU Common Foreign and Security Policy

CHCs – Community Health Councils

Cm – Parliamentary Command Paper

Cmnd – Parliamentary Command Paper

COI – Central Office of Information

COSAC – Conference on the European Affairs Committee

CPF – Conservative Policy Forum

CPS – Crown Prosecution Service

CRC – UN Convention on the Rights of the Child

CRE – Commission for Racial Equality

DIS – Defence Intelligence Service

DOH – Department of Health

DTI – Department of Trade and Industry

DUP – Democratic Unionist Party

DV – Deviation from proportionality

EAC – European Affairs Committee (in the House of Commons)

ECHR – European Convention on Human Rights

ECHR – European Court of Human Rights

ECJ – European Court of Justice

ELDR – European Liberal and Democratic Reform Group

EOC – Equal Opportunities Commission

EPP – European Peoples Party

FETO – Fair Employment and Treatment Order

FOI – Freedom of Information
FPTP – First Past The Post (electoral system used for Westminster elections)
FRU – Free Representation Unit
GCHQ – Government Communications Headquarters (the secret surveillance agency)
GEC – General Electrics Company (now Marconi)
GIS – Government Information Service
GLA – Greater London Assembly
GRECO – Groupes d'Etats contre la corruption (anti-corruption consortium)
HC Deb – House of Commons Debate
HC Deb, WA – House of Commons Debate, written answer
HL Deb – House of Lords Debate
ICESCR – UN International Covenant on Economic, Social and Cultural Rights
ICM – A UK polling organisation
IDEA – The International Institute for Democracy and Electoral Assistance, Stockholm
ILO – International Labour Organisation
INLA – Irish National Liberation Army
IPCC – Independent Police Complaints Commission
IPPR – Institute for Public Policy Research
IRA – Irish Republican Army
ITA – Independent Television Authority
ITC – Independent Television Commission
ITN – Independent Television News
ITV – Independent Television
IVS – International Voluntary Service
JHA – Justice and Home Affairs (an EU pillar)
JMC – Joint Ministerial Committee
JP – Justice of the Peace
LCD – Lord Chancellor's Department
LGA – Local Government Association
LVF – Loyalist Volunteer Force
MI5 – The domestic security service
MI6 – The foreign security service
MIG – Minimum Income Guarantee
MIND – The mental health charity
MLA – Member of Legislative Assembly (NI)
MMP – Multi-member proportional (another name for AMS)
MOD – Ministry of Defence
MORI – A UK polling organisation
NDPB – Non-Departmental Public Body (or quango)
NCVB – National Coalition for Black Volunteering
NEC – National Executive Committee (of the Labour Party)
NI – Northern Ireland

NICE – National Institute for Clinical Excellence
OECD – Organisation for Economic Co-operation and Development
NOP – A UK polling organisation
OXFAM – Oxford Committee for Famine Relief
PASC – Public Administration Select Committee
PBS – Public Broadcasting Service (US)
PCA – Parliamentary Commissioner for Administration (the Ombudsman)
PCA – Police Complaints Authority
PCC – Press Complaints Commission
PES – Party of European Socialists
PFI – Private Finance Initiative
PIIC – Public Interest Immunity Certificate
PLP – Parliamentary Labour Party
PPB – Party Political Broadcast
PR – Proportional Representation
PSAs – Public Service Agreements
PTAs – Prevention of Terrorism Acts
QC – Queen's Counsel
QMV – Qualified Majority Voting
RIPA – Regulation of Investigatory Powers Act 2000
RDAs – Regional Development Agencies
RUC – Royal Ulster Constabulary
SAS – Special Air Service
SDA – Sexual Discrimination Act 1975
SDLP – Social Democratic and Labour Party
SEN – Special Education Needs
SEU – Social Exclusion Unit
SIS – Secret Intelligence Service
SNP – Scottish National Party
STV – Single Transferable Vote (a proportional voting system)
SV – Supplementary Vote (a disproportional voting system)
TUC – Trades Union Congress
UNICEF – United Nations Children's Fund
UDA – Ulster Defence Association
UN – United Nations
UUP – Ulster Unionist Party

Introduction

Why audit democracy in the UK?

This is the second 'audit' of the state of democracy in the UK by Democratic Audit, a research body attached to the Human Rights Centre, at the University of Essex. The first was conducted in the mid-1990s at the end of the long period of Conservative rule and was published in two parts.[1] This audit assesses the condition of democracy and human rights in the country after five years of government under Tony Blair.

Obviously, much has changed. We now have a Bill of Rights, devolved government for Scotland and Wales, a partial settlement in Northern Ireland, a freedom of information law, a half-reformed House of Lords, other reforms to Parliament and much else. Labour's programme of constitutional reform has sought to address many of the democratic deficiencies highlighted by our first audit. At the same time other deficiencies, such as the dominance of the executive over Parliament, the unaccountable 'quango state', and the decline in voter turnout, have persisted if not intensified. More visible business influence in government, the prevalence of money politics, cronyism and allegations of 'cash for favours' seem to have further reduced public confidence in government and the political class. The events of 11 September have encouraged government to increase the powers of the security forces and police to encroach on liberties and intensify official surveillance of the public. The government response to the obvious dangers which ministers must confront calls into question their commitment to international law and their own Human Rights Act. The aim of this volume is to assess the impact of reform, change and continuity on our public life since 1997 from a democratic perspective.

Why conduct such an audit at all? After all, political and specialist writers have already covered a number of the issues that we address in this book. The media devote unprecedented attention to the political process. But they do not necessarily do so from the standpoint of democratic values, nor do their findings and views harden into a systematic overview of the country's democratic condition. The purpose of this democratic audit is to fill the gap – to give the public a systematic assessment of democracy in the UK, of its strengths and weaknesses, so that people can get a clear sense of how we stand at the start of the new century. How justified is the sense of democratic malaise referred to by many commentators? Which aspects of our public life should give us most concern from a democratic point of view? How do we rate in comparison with our European partners? These are the kinds of question we seek to answer in this book. In making our assessment, we look backwards, to identify and evaluate what has changed since our first audit; we also look to standards of best practice internationally against which to measure ourselves.

As in our first two-part audit, our starting point is with the key democratic principles of popular control and political equality: that is, that ultimately the people should control our political decision-makers and the decisions they take; and that we should all be equal in the exercise of that control and in our citizenship rights more generally. These principles are realised through 'contributing values', such as accountability, equality, representation, participation, and so on. The mere existence of political institutions – regular elections, parliamentary government, the judiciary, local councils, and so on – does not in itself deliver democracy. How democratic these institutions are in practice – and how democratic is the whole of which they are a part – depends on how effectively they realise these principles and values. For example, Parliament may or may not be properly representative of people's votes or of the currents of popular opinion. It may or may not reflect the social composition of the public. It may or may not make government accountable and subject it to effective scrutiny.

The auditing framework

In some key respects, however, this audit differs from the previous one. The first two volumes dug a narrower trench more deeply. This book covers a wider range of aspects of democratic life, and uses a much more comprehensive assessment framework. The new framework was developed in partnership with an international panel of experts and is being and has been used by in-country teams of assessors in such countries as Australia, Bangladesh, Canada, Italy, Kenya, New Zealand, Peru, South Africa and South Korea. It can thus be said to have achieved a measure of international credibility.[2]

The expanded framework comprises 14 sections covering every aspect of democracy. Each section contains a list of questions that the audit aims to answer. All of these questions are phrased comparatively (how much? how far? to what extent? etc.) to reflect the view that democracy is a matter of degree, not an all-or-nothing affair. The sections are grouped in turn into four main blocks. These begin with the citizen and his or her rights, move on to the institutions of decision-making, representation and accountability, consider the contribution of civil society to the realisation of democratic values, and conclude with the external profile of the country from a democratic perspective. An overview of the framework is given in the accompanying table, to show how the audit has been structured. At the end of the audit we have summarised the findings of each section for easy reference.

1. The framework for assessing democracy

I. Citizenship, Law and Rights	II. Representative and Accountable Government	III. Civil Society and Popular Participation	IV. Democracy Beyond the State
1.0 Nationhood and citizenship Is there public agreement on a common citizenship without discrimination?	*5.0 Free and fair elections* Do elections give the people control over governments and their policies?	*10.0 The media in a democratic society* Do the media operate in a way that sustains democratic values?	*14.0 International dimensions of democracy* Are the country's external relations conducted in accordance with democratic norms, and is it itself free from external subordination?
2.0. The rule of law and access to justice Are state and society consistently subject to the law?	*6.0 Democratic role of political parties* Does the party system assist the working of democracy?	*11.0 Political participation* Is there full citizen participation in public life?	
3.0 Civil and political rights Are civil and political rights equally guaranteed for all?	*7.0 Government effectiveness and accountability* Is government accountable to the people and their representatives?	*12.0 Government responsiveness* Is government responsive to the concerns of its citizens?	
4.0 Economic and social rights Are economic and social rights equally guaranteed for all?	*8.0 Civil control of the military and police* Are the military and police forces under civil control?	*13.0 Decentralisation* Are decisions taken at the lowest practicable level of government for the people most affected?	
	9.0 Minimising corruption Are elected representatives and public officials free from corruption?		

Many of these sections cover ground in common with the first UK audit. If they did not, it would be impossible to use the first audit as a benchmark against which to assess the changes introduced under New Labour. Three additional sections, however, deserve particular mention. The first (Section 4) covers economic and social rights. The underlying rationale from a democratic perspective is that people cannot exercise their civil and democratic rights and opportunities effectively in practice without economic and social security; and that ordinary people tend to judge the quality of a country's democracy by its ability to secure them the basic economic and social rights on which a decent life depends.

A second new section (Section 9) examines the extent of corruption in the UK. There is considerable complacency within the British political class about the comparative absence of corruption in public life. But it is vital for every society to examine its politics for the cancers of corruption and to take instant remedial action. Finally, Section 14 covers the international dimensions of the country's democracy. The rationale here is not only to identify the extent to which domestic decision-making is limited or compromised by bodies external to the state, but also to assess how consistently a country supports democracy and human rights abroad.

Two of these new sections have a particular relevance to the UK. The recognition that the principle of equal citizenship is compromised by gross economic and social inequalities underlies the Labour government's programme to combat 'social exclusion'. Moreover, analysis of economic and social rights in the UK gives us an accurate picture of the impact of discriminations and disadvantage in British society at its rawest. We have devoted particular attention to policies on social exclusion, therefore, and to an assessment of the conditions to which they are a response. This constitutes the first systematic assessment of economic and social rights in the UK, measured against international standards. A fuller version of this section of the audit is to be published separately. At the international level, we have used Labour's own claims to an 'ethical dimension' in its foreign policy to assess Britain's contribution to supporting democracy and human rights abroad. At the same time we recognise that much of the legislation affecting the lives of UK citizens takes place beyond our borders at the European level. We examine the contribution that EU law-making has made to human rights in the UK as well as how far the links between the UK government and the EU are democratically accountable.

A systematic audit of so many aspects of public life in the UK could only have been achieved with the collaboration of contributors with a wide range of expertise, including law, human rights, electoral and regional politics, the core executive and its relations with Parliament, the gender, racial and ethnic dimensions of public life, and so on. These contributions are all acknowledged on pages vii and viii. So far as has proved possible, we have attempted to keep the whole audit up-to-date, but the cut-off points for each section necessarily vary. In addition, the audit has built on a number of earlier specialist studies undertaken by Democratic Audit.

Findings and conclusions

In the last analysis, conducting a democratic audit or assessment is a matter of making judgments – judgments about how far public life measures up to given standards of democracy in its various aspects. There is an intricate mesh of such judgments through every section of the audit. But at the end of the book we have collected a series of the most significant judgments in the Findings section; and have then gone on to reach a final set of judgments and recommendations in the Conclusions section. In a sense, these two sections perform the role of an executive summary.

By taking principled democratic criteria as our measuring rods, we are obviously setting high standards. We acknowledge that in practice governments do fall short of such standards, often in their search for popular backing. But we could not fulfil our purpose if we compromised those standards. We have however made our judgments transparent so that they can be challenged at a number of levels: for their selection and interpretation of facts; for their definition of what counts as a good or adequate level of attainment; for their basic understanding of democracy and how it can be realistically realised in practice. We hope we have avoided the most obvious errors and biases by exposing the audit in draft stage to the critical eye of commentators of different persuasions, and by discussing it with a seminar of experts drawn from abroad as well as the UK. We have also taken care to identify strengths as well as weaknesses in the UK's democratic life, since the quality of democracy in the UK is relatively high. Where our judgments remain controversial, we hope we have taken good care to explain the basis on which they have been made, and to identify the evidence on which we have relied.[3]

Finally, we have undertaken this audit in the belief that the quality of a country's democracy matters to its people. It matters that people should have the opportunity and resources to shape the conditions of their collective life at its various levels; that governments should be responsive to their needs and concerns, and that its decision-making should be open and effective; that public life should be inclusive of the different communities, identities and opinions in the country; that public officials should be clearly accountable; that people should be able to maintain trust in their representatives and their fellow citizens. All these are part of what we mean by 'democracy'. However much we may choose to live our lives privately, the character of the public sphere inevitably shapes the conditions under which our private lives are conducted. It is this character that the present audit seeks to assess.

Notes

1   The first, *The Three Pillars of Liberty*, analysed citizens' civil and political rights (Klug, Starmer and Weir, Routledge, 1996); the second, *Political Power and Democratic Control in Britain*, dealt with the central institutions of government (Weir and Beetham, Routledge, 1999).

2   The International Institute for Democracy and Electoral Assistance (IDEA), Stockholm, sponsored the expansion of the audit framework. Under the auspices of IDEA, the Centre for Democratisation Studies, University of Leeds, and Democratic Audit worked with in-country partners in eight nations to test the audit framework in practice. IDEA has promoted a handbook on democracy assessment, which explains our methodology so that it can be used by anyone interested (Beetham, Bracking, Kearton and Weir, Kluwer Law International, 2002). A comparative volume of country assessments and findings is to be published shortly (Beetham, Bracking, Kearton, Vittal and Weir (eds)., Kluwer Law International, 2002). Assessment teams in Australia, Austria, Canada and South Africa have carried out or are working on democratic audits independently of IDEA. We see the present democratic audit of the UK as an addition to this global enterprise, as well as being addressed to concerned citizens of the UK itself.

3   For various sections, we have been obliged to present a condensed version of the evidence drawn from a greater body of original research. In such cases, this information will be published on the Democratic Audit website., http://democraticaudit.essex.ac.uk

Section one: citizenship, law and rights

One: Nationhood and citizenship

Civis Britannicus sum

Is there public agreement on a common citizenship without discrimination?

It would presumably be politically impossible to legislate for a colour bar, and my legislation would have to be non-discriminatory in form. On the other hand, we do not wish to keep out immigrants of good type from the old Dominions.
Sir Alec Douglas Home, former Prime Minister, 1955

Introduction

Democracy as rule of the people pre-supposes agreement on who constitutes 'the people'. Such agreement must necessarily distinguish between those who enjoy the rights of citizenship and aliens. For the most part this distinction is made on the basis of the borders of the state in which people live and agreement on those borders.

The basic decisions on citizenship, then, necessarily have an externally exclusive dimension. At the same time, democratic principles require that citizenship should be internally inclusive, in the sense that there is mutual respect between the different communities or identities that make up the nation, and that all citizens enjoy effective equal rights under the law. How a country manages the potential tensions between the requirements of equal citizenship and the distinctiveness of its different communities, and between internal inclusiveness and external exclusivity, is an important indicator of the quality of its democracy. This is especially so in its immigration procedures, rules governing asylum and the processes for acquiring citizenship – all of which are issues of intense public debate in the UK and western Europe as a whole. Also of democratic significance are a country's procedures for resolving disagreement about the state borders and its constitutional arrangements, and how inclusive these are.

1.1. How inclusive is the political nation and state citizenship of all who live within the United Kingdom?

The UK does not have a fully written constitution, as most other countries have, nor a clear statement of the rights and duties of citizenship. Even the most basic right of citizenship – the right to reside in the country and to leave and return to it without restriction – is subject to laws of considerable complexity, which have long been racially discriminatory both in their intention and in their day to day operation. Thus the British Nationality Act of 1948, which created a category of citizens of the UK and colonies, with equal rights of abode in the UK, was amended by successive immigration acts from 1962 onwards to limit immigration from former colonies in Africa, Asia and the West Indies, while allowing it as of right to citizens of any Commonwealth country who could show British descent. These so-called 'patrials' were almost exclusively white.

The concept of 'patriality' was dropped in the British Nationality Act 1981, but the Act's definition of British citizenship with the right of abode in the UK maintained the racially discriminatory character of previous immigration acts by distinguishing between those born abroad to British parents and others. The Act also created a number of categories of British 'nationals' who have no right of entry to the UK, some of whom have been rendered de facto stateless (though this anomaly was removed for residents of dependent territories in May 2002). The position is further complicated by European legislation which gives citizens of any EU country the right to enter and remain in the UK, and to seek work here.

The cumulative effect of this legislation, and the key link it makes between citizenship and immigration status, has been to reinforce the view that immigration from the New Commonwealth is undesirable, with significant consequences for equality of respect between communities within the UK. It is particularly immigrants from the New Commonwealth who are liable to forcible deportation without appeal, regardless of their circumstances, if they cannot prove that their continued residence is lawful.

Naturalisation
British citizenship can be acquired either through parentage (if one parent is a British citizen or legally 'settled' in the UK), or through naturalisation. People who have been resident in the UK for at least five years may be naturalised at the discretion of the Home Office. They must be 'of good character', and have a sufficient knowledge of English, Welsh or Scottish Gaelic. Those born in the UK to parents whose immigration status may be limited or uncertain, and who therefore do not count as 'settled', may end up stateless. British citizenship confers no right for spouses or other family members from abroad to join the citizen in the UK, and requests to do so are disproportionately denied to black and Asian

applicants, who have greater difficulty in proving that their family members can be supported in the UK without resort to public funds. Citizens of other EU countries resident in the UK, in contrast, enjoy an automatic right of family reunion under EU law. Spouses of British citizens who have joined them from abroad have no automatic right to British citizenship themselves, however long they may have lived here. Like all applicants for naturalisation, they are subject to tests and Home Office discretion, from which there is no right of appeal. Under the current Nationality, Immigration and Asylum Bill, applicants for naturalisation will now be required to 'demonstrate sufficient knowledge about life in the UK' as well as proficiency in a UK language (see Section 14.4 for fuller analysis).

Citizenship rights

Apart from the right to residence and unrestricted return from abroad, British citizenship confers few other rights that are unconditional or exclusive to British citizens. Any citizen of a Commonwealth country or the Republic of Ireland who is resident in the UK, for whatever reason, can vote in all types of election; EU citizens resident here can vote in Euro- and local elections; other aliens have no voting rights however long they may have resided in the country. On the other hand, long-standing denials of the right to vote to British citizens who are homeless or travellers, or resident in hospital suffering from a mental disorder, have been rectified by the Representation of the People Act 2000. But most convicted prisoners are still denied the vote while they are in prison.

European Union citizenship

Under the EU Amsterdam treaty which came into force in 1999 everyone who holds UK nationality is a citizen of the European Union. Nationality is defined according to UK laws. Citizenship of the Union is complementary to national citizenship and comprises a number of rights and duties in addition to those stemming from UK citizenship. For all citizens of the Union, citizenship implies the following rights:

- to move and reside freely within the territory of member states;
- to vote and to stand as a candidate in elections to the European Parliament and in municipal elections in the member state in which they reside, under the same conditions as nationals of that state;
- to diplomatic protection in the territory of a third country (non-EU state) by the diplomatic or consular authorities of another member state, if their own country does not have diplomatic representation there; and
- to petition the European Parliament and to apply to the European Parliament's Ombudsman about maladministration by EU institutions or bodies (with the exception of the Court of Justice and the Court of First Instance).

1.2. How far are ethnic, cultural, gender and other differences recognised, and how well are disadvantaged minorities protected?

There is increasing recognition of ethnic, cultural and other differences in an obviously diverse society in which one in 15 people regard themselves as 'non-white'. Women and members of all kinds of minorities – for example, young Asian men and gay pride activists – increasingly demand equality both in law and practice. The Commission for Racial Equality (CRE) is the chief agency for achieving race equality and acting against racial discrimination; the Equal Opportunities Commission performs the same role for women and the Disability Rights Commission for people with disabilities. The government now proposes to establish an Equality Commission that will combine the three existing bodies. Lobbying organisations want the government to cement the new Commission's future by linking its creation to a new general equality right and the extension of the new duty on public bodies to promote racial equality (see below) to across-the board protection for all minorities and promotion of their rights..

Racism and racial and other discriminations persist in British society and we examine their prevalence in the following sections of Section1. Here, we briefly note that riots and disturbances, principally involving young white and Asian men, in various north English cities after the 2001 election, gave a dramatic warning of the racial divisions in British society and the depths of feeling within the various communities involved. In the election itself, the British National Party fought only 34 seats, but ignited heated racial conflagration and won significant votes in the two Oldham seats. In the local elections in May 2002, the BNP won three seats in Burnley.

It is notoriously difficult to measure racism and discrimination. Discrimination can be overt and open but it is also often covert and subtle; it can be both intentional and unintentional. Formal complaints of racial discrimination are minute compared to the evidence of the extent of discrimination (Hepple et al, 2000; Sanders 1998). The disproportionately high levels of economic and social exclusion, low work status and levels of unemployment, linked to race and ethnic origin (see Section 4), are not of themselves evidence of the levels of discrimination in British society. But in the absence of other explanations for such levels of disadvantage they provide a *prima facie* indication of the presence of pervasive discrimination.

The Runnymede Trust Commission on the Future of Multi-Ethnic Britain (chaired by Professor Bhikhu Parekh) explored extensive evidence of discrimination in several areas, including employment, criminal justice and policing, health and welfare, education, the arts, media and sport (the Parekh report, 2000). Other reports have also highlighted the persistence of racial discrimination in the health service and the Crown Prosecution Service (*Guardian*, 19 June 2001).

Anti-discrimination laws

Governments have passed laws against discrimination of various kinds since the mid-1970s with the aim of promoting a 'human rights culture' of respect for the dignity and values of the diversity of people in the United Kingdom. However, the legal reality in England, Scotland and Wales is that these laws protect only racial and ethnic differences; cultural and religious differences are partially protected only where they intersect with people's racial origins. In Northern Ireland, fair employment legislation offers protection against discrimination on the basis of religion or political opinion. There is thus no general principle of non-discrimination in the UK. The common law guarantees equality before the law in the sense that no one is exempt from the law. This principle, while important, does not provide protection against discrimination that is not prohibited by specific anti-discrimination laws. Outside those areas to which anti-discrimination legislation applies, discrimination is perfectly lawful. The key criticisms are that the present legislative regime is fragmented and inconsistent, and that it focuses on a negative prohibition on discrimination rather than a positive duty to promote equality.

The Race Relations Act 1976

The Race Relations Act 1976 put in place legal protection against discrimination in employment, education and the provision of goods, facilities and services. The act protects against:

Direct discrimination less favourable treatment on 'racial grounds' (defined as colour, race, nationality or ethnic or national origins) and;

Indirect discrimination when a detrimental requirement is applied in any of these areas that means that far fewer people of any one racial group can comply with it than the proportion of people of another racial group; and the requirement cannot be justified irrespective of the colour, race, nationality or ethnic or national origins of any person to whom it is applied. There is no protection against discrimination based on a preference only.

The Act also protects people who bring proceedings, or give evidence, under its provisions from being victimised or deterred by 'less favourable treatment' as a result. But the Act does not give protection against direct discrimination on cultural and/or religious grounds if it is not also on racial or ethnic grounds (Mandla v Dowell Lee, 1983). To be protected, people must belong to an ethnic group that is regarded as a distinct community with a long shared history, and cultural tradition of its own. Additionally it may have a common: geographical origin, or descent from common ancestors; language; religion, or have a sense of being a minority or being an oppressed group within a larger community.

Through a series of cases, the courts have decided that Jews, Sikhs and gypsies qualify as ethnic groups, but not Rastafarians or Muslims (though Muslims have been able to seek protection against indirect race discrimination under the Act if they come from the Indian subcontinent).

Legislatives changes since 1997

The official inquiry into the murder of the black teenager Stephen Lawrence inspired a major advance in seeking to eliminate racial discrimination. The inquiry report recommended that public authorities should be made subject to the obligations of the 1976 Act in respect of all their functions (the Macpherson report, 1999). Jack Straw, then Home Secretary, grasped this issue at once and introduced the Race Relations (Amendment) Act 2000. Initially the intention was to extend the 1976 Act only to direct discrimination, but pressure from MPs and race and civil liberties groups ensured that the amending Act also outlawed indirect discrimination. It is worth noting however that this deficiency still remains in sex discrimination law.

The 2000 Amendment Act introduced a general duty on specified public authorities to 'have due regard to the need to eliminate unlawful racial discrimination and to promote equality of opportunity and good relations between persons of different racial groups when performing their functions.' The intention is to extend protection against race discrimination in the public sphere and to prevent official discrimination before it occurs. With the notorious exception of immigration and asylum, virtually all public services are involved – from primary schooling and housing allocation to the courts and prisons. The Act limits the circumstances in which the grounds of 'safeguarding national security' can be used to justify discrimination; and also creates a new duty on specified public authorities to take action to eliminate racism. Chief police officers are now liable for the discriminatory acts of officers under their control. Complaints of race discrimination in education may now be brought in the county courts (in England) or the sheriff courts (in Scotland), without having to be referred to the Secretary of State for Education. Complaints of race discrimination in some immigration decisions may be heard as part of the immigration appeal.

In March 2000 the government required all public bodies to publish race equality plans by May, monitor their recruitment and promotion policies, and measure the impact of their services on the communities they serve. In effect, public authorities are now obliged to eliminate unlawful discrimination, and promote equality of opportunity and good race relations. They also have to consider the race relations implications for every decision that they make. The Commission for Racial Equality has back-up powers to drive this major exercise forward and can impose compliance orders on failing authorities. Whitehall, however, is one area where inspection will be weak and unclear; and the duties to eliminate racism and promote equal opportunities and good race relations are confined to the public sphere.

Immigration controls and decisions by definition discriminate on grounds of nationality. The most alarming aspect of the Amendment Act allows the Home Secretary himself to discriminate on grounds of nationality, or national or ethnic origin, or to authorise his officials to do so through instructions or guidelines. Immigration law of course allows discrimination on grounds of nationality. But as the Parekh report notes:

> The exemption goes further than this, specifically permitting institutionalised discrimination on grounds of ethnicity or national origin, without the need to justify differential treatment (Parekh, 2000).

The government originally justified this exception by stating that it would allow officials to discriminate positively in favour of groups such as the Kosovans (HC Deb, 30 October 2000). However the Home Secretary has since authorised immigration officers to discriminate specifically against particular ethnic or national groups (HC Deb, WA, 1 May 2001). The post of a race monitor who was to oversee the operation of authorised exceptions has not been filled.

Remedies under race relations laws

Wronged individuals may obtain damages for direct discrimination and intentional indirect discrimination under the 1976 Act. It is up to the people affected to issue proceedings against employers, since the Act does not make provision for class actions.

Race hate and harassment

The Public Order Act 1986 created an offence of incitement of racial hatred through words, behaviour or display of written material that uses 'threatening, abusive or insulting' terms. But the material has to be blatantly abusive for the authorities to act and there have been very few prosecutions for race hate. The Act shows a proper concern to balance freedom of speech and the protection of racial minorities from injury and hurt resulting from the incitement of racial hatred, but perhaps the protection of public order from disruption was the paramount concern. The Crime and Disorder Act 1998 created new offences of causing harassment and causing fear of violence and a new offence of racially aggravated violence and harassment; racial motivation can now be considered as an aggravating factor that merits an increased sentence.

Sex discrimination legislation

The Sex Discrimination Act 1975 (SDA) prohibits direct and indirect discrimination and victimisation in the areas of employment, education, and the provision of goods and services. The Equal Pay Act 1970 was introduced to address the differential in women's earning power. However, as with race discrimination, women are still considerably disadvantaged despite the introduction of legislation outlawing discrimination,. They are under-represented in politics and public life (see Section 11.3); are paid significantly less than men (their income as a whole represents only 53 per cent of men's); are over-represented in part-time work; and tend also to be excluded from benefits such as pensions (see Section 4.1).

Disability discrimination

The Labour government passed the UK's first Disability Discrimination Act in 1995, and set up a Disability Rights Commission in 2000. The Act's scope is limited: it deals only with direct discrimination and victimisation, in certain circumstances, such as employment and the provision of services. It applies only to organisations and businesses with over 15 employees. Its rules for the access of disabled people to public transport are very weak, and there is no commitment to disabled access in mainstream schools. The Disability Rights Commission has been widely welcomed as a voice for disabled rights within society.

Sexuality discrimination

No legislation currently protects gay men and lesbians from discrimination in the UK. There have, however, been major advances in recent years in securing rights for gay men, lesbians and transsexuals, most of which have come about through judgments of the European Court of Human Rights or the European Court of Justice (ECJ). As a result of a judgment of the ECJ in 1996 (P v S & Cornwall County Council), transsexuals are now protected against employment discrimination in UK law. A European Court of Human Rights decision brought the ban on gays and lesbians in the UK armed forces to an end (Smith and Grady v United Kingdom, 1999).

The government itself passed legislation to equalise the age of consent for heterosexual and homosexual sex after an adverse finding by the European Commission on Human Rights (Sutherland v UK, 1997). The domestic courts decided in 1999 that long-term homosexual relationships could constitute a 'family' for certain purposes' (Fitzpatrick v Sterling Housing Association, 1999) and have sanctioned fostering and adoption by gay couples (Re T, Petitioner, 1997). It is worth noting that these reforms were findings of the courts, not of elected representatives or the executive.

Gay men and lesbians, however, may still face discrimination at work, and it is still a crime for gay men to have sex in circumstances where it would not be a crime for heterosexual couples. In the case of ADT v UK in July 2000, the European Court of Human Rights found that the UK had violated Article

8 of the European Convention, the right to a private life, by convicting a gay man for an act of gross indecency involving sexual acts with up to four other men. The government initiated a sex offences review in January 1999, which recommended that this offence should be repealed, and is now considering reform (but no legislative changes have been made). No such offence of gross indecency exists for either lesbians or heterosexuals.

Age discrimination

Awareness of age discrimination has increased substantially in recent years. There is pressure on employers and service providers from the European Union, government and non-governmental organisations not to impose unnecessary age limitations. However older workers still have less access to training and promotion and find it more difficult than younger people to find employment. In 1999 the government published a voluntary Code of Practice for Age Diversity in Employment to encourage employers to remove unnecessary age limitations. Research published by the Employers Forum on Age in 1999 indicated that this was having little effect on the way employers were running their organisations and businesses. Employers openly reject job applicants on the sole ground of age as a matter of routine 'company policy'. The government has now set up an age advisory group to start the process of consulting about new forms of legislation to outlaw age discrimination.

Age Concern and other groups working with the elderly point to significant discrimination against older people in the provision of health-care, with resources being prioritised towards younger people, and under-resourcing of social care for the elderly. Violence towards old people in private or residential homes is now increasingly recognised to be a problem, and there have been calls for legislation to provide protection for this vulnerable group.

Developments in the European Union

UK anti-discrimination legislation has developed under the influence of EU law. Traditionally the law of the European Community (EC) has provided protection against discrimination on the basis of sex and, for EU citizens, nationality. Article 13 of the EU Treaty, as introduced by the Treaty of Amsterdam, provides a legal basis for the Council of Ministers to 'take appropriate action to combat discrimination based on sex, racial or ethnic origin, religion or belief, disability, age or sexual orientation'. In June 2000 the Council adopted a Race Directive that prohibits discrimination against racial or ethnic groups in the areas of employment and occupation, the provision of goods and services, education and social protection. It defines race in the same way as the 1976 Act in the UK, so that certain religious groups will again be at an advantage compared with others and be given greater protection from discrimination. To ensure that these anomalies are not intensified the government will have to introduce legislation that covers all ethnic groups and areas of potential discrimination within the framework and race directives.

In November 2000 the European Union also agreed a new Employment Framework Directive that requires member states to introduce legislation against discrimination at work on the grounds of religion, belief and sexual orientation by 2003, and discrimination on grounds of disability or age by 2006. So many of the shortcomings identified here should be eliminated by at least 2006.

The Race Directive is wider in scope than the Employment Framework Directive because, in addition to employment, it covers social protection, social advantages, goods and services. Neither directive extends protection to discrimination on the grounds of nationality against citizens of non-EU countries.

The employment directive also has specific exemptions in relation to discrimination based on age, disability and religion or belief. Thus significant gaps are developing between UK law and developing EU law, specifically between existing UK legislation and the requirements of the two directives. Most obviously the Employment Framework Directive covers discrimination on the grounds of age, sexual orientation, religion or belief. Except for Northern Ireland (where the Fair Employment and Treatment Order prohibits discrimination on the grounds of religion or belief) UK legislation does not extend to these grounds. There is also a danger that in implementing the employment directive the government will create inconsistent and differing levels of protection for different religious groups.

The European Union proclaimed a Charter of Fundamental Rights in December 2000. Chapter 3 affirms a general principle that 'everyone is equal before the law' as well as prohibiting discrimination on 'any ground such as sex, race, colour, ethnic origin or social origin, genetic features, language, religion or belief, political or any other opinion, membership of a national minority, property, birth, disability, age or sexual orientation'. There are also articles proclaiming equality between men and women and respect for 'cultural, religious and linguistic diversity'. The impact of the Charter and its precise legal nature remains to be clarified. The UK government has stated that the Charter is not intended to have legal status, but the EU Commission says it will have influence in the EU Court of Justice.

Populist media and politicians

The business of selling newspapers has sometimes meant that editors pander to and excite populist viewpoints on race and minorities in order to tap into their perceptions of the popular mood and to boost circulation. In doing so, they sometimes distort the facts and misinform the public and expose themselves to the charge of exacerbating already delicate situations. The Refugee Council website includes a section entitled 'Press Myths' which corrects some of the inaccurate and misleading claims about asylum seekers that have been made in the national press. Some politicians are broadly guilty of similar conduct.

The Second Report on the UK from the European Commission against Racism and Intolerance (16 June 2000) drew particular attention to negative press comment on asylum seekers and refugees in the UK, stating that, 'Opinion polls suggest that asylum and immigration issues feature increasingly high in the list of concerns of the British electorate.' The report found that 'Many politicians have contributed to, or at least have not adequately prevented, public debate taking on an increasingly intolerant line with at times racist and xenophobic overtones.' The commission also criticised 'the consistent inflammatory attacks on asylum seekers and migrants coming in to the United Kingdom, which have appeared in local but also in some national mainstream newspapers'. The importance of a free press that investigates and raises issues of public concern should not distract from its responsibility to ensure that its articles and reports do not provoke harmful and excessive reactions against particular elements of society.

Summary

In spite of over 25 years of anti-discrimination legislation, it is clear that ethnic minorities are disproportionately represented among the unemployed, low-waged and socially excluded (see Section 4), though some groups are more disadvantaged than others. Women are still grossly disadvantaged at work and in public life by comparison with men (see Sections 4.1 and 11.3). As recently as 1997, the UN

Committee on Economic, Social and Cultural Rights found that 'despite the elaborate machinery and legislation for protection against discrimination, there continues to exist to a significant degree de facto discrimination against women, Blacks and other ethnic minorities'. For example a survey of 500 people representing diverse ethnic minority groups for the government's People's Panel found that one in six of those surveyed felt that even public services, including the NHS, schools and benefit agencies, discriminate against them; and that in a quarter of cases discrimination amounted to verbal racial abuse (see also Section 4).

Part of the problem is that the UK's anti-discrimination legislative framework has so far failed to provide comprehensive protection, being as we have seen, outdated, inadequate and inconsistent. Arbitrary discriminations on grounds of age, sexual orientation and religion or belief (apart from Northern Ireland) are not prohibited at all. There has been consistent international criticism of the failure to introduce race relations legislation in Northern Ireland. Possible reforms could include a single equality act or, at least in the short term, the ratification of Protocol 12 of the European Convention of Human Rights which prohibits all forms of discrimination. However, the UK failed to sign up when it was opened for signature in November 2000 (in contrast to 25 other Council of Europe members). The government claims that this is because the right as formulated in Protocol 12 is 'too general and open-ended'.

1.3. How much consensus is there on state boundaries and constitutional arrangements?

The United Kingdom consists of both Great Britain (England, Scotland and Wales) and Northern Ireland. The Hebrides, Orkney and Shetland Islands, Anglesey and the Isles of Scilly are part of the UK, but not the Isle of Man in the Irish Sea and the Channel Islands which are largely self-governing. The UK is part of the European Union. Within Great Britain the borders between England and Scotland and England and Wales are settled and accepted, although should Scotland ever become independent the precise location of the boundary in the North Sea between it and England would certainly give rise to serious debate (because of oil and gas deposits).

The border, however, between Northern Ireland, as a part of the United Kingdom, and the Republic of Ireland has been very seriously contested. A Boundary Commission which produced a report in 1925 (but not actually published until 1968) recommended a certain movement of territory from Northern Ireland to the then Irish Free State and *vice versa*. The report was not implemented and since then the major debate has concerned not so much the actual line of the border as its very existence. The resolution of this issue is now formally regarded, in both Great Britain and the Republic of Ireland, as being a matter for the people of Northern Ireland to decide by a simple majority vote whether to be a part of the United Kingdom or of a united Ireland (outside the United Kingdom). The current formal position, however, masks considerable debate and developments concerning three key principles: (a) the *de jure* and *de facto* status of Northern Ireland according to both British and Irish law; (b) the question of whose consent should be sought; and (c) other constitutional options.

The current position is contained in the Northern Ireland Act 1998, as read with the multi-party Belfast and the British-Irish Agreements of April 1998. Section 1 of the Act declares that the territory of Northern Ireland *in its entirety* remains part of the United Kingdom and shall not cease to be so without the consent of a simple majority of the people of Northern Ireland voting in a constitutional referendum or 'border poll'. The Act also imposes an obligation on the Secretary of State for Northern Ireland to direct the holding of a border poll 'if it appears to him likely' that a majority of those voting would support a united Ireland.

Thus it is the Northern Ireland Secretary, subject to the approval of the Westminster Parliament (and for some matters after consultation with the Irish Government), and the people of Northern Ireland who will decide. The procedures do not involve the Northern Ireland Assembly. The British-Irish Agreement sets out the principles agreed between the two governments on the issue of consent regarding the status of Northern Ireland; and states that whatever choice is made by the people of Northern Ireland, 'the power of the sovereign government with jurisdiction there' shall be exercised in accordance with the principle of parity of esteem between communities.

As far as the more general question of consensus on constitutional arrangements in the United Kingdom is concerned, in essence all such matters are dealt with by the Westminster Parliament without or (increasingly) with the 'advice' of the electorate as manifested in a referendum (see Section 1.5 below).

1.4. How far do constitutional and political arrangements enable major societal divisions to be moderated or reconciled?

Within the United Kingdom and specifically Northern Ireland, nationalism or the desire for independence is the major societal division either accommodated within or addressed by constitutional arrangements. In general, societal divisions within the United Kingdom are addressed through the substance of the law, for example anti-discrimination laws, rather than through political or institutional change. Devolution is in part an exception to this, especially through the adoption of more representative electoral systems for elections to the variously devolved bodies in Scotland, Wales and Northern Ireland.

Within Scotland and Wales about a quarter of both electorates tell pollsters that they are in favour of independence from the UK (but generally within the EU). The quite different systems of devolution as contained in the Scotland Act 1998 and the Government of Wales Act 1998 do not as such deal with nationalist aspirations. What they seek to do is to strengthen the Union by formally recognising the Scottish and Welsh national dimensions in the context of a legislative and administrative structure which holds the Union together (see Sections 13.1 and 13.2). Nationalists may be prepared to accept devolution as a temporary expedient or as a half-way house to independence, but devolution is not as such a 'vehicle' which itself recognises or accommodates separatism. It may serve either as a stimulus to independence or may serve to weaken it, but it remains distinct from it.

By contrast, devolution to Northern Ireland under the Northern Ireland Act 1998 was not presented by the Westminster government in terms of strengthening the Union; alone of the three devolution Acts, it contains a provision which could trigger the dissolution of the Union. No formal recognition at all is given within the political and constitutional arrangements of the United Kingdom to the English dimension (though the government announced cautious plans for English regional assemblies in 2002).

Proportional elections to devolved assemblies

The three systems of devolution are different, the main difference being that devolution to Scotland and Northern Ireland entails considerably more powers than those devolved to Wales. In this Section, the most significant differences to note are the proportional electoral systems used for the elections to the Scottish Parliament and the Northern Ireland and Welsh Assemblies. In Scotland and Wales, the government chose the additional member system (AMS) principally to prevent the unrepresentative domination of both devolved bodies by the Labour parties of the Scottish Central Belt and South Wales that would have occurred under the conventional plurality-rule (or 'first-past-the-post') elections employed for Westminster. But the proportional AMS elections have by the same token facilitated a much wider political representation than is possible under plurality-rule elections, thus enabling more parties, including the nationalist parties, to play a much fuller part in devolution than would otherwise be the case. This carries the possibility of resolving political differences, maybe even differences of conflicting constitutional aspirations, more through consensus and inclusive politics than would otherwise be the case (see also Section 13).

In Northern Ireland, proportionality in government is a statutory requirement. Elections to the Northern Ireland Assembly are conducted under the single transferable vote, a broadly proportional system that is designed to ensure the representation within the Assembly of both communities and most community and political forces in the province. The Northern Ireland multi-party Executive proportionately reflects the number of seats held by the (largest) parties in the Assembly. Currently four different parties are represented in the Executive.

Devolution, thus both in itself and its key details, reflects a variation from the dominant United Kingdom approach of addressing the divisions within society through the ad hoc substantive law rather than through institutional change. In Northern Ireland, for the past 30 years, there has been an awareness of the need for both substantive and institutional law to address major societal divisions. Furthermore, the substantive law incorporates both anti-discrimination law and the enhancement of positive rights. It is likely that the new Bill of Rights for Northern Ireland will include social and cultural rights on education, culture and identity, and language (see also Section 4).

1.5. How impartial and inclusive are the procedures for amending the constitution?

Governments in Britain possess a wide measure of discretion on whether or not to put proposals for constitutional change to the electorate. The normal procedure for gaining public approval for constitutional changes has more recently been to hold a referendum, but there are no rules whatever, other than political expediency, governing the issues on which a referendum should be held. The conduct of referendums however is now to be supervised by the new Electoral Commission.

The growing use of referendums

Traditionally, referendums were considered to contradict the basic principle of parliamentary sovereignty (see Section 7) and the very idea of representative democracy. A V Dicey, the Victorian constitutional authority, came in later life to favour referendums as a check on single-party government, but this was one Dicey view that never hardened into political orthodoxy. However, 1975 proved to be a watershed in the use of referendums. The then Labour government, thoroughly split on continued membership of the European Economic Community, held a referendum on EEC membership. This was the first nationwide referendum in the United Kingdom. In 1973, a referendum was held in Northern Ireland over remaining part of the United Kingdom after a statutory rule that the constitutional status of the province would not change without the consent of the Stormont parliament was transmuted into the consent of the people after the collapse of Stormont. Referendums were also held in Scotland and Wales on devolution in 1979.

Since 1997, referendums have been held in Scotland on the proposal to establish a Scottish parliament with tax-raising powers; in Wales, on setting up a Welsh assembly; in London, on having a Mayor and Greater London Assembly; and in Northern Ireland over the peace agreement and a devolved assembly (see Section 13); and in various cities over adopting mayors. The referendum on the Belfast Agreement is a major landmark and has led to the uneasy peace that still remains in place in Northern Ireland. A parallel referendum on the peace agreement and consequent constitutional changes was held in the Republic of Ireland; and any change to the status of Northern Ireland will now be determined by a referendum in the province.

There was some debate about the propriety of excluding the English public from the devolution referendums in Scotland and Wales, since the proposals clearly affected England and the balance of representation of English, Scots and Welsh people in Parliament. The government was also criticised for holding the Scottish and Welsh referendums before the form and powers of the devolved assemblies were determined. The established principle seems to be that only the views of the electorate in that part of the United Kingdom directly affected by proposed constitutional changes need to be ascertained. There has been no acceptance of the principle that reform of a part constitutes a reform of the whole necessitating the consent of all constituent parts.

The Labour government is committed to two further referendums – a major referendum on joining the European single currency, that may take place in 2003; and another on the voting system for elections to the House of Commons, which was to have been held in the 1997-2001 Parliament, but now looks likely to be long delayed.

One major constitutional change has taken place since 1997 with no referendum or genuine process of public consultation at all. The Human Rights Act, almost certainly the most profound constitutional change in postwar Britain, was passed without fuss in 1998 and came quietly into effect in Scotland, and then in the rest of the UK. The government feared a public backlash, inspired by the tabloid press, and so played down the implications of the Act.

Fixing constitutional change
The Blair government has been very ready to manipulate the processes of constitutional change to get the results that it wants. The most extreme examples were the *Independent* Commission on the Voting System (under Lord Jenkins) and the *Royal* Commission on the Reform of the House of Lords (under Lord Wakeham). In both cases, the italics are ours: the Jenkins commission was anything but 'independent', being subject to continual party political negotiation between Blair and Peter Mandelson, Blair's adviser; Paddy Ashdown, then the Liberal Democratic leader, and Lord Holme, his adviser; and Jenkins himself. In British politics, 'Royal' signifies a body or process that is supposedly above party politics, but the commission was run and organised by Lord Wakeham and the Labour party's nominee,

Gerald Kaufman MP, fixers both, to deliver a report that recommended a largely appointed second chamber in accordance with the wishes of 10 Downing Street at that time.

The Jenkins commission was set up within the context of Blair's desire for a realignment of centre-left politics in Britain and a closer alignment between Labour and the Liberal Democrats; its remit, composition and recommendations were subject to intense negotiations over 16 months between Blair, Ashdown and Jenkins, on occasion over a bottle of wine in Downing Street. Ashdown insisted that 'broad proportionality' should be part of the remit; Blair insisted that it should not be so 'broad' as to produce near permanent coalition government. A formula was agreed between the two sides at a Downing Street dinner: broad proportionality meant that a party which won 45 per cent of the vote at a general election should receive 50 per cent or more of the seats in the House of Commons. Jenkins discussed the report's proposals with Blair and Ashdown, and personally showed the final draft of the ingenious compromise report to Blair (Ashdown, 2001). Finally Blair was unable to win over hostile 'big beasts' in the cabinet; and the deal fell through. The referendum which was to be put to the public before the 2001 election was postponed, probably indefinitely (see further, Section 5.4).

The composition of the royal commission on the House of Lords was fixed carefully to ensure that no member was a known believer in an elected chamber rather than the wholly-appointed body that the Prime Minister wanted; and to avoid the danger of a more democratic minority report. Gerald Kaufman was appointed as keeper of the New Labour position and he and Wakeham later formed the core of an 'inner Commission'. Lord Plant, a highly-respected constitutional expert close to the Labour party, was rejected as a potential member once it was clear that he was committed to the principle of election; so, too, was Shirley Williams, an early Liberal Democrat nominee, for the same failing.

The weight of evidence to the commission was for election rather than appointment, but in January 2001, Lord Wakeham was able to deliver a report in favour of a largely appointed House of Lords; and in late 2001 the government produced a white paper, Completing the Reform (Cm 5291), that came out again for a largely appointed House, but without the independent scrutiny and control of appointments that Wakeham recommended. The white paper was also deliberately misleading about the prevalence of elected second chambers around the world (see further, Democratic Audit 2002).

In February 2002 the all-party Public Administration Select Committee in the House of Commons published a unanimous report arguing that a 60 per cent elected second chamber offered a way forward that represented (in its words) the 'centre of gravity' of political and public opinion (PASC 2002). This claim was based on PASC's own poll of MPs and an ICM opinion poll for Democratic Audit in December 2001. The government is in a dilemma: it is utterly opposed to a largely elected (and so more legitimate) second chamber, but its own proposals are so unpopular in Parliament that Lord Lipsey, a Labour loyalist who saw merit in the white paper's proposals, described them 'as a dead duck . . . on its back in Parliament with its legs in the air'. For the moment the government has passed the poisoned chalice to a joint committee of MPs and peers. But the manner in which it finally resolves its dilemma will say much about the inclusive and impartial nature in which such constitutional issues are determined.

Meanwhile, only one voice has been raised – that of Charter 88, the constitutional reform group – calling for a referendum on second chamber reform. The government is therefore under no political pressure to hold a referendum and there is no provision in the unwritten constitution to prevent any government from making such a fundamental constitutional change on the authority only of an unrepresentative parliamentary majority (see Section 5.4).

The absence of constitutional checks on the executive
In the absence of a fully written constitution, there is no constitutional authority which has the power to determine the processes by which any constitutional change should be made, or even what constitutes a constitutional issue. Any government has royal prerogative powers enabling it to make fundamental changes in the state bureaucracy without recourse even to Parliament, even though such changes have a major effect on central constitutional questions such as ministerial responsibility to Parliament; and can for example make Alastair Campbell, an unelected special adviser, the de facto Minister of Information in the Blair government (see Section 7.8). The fact is that governments are free to take decisions in a constitutional and legal void, and generally possess the legislative and prerogative power to carry them through. They are not required to gain an enhanced majority in Parliament for major constitutional changes, as in many other countries, nor is the second chamber to be given a particular role as a constitutional watch-dog, as many who gave evidence to the Wakeham commission suggested.

There is likely to be more use of referendums – for example, on regional authorities throughout England – but questions of if and when a referendum should be held, and what constitutes a relevant issue, will continue to be decided by the government and its party managers in the light of political expediency, the salience of the issues, political party considerations and the likely attitude of the public. Even the results of referendums are not formally binding on governments, though the political consequences of ignoring them would probably be severe.

The Political Parties, Elections and Referendums Act 2000 introduced a few minimal rules for the conduct of referendums. Referendum campaigns are not made subject to any overall limit on spending, but come under the supervision of the new Electoral Commission (see Sections 5.2 and 5.3). The commission's basic role is to try and maintain a level playing field, especially with regard to campaign spending. The commission can give up to £600,000 to designated 'yes' and 'no' umbrella organisations which also have the right to a free mail-shot to all voters. Each campaign can spend up to £5 million in all. Political parties must keep within spending limits set between £500,000 and £5 million (depending on their share of the vote at the previous general election); and 'permitted participants' can spend up to £500,000 each. Those that spend more than £10,000 must register with the commission.

The Act recognises the need to restrain the power of government to influence the results of a referendum. The government must therefore observe a 28-day 'purdah' before any vote is taken, but critics of the Act argued strongly that governments have such powerful resources in communications that it would still have ample time in which to exercise strong influence over a referendum. Another significant issue concerns the wording of any referendum question. The framing of the question obviously carries with it the potential to influence the public response. Yet the Act leaves control over the wording to the government, and gives the Electoral Commission power to intervene simply on grounds of intelligibility. Other questions are left unaddressed. For example, should there be a threshold for turnout, or the margin of the majority vote, below which a referendum result would be void?

Overall, our view is that governments retain so much control over what constitutional issues should be put to the public, or left within their grasp, and so much power to determine the timing of referendums, pre-publicity and the framing of referendum questions, that there is no impartial means for consulting the public on constitutional amendments, though the growing use of referendums has led to a partial increase in the inclusivity of some decisions.

Two: justice and the rule of law

Equal before the law?

Are state and society consistently subject to the law?

Here every man, whatever be his rank or condition, is subject to the ordinary law of the realm
A V Dicey, Victorian constitutional authority, 1885

Introduction

The idea of the rule of law is a long-standing one that pre-dates the advent of democracy. It expresses the powerful idea that law, not the arbitrary will of particular people, whether in government or not, should rule society. The idea comprises the following distinct elements:

- no one should be above the law, whatever their position or social standing, and everyone should be equal before it;
- all public officials should be subject to the law, and act within the terms of legally prescribed duties, powers and procedures;

- parliamentary law-making should itself conform to constitutionally defined procedures and limits;
- the judiciary should be institutionally and personally independent of both executive and Parliament, so that it can interpret and enforce the law without fear or favour;
- all law should be certain, and its provisions and penalties known in advance;
- no one should be punished without a specific charge and a fair hearing before a duly constituted court.

These ideas form a cornerstone of democratic government. However, citizens in a contemporary democracy also expect more from the 'rule of law' than this traditional understanding implies: for example, that parliamentary legislation should uphold the rights fundamental to democratic citizenship; that the police should enforce the law effectively and fairly; that no one should be denied the protection due them under the civil or criminal law because they cannot afford the cost, or because of gross delays in the administration of justice.

2.1.   How far does the rule of law operate throughout the United Kingdom?

In the main, the idea of the rule of law is respected in the UK and operates across the country. However, there are significant exceptions under each of the items mentioned above, and these will be summarised here, although some will be covered in more detail in later questions.

The reach of the law

People in all countries complain that there are not enough law enforcers (police, health and safety inspectors, etc) to give them the protection they expect. More serious are areas where the law hardly reaches at all, as in the case of 'punishment beatings' in Northern Ireland, or shootings between rival drug gangs in various British cities. In many inner cities prosecutions fail or are not attempted because witnesses are afraid to come forward: this failing was illustrated dramatically in the investigation into the killing of the Nigerian boy, Damilola Taylor, in south London and the subsequent trial. In the economic field there is a substantial parallel economy, not only in the drugs trade, which evades tax altogether; and there are all kinds of opportunities for the wealthy to evade tax that are not open to the average citizen. According to a *Guardian* special report, the Inland Revenue readily connives in the tax avoidance schemes for large international companies which are not available to small businesses and individual taxpayers (23 July 2002). There are also off-shore islands, nominally under UK jurisdiction, such as the Isle of Man and the Channel Islands, which comprise attractive tax havens because they remain beyond the UK's tax regime.

Equality before the law

Everyone in the UK, whatever their race, gender, class or other difference, does formally have equal access to the courts, and the same remedies, under the same legal system. But this principle is limited in practice. First, the common law has proved inadequate in modern Britain to protect people against various discriminations on grounds of race, gender, etc. Most anti-discrimination and race relations law is the work of Parliament rather than the courts and the common law; and is patchy in its coverage. The

Human Rights Act 1988, which provides a new foundation for the protection of civil and political rights in this country (see below and Section 3), contains a general anti-discrimination clause. But it applies only to the rights and safeguards set out in the Act (and behind it the European Convention on Human Rights). UK governments have refused to ratify Protocol 12 of the ECHR that guarantees a wide-ranging protection against discrimination (see Section 1.2 above). In addition, much higher proportions of the black and Asian minorities have been subject to police stop and search, to arrest and prosecution than whites, and are hugely over-represented in the prison population.

However much the law may treat individual citizens and institutions as equals, it does so in a purely formal way, and cannot by itself alter the profound inequalities within their actual relationships. One consequence of such inequalities is that not everyone can afford the costs and risks of going to court; and the legal aid system is insufficient to meet the widespread unmet legal needs of the population (see Section 2.4).

Executive dominion

The doctrine of parliamentary sovereignty makes Parliament the highest court in the land; and, as the two previous Democratic Audit studies have shown, in practice also raises the executive above the judiciary by virtue of its control of Parliament through its disciplined party majority in the House of Commons. Thus Britain's constitutional structure has not been conducive to effective oversight of the conduct or legislation of the executive and has historically failed to protect individual civil and political rights (Weir and Beetham, 1999; and Klug, Starmer and Weir, 1996). Even now the Prime Minister, ministers and their officials both exercise pre-democratic discretionary powers inherited from the monarch (royal prerogative powers) and may use Parliament's legislative powers to accumulate new powers (see Section 7 further). Judicial review does oblige the executive to observe rules of due process in its decision-making and to avoid arbitrary, unfair or unreasonable decisions. But the courts are powerless in the face of primary legislation and we must await the outcomes of judicial intervention to declare Acts incompatible with the new Human Rights Act to judge how far the executive will be subject to judicial restraint in the future. At present, if it so wishes, the executive can reject judicial declarations of incompatibility, and could, for example, continue to hold the nine foreign Muslim terrorist suspects in detention under the Terrorism Act 2000 in spite of court rulings. The executive's domination of Parliament through its party majority also allows it to rush through primary legislation on occasion without it being properly checked, thus reversing the principle of the rule of law that the executive branch of government should be effectively subordinate to the legislature, and not merely in name. Further much legislation at the European level that is binding on UK citizens is decided on by ministers in the EU Council of Ministers without genuine parliamentary approval (see Sections 2.2 and 7.5).

Legal regulation of public officials

Although the Human Rights Act has done much to improve the legal accountability of public officials, there remain significant areas of administration whose procedures are unclear, or which are subject to legal immunities. Much administrative practice is also regulated by secondary legislation, which the executive generally introduces free from effective parliamentary scrutiny.

The separation of powers

Judges in the UK have an impressive tradition of independence from the executive. However, the Lord Chancellor's pivotal position in all three branches of government breaches the principle of the separation of powers. The Lord Chancellor is a powerful member of the Cabinet; and yet, as a prominent member of the executive, he is also head of the English and Welsh judiciary; speaker of the House of Lords in its legislative capacity; and may sit with the law lords in the highest court of appeal. He also has a strong influence over the composition of the judiciary; has political and administrative authority over criminal and civil justice policies; is responsible for appointing or advising on the appointment of judges in England and Wales at all levels above that of magistrates; and appoints Queen's Counsel (the senior rank of barristers and usually a necessary stage towards becoming a senior judge). The present incumbent is also an influential figure in party politics and has been involved in Labour party fund-raising activities that have raised questions of conflict of interest (see further Section 2.3).

Certainty in the law

The bulk of UK law derives from the common law – legal principles and rules that have been developed through the accumulated decisions of the higher courts over time, in contrast to statute law enacted by Parliament. The doctrine of *stare decisis*, by which decisions of the higher courts are binding in subsequent cases, is generally held to ensure a measure of legal certainty and consistency in the common law. However, the discretion given to judges in the interpretation of common law can sometimes result in wholly unexpected judgments which transform the legal landscape, as for example the decision for policy holders against Equitable Life, which altered the responsibilities of mutual bodies without the consultation and public debate which usually attends parliamentary legislation.

Due process

There are a number of situations where people are specifically denied access to the courts for review of adverse administrative decisions. Typical are decisions over deportation, family reunion and naturalisation under nationality and immigration legislation, and detention under successive Terrorism Acts.

2.2. To what extent are all public officials subject to the rule of law and to transparent rules in the performance of their functions?

Britain's constitutional arrangements give the executive a wide measure of 'flexibility' and facilitate 'strong' government, which too often in practice amounts to unchecked government. Ministers extend their flexibility to officials acting in their name. Formally, ministers and public officials are subject to the rule of law through judicial review in the courts and through the private law of liability for tort (that is, a breach of duty). Bodies such as the Police Complaints Authority and the Commission for Racial Equality exist to review, challenge and control the conduct of public servants, police officers, etc. But they do not always possess sufficient independence from the executive and are not necessarily able or willing to challenge the authorities under review.

The Human Rights Act should make a strong contribution to making public officials accountable for their actions and governing the conduct of the executive as a whole. First, the Act is likely to oblige public authorities to give reasons for their decisions in most circumstances. This could prove to be a major advance for many citizens who have dealings with government at all levels. Secondly, in the past the limited powers of scrutiny under judicial review has restricted the ability of the courts to make public officials accountable; and the existence of broad privileges and immunities for public bodies and officials has prevented the courts from holding them liable for negligent decisions. The 1998 Act makes all public officials (acting in their capacity as 'public authorities') directly accountable in the courts for actions that interfere with basic civil and political rights set out in the European Convention. Anyone who believes that an official has violated their Convention rights may now seek a legal remedy. The Act thus considerably enhances public accountability by providing a principled basis on which public policy and practice can be assessed. It places civil and political rights at the heart of the daily business of public authorities, not only in Whitehall where officials have long been schooled to 'beware the judge on your shoulder', but in the NHS, Inland Revenue, the police, local authorities and all other agencies with a public role (including some private bodies with a public function, such as universities or trade unions). Moreover, government and public authorities will probably at last be obliged to furnish citizens with the reasons for public decisions that affect them and are likely to have to improve the objectivity of their decision-making.

The Act also strengthens the law of judicial review. Previously, judicial review enabled the courts to impugn the actions of a public body on three broad grounds: that the body had exceeded its powers; that it had acted in breach of rules of procedural fairness; or that its course of action had been irrational: i.e., so unreasonable that no reasonable person could have taken it. The inadequacy of these extremely limited grounds of review was illustrated, for example, when three male homosexuals and a lesbian, who were discharged from the armed forces because of their sexuality, challenged the policy of the Ministry of Defence in a 1995 case (R v Ministry of Defence, *ex parte* Smith and Grady, 1996). The courts very reluctantly upheld government policy by applying the simple test – was it so unreasonable that no reasonable body would operate it? i.e., in the view of the courts, it was not an outrageous defiance of logic. Here lies the nub of the difference that now governs law in the UK: the Convention accepts only decisions that are reasonable and defensible, not any decision that is not absurd.

The Act also requires a more searching review of the quality of public policy and practice. Under judicial review the courts must now inquire whether the action under review interferes with Convention rights; and if so, whether the official or public body can justify it as a permissible limitation on rights. And where the actions of a public body affect human rights, the courts have made it clear in three recent cases involving the Home Office (*ex parte* Sezek, 2000; *ex parte* Isiko, 2000; and *ex parte* Daly, 2001) that they must be justified against more than a minimum standard of rationality, and that the burden is on the public body to demonstrate that there has been no breach of Convention rights.

But how intense will such reviews be? The judiciary observes a long tradition of reluctance to interfere in the functions of government, partly out of a desire to avoid making the law as opposed to interpreting it. Public policy is said to be 'an unruly horse, and once you get astride it you never know where it will carry you' (Lester and Bindman, 1972). More recently the judiciary has shown a tendency to accord a broad 'discretionary area' for executive action into which they will not inquire; and also appears to defer to the executive where it exercises its royal prerogative powers (though it at least now regards their deployment as justiciable).

The effects of private law

The laws of tort (breach of legal duty) and negligence are important instruments for securing redress for public wrongs. Public officials may be sued for breaches of their legal duty where their actions amount to assault, trespass or similar wrongs. For example, legal actions for tort can provide redress for misconduct by the police or other law enforcement agencies, in cases of false imprisonment, malicious prosecution and wrongful arrest; and damages may be awarded against public authorities in such actions.

Restrictions on the rule of law

However, public officials can often shelter behind immunities against such private actions, under both the common law and statute. Certain of these immunities can be justified on constitutional and public interest grounds. For example, the immunity of MPs from defamation, other civil actions and criminal prosecution for statements they make 'in the course of Parliamentary proceedings' (which covers not only speeches in Parliament, but letters to ministers, etc.) derives from the importance attached in the Bill of Rights 1689 to freedom of parliamentary debate. The immunity of judges from liability for acts within their judicial competence may also be justified as protecting the authority of the judiciary. But the immunity of certain public authorities, such as the police and social services, from actions for negligence in criminal investigations or child protection work, is more difficult to justify. The European Court of Human Rights has recently restricted such immunities (in a case involving social workers' failure to check child neglect and abuse, Z v UK, 2000) and the rules excluding the liability of public servants, such as the police and social workers, are no longer absolute.

The liability of certain public authorities and officials is also restricted by statute. Under the Mental Health Act 1983, for example, mental health workers are not liable in either civil or criminal proceedings for their work under the Act, unless they have acted in bad faith or without reasonable care.

The rule of law is additionally restricted for officials acting in cases involving national security, surveillance, bugging, etc., or in immigration and asylum cases. In such cases, the courts are unwilling to look behind the government's arguments justifying measures on very broadly-defined national security grounds. Their reluctance to challenge the authorities has detracted from the quality of their reviews of public actions (see for example the recent case, Secretary of State for the Home Department v Shafiq ur Rehman, currently awaiting judgment in the House of Lords). Here again the absolute nature of public interest immunity has been qualified by decisions of the European Court of Human Rights. The very broad definition of terrorism in the Terrorism Act 2000 similarly weakens the rule of law. The Act allows exceptional measures against a much broader and uncertain range of dissenting activity than that normally considered as terrorist; and normal safeguards and procedures may be set aside by the authorities across this potentially wide and uncertain area of civil and political activity.

Transparent rules

Another consequence of the Human Rights Act has been that previously opaque or uncertain administrative practices have been subjected to publicly available guidelines, or have been given a statutory basis. Under the principle of legality which is fundamental to the European Convention, the Act requires that any restrictions or interferences with rights should have a clear legal basis that is sufficiently certain and foreseeable to be 'prescribed by law'. This rule has brought about legislation to regulate sensitive public activity that affects human rights – for example, the Regulation of Investigatory Powers Act 2000 (RIPA) which now governs surveillance and the interception of communications (see also Section 3.4). The Act has also prompted the publication, for the first time, of guidelines for police actions, such as the use of firearms.

However, much administrative practice is still regulated by secondary legislation or guidelines rather than by primary legislation. Government increasingly passes 'framework legislation', in which Acts set out a statutory framework for later secondary orders which introduce detailed regulations and provisions, which may very well substantially alter the scope or direction of the Act, but escape effective parliamentary scrutiny. Democratic Audit is concerned about the extent of the reliance on guidelines and delegated legislation in relation to, for example, the Immigration and Asylum Act 1999 and RIPA.

2.3. How independent are the judiciary and courts from the executive and how free are they from all kinds of interference?

The highest court of appeal for England and Wales is the Judicial Committee of the House of Lords, which is at the head of a system of courts including magistrates' courts, crown courts and county courts at first instance, and the High Court and Court of Appeal. Under Scotland's separate legal system the highest court of appeal is the Scottish High Court of the Justiciary, with an appeal to the Judicial Committee of the Privy Council (open in certain cases to decide whether the devolved parliament has acted within its competence, or in breach of human rights standards).

In general, the courts are considered to be independent of the executive; judges have a tradition of fierce independence and they are protected at an individual level from many of the risks of reaching controversial or politically unpopular decisions. The measures that protect them include security of tenure; judicial immunities in legal proceedings; the law of contempt of court, prohibiting scurrilous criticism or imputations of partiality amounting to bad faith; and the convention that members of the executive do not criticise their actions. Rules of order in both Houses of Parliament also prevent criticism of their decisions. Criticisms must take the form of an actual resolution and a High Court judge can be dismissed only as a joint resolution of both Houses (which has happened only once – in 1830).

The imperfect separation of powers
We have already drawn attention to the hydra-headed role of the Lord Chancellor (see Section 2.1). As we stated there, he may sit as presiding judge with the law lords in the highest court in the land. In controversial cases, the composition of this court is of great significance. Three years ago Lord Irvine refused to lay down detailed rules as to when he might sit as presiding judge, saying that there is no category of cases that could be labelled 'constitutional' and 'no-go areas' for the Lord Chancellor (HL Deb, 17 February 1999). However, in 1999 a working group of eminent lawyers, set up by JUSTICE to give evidence to the Royal Commission on the Reform of the House of Lords, identified three cases of 'constitutional importance' over which Lord Irvine himself or his Conservative predecessor, Lord Mackay of Clashfern, had presided (JUSTICE working party, 1999). The cases, which they argued affected the 'the respective functions of the legislative, executive and judicial branches of governments', were:

- Pepper v Hart (1993). Lord Mackay dissented from the six other law lords who held that the courts could have recourse to ministerial statements to Parliament to resolve statutory ambiguities;
- Boddington v British Transport Police (1998). Irvine took part in this case which delineated the scope of judicial review – an issue of great importance for the executive;
- Director of Public Prosecutions v Jones and Another (1999). Irvine presided over this case 'interpreting a politically controversial change made in 1994 to the Public Order Act 1986 in light of the Convention right to freedom of peaceful assembly'.

The working group concluded that 'the present arrangements are inherently flawed, and that reform of the judicial functions of the Law Lords and of the Lord Chancellor is not a luxury but an urgent practical necessity'.

Judicial appointments

The Lord Chancellor has a determining influence on the composition of the judiciary. Yet in early 2001, Lord Irvine hosted a fund-raising dinner for the Labour party, to which lawyers who were potential candidates for judicial appointment were invited. Yet the Lord Chancellor 'advises' the Prime Minister (and in effect normally determines) on appointments to the senior judiciary and in effect appoints all judicial posts in England and Wales below the level of High Court judge. The 'cash for wigs' controversy was debated in the House of Lords (21 February 2001). No doubt no corrupt intent was involved; yet the occasion was ill-advised and demonstrated the potential for corruption of judicial office that lies in the present untidy arrangements.

The Lord Chancellor has set out 'three fundamental principles' on the LCD website which underpin the selection of candidates for judicial appointment: first, merit; usually part-time service before a full-time appointment; and soundings of 'the independent views' of senior lawyers and others as to the suitability of candidates. The last of these elements – a confidential process – is rightly criticised. Research for the Department into why so few women and ethnic-minority practitioners do not apply to be judges uncovered 'a fear that there was a need to network and socialise in the right circles to get known' (see the *Judicial Appointments Annual Report, 1999 – 2000*). Not easy for them in a profession which has no High Court judge from an ethnic minority, no female law lords and only two women among 35 Lord Justices of Appeal.

A Commission for Judicial Appointments is being established. But its role is confined to scrutiny and its remit won't run to monitoring the appointments of the Lord Chief Justice and the law lords. The First Commissioner was appointed in March 2001. The commission may contribute to greater transparency, but it falls far short of the fully independent Judicial Commission responsible for determining candidates for judicial office that a modern democracy requires. Meanwhile, the judiciary as a whole is hardly properly independent, nor even representative of the legal profession, while prominent members of the executive control its composition with secret advice from a relatively small professional elite. It should finally be noted that the Lord Chancellor is not elected, but appointed personally by a Prime Minister; and can be, like Lord Irvine, a friend and former colleague. The only constitutional stipulation, in fact, is improper: people of various Christian persuasions and non-Christians are disbarred from holding the office; and in practice no Lord Chancellor has been a woman.

2.4. How equal and secure is the access of citizens to justice, due process and redress in the event of maladministration?

The Blair government has acted to try and improve access to justice while at the same time seeking to restrict legal aid provision and spending. Recent changes include:

- New Civil Procedure Rules are now in place with the stated aim of making access to the courts simpler, quicker and more cost-effective. These rules allow for a 'fast-track' for relatively simple small claims;
- The Access to Justice Act 1999 established a Legal Services Commission responsible for the Community Legal Service (a network of legal services providers including firms of contracted solicitors, law centres and Citizen's Advice Bureaus) and the Criminal Defence Service;
- The old system of civil legal aid organised by the Legal Aid Board has been abolished.

The government's stated objective is to ensure a high standard of quality in the legal assistance made available to people, and to assess and meet developing needs through a more focused and planned service. However, far fewer solicitors' firms now provide publicly-funded legal services. Citizen's Advice Bureaus (CABs) have reported increased difficulties in finding firms to assist clients, particularly in rural areas (Green and Philo, 2000). There is also considerable concern about the level of resources being made available for civil legal aid. Under the new system, there is now a cap on total legal aid funding, with civil legal aid being funded out of the moneys remaining once criminal legal funding has been catered for.

Low levels of eligibility for legal aid clearly restrict access to justice. In 1995, the Legal Action Group indicated that legal aid eligibility on income grounds had fallen from more than three quarters (77 per cent) of households in 1979-80 to less than half (47 per cent) in 1994-95. Under new financial conditions, which determine eligibility for legal aid, an applicant with equity above £3,000 must now make a capital contribution towards legal costs under the scheme. The rules also introduced a gross income cap beyond which an applicant will not be eligible for legal aid. There are also fears that a new eligibility test of 'sufficient benefit' – an assessment of the likely success of an action and the cost of funding it – will further restrict access to justice. On the other hand, legal aid officials now have the discretion to grant legal aid under a wider public interest test, where litigation could benefit far more people than those involved in a case.

The government has sought to redress such restrictions on eligibility for legal aid by developing conditional fee agreements to fund litigation for those on low to middle incomes. These agreements with their lawyers allow people to recover fees and any insurance premium from the other party if their case succeeds. But they are unlikely to provide a suitable alternative to legal aid; and people may be refused public funds if officials consider that such an agreement would be appropriate.

In March 2001, the Lord Chancellors's Department published an early evaluation of the operation of the new civil procedure rules (LCD, 2001). Their findings indicated that that the new rules had led to fewer claims; more use of alternative dispute resolution; and faster trials. However, the findings also suggest that the new 'case management system' may have resulted in higher litigation costs, particularly at the outset of cases, which has had the effect of discouraging potential claimants.

Fair hearings

Due process in the UK is protected at common law and now also by the further right to a fair hearing under the Human Rights Act. The Act brings into force Article 6 of the European Convention that guarantees the right to a fair hearing in criminal trials, civil cases and administrative decisions where 'civil rights and obligations' are determined. The Act adds considerably to the protection available to people adversely affected by administrative decisions, made by government departments, local councils or other public authorities. It requires first that the body – either an internal review body or a tribunal – that hears and determines cases of civil rights and obligations arising out of administrative decisions must be impartial and independent of both the executive and any parties to the case. Such bodies must also:

● come to their decisions within a reasonable time;
● give adequate reasons for their decisions to the people who are affected by them;
● keep all parties informed of the progress of a case and give them adequate access to documents; and
● give the people who complain the opportunity to make representations regarding the case, at an oral hearing if appropriate.

As many administrative review bodies and tribunals are not, of their nature, independent and impartial, aggrieved people should be able to appeal to an independent court or tribunal. However, the extra protection of Article 6 doesn't apply to asylum decisions, leaving a very vulnerable group of people relatively unprotected (see 14.4). It remains to be seen whether the British courts will broaden their interpretation of Article 6 to redress this imbalance.

In December 2001, the UN Human Rights Committee, the guardian of the UN Covenant on Civil and Political Rights, recorded that it was 'troubled' by the fact that juries may draw negative inferences from the silence of accused people on trial and asked the government to re-consider this in order to ensure compliance with the rights to fair trial guaranteed under Article 14 of the Covenant. The Committee was also concerned that, under the Criminal Procedure and Investigations Act 1996, the prosecution can seek a non-reviewable decision by a court to withhold on public interest immunity grounds sensitive evidence that would otherwise be disclosed to defence lawyers acting for someone on trial. The government failed to justify this power – that clearly prejudices a citizen's right to a fair trial – to the Committee. The use of public interest immunity certificates (PIICs) caused great concern during the 1990s 'arms to Iraq' cases when they were very widely drafted, to avoid disclosure of discreditable information and often simply for administrative convenience; and did not necessarily refer to the national interests that disclosure of information might damage (Richard Norton-Taylor et al, 1996). In his report on the export of defence equipment to Iraq and Iran in 1996, the High Court judge Sir Richard Scott condemned the use of 'class' PIICs (i.e., across-the-board refusals to disclose whole classes of documents to defence lawyers).

Redress for maladministration

Outside the courts, ombudsmen and other complaints bodies exist to investigate maladministration in the public service. They possess varying powers which do not always include the capacity to award compensation or other redress. The Ombudsman with the most wide-ranging remit is the Parliamentary Commissioner for Administration (PCA), whose terms of reference are to investigate complaints by individual people who claim to have 'sustained injustice in consequence of maladministration' by specified government departments, executive agencies, quangos and any bodies or officials acting on their behalf (see a fuller account in Weir and Beetham, 1999; see also De Smith and Brazier, 1998).

Here we discuss the role of the Parliamentary Ombudsman (PCA) in relation to scrutiny of public decisions.[1] Strictly speaking, he cannot accept complaints directly from individual citizens; complaints should be referred to him through an MP. However, for many years the PCA has passed important cases from the public on to sympathetic MPs for their sponsorship. The Ombudsman cannot overturn the decisions of public bodies and the response to his findings is at the discretion of the public body concerned. But he has wide powers of investigation and can also report on his findings to both Houses of Parliament. In some cases, government departments have made *ex gratia* payments to individuals who have had their claims upheld (see further Weir and Beetham, 1999).

2.4. How far do the criminal justice and penal systems observe due rules of impartial and equitable treatment in their operations?

The Criminal Justice Act 1994 requires the Home Secretary to publish annually information that will help criminal justice agencies in England and Wales to avoid unlawful discrimination. The resulting statistics provide a wealth of information about the age, gender and ethnicity of people passing through all stages of the criminal justice and penal systems: from arrest, through charge, to court and beyond.

The power of the police to stop and search people on suspicion has long been the focus of criticism. The potential for these powers to be used disproportionately against ethnic minorities has been highlighted most recently in an internal Metropolitan Police report, published in January 2001, into the treatment of Delroy Lindo and his family. Police officers stopped Delroy Lindo, a black man from north London, 37 times in eight years. He has had 17 charges against him quashed and suffered one wrongful conviction. The report concluded that he and his wife had been subjected to 'unwarranted and unreasonable treatment'. This report is to be read against the background of Home Office statistics (Home Office, 2000a) showing persistent bias against black people in the use of these powers (see Section 3.1 below). Black people were four times more likely to be stopped than white people and four times as likely as whites to be arrested.

At court, Home Office figures showed that young ethnic minority defendants were less likely to be convicted and more likely to have their cases terminated before trial than young whites (Home Office, 2000b). However, these apparently favourable findings probably reflect the fact (as indicated in research cited by the Commission for Racial Equality in 1999) that black and Asian people tend to be arrested and charged on weaker evidence than whites. In 1993-94, there was sufficient evidence to support nearly two thirds of white arrests, but nearer half of black (56 per cent) and Asian (52 per cent) arrests.

Further, research has found that it is only when the judge and prosecuting counsel introduce 'a truly objective and independent element' into case reviews at the Crown Court that the original charges and the evidence for them are properly appraised. Defendants also believed strongly that there was less potential for racial bias in front of a Crown Court judge and jury – not necessarily because magistrates are biased, but because they believed that 'the collective decision-making of the jury, rather than that of the single stipendiary magistrate or bench of lay justices, provides a better chance of bias on the part of any individual being balanced out' (Bridges et al, 1994). The avoidance not just of bias itself, but also of the appearance of bias, plays an important part in the contemporary conception of the rule of law and in maintaining confidence in the legal system. The Fawcett Society has also raised this issue in relation to gender. The Society applied, unsuccessfully, in 2001 to the law lords for permission to intervene in their hearing of a case in which they were considering the admissibility of evidence in rape trials of a complainant's previous sexual activity. The Society argued that on such a gender-sensitive issue, an all-male tribunal such as the law lords gave rise to a reasonable apprehension of bias; and, as it transpired, they were right (see below).

Post-trial, despite favourable rates of acquittal, ethnic minorities are still statistically over-represented in prison. Home Office findings show that in June 1999, ethnic minorities accounted for 18 per cent of the male prison population (compared with 5.2 per cent of the general population) and 25 per cent of the female prison population. Black prisoners also tended to be serving the longest sentences. It is also cause for concern that about two thirds of all remand prisoners and two-fifths of the sentenced population suffer from some form of mental disorder; and that ethnic minorities and poor and vulnerable members of the community are also over-represented among the victims of crime as well as among those who are arrested, convicted and sentenced. Overall in the criminal justice system, ethnic minorities are under-represented in only one aspect – its staffing. In 1998, 2 per cent of police officers in England and Wales were from ethnic minority groups, nine out of ten of them being constables; 8.2 per cent of solicitors and 8.5 per cent of barristers, and a mere 1.7 per cent of QCs were from ethnic minority groups. Beyond the five ethnic minority circuit judges, 13 recorders and 13 assistance recorders there are no ethnic minority members amongst the senior judiciary.

Being 'tough on crime'

The question of law and order is clearly one of the greatest concerns within communities. A government's determination to be 'tough on crime' may sometimes place them in conflict with the civil and political rights of suspects and the accused. A government has also the responsibility of legislating in a manner that addresses social ills and problems. However, the fair and impartial administration of justice is vital to a democratic society, which means that it is important not to dilute important fair trial rights.

The government has now abandoned plans to restrict jury trials, but other proposals to toughen the law and impose stricter sentences will require close monitoring. For example, the government plans to place greater restrictions on the rule against 'double jeopardy' (preventing someone from being tried twice for the same offence). The argument against relaxing the rule against double jeopardy has been that it could result in sloppy police investigations since the police could always bring an action again; and that it would place an acquitted person in the intolerable position of never knowing whether they could be re-charged for the same offence. On the other hand, scientific advances, like those in DNA technology, can provide strong new evidence that was not available at the time of an original trial. The government's proposals for change are likely to follow a Law Commission report that suggested a new trial should be allowed where new and compelling evidence comes to light after an acquittal. But can a fair conviction be achieved in a re-trial, especially in high-profile cases, without breaching the right of the accused to be presumed innocent?

Rape trials

The courts are sometimes required to work out approaches to the law that strike a balance between the rights of the defendant and the interests of the victim. One such area concerns the allegation of rape that is notoriously difficult to prove. The vital question before the jury is often whether to believe that the woman consented to intercourse or not. The Youth Justice and Criminal Justice Act 1999 attempted, in the face of opposition from the House of Lords, to restrict the scope of such evidence. Cross-examination on the previous sexual history of a victim is now supposed to be allowed only in exceptional circumstances and with the consent of the judge. The law lords recently had to consider whether the restrictions were capable of preventing an accused from putting forward evidence which may be critical to his defence, thereby preventing him from receiving a fair trial (R v A, 2001). In this case, the defendant said that they had had sex before and she denied it. Remarkably, the four male judges reinterpreted the repugnant and now discredited belief that if a woman had previously consented she was more likely to have consented again. They concluded that it was 'common sense' that if a woman had had sex with a man before, she was more likely to have consented to sex on the occasion when she testified that she had been raped. Thus his 'evidence' of a previous relationship was deemed admissible. In each case trial judges would need to hold the balance between protection of the woman and the relevance of evidence to ensure that the trial is fair. The law lord, Lord Hutton, hinted at where he believed the boundary between the right to a fair trial and the interests of an individual and society when he commented that:

> the rights of a defendant to call relevant evidence, where the absence of such evidence may give rise to an unjust conviction, is an absolute right which cannot be qualified by considerations of public interest, no matter how well founded that public interest may be.

As the Fawcett Society, or any woman judge, could have told the four men, any number of factors might have made a woman less likely to repeat such an experience, and equally there may have been factors that made it more likely. Common sense should not point only one way (see also pages 34-5 above and barrister Vera Baird in the *Guardian*, 6 August 2001).

2.6. How much confidence do people have in the legal system to deliver fair and effective justice?

In 1999, researchers from University College, London, and the National Centre for Social Research published the results of the most comprehensive survey to date of public perceptions of the civil law. They found:

- 'a widespread perception that legal proceedings involve uncertainty, expense and potential long-term disturbance and that only the most serious matters could justify enduring those conditions';
- 'Fears about the cost of embarking on legal proceedings and a belief that resources are crucially important to the outcome of litigation lead many people to feel that the courts are largely irrelevant to their lives and to the resolution of their problems.' (Genn, 1999).

Civil justice
Over five years one in four people experienced common problems which had the potential to be solved

through the civil law: faulty goods and services; money problems; owning residential property; injury and work-related health problems; living in rented accommodation; relationships and family matters; employment problems; divorce; problems involving children; negligent medical treatment; unfair treatment by police; discrimination on grounds of race, sex or disability; and immigration. Many people experienced more than one of these problems. But only just over half of these people sought legal advice about their problem. Few cases went to a court, tribunal, ombudsman, or other formal resolution. The research concluded that a large 'dark figure' of hidden potential demand for civil justice existed.

Barely half of the people questioned were confident that they would get a fair hearing in court and, worryingly, people with past experience of the legal system had less confidence in it than those who had never sought legal advice. Nearly three quarters of people said that lawyers charged too much for the work they do; and the same proportion agreed, 'The legal system works better for rich people than for poor'. Two thirds thought judges were remote, insensitive, inconsistent in sentencing, and 'out of touch with ordinary people's lives'.

Criminal justice

Political manipulation of crime figures and fear of crime causes strong anxiety and anger about the perceived prevalence of crime. There is particular fear in some cities about violent 'street crime', which is often drug-related. Low police clear-up rates and the perceived absence of police officers 'on the beat' fuel such concerns. Incompetent police investigations in high-profile murder cases, like those of Stephen Lawrence and Damilola Taylor – and the Yorkshire Ripper in an earlier era – undermine confidence in the criminal justice system as well as in the police. One woman in four is either raped or suffers an attempted rape during her life, but women have so little confidence in the sensitivity and effectiveness of criminal justice that victims frequently do not report being raped. There is a well-founded fear that they will be fiercely cross-examined and asked intrusive questions about their past sexual behaviour. Low conviction rates compound the problem (see also Sections 2.4, 2.5 and 3.1).

There are another two concerns about the criminal justice system. The Crown Prosecution Service was under-funded from its launch in 1986 and its performance is only slowly improving. The CPS inspectorate published the results of a survey in May 2002 which suggest that the service wrongly abandoned about 11,000 cases in 2001, some 'with little or no record of any analysis or reasons for the decision'. The inspectorate also called for action to monitor and reduce the number of 'ineffective' trials and those that do not go ahead ('cracked trials') in magistrates' courts – between 55 and 80 per cent of the total (*Guardian*, 4 May 2002).

Wrongful convictions are another major concern. After a run of high-profile miscarriages of justice in the 1980s, the Criminal Case Review Commission was established to take over the task of reviewing possible wrongful convictions from the Home Office. The Commission took over a backlog of some 250 cases from the Home Office; 'the files arrived in a pantechnicon,' an official said (*Times Law Reports*, 30 April 2002). The Commission has since received some 800 cases a year. Five years later, the Commission has referred just 161 cases (4 per cent of the total) to the Court of Appeal for review. But referral to the Court is only a stage in the process. The appeal judges then decide if a conviction should be quashed or a case sent for re-trial. The Commission only sends on appeals that it believes are likely to be allowed, in effect second-guessing the Court of Appeal. Even then, the Court is very rigorous: of the 161 cases sent so far, 95 have been heard. Two thirds of convictions have been quashed; the rest upheld. But rejected appeals have been rising, prompting concerns that the Court is taking a tougher line and defending the criminal courts' record. One lawyer for a rejected appellant has argued that convictions are now sustained even in 'the face of compelling new evidence' (*TLR*, 30 April 2002). Many lawyers are now arguing that the court that considers appeals should be independent of the constraints and loyalties of the present criminal justice system.

Creating confidence in Northern Ireland

Police reforms and the new independent Police Ombudsman in Northern Ireland aim to create new confidence among the Catholic community while not alienating the Protestant majority. A judicial inquiry into the shootings of Republicans in Derry on 'Bloody Sunday' in 1972 is being held to reassure Catholics about the impartiality of UK rule. Sir John Stevens, now Metropolitan Police Commissioner, has now held three police investigations into the murder of human rights lawyer, Pat Finucane, over a period of nine years (see Section 8.4). However, the government has failed to hold public inquiries into the significant number of unsolved sectarian murders, including those of Finucane and another human rights lawyer, Rosemary Nelson, even though years have elapsed and few people have been prosecuted. The UN Human Rights Committee remarked that this neglect is 'doubly troubling' while 'persistent allegations of involvement and collusion' by the security forces, including the Force Research Unit, remain unresolved. The Committee demanded urgent measures to ensure 'a full, transparent and credible' account of the circumstances surrounding these murders (UN Human Rights Committee, 2001). Amnesty International's annual report in May 2002 complained that no action had been taken against RUC officers accused of issuing death threats against Rosemary Nelson.[2]

Leniency of sentences

The public hold strong views about the perceived leniency of sentences for causing death by dangerous driving; legal aid for rich defendants, such as the Maxwell brothers in 1996; and expensive fraud trials. The high-profile case of Robin Peverett, former headmaster of Dulwich College, who received a suspended sentence of 18 months in October 2000, thanks to a plea bargain after pleading guilty to nine charges of indecent assault against his pupils, provoked a public outcry. As Lord Williams of Mostyn told the *Observer*, 'the public have the view: 'What is going on here? What is going on behind the back door? Would such a bargain be available to someone with a different social background?' (22 October 2000). But it is not only those of higher social status who escape sentences for drunk and dangerous driving, for example, that the public regard as inadequate to express society's disapproval.

---

1   For convenience, we use the words 'he' and 'his' in all references to an ombudsman service.

2   As we go to press, the government has asked a Canadian judge to examine six cases where security force collusion with terrorists is alleged, including the murders of Pat Finucane and Rosemary Nelson and those of victims of the IRA and INLA.

Three: civil and political rights

Protecting political freedoms

Are civil and political rights guaranteed equally for all?

Human rights are now probably as significant as the Bible has been in shaping modern, western values. With the coming into force of the Human Rights act their influence in Britain is set to expand significantly.
Francesca Klug, human rights author, 2000

Introduction

Democracy cannot work without effective civil and political rights. Citizens must be able to join together in associations and to meet freely to discuss their aspirations and needs, their concerns and possible remedies. They must be able to express their views freely. They must have access to uncontaminated information from government and a variety of independent sources. Open government and free media are essential underpinnings of these rights.

Moreover, citizens must be equal in their enjoyment of such rights, whatever their gender, race, religion, ethnic origin, sexual orientation or economic or other status. Minorities of all kinds must feel secure in their freedom to use their own language and to practise their own religion and culture. Otherwise there can be no political equality to ensure that the needs and views of all sections of society are given voice and taken into account. Above all, all citizens must be free from intimidation and violence, and the fear and threat of violence. Physical security of the person is the basis for the exercise of all other rights.

The Human Rights Act 1998

The first democratic audit of political freedom in the UK in 1996 showed that the structure for safeguarding fundamental civil and political rights in the UK was seriously inadequate, and offered less protection than ordinary citizens were entitled to expect (Klug et al, 1996). The audit identified 42 violations of international human rights standards in British law, and a further 22 examples of UK law or practice which came close to infringing those standards, or which gave cause for concern. In similar vein, the report of the authoritative UN Human Rights Committee – the guardian of the International Covenant on Civil and Political Rights (to which the UK is a signatory) – in 1995 found that the UK failed both to protect civil and political rights and to provide an effective remedy for violations of such rights. The only remedy for people denied the protection of Convention rights was first to exhaust all domestic legal processes and then to take their case to the European Court of Human Rights – a costly and long drawn-out trek that usually provided redress too late for the aggrieved petitioner.

The Human Rights Act 1998 has gone a long way to remedying these deficiencies. The Act, which incorporates into British law the European Convention on Human Rights. Citizens will now be able to appeal to UK courts directly for protection of their rights, or for remedy in case of their violation. The Convention covers such rights as the right to life, to liberty and security of the person, to fair trial, to freedoms of thought, expression, assembly, association, and so on. Although most of these rights are subject to such limitations 'as are prescribed by law and necessary in a democratic society', these limitations are themselves subject to interpretation by the courts, not just to the government's say -so. And in interpreting the Convention's safeguards, the courts will be able to make use of the rich case law developed over 50 years of the European Court's existence.

For the first time, UK courts will be able to apply Convention standards to parliamentary legislation as well as to administrative and executive decisions at all levels of government. Although the Act does not give judges the power actually to strike down laws passed by a democratically elected Parliament, they have the power to issue a 'declaration of incompatibility' between legislation and rights under the Convention, which ministers must address either by changing the law or explaining why they will not do so. The principle of parliamentary sovereignty is thus preserved in form, and it remains to be seen whether ministers will persist with legislation once it has been publicly declared to be in violation of human rights standards. In the case of the Scottish Parliament, and the assemblies of Wales and Northern Ireland, legislation is fully subordinate to the Act's provisions.

The Human Rights Act is a landmark in British constitutional reform that ranks in significance alongside the Magna Carta and the 1689 Bill of Rights. For the most part, the Act and the rights it enshrines mark a radical shift in how government is required to operate, as will be discussed in detail in the answers to the questions that follow. However, ministers themselves seem not to have fully appreciated the significance of their own Act. Home Secretaries Jack Straw and David Blunkett, who has made no secret of his view that unelected judges should not dictate to elected politicians, have persisted with measures that seem *prima facie* to contravene the Act's provisions, such as restricting 'football hooligans' from travelling abroad, imposing child curfews on older children, storing DNA samples and finger-prints from suspects indefinitely and demanding official access to website, email and telephone logs (indeed, legal advice to the Information Commissioner warns that the government's electronic surveillance regime may be illegal; *Guardian*, 31 July 2002).

The events of 11 September severely tested the government's commitment to the protection of civil and political rights under the Act. David Blunkett had recently passed the Terrorism Act 2000 through Parliament to give the authorities strong and wide powers to deal with terrorism. However, he at once rushed the Anti-Terrorism, Crime and Security Act 2001 through Parliament; shovelled extra powers for the police and security forces into the Act; and declared a complete derogation from the terms of the Human Rights Act, to enable him to lock up foreign terrorist suspects of being terrorists without charge or legal appeal, on the grounds of 'public emergency threatening the life of the nation'. There is some doubt whether the derogation would survive a legal challenge. In December 2001, the UN Human Rights Committee criticised the 2000 Act's powers of detention and questioned their compatibility with the UN Covenant.[1] The Committee also warned that the legislation 'may have potentially far-reaching effects on rights guaranteed in the Covenant'.

3.1. How free are all people from intimidation and fear, physical violation of their person, arbitrary arrest and detention?

Freedom from fear and intimidation are the pre-requisites of any participatory democracy. The circumstances in which the state can deprive citizens of their life or liberty determine how far they are able to enjoy, if at all, their civil and political rights. English law has long had protections in place to protect citizens from the coercive power of the state. The Habeas Corpus Act 1641 gave people detained by the authorities the right to apply to the courts for immediate release from custody. The well-established obligation upon the state not to inflict 'cruel and unusual punishment' was part of the 1689 Bill of Rights. In 1996, the Democratic Audit found that the formal laws on the use of lethal force and the powers of the police and security forces generally met international human rights standards, but there were significant exceptions:

- abuses in practice from fatal shootings in Northern Ireland and Gibraltar to discriminatory use of police 'stop and search' powers violated those standards;
- the scale of evidence of ill-treatment of suspects in police custody; and
- powers of prolonged detention under the Prevention of Terrorism Acts (PTAs), which then gave rise to the UK's only derogation from its human rights obligations, were misused for information gathering only (Klug et al, 1996).

Powers of arrest, stop and search and detention
The police's general powers of arrest are set out in law and codes of practice, as required by the European Convention, and usually require police officers to act on a warrant or 'reasonable suspicion'. But they are nevertheless broad: police officers may arrest people for 'obstruction on the highway' or to prevent a breach of the peace – a concept that is so vague and undefined that it probably itself breaches the European Convention. Police officers also possess general powers to stop and search people or

vehicles if they reasonably suspect that they will find evidence of an arrestable crime. If the police are about to question someone about an offence, they must first caution them. Suspects for an arrestable offence may be held in police custody for up to 24 hours without charge, and for up to 96 hours if the offence is serious (but not beyond 36 hours without a magistrate's warrant).

The use of police powers of stop and search aroused concern and resentment when it became clear that these powers were used more heavily against black people than against whites. The Macpherson report on the racial murder of black teenager Stephen Lawrence urged more sensitive use of these powers. The use of stop and search powers fell in the wake of the report, creating concerns that the police were being hampered in their efforts to stop street crime and burglary. At the same time, black people were five times more likely to be stopped and searched than whites (*Guardian*, 11 March 2002). In 1999, the *Statewatch* bulletin published analysis of the incidence and effect of police stop, search and arrest activities that showed great discrepancies in their use between police forces and consistent bias against black people. The report questioned the value of police activities on the street in combating crime (vol 9, No. 1, January–February 1999).

Anti-terrorism legislation

The incorporation of the European Convention into British law should strengthen and systematise the safeguards that already exist in the procedures for arrest, stop and search, and detention. However the government's recent anti-terrorism and criminal justice laws weaken that protection and may very well lead to abuses. The 2000 Act gives the police:

- 'a special arrest power' to enable them to arrest without warrant or evidence of any offence someone they suspect of 'involvement with terrorism';
- general powers to stop and search people and vehicles 'for the prevention of terrorism' in Northern Ireland; and
- power to detain suspects for 48 hours without access to a lawyer if they believe that this access would lead, for example, to interference with evidence or alerting another suspect.

The 2000 Act also:

- contains a very wide definition of terrorism that could, for example, be misused in the wrong hands;
- authorises the continued use of 'Diplock courts' in Northern Ireland. These courts consist of only a judge, sitting without a jury. People charged with a range of 'scheduled offences'- e.g., murder, riot, kidnapping, etc. – that may be acts of terrorism are subject to a separate regime of criminal procedure and are likely to be tried in a Diplock court;
- gives the Home Secretary the power to proscribe an organisation as terrorist without having to prove a case against it in court. The right of appeal against proscription is only to a special commission, not to the courts; and
- creates offences where the burden of proof may be placed on the accused to prove their innocence.

The UN Human Rights Committee argued in its report of December 2001 that the UN Covenant on Civil and Political Rights requires the British authorities to provide 'objective and reasonable grounds' to justify the use of Diplock courts and questions whether the exigencies of the uneasy peace in Northern Ireland continue to justify their use. The Committee also warned that the power to hold suspects in detention for 48 hours may violate Articles 9 and 14 (on arrest and fair criminal process); and stated that other less intrusive means for achieving the same ends exist (UN Human Rights Committee, 2001).

The Anti-Terrorism, Crime and Security Act 2001 also contains powers bearing on people's physical security that provoke human rights concerns. For example, the Act gives the police the power to search anyone detained at a police station in order to determine his or her identity, and likewise to photograph them for the same purpose, using force if necessary. Constables on the street are also now empowered to require any person to remove face coverings or other items that concealed their identity. The parliamentary Joint Committee on Human Rights questioned whether such powers were proportionate to the problem they sought to address, pointing out potential interference to the rights guaranteed to ordinary citizens under the European Convention, such as the right to privacy (paras. 61-64, 2001).

The derogation that Blunkett applied for was to allow the government, contrary to human rights law, to continue to detain foreign suspects whom they cannot send back to a country where they may be executed or tortured. At time of writing, nine suspects, all Muslims, were being held. Organisations like Liberty fear that the detention powers give too much credence to what intelligence experts speculate a suspect might do, rather than on what a person actually has done (Liberty briefing, November 2001). MPs on the Home Affairs Select Committee echoed concerns about the quality of intelligence information and cited as a cautionary tale the over-enthusiastic detention of Iraqis during the Gulf War – many, if not all, of whom were eventually released without charge, some later receiving compensation (HC 352, 15 November 2001).

Police custody and prison

In its annual report for 2001, Amnesty International drew attention to deaths in police custody, ill-treatment and disputed killings by the police, including the death of Harry Stanley, shot dead by officers in September 1999 in east London, while walking home carrying a repaired table leg in a bag. The Crown Prosecution Service decided not to prosecute any officer. The inquest in June 2002, more than two years later, failed satisfactorily to resolve the issues that the shooting raised. The coroner refused to allow the jury to return a verdict of 'unlawful killing' and gave them a choice between an open verdict and one of lawful killing. The jury returned an open verdict, apparently refusing to justify the shooting.

The UN Human Rights Committee was also disturbed at the sharp increase in racist incidents within the criminal justice system, particularly those reported as having been committed by police or by prison staff against inmates. There is a need for more transparent reporting and investigation of racist incidents within prisons and reform of the inquest system.

Meanwhile, more than 71,000 people are now in prison in England and Wales and this figure will rise still further to 78,000 by 2007 unless major changes are made. The number of women in prison has risen by 21 per cent in the past year and on current trends will double by 2007. England and Wales has the highest imprisonment rate – 133 inmates for every 100,000 people – of any country in western Europe, except for Portugal, and proportionately more people in prison than China, Saudi Arabia and Turkey. The rate for Scotland is 120 per 100,000, also very high by European standards, and for Northern Ireland it is 50 per 100,000.

Our prisons are also grossly overcrowded. The official capacity of prisons in England and Wales is 63,986. Thus the occupancy rate (in May 2002) was 111 per cent. Overcrowding breaches both UN standards and European Prison Rules. It forces prisoners and their families hundreds of miles apart, separates mothers from their children, perpetuates squalor and 'slopping out', disrupts education programmes and encourages disciplinarian regimes. Magistrates sentence thousands of people to a week or less in prison, often creating family breakdown and job loss.

Ever since the prison riots and anarchy of 1991, Home Secretaries have promised to reform the prison and penal system, and David Blunkett is no exception to this rule. There are positive elements. The prison inspectors have issued remarkably robust independent reports on conditions in prisons and the Prisons Ombudsman takes up prisoners' complaints. The service at its senior levels is self-critical and committed to reform. But inspectors' reports and reforms are engulfed by the sheer weight of numbers. British prisons are at crisis point. Winston Churchill once said that the way we treat our prisoners reflected the 'moral fibre' of the nation. Our prisons now are a glass through which we observe ourselves darkly.

Over 600 women and young people committed suicide in prison in England and Wales in the 1990s –roughly a third of whom had previously been in touch with mental health services. Of the 91 suicides in 1999, 64 were not being given psychological or practical assistance. Further, more than 50 people kill themselves each year shortly after leaving prison because the prison and probation services neglect them (figures from the Howard League for Prison Reform).

Uneasy peace in Northern Ireland

Since the Belfast Agreement in April 1998, the government, Stormont and most political forces in Northern Ireland have sought to move away from organised sectarian violence and the extraordinary security measures in place there towards higher promotion of respect for human rights and fundamental freedoms. The government has introduced police reforms and is seeking to make the police there more representative of both communities (see also Section 8). A Human Rights Commission has been established. But incidents of sectarian violence and intimidation continue to occur.

Racial riots and violence

Though the government has introduced new criminal offences of racially aggravated violence, harassment or criminal damage, recent violent outbreaks of serious race rioting in Burnley and other north English cities seriously endanger the security and property of people of minority ethnic origins. The government has a duty under the European Convention to protect the security of residents of such towns and to facilitate dialogue between different communities. The UN Human Rights Committee recommends that the government 'should also consider facilitating inter-political party arrangements to ensure that racial tension is not inflamed during political campaigns' (2001). Since 11 September, there have been unprovoked attacks on people of Asian origin, usually on the basis of their religious beliefs.

Asylum-seekers

Asylum-seekers have been detained in various facilities for administrative convenience and other grounds that are not acceptable under the European Convention or the International Covenant. Some are wrongly detained in prisons. Asylum-seekers refused entry to the UK have been held in detention for a prolonged period when deportation is impossible for legal or other reasons. The forced dispersal of asylum-seekers may have adverse effects on their ability to obtain good legal advice. Dispersal and the system of vouchers for asylum-seekers (that is now being abolished) have on occasion put their physical security at risk. The government is reforming the system for considering the claims of asylum-seekers (see Section 14.4).

Protecting people from harm

The Convention not only prohibits 'torture, inhuman or degrading treatment or punishment' under Article 3, but also places a positive obligation on the government to protect individuals from harm. There is an evident need in the UK fully to protect children in abusive families. On 10 May 2001, the European Court held that the failure of social services to place four seriously neglected children into care, despite monitoring their situation for nearly five years, contravened Article 3 (Z v UK, App. No.29392/95, unreported). The European Court acknowledged that social services had to resolve difficult and sensitive issues and observe the 'countervailing principle of respecting and preserving family life', but the protection of human life was one of the most fundamental values of a democratic society. The state must therefore:

> provide effective protection, in particular, of children and other vulnerable persons and include reasonable steps to prevent ill-treatment of which the authorities had or ought to have had knowledge.

This positive obligation on the authorities was also highlighted in the case of Keenan v UK, another recent unreported case (3 April 2001, App. No. 27229/95). Keenan was a prisoner with a history of paranoia, aggression and deliberate self-harm. He committed suicide after being placed in segregation following attacks on two hospital officers. The European Court found that significant defects in the medical care provided to a mentally-ill person who was known to be a suicide risk amounted to a violation of Article 3.

Corporal punishment

Under the European Court, children are now protected against excessive corporal punishment in the home. British governments have traditionally refused to act on domestic corporal punishment, but in 1998 the European Court ruled that a step-father who beat a child with, among other things, a garden cane, had violated the child's rights (although it did not advocate an outright ban on corporal punishment in the home; A v UK). The government still refuses to outlaw all forms of corporal punishment against children, but will seek to define 'acceptable' physical punishment.

3.2. How effective and equal is the protection of the freedoms of expression, information, association and assembly?

It is largely the police who patrol the boundary between the lawful and unlawful exercise of these basic freedoms. We are concerned that the anti-terrorism and criminal justice laws, passed by the Labour government since 1997, may put these freedoms at risk, even though they should now have systematic protection under the European Convention. We describe the new police powers in some detail in Section 3.1. above; and we fear that the new laws do not contain sufficient safeguards to prevent their use against people peacefully exercising their rights to free assembly, protest and association.

Freedom of expression

Speakers' Corner in London is a popular but misleading symbol of the British tradition of free speech. In fact, free speech in the UK is prized and tolerated only within legal and official -often unspoken or unseen – constraints. Parliament, governments and the courts have long been criticised for adopting the view that 'free speech is a good thing so long as it does not cause trouble' (Robertson and Nichol, 1992). It is governed by the Official Secrets Act and laws of government secrecy (over 300 of them; see section 7.7); laws of defamation, sedition, blasphemy, and copyright. It is constrained by the media regulatory authorities and other bodies, such as the Defence, Press and Broadcasting Advisory Committee (hereafter, 'the defence advisory committee').

Freedom of expression is of course not absolute anywhere. But British law has not until now accepted that free speech should be protected and that restrictions should be exceptional; and that they should not outweigh the basic principle of freedom of expression unless the need for them is convincingly established. These principles are embodied in the European Convention (see further Klug et al, 1996) that now forms part of UK law.

The European Court places great value on the role of the media as essential public watchdogs and producers of information on matters of political and public interest. Recently in the House of Lords, the law lord, Lord Nicholls, echoed this view, commenting that without free media, 'freedom of expression would be a hollow concept'. But governments here frequently challenge the right of television programmes and journalists, like the BBC's *Panorama*, Kate Adie and John Simpson, to report on air on the conflict in Northern Ireland, or the bombing of Libya or Serbia, or of television channels to broadcast Osima bin Laden's videos. In addition, a new public consensus seems to be emerging to the effect that free speech ought not to cause offence.

But in a democratic society, as the European Court stated in reviewing the prosecution of the publisher of *The Little Red Schoolbook* in the 1970s, the right to freedom of expression must protect not only information or ideas that are agreeable to the state and others, but also those that may 'offend, shock or disturb the state or any section of the population' since democracy is characterised by 'pluralism, tolerance and broadmindedness' (Handyside v UK, 1976).

Government interference

In July 2000, the UN Special Rapporteur on Freedom of Expression reported that the Official Secrets Act and the defence advisory committee were 'incompatible with media freedom'. The Act was used to 'stifle legitimate debate and to penalise writers and journalists who refuse to reveal their sources.' The UN Human Rights Committee has also expressed its concern about the use of powers under the Act 'to frustrate former employees of the Crown from bringing into the public domain issues of genuine public concern, and to prevent journalists from publishing such matters'.

The government can turn to the law to restrain media publication of information that they dislike, and especially information on defence, counter-terrorism and 'national security'. But it also uses the defence advisory committee, an official MOD body (which is not listed in the official directory, *Public Bodies*), to give 'guidance' to the media on what information they may publish on security, defence and counter-terrorism issues. The committee is in essence a censorship body that encourages self-censorship in the media, including publishing.

The committee dates from 1912 but its existence first came to light only in the 1960s. Its remit and workings were revised in 2000 following the break-up of the Soviet Union and Warsaw Pact. It is largely made up of media representatives, but a senior MOD official occupies the chair and its secretary is a high-ranking retired officer (currently a former rear-admiral). The committee issues five standing 'DA' notices containing its guidance and specific 'DA' notices as required; and the media can seek the secretary's advice and negotiate with him over the substance or details of stories they wish to publish. The defence advisory system is avowedly voluntary, and its notices have no legal force. But they issue forth under the sword of the punitive Official Secrets Act, and thus the system is not truly voluntary. Even if the media comply with the secretary's advice, they can still fall foul of the Official Secrets Act.

According to Article 19 and Liberty, the current secretary has argued that negotiation with him is preferable to slow and expensive litigation that 'tends to . . . end in blanket suppression of a story or source, rather than the removal of just a few details' (November 2000). But journalists have found that entering into negotiation with him can lead to an early injunction or investigation under the Official Secrets Act. The treatment of Tony Geraghty, author of *The Irish War*, on the surveillance work of intelligence agencies in Northern Ireland, is a case in point. Geraghty refused a request from the secretary to submit his manuscript for clearance under DA notices, fearing that the request was made to facilitate identifying his sources. The secretary expressed his hope that Geraghty 'would not come to regret' his non co-operation. When the book was published, MOD police raided Geraghty's house in December 1998, and Geraghty was charged under the Official Secrets Act. (The prosecution was later withdrawn after sustained and hostile publicity).

Governments can interfere politically as well. We discuss recent government interference in the media, and especially in the BBC and television, from Mrs Thatcher's heyday to Alastair Campbell's media management on behalf of Tony Blair, later in Section 10.2.

Censorship through the courts

The law of defamation ensures that the media and publishers adopt a high degree of caution before submitting anything to print or the air waves. The threshold for what constitutes a libel is low and uncertain – it need simply lower a plaintiff in the eyes of right-thinking people, or expose them to hatred, ridicule or contempt. It is then up to the defence to prove that was said is both true and published without malice, or is 'privileged' by law.

Defamation is the one branch of the common law for which legal aid is unavailable. The costs and complications of defending a libel action are huge; and actions launched by wealthy individuals, corporate bodies and professional organisations can cost hundreds of thousands of pounds to defend. Small magazines can be either forced to apologise or be extinguished by the size of defence costs alone; even national newspapers are often cowed by a writ. The comparatively low level for complaint, for example, forces American and British publishers to censor US books and magazines distributed in the UK to avoid being sued over statements that are part of normal public debate in the USA.

Thus, powerful and wealthy people or bodies have privileged access to a strong weapon of restraint or redress. The media are not afforded a public interest defence as of right (which exists in many other countries, such as Australia, New Zealand and India) – though the House of Lords, in refusing to accept the legitimacy of a public interest defence, accepted in 1999 that it would do so where the media established that there was a 'right to know' (4 All ER 609). The direction of developing case law in the European Court of Human Rights also suggests that journalists will be entitled to use a public interest defence where issues of legitimate public concern are raised (see Bergens Tidende v Norway, 2 March 2000). This seems similar to the robust approach of Lord Nicholls in the case Albert Reynolds, the former Irish prime minister, brought against the *Sunday Times* the same year:

> The press discharges vital functions as a bloodhound as well as a watchdog. The court should be slow to conclude that a publication was not in the public interest and, therefore, the public had no right to know, especially when the information is in the field of political discussion. Any lingering doubts should be resolved in favour of publication.

Nevertheless, the media are often intimidated into either silence or apology by powerful figures or interests who are prepared to sue for defamation through the courts. Often the mere issue of a writ serves to deter publication or force an apology.

Injunctions

Pre-trial court injunctions to prevent publication of material to which someone (usually a strong corporation or rich person) objects, have been a major obstacle to media freedom. One of the main objects of section 12 of the Human Rights Act is to limit their scope in future. In particular, there was concern that there should be no pre-trial prohibition on publication unless a court is satisfied that it is likely that the publication would not be allowed when the matter came to trial. The Home Secretary emphasised this measure during the debates during the bill stage of the Act:

> no relief is granted to restrain publication pending a full trial of the issues unless the court is satisfied that the applicant is likely to succeed at trial ... we believe that the courts should consider the merits of an application when it is made and should not grant an interim injunction simply to preserve the *status quo ante* between the parties (HC Deb, 2 July 1998).

However, this does not give editors or others a right to publish that overrides other rights and, in particular, the right to privacy (see Section 3.4).

Governments have obtained injunctions to suppress information in the past: for example, in 1987, both to stop a BBC radio series about the security forces, *My Country Right or Wrong*, and to ban mention of the allegations of former MI5 officer Peter Wight in his memoir, *Spycatcher*. In particular, governments are still likely to seek to protect the security services from unwanted or embarrassing publicity that is not necessarily harmful to national security. In any event, governments and major interests alike will still be able to take civil actions to prevent publication on the grounds of breach of confidence.

Blasphemy and anti-religious argument

The existing law of blasphemy protects only the Anglican church from 'vilification, ridicule or indecency'. The law was created originally to protect society against the dangers of disbelief and it was used vigorously in the nineteenth century to imprison free-thinkers and publishers. In 1985, the Law Commission recommended that the law should be abolished because of its 'serious and fundamental' deficiencies. There is no 'public interest' defence. In the last blasphemy prosecution in 1979 – against Gay News over a poem about the body of Christ – the defence lawyer, John Mortimer, could not call evidence on the merits of the poem and the poet could not explain his intentions in court. The judge in his autobiography said that he felt the hand of God had guided him through his summing up (Mortimer in the *Daily Mail*, 18 October 2001). The government has recently abandoned a commitment to extend the law rather than repeal it.

Freedom of information

Freedom of information is a vital partner of free speech. Article 10 of the European Convention on Human Rights – now part of UK law – does not explicitly refer to the right to seek, receive and impart information, unlike Article 19 of the International Covenant. But the European Court has made it clear that the right to know is a significant element in freedom of expression. The UK has been slow to enact freedom of information legislation; and we deal with the restricted nature of the Freedom of Information Act 2000 in Section 7.8.

Freedom of assembly

The associated freedoms of assembly and association constitute active social use of the freedoms of expression and information. Public demonstrations are an increasingly visible form of political expression and recently have involved protests against the international order or companies, groups and individuals. The public overwhelmingly believe that protests are a 'legitimate way of expressing popular concerns' and more than half the public broadly agreed that protests like the destruction of GM crops and petrol blockades in 2000 were justified when 'governments don't listen' (Dunleavy et al, 2001). Protests run wider of course. Some, like the 'Stop the city' protests and demonstrations against people believed to be paedophiles, do not command so much public support.

However, freedom of assembly can provide a degree of pluralism which is often missing in the media, political parties and other orthodox channels of opinion; and which seems to be increasingly prized. But the rights of people to engage in protests like those set out above must be balanced against the rights and freedoms of other citizens. The state must strike a justifiable balance between public order; the protection of individuals and property; and the exercise of this collective form of freedom of expression.

In the UK, freedom of assembly existed only as a negative right up until the Human Rights Act came into force. People were held to be free to use the highway in a 'reasonable' manner, but the courts did not recognise a general positive 'right' to hold assemblies on the highway. Under the Act, the right of free peaceful assembly is now positively defined and guaranteed– and then specific exceptions to the right are allowed. Thus the balance will shift over time in the UK to a more positive recognition of the right of assembly while for example recognising the potential danger that sectarian marches pose by exacerbating community tensions and possibly sparking off violence.

As we have seen, the police possess a variety of powers that may be used to prevent protests, or to criminalise those involved. In 1998, the European Court assessed these powers in reviewing the arrests of protesters in the UK, some of whom had taken direct action (Steel v UK). One protester had joined in obstructing and disturbing a grouse shoot; another had protested against the building of a motorway extension by repeatedly breaking into a construction site, climbing trees and standing in front of machinery until he was removed (without offering any resistance). Three others had protested outside an arms conference, handing out leaflets and holding up banners saying: 'Work for Peace and not War.' The Court found that the arrest and detention of the first two protesters were lawful since police fears that their behaviour might provoke others to violence were justified. But the arrests of the other three protesters violated the Convention since their protest was entirely peaceful and was not likely to cause a breach of the peace.

However, the authorities are still willing to obstruct the right of peaceful protest where it may cause some political embarrassment. During the state visit by the Chinese President to London in October 1999, the police removed flags and banners, and positioned police vans in front of protesters peacefully demonstrating against the Chinese occupation in Tibet. When the actions of the police were challenged in the courts they conceded that they had acted unlawfully.

The recent tendency for protests to be more organised, sophisticated and often confrontational does create dilemmas for the authorities, especially when violent groups infiltrate otherwise peaceful protests. During the 2001 May Day protests in London the police boxed in several hundred people in Oxford Street, preventing them from leaving for more than four hours. When eventually people were allowed to leave they could only do so once their photographs had been taken. Those 'detained' included not only demonstrators, but shoppers, tourists and passers-by. This indiscriminate and prolonged detention in Oxford Street suggests that the police strategy went beyond what is 'necessary in a democratic society' to protect law and order and the rights and freedoms of others. However, following a relatively peaceful day, politicians were quick to praise the police strategy as a successful tool in crowd control. Others were more critical of the 'subversive' methods employed. As yet there have not been any legal proceedings connected with the 2001 May Day protests.

In rare circumstances damage to property may be regarded as a justifiable response to a particular situation. In September 2000, 28 defendants including the executive director of Greenpeace, Lord Melchett, were charged with criminal damage for destroying a field of genetically modified maize. The jury accepted the protesters' defence that they had acted in order to prevent pollen from the genetically modified maize from polluting neighbouring crops and acquitted them.

Freedom of association

The Terrorism Act 2000 gives the Secretary of State the power to proscribe an organisation as a terrorist organisation (see above), with the consequence that anyone who supports the organisation commits a criminal offence. Support includes the wearing of badges and attendance at meetings. This disproportionate erosion of freedom of expression and assembly through the guise of anti-terrorism seems very hard to justify. These new offences may lead to violations of safeguards that protect private life and freedoms of expression and assembly under the European Convention. (See Section 4.5. for trade unionism.)

3.3. How secure is the freedom for all to practise their own religion, language and culture?

Any person's freedom to practise his or her own religion, language or culture is largely determined by the degree of discrimination he or she faces in doing so. Here we focus on the freedom to practise religion, to use minority languages and to follow minority cultures, while recognising that such freedoms are intimately linked to prejudice and discrimination on the grounds of race and ethnic origin. The following analysis is based on the Cambridge University review of the effectiveness of UK anti-discrimination legislation (Hepple et al, 2000; and see Section 1.2).

Religion and belief

A Home Office research study (Weller et al, 2001) of religious discrimination in England and Wales paints a complex picture of diverse levels and patterns of discrimination experienced by different faith communities:

- A consistently higher level of unfair treatment was reported by Muslim organisations than by most other religious groups. They made proportionately more complaints and proportionately more were of frequent rather than occasional unfair treatment. Most Muslim organisations reported cases of unfair treatment in education, employment, housing, law and order, and in access to local government services;
- Sikh and Hindu organisations also reported a high level of unfair treatment and tended to highlight the same areas of concern as Muslims;
- Christian organisations in the survey were generally much less likely to report unfair treatment than Muslims, Sikhs and Hindus, and nearly all the cases they reported were 'occasional' rather than frequent;
- However black-led Christian organisations and those representing groups such as Mormons and Jehovah's Witnesses were much more likely to report unfair treatment in nearly all walks of life than 'mainstream' Christian organisations;
- Jewish organisations, in common with other religions, reported unfair treatment by journalists and the coverage of their religion by the media. In education, they singled out the behaviour of school pupils and higher education students and arrangements for collective worship;
- Even though Muslims, Hindus, Sikhs and Jews report considerable discrimination, some of the traditions with fewer adherents – Bahá'ís and Zoroastrians, for example – regret that they lack the degree of recognition given to these groups. They have a feeling of being constantly overlooked as 'minorities within minorities'; and
- Pagans and people from the New Religious Movements complained of open hostility and discrimination, and of being labelled as 'child abusers' and 'cults'.

Language and culture

Discrimination on the grounds of language and culture is closely linked to discrimination on the grounds of race, religion and belief. Professor Tariq Modood refers to the emerging recognition of 'cultural racism' that uses 'cultural difference to vilify or demand cultural assimilation' (Modood, 1997).

Measures are in place for the protection and promotion of minority indigenous languages, particularly Scottish Gaelic, Welsh, Irish and Ulster Scots.

Anti-discrimination laws

There is legal protection in place aimed at preventing discrimination and at providing redress in some situations where discrimination occurs, but as stated above, such protection applies unevenly in the areas of religion, language and culture (see Section 1.2). Under the Fair Employment and Treatment Order (FETO) discrimination on the basis of religious belief or political opinion is prohibited in Northern Ireland in relation to employment and in the provision of goods, service and facilities. However, there is no equivalent legislation in Great Britain. In addition under the Northern Ireland Act 1998, public authorities there must have due regard to:

- the need to promote equality of opportunity 'between persons of different religious belief, political opinion, racial group, age, marital status or sexual orientation; between men and women generally; between persons with disability and persons without; and between persons with dependents and persons without'; and.
- 'the desirability of promoting good relations between persons of different religious belief, political opinion or racial group'.

These duties go beyond avoiding discrimination. Public bodies are required to actively seek ways to encourage greater equality of opportunity.

European law

The EU Council of Ministers issued Race and Employment Framework Directives in 2000 that are designed to give wider protection against discrimination in member states (see Section 1.2). The directive establishes a general framework for equal treatment in employment and occupation without discrimination 'on the grounds of religion or belief, disability, age or sexual orientation'. The UK must implement the Race Directive and Framework Directive, in respect of religion or belief, by 2003.

But the directive will ensure only that all religious groups would be protected in the area of employment. Discrimination would remain lawful in the provision of goods, services and facilities. Religious groups that are recognised as ethnic groups, like Sikhs and Jews, would be protected from discrimination in these areas; other religious groups would be protected only where they could show that the discrimination against them constituted indirect race discrimination.

Promotion and protection of languages

English is the predominant language in the UK, but it exists alongside several officially recognised minority indigenous languages. There are official bodies and other measures in place for the promotion and protection of Scottish Gaelic, Welsh and more recently, Irish Gaelic and Ulster Scots. The UK has ratified the European Charter for Regional and Minority Languages and it came into force in July 2001. The Charter applies to languages that are traditionally used by a minority group within the state but does not apply to the 'languages of migrants'. Under the Charter, the UK undertakes to eliminate any unjustified distinction or preference that would restrict or discourage the use of a recognised indigenous minority language.

3.4. How free are individual citizens from invasions of their privacy?

Privacy rights in English law are being transformed, as the Human Rights Act 1998 makes itself felt. Traditionally, UK law has not recognised a general right to respect for privacy. Rather, it has protected some aspects of the individual's 'right to be let alone' through a patchwork of civil actions and legislative measures. Measures available to redress certain invasions of privacy include a civil action against harassment, for trespass to land or goods, for breach of confidence, or for defamation (see Section 3.2 above). Thus some elements of the right to privacy have been well protected: but the absence of a general privacy right has left significant gaps.

The disparate measures described above continue to apply: now, however, they must now be seen in the light of the right to respect for private life set out in Article 8 of the European Convention, following its incorporation into UK law. This right is 'qualified' and may be legitimately interfered with in the public interest as long as the intrusion is 'necessary in a democratic society' and proportionate to a legitimate aim: e.g., the prevention or detection of crime. Other human rights may also condition rights to privacy. For example, the Human Rights Act gives particular importance to freedom of expression – to reassure media interests that privacy rights would not interfere too much with their freedoms to publish.

But the strength of Convention privacy rights should not be under-estimated: Article 8 protects not only the 'right to be let alone', but also a broader notion of privacy, that extends to the individual's right to develop their personality in community with others. It therefore has great potential to form the basis for a newly comprehensive and coherent protection against intrusions into private life in UK law.

Under the Act, all public authorities, including for example the police and law enforcement authorities, are required to comply with Article 8 rights. In addition, the courts have made clear in recent cases that they will also ensure that the media and private organisations must comply with these privacy rights. In Douglas v Hello!, the Court of Appeal found that it had power to grant an injunction, preventing the magazine from publishing photographs of the wedding of Michael Douglas and Catherine Zeta-Jones in breach of the right to respect for private life (though it didn't do so). Lord Justice Sedley said that English law had reached a point 'at which it can be said with confidence that it recognises and will protect a right of personal privacy' (Douglas v Hello!, 2000).

In 2001, Dame Elizabeth Butler-Sloss, the Appeal Court judge, also granted an injunction to prevent the media from identifying the child killers of James Bulger when they were released as teenagers from custody (Venables and Thompson v News Group Newspapers Ltd). She took the view that information about their new identities would put their right to life at risk; and gave pre-eminence to the right to life – just as another court had done when overturning the decision to require soldier witnesses to give evidence to the Bloody Sunday inquiry without revealing their identity.

Privacy of personal information
The Data Protection Act 1998 provides particular protection for privacy and access rights in relation to personal information. The Information Commissioner oversees access to data records with enforcement powers and a mandate to encourage good practice. The Act:

- regulates the processing of personal data, and establishes a right of access by individuals to personal information held on them;

● enshrines a number of basic principles that seek to ensure that personal data is processed fairly and accurately, that it is not retained unnecessarily, and that it is kept securely; and

● gives people a right of access to ascertain whether a body holds personal information on them, and then to be informed of the nature and contents of the information. The right of access to personal information is not absolute however: it is subject to a range of exemptions, for example on grounds of national security and prevention of crime. These exemptions nullify much of the protection the Act offers.

The Freedom of Information Act 2000, yet to come into force, will extend data access rights to cover both personal and non-personal information. It provides for a general right of access to information held by public authorities, with a number of exceptions. Several of the exemptions to the right of access to information under the Act are designed to protect privacy, including exemptions in relation to court records and trade secrets.

Surveillance and the interception of communications

A comprehensive statutory framework regulates covert surveillance and the interception of communications – comprising the Police Act 1997, the Security Services Act 1989, the Intelligence Services Act 1994, and the Regulation of Investigatory Powers Act 2000 (RIPA). The 2000 Act was a partial response to a breach of the right to privacy when personal telephone calls made by Alison Halford, the assistant chief constable of Merseyside, were tapped at a time when she was bringing a case of sexual discrimination against the force. However, the new Act has faced immediate criticisms for not keeping pace with more sophisticated surveillance techniques.

Together, these Acts establish a system of warrants governing surveillance by public authorities, interception of communications, acquisition of 'communications data' (including for example e-mail addresses or records of telephone numbers dialled) and the use of undercover agents by police and others. The RIPA also allows investigating authorities to obtain a court order requiring the disclosure of a key (such as a password) to encrypted information, so that the information can be de-coded.

The police, the intelligence services, Customs & Excise and the Inland Revenue currently have the right to demand access to the communications records of telephone and Internet users. But in June 2002 the government planned to issue parliamentary orders under RIPA extending the range of public bodies able to gain access to detailed communications logs, including individual people's email records and mobile telephone location data. Government departments, local councils and quangos would have been entitled to demand access, on their own authority, and to authorise themselves to conduct surveillance against individuals and to use informers. Bowing to intense public and political pressures, the Home Secretary withdrew the orders in July and shelved them until at least autumn 2002 to allow time for public consultation. It emerged at the same time that Sir Andrew Leggatt, the chief surveillance commissioner, had reported earlier in 2002 that his tribunal had a staff of only 22 to oversee the activities of 1,039 public bodies. He warned, 'I clearly cannot carry out any meaningful oversight of so many bodies without assistance' (*Guardian*, 3 July 2002).

Judges must authorise police surveillance of a home, hotel room or office where legally privileged material (e.g., correspondence with a solicitor), or confidential personal or journalistic material may be acquired. The intelligence services are similarly bound under the Intelligence Services Act 1994. But other covert surveillance by the authorities and intelligence services does not require judicial approval so long as it does not involve interfering with property rights or is not directed at someone's home or private vehicle. This absence of safeguards, allowing the authorities to undertake extensive surveillance that is only authorised internally, raises concerns that privacy rights are not adequately protected by the legislation.

RIPA also governs the interception of communications, for example by telephone tapping, on both public and private communications systems. It imposes criminal and civil liability for unlawful interception, and creates a system of warrants, authorised by the Home Secretary. In principle, a warrant will be issued only where it is necessary for specified purposes and is proportionate to its aims. However, once again, there is no judicial control; approval is in the hands of the executive. There is another cause for concern. RIPA allows employers to monitor calls or e-mails of their employees at work. Abuse of such powers will not incur criminal liability, though an employee may sue an employer who acts unreasonably. Regulations made under RIPA require an employer to warn employees that their calls or e-mails may be monitored.

Legislative restrictions on privacy

An increasing and worrying trend has seen the granting of extensive investigatory powers to law enforcement agencies to build up data-bases of personal material gleaned from private institutions such as banks and service providers. A number of recent or proposed legislative measures of this type have the potential to impact adversely on privacy. The Social Security Fraud Act 2001 permits the gathering of personal data from private bodies to assist in investigating benefits fraud. The Act requires specified private organisations such as banks, insurance companies, schools and colleges, gas and electricity service providers, to disclose on request information held by them to officers authorised by the Secretary of State for Social Security, or by a local authority, for the investigation of cases of benefit fraud.

EU measures and privacy

Data-bases and mechanisms of information exchange established at an EU level also have the potential to impinge significantly upon privacy rights in the UK. The Schengen Information System, established in 1995, holds extensive personal information relevant to criminal investigations as well as asylum and immigration. In 2000, the UK joined the system for policing only. Police and law enforcement agencies in participating countries place personal information on a joint data-base that is then distributed to every national system. The SIRENE data-base also allows additional information such as fingerprints and photographs to be exchanged.

These systems are obviously important for preventing and investigating increasingly international crime. But they are equally obviously liable to intrude into privacy, particularly given the lack of constraints as to the information entered on the system, the lack of rigorous data protection controls, and the absence of judicial oversight.

Redress under the Human Rights Act

For all the deficiencies of the legislation and practice described above, the Human Rights Act now offers the possibility of redress for people whose privacy has been invaded. They may take an action against any public authority or private organisation or body that breaches their privacy rights, and damages may be awarded if a breach is found. All courts and tribunals are also obliged by the Act to respect Convention rights, including the right to privacy.

Media self-regulation

Media intrusions on private life are addressed by the Press Complaints Commission (PCC), a private body, and the Broadcasting Standards Commission (BSC), a public body that is to be subsumed within Ofcom, the proposed new communications commission (see Section 10). The PCC enforces a voluntary code of practice for newspapers and similar publications. The code includes protections against interference with privacy rights, and against harassment, warning newspapers that they 'will be expected to justify intrusions into any individual's private life without consent'. It also prohibits the use of long-lens photography to take pictures of people in private places, defined as places where there is a reasonable expectation of privacy. The commission can adjudicate on complaints alleging breach of the code, and can require a newspaper to print the results of its adjudication on any such complaint. But it is not independent of the print media and compromises its own principles in practice. Even editors on the PCC infringe the code and afterwards offer specious excuses. It is perhaps no surprise that celebrities like Sara Cox and Amanda Holden who have experienced blatant invasions of their privacy are turning to the courts.

Stalking and protecting whistle-blowers

There has been an increasing recognition that people may suffer harassment or intimidation in all walks of life. The growing awareness of stalking and its effect on the victims was recognised in the Protection from Harassment Act 1997. Similarly, the Public Interest Disclosure Act 1998 has been put in place to try and prevent the victimisation of whistle-blowers who speak out against illegal or irregular practices or individuals at work. One example is provided by Alison Taylor who lost her job for revealing the scale of abuse in child-care homes in 1991, only to have been vindicated a decade later by the Waterhouse inquiry at a cost of £14 million.

Identity cards

The issue of identity cards came to the fore in the wake of the 11 September massacres when the Home Office, which has long wanted to introduce identity cards, persuaded the Home Secretary that they would be a useful precaution against terrorism. A short period of public debate forced the Home Secretary to spike the idea, but it is constantly being resurrected, lately as an 'entitlement card'. As we write, the government is proposing to hold a 'public debate' on introducing them. The obligation to carry an identity card and to show it to the police whenever requested does not necessarily constitute an interference with the right to respect for private life; and the government has pledged that it would not be an offence (except for asylum-seekers) not to carry one. They are also common in continental Europe. However the idea of their use contradicts deeply felt notions of civil liberties in Britain.

3.5. How free from harassment and intimidation are individuals and groups working to protect human rights?

British society is rich in organisations, independent of government, that exist to protect and advance human rights. Among them, for example, are JUSTICE, Liberty, MIND, the Runnymede Trust, Child Poverty Action Group, and Shelter. Britain is the birthplace of Amnesty International and a UK branch is based in London. All such organisations seem free to organise, lobby and publish their views without their workers being harassed or intimidated by the authorities. Indeed, many have judges and former judges, former senior civil servants, MPs, and peers among their active members; others have advanced through them to the House of Commons, judicial and ministerial office. In the 1970s, the intelligence services did keep staff and members of the National Council for Civil Liberties (now known as Liberty) under surveillance, largely because of the organisation's Communist roots. Two staff members kept under scrutiny have both since become cabinet ministers.

1   As we go to press, the monitoring body for the act, the Special Immigration Appeals Commission (SIAC), has ruled that the detention of the nine Muslims still in custody is unlawful. The chairman of SIAC said, their detention was 'not only discriminatory and so unlawful . . . But it is also disproportionate'. However the government is to appeal to the Court of Appeal and need not release the men even if the UK courts find against it.

Four: economic and social rights

Unequal Britain

Are economic and social rights equally guaranteed for all?

My vision of Britain is of a nation where no-one is left out or left behind, and where power, wealth and opportunity are in the hands of the many, not the few
Tony Blair, foreword to social exclusion consultation document, 2000

Introduction

Paid work with fair rates of pay and good working conditions, safe and secure housing, education for life, access to high-quality health care, benefits, pensions and services for people who are out of work, injured, disabled and elderly – in brief, economic and social rights – are vital to political equality and social inclusion. The democratic principle of equal citizenship requires that no-one should be allowed to fall below a minimum acceptable level of economic and social existence; and economic and social well-being create self-confident citizens able and willing to play a part in the democratic life of their society; to know and exercise their civil and political rights; and to enjoy personal and political freedoms. By the same token, poverty – or economic and social exclusion – leads not only to alienation, social tensions and crime, but also hinders people from being active citizens or even registering or using their right to vote (see Byrne 1997; Weir and Beetham, 1999: 41).

We adopt the concept of 'social exclusion', as well as poverty, as our guiding stars for this review of economic and social rights in the UK. Social exclusion places poverty within the idea of a modern European society of people bound together by rights and obligations that reflect a shared civil, political and moral order. It is a broader concept than poverty. Social exclusion describes not just poor material means, but also people's inability to participate fully and effectively in everyday life and individual and communal alienation from mainstream society. It embraces a broad range of inter-connected issues and policies – education, health, housing and work conditions as well as employment and social security. Social exclusion can therefore be defined in terms of the denial of human rights – civil, political, economic, social and cultural.

The higher a person's socio-economic status, the more able and likely they are to engage with civil society and politics. A recent survey of poverty and social exclusion in the UK found that 43 per cent of those who do not participate at all in civic life are poor. Only 18 per cent of poor people participate to any great extent (Bradshaw, 2000: 29). A study of social exclusion during the 1990s also found first that low incomes are often associated with exclusion on other dimensions, especially engagement in a productive or socially valued activity, and political engagement (Burchardt et al, forthcoming).

Social exclusion is seen in the UK as a quintessentially New Labour idea. In fact, the Social Exclusion Unit was set up in 1997 as part of a joint European Union strategy against poverty and social exclusion which the UK signed up to in the Amsterdam treaty in October 1997. At the Lisbon summit in 2000, the UK agreed to the target of eradicating poverty in the EU by 2010.

Enforcing economic and social rights in the UK

People do not in general have enforceable economic and social rights in the UK. This country has ratified the central international treaties for economic, social and cultural rights, but like most other countries, refuses to incorporate them into British law. Governments and the judiciary justify this refusal on the grounds that such rights depend on the resource priorities and spending decisions of elected governments and their administrations. They agree that the courts are not fit bodies to review such decisions. Legislation rather obliges a variety of authorities – often local councils – to provide social and welfare entitlements, but gives them a wide degree of discretion over how they do so. Very few entitlements other than benefits are mandatory; and entitlements to benefits are strictly de-limited and leave room for officials to interpret the rules that apply in a negative way. Thus few socio-economic rights are legally protected and enforceable in the UK; those that are largely derive from EU directives, such as the right to equal pay for equal work.

The UK has ratified the UN International Covenant on Economic, Social and Cultural Rights (ICESCR) that seeks to define and protect such rights generally. It sets out rights on employment; working conditions; social security; adequate standards of living (including housing); health; and education. These are the rights on which this section concentrates.[1] Three further UN treaties ratified in the UK reinforce the ICESCR: the Convention for the Elimination of Racial Discrimination (CERD); the Convention for the Elimination of Discrimination Against Women (CEDAW); and the Convention on the Rights of the Child (CRC). These treaties insist that there should be no discrimination in the way economic and social rights are met. We also refer here to the 200 conventions of the

International Labour Organisation and the 31 articles of the European Social Charter on workers' individual and collective rights, social assistance, poverty and housing.

The UK has ratified the important ILO conventions and signed the original European Social Charter. But the government has refused to sign the 1995 Additional Protocol to the Charter, allowing British citizens to bring complaints and has not yet ratified the significant 1996 revision of the Charter. UK domestic law does not afford consistent protection of the economic and social rights contained in the ICESCR.

We adopt the obligations set out in these treaties as benchmarks for our audit (which we apply with reference to EU norms). Polls for the Rowntree Reform Trust have shown that the public overwhelmingly believe that economic and social rights should have a high place in a UK Bill of Rights; and that social equality is widely regarded as an important part of British democracy (Dunleavy et al, 2001). However, as the government report to the UN's oversight committee in December 1997 explained, the UK authorities regard economic and social rights as 'programmatic objectives rather than legal obligations'.

The government has resisted pressure to establish a Human Rights Commission in the UK to keep watch over progress under the Human Rights Act and to encourage a human rights culture in the UK. There is, however, a Human Rights Commission in Northern Ireland. In 2001, the Commission published a draft Bill of Rights for Northern Ireland in 2001 that includes social and economic rights (Northern Ireland Human Rights Commission, 2001).

The Commission consulted widely on this proposal and found strong public backing for including rights to health, housing and employment in the Northern Ireland Bill of Rights. In the consultation paper, the Commission expressed the view that:

> Since poverty and social exclusion represent a fundamental denial of human dignity, the protection of social and economic rights is an integral part of the delivery of effective human rights.

The draft bill would require all Northern Ireland public authorities to develop programmatic measures to give effect over time to its socio-economic provisions, and to allocate resources to such measures in a proportionate and non-discriminatory way.

The international audit of economic and social rights in the UK

Just what progress is the UK making on its international obligations? The UN oversight committee's report in May 2002 on the government's record praised some initiatives including the New Deal, the minimum wage, measures taken to reduce homelessness, rough sleeping and permanent exclusions from school, and the halving of overcrowding in prison cells. However, 'principal subjects of concern' were:

- the persistence of de facto discrimination of some marginalised and vulnerable groups in society, especially ethnic minorities and people with disabilities, in employment, housing, education and other areas of life;
- the minimum wage was not set, in the Committee's view, 'at a level that provided all workers with an adequate standard of living'; did not protect workers under 18 years old; and discriminated against workers aged 18-22 by giving them less than the standard minimum;
- the failure to incorporate the right to strike into domestic law;

- the increasing incidence of domestic violence;
- the persistence of considerable levels of poverty, especially among older people, ethnic minorities and people with disabilities, and in certain regions;
- the increasing gap between rich and poor;
- high levels of child poverty;
- the persistence of homelessness, especially among ethnic minorities; and the large number of alcoholics and the mentally ill in their ranks;
- poor quality housing and 'fuel poverty';
- the introduction of tuition fees and student loans for university education that has 'tended to worsen the position of students from less privileged backgrounds'; and
- the heavily segregated structure of school education in Northern Ireland, despite the increase in demand for integrated schools.

In particular, the Committee pressed the government to adopt 'comprehensive legislation on equality and protection from discrimination'.

Other international scrutiny bodies have expressed strong concerns about the UK's record on socio-economic rights. Their reports are neglected by the government and media in the UK. But they give strong warnings to the current government on how much needs doing, even to lay the foundations of the meritocratic society they aim for. Poverty, race and class are disabling too many people's lives.

Making economic and social rights legal

The British courts display very little understanding of economic and social issues as rights which is not untypical among European countries. The courts in the UK have on occasion upheld ideas of economic and social entitlement, but in the absence of inscribed rights they have scarcely any purchase within the discretion that social and welfare legislation gives to public authorities. Even when the courts uphold people's entitlements, governments have been able to reverse their decisions by further legislation.

The judge-made common law has systematic weaknesses in the realm of modern positive rights (see Klug, Starmer and Weir, 1996). The expansion of judicial review may seem to offer the prospect of justiciable economic and social rights, but in practice there has been scarcely any advance. Judicial review generally remains limited to making the exercise of executive discretion comply with standards of 'reasonable' process, legality and procedural propriety. Homelessness and immigration cases bulk large in the judicial review caseload, but they rarely make headway. Nor do the very few social security, health-care and family cases. The courts are very reluctant to intervene on the economic and social front, regarding such cases as largely matters for the executive and administrators to decide. The 'test case strategy' of the Child Poverty Action Group in the 1970s, focusing on benefit and homelessness cases, encountered 'judicial hostility' and 'procedural and institutional inadequacies' (Prosser 1983).

In the 1980s and early 1990s, the courts acquiesced in the Conservative government's disengagement from welfare and social provision, denying for example appeals from homeless persons, upholding refusals of benefits and endorsing cuts in local authority social services. Recently, however, there have been more positive developments, especially under the impact of EU law. For example, the Equal Opportunities Commission won a case on women's employment rights in 1994 that brought even wider gains (R v Employment Secretary *ex parte* EOC). First, the law lords ruled that aspects of UK law that are incompatible with EU law may be declared illegal or unconstitutional. Secondly, they said that interested bodies, like the EOC, could initiate judicial review cases.

But it is also increasingly the case that the courts no longer regard challenges that raise issues of resource allocation as non-justiciable for that reason alone. In the later 1990s, there have been politically sensitive challenges on community care, health treatment and education. But the courts remain acutely aware that public resources are scarce and are inhibited by the knowledge that to insist on re-housing, hospital treatment or other public service in any one case will have budgetary repercussions that may affect the rights of others. So they rarely interpret the usually discretionary statutory obligations for the delivery of services or facilities as absolute. In fact, the courts are reluctant even to enforce mandatory obligations set in statute law to provide community care if it is refused on grounds of lack of resources. It is true that they do on occasion give precedence to the needs of individual users. In 2000, for example, the Court of Appeal ordered a health authority to keep open a residential home they intended to close so that the authority would keep its promise to six disabled residents that it would remain their home 'for life' (the Coughlan case, 51 Butterworths Medical Law Reports, 2000).

However, the resource implications in this case were limited. Generally the courts take the view, as expressed by the same court in the notorious case of Child B in 1995, a young girl dying of leukaemia, that:

> Difficult and agonising judgments have to be made as to how a limited budget is best allocated to the maximum advantage of the maximum number of patients. This is not a judgment that the court can make.

The future role of the Human Rights Act

The protection that the Human Rights Act now gives to civil and political rights in the UK does overlap with economic and social rights where the right to life (Article 2 of the European Convention) and to respect for family and private life (Article 8) are concerned.

Protection of the right to life is the central Convention right so far as economic and social rights are concerned. The European Commission of Human Rights has established that a state must not only refrain from taking life but that it must also take appropriate steps to safeguard life (X v United Kingdom, 1978). However, there is nothing in the jurisprudence of the European Court to guide UK judges on what may justify overturning the decisions of local authorities or of a national standards body such as NICE when they have accepted that the right to life is engaged.

The European Convention also strays into economic, social and cultural territory with its guarantees of the right to education; prohibitions against discrimination; and protection of people from 'inhuman and degrading' treatment. The European Court has held that there is no watertight division separating Convention rights from socio-economic rights. But in 2001 a pregnant single parent with three young children sought the protection of Article 8 against eviction in the UK courts and failed. The fact that four children would ultimately share the desperation of homeless conditions with their mother did not weigh very strongly against the interests of a housing association in the midst of the severe shortage of rented accommodation for poor households in the UK.

Finally, the growing involvement of the private and voluntary sectors in the delivery of health and welfare services creates a serious gap in the accountability of providers towards their clients. The recent case of R v Leonard Cheshire Homes and HM Attorney General *ex parte* Heather and others (unreported, 15 June 2001) shortly to be heard on appeal, has established that decisions by independent contractors engaged by local authorities to provide services are generally outside judicial review and public law proceedings for violations of Convention rights.

Overall, applying traditional principles of judicial review to cases of economic and social rights is very different from the courts being given primary jurisdiction to determine the scope of constitutionally enshrined rights to enjoy an adequate standard of food, shelter, health or education. In South Africa, the constitution incorporates a wide range of legally enforceable socio-economic rights in a Bill of Rights. Most of these rights are described as 'progressively realisable' – that is, they depend on what resources are available to meet them. In this way the drafters of the constitution, itself a remarkable product of very widespread consultation, attempted to square the circle –giving citizens justiciable socio-economic rights while acknowledged that the South African state cannot deliver such basic rights immediately to all citizens. The case law so far suggests that inscribed economic and social rights give citizens the opportunity to assert basic needs to shelter and health-care without swamping public authorities with far fewer resources than their UK counterparts can call upon, based on the principle of whether the state has done everything reasonable in the circumstances to realise the right.

Other means of enforcing rights

Social and welfare legislation usually gives people a right of appeal to networks of national and local administrative tribunals, as opposed to the right of appeal to courts, when they are denied social or economic entitlements by public authorities. These tribunals hear cases involving, *inter alia*, social security, employment, equal opportunities and housing. Most tribunals hear appeals against the decisions of government departments and other public bodies, and are constrained by government policies.[2] They may not consider 'free-standing' points of EU law (i.e., those outside their statutory competence). These go instead to the UK courts, and may ultimately reach the European Court of Justice. Devolved administrations have similar tribunals, as well as others like, for example, the Children's Panel in Scotland and an Industrial Court in Northern Ireland (which enforces the provision of information from employers to trade unions).

Tribunals deal with more cases every year than all the civil courts put together. There are over 270,000 social security appeals each year. Two major failings of the UK tribunal model are:

- Tribunals are often not independent from their sponsoring departments. Independence and impartiality are crucial qualities if individuals are to receive fair hearings. Government departments typically pay tribunal members' salaries and expenses and may even have a role in appointing members; and
- Only a meagre amount of legal aid is available to individuals pursuing cases. There is no funding for legal representation, except for cases coming before land tribunals, immigration and employment appeal tribunals, and mental health review tribunals. So usually poor appellants must pay for legal representation, unless they are trade union members or can get aid from a citizen's advice bureau, welfare rights or law centre. Increasingly complex laws and expanding jurisprudence in most areas put applicants without legal assistance at a serious disadvantage (Law Society, 2000a; Citizen's Advice Bureau Service, 2000).

The Ombudsman service may receive complaints from citizens about maladministration in central government, the NHS and local authorities. There is also an official Pensions Ombudsman who oversees occupational pensions.

Within government, departments, executive agencies and quangos have introduced complaints procedures as a substitute for legally enforceable rights and arrangements. But there is no systematic appraisal of access to them, nor of their independence or quality. By their very nature, they are not fully independent of the authorities that establish them. The best known of these is the NHS complaints procedure, introduced in 1996. This has been widely criticised for being incompetent, opaque, ineffective and (in the words of a recent Health Secretary) 'a bit of a shambles' (see the Hutton Commission, 2000). The NHS procedures are undergoing reform, as are the complaints processes operated by professional bodies within the NHS. Arrangements of this kind are no substitute for legally enforceable rights in the hands of citizens, individually or collectively.

Various public bodies and agencies are charged with protecting and promoting different aspects of socio-economic rights in the UK. Chief among them are the Commission for Racial Integration, the Disability Rights Commission, the Equal Opportunities Commission, the Northern Ireland Equality Commission, and the Health and Safety Commission and Executive, as well as advisory quangos like the Disabled Persons Transport Committee.

Government social and welfare policies

The 1945-51 Labour government aimed to create a universal statutory approach to 'social citizenship' and economic and social rights through the welfare state. The weaknesses of the initial approach have been well documented since, but the government's goals were at least inclusive in intent. But it was statist and bureaucratic, and unpopular as a consequence (the NHS apart). Since the crises of the 1970s and the advent of a neo-liberal government in 1979, the statutory framework has been diminished over time by Conservative and Labour governments, which are progressively shifting the burden of economic, social and educational provision onto the shoulders of individuals.

The current government has returned to policies of full employment (though not to neo-Keynesian economics), introduced a national minimum wage in April 1999 and is seeking to retain free and inclusive treatment within the NHS. But it has abandoned the previously universalist Labour approach to social security and adopted policies of 'targeted', or means-tested, benefits (consequently problems of low take-up and stigma are likely). In some areas it has reversed previous Labour policies – for example, over fees and grants for university education. At the same time, the government is making significant advances, such as the minimum wage, the New Deal employment and training programme, and the social exclusion project.

Public services and social security – the NHS, education, benefits, pensions, social housing, etc – are suffering still from prolonged under-investment in the public sphere. The government still has a decades-long backlog of neglect to make up for. Its efforts to improve services had a slow start owing to the decision to adhere to the previous government's spending plans for its first two years after 1997; but it has also been handicapped by its ambition to create effective public services on the European model, but also to emulate low US tax rates. However, the huge boosts given to public investment in the NHS, education, transport, etc, in 2002 seems to have reversed this policy. The government may, for example, fulfil the pledge to match average health spending levels in the EU.

However, Gordon Brown's means-tested strategy for re-constructing social security and eradicating poverty is markedly less universalist in spirit. His 'targeted' approach relies first of all on employment, and secondly on wide-ranging means-testing. Very early in the Labour government's life, a public debate between Brown and the former Labour minister, Roy Hattersley, set out the framework within which Brown's strategy will ultimately be judged (see Timmins, 2001). Roy Hattersley accused the government of apostasy on poverty and equality. The goal of equality had been abandoned (*Guardian*, 26 July 1997). Brown replied angrily that the government did indeed reject 'an unrealisable equality of outcome', a goal that was neither 'desirable nor feasible'. He stressed the need to respect and respond to diversity. The government would always defend the sick and elderly, but by ensuring that work always paid, by enhancing skills and introducing life-long learning, Labour would 'tackle inequality and poverty at source'. The government was committed

> to tackling the causes of poverty – unemployment, low skills and low wages – and not simply the consequences (*Guardian*, 2 August 1997).

Hattersley replied that true diversity was only possible in a society 'which avoids great discrepancies in wealth and income'. The Labour government would have to tax the better-off more heavily to achieve a 'more equal society' through redistribution (*Guardian*, 6 August 1997).

The current position

This Section goes on to examine the current position with regard to significant economic and social rights. It does not offer a comprehensive analysis, nor can the following paragraphs be regarded as a critique of the current government, given the long time-lags in economic and social policy. Through searching questions, as in previous Sections, we focus on the following rights and issues: social exclusion; health and education; standards of living; the situation of ethnic minorities; elderly people; people with disabilities; the position of women and children; the efficacy of the benefit and pension system; rights to work; just and decent working conditions; and trade union rights.

4.1. How far are economic and social rights, including equal access to work, guaranteed for all?

As we record above in Section 3 there is no free-standing right to equality in the UK. Anti-discrimination and equality laws deal with sex, race, religion, employment and disability, but are incomplete and inconsistent. Their inadequacies and omissions impact on economic and social citizenship. One major effort to rectify the effects of discrimination is the government's campaign to act on the Race Relations (Amendment) Act 2000 and to require most public authorities, including the police, local authorities, schools and hospitals, to eradicate 'institutional racism' in the services and facilities that they provide.

This is a welcome initiative to make anti-discrimination laws work. But generally these laws cannot – and too obviously do not – of themselves secure economic and social equality for people from the ethnic minorities, women, people with disabilities and others in the social and economic sphere. Poverty, class, sickness and age also discriminate against people in employment, housing, security, education and health. Even where people live can count against them. Continuing discriminations, failures in government policies and public services, and cycles of disadvantage contribute to widespread social exclusion and multiple deprivations. In addition to suffering from an alarmingly high degree of prejudice and discrimination, people from ethnic minority backgrounds are often disadvantaged by class, gender and other factors too.

Disability and age are two major obstacles to economic and social well-being. The Disability Discrimination Act 1995 made it unlawful to discriminate against people with disabilities in the areas of employment, access to goods, facilities, property and some services, except in certain sectors (the armed forces, police, etc). In 1999, the government established the Disability Rights Commission that has a duty to work towards the elimination of discrimination against disabled persons; to promote their equal opportunities; to give practical encouragement to good practice in the treatment of disabled persons; and to review the workings of the 1995 Act. There is no legal framework in the UK for the protection of the rights of the elderly. The Northern Ireland Commission for Human Rights recently reviewed the rights of the elderly in Northern Ireland to try and identify and remedy the failures of the state fully to protect their rights.

Discrimination against travellers
Travellers are one group that suffers constant, but rarely acknowledged, discrimination in the UK. A report in 2001 by the Scottish Parliament's Equal Opportunities Committee highlights the nature of the discriminations against them in all areas of life. This includes accommodation, education, the provision of health, personal and social services and in policing and the criminal justice system. A key source of much of the discrimination and disadvantage is a failure by the settled community to understand and accommodate to the needs of their culture and lifestyle. The report notes that 'having no address (or an address identified as Gypsy Traveller site accommodation) may lead to subsequent refusal or difficulties in accessing service provision and the general disenfranchisement from the democratic process'.

The right to work
International human rights conventions emphasise not only the right to work, but to genuine choice of employment and access to vocational training. The government's full employment policies have reduced unemployment in the UK well below the average for the EU as a whole. However, the official figure – currently around one million- under-estimates the full extent of joblessness, as it counts only unemployed people drawing benefit. Further, a survey by the Work Foundation (formerly the Industrial Society) found that faulty counting methods used to calculate the official figure excluded certain groups of working-age women and part-time workers. This study suggests that joblessness is twice as high as the official figures show and 10 per cent higher still in poorer areas (Nathan, 2000). The fuller ILO definition of joblessness, which is based on labour market inactivity, produces a figure of 1.6 million people.

There is some progress on women's employment. In 1970, women represented a third of the workforce; now they are close to half. But fewer women of working age are in work in the UK than in the EU as a whole; and those in work are generally in poorly paid work.

The New Deal is a lynch-pin of the government's welfare to work strategy. It originally gave 18-24 year-olds training and subsidised employment opportunities in the private sector, with special assistance to ethnic minorities. It is being extended to all unemployed people aged 25-50, with strong emphasis on skills training and denial of benefit to those who refuse either subsidised work, training, voluntary work or a place on an environmental taskforce. At present, people over 25 have to wait two years to be admitted to government retraining schemes. This will be reduced to 18 months in 2002, a long wait. British industry is investing in training at only two-thirds of the rate of France, Germany and the USA.

Overall, people's work opportunities depend heavily on their age, location, previous job and ethnic origin: for example,

- After five years of Labour government, ethnic minority workers are up to five times as likely to be unemployed than their white counterparts and more likely to be in low-paid work;
- Bangladeshi and Pakistani women have the highest rate of unemployment in the UK at 23.9 per cent – nearly four times the average rate;
- Black and Asian graduates are heavily discriminated against on seeking work in England and Wales;
- Strong regional disparities persist and rural unemployment has increased markedly. Some 24,000 agricultural jobs were lost in 2000, an increase of nearly 30 per cent (*Guardian*, 19 December 2000).

4.2. How effectively are the basic necessities of life guaranteed, including adequate shelter and heating?

Most people in the UK do not suffer absolute poverty. The two principal causes for concern are the absence of sufficient affordable housing and of warmth in the home. One major reason is the huge slowdown in house-building – especially of public housing for rent – since the 1980s. Shelter, the housing charity, estimates that more than 100,000 'affordable' homes will have to be provided by 2011. John Prescott is now reported to be considering to put a stop to the sale of public housing to sitting tenants – a policy that would save millions of pounds as well as shoring up the pool of affordable housing for rent. The inability of poor people, especially the elderly, to heat their homes contributes to some 40,000 excess deaths every winter, two thirds of which are attributable to cold. This death rate is greater than that in most of continental Europe and Scandinavia, even though winters in Britain are comparatively mild (Wilkinson et al, 2001).

Homelessness

Homeless people have no legal right to a home in the UK, even though three quarters of the population believe that their right to be rehoused should be enshrined in a British Bill of Rights (Dunleavy et al, 2001). Instead, the National Assistance Act 1948 provides that local authorities may (under the government's direction) make arrangements for the housing of adults 'who by reason of age, illness, disability or any other circumstance are in need of care and attention which is not otherwise available to them'. The Act does not offer protection against homelessness or destitution to asylum-seekers or immigrants who are unable to leave the UK because of a risk of death, torture or inhumane treatment abroad. The ineligibility of some immigrants for social housing may violate their right to be free from discrimination once admitted to the UK.

More recent legislation defines the duty on local authorities more closely. Under the Housing Act 1996 they must provide 'temporary' accommodation only for families with children and other vulnerable 'priority' groups. But they have a wide measure of discretion and may refuse accommodation to people they believe have made themselves 'intentionally homeless' (e.g., by falling into rent arrears). Children's legislation allows social services to provide housing to prevent families with children being split up. The Homelessness Act 2002 requires local authorities to prepare five-yearly strategic plans to prevent and deal with homelessness. It gives applicants for public rented housing a right to a review of a council's decision on their case and a right of appeal to the county court against the refusal of re-housing or a time-limit on emergency accommodation. But families or individuals that refuse a housing offer can lose the chance of a further offer. The parliamentary Joint Committee on Human Rights complained in 2001 that the original Bill did not specify clearly enough that an offer 'must be appropriate to the needs of the homeless person or family'.

Official statistics show that local authorities recognised 166,760 households as being homeless in 1999-2000 – that is, as being entitled to emergency accommodation, even if it is only in a bed-and-breakfast hotel. Shelter adopts a standard higher than that of immediate emergency – including for example people in shared or unfit housing – and calculates that more than five million people are homeless on this standard.

Rough sleeping

The government has given priority to eliminating the scar of people who sleep on the streets. There is a homelessness 'czar' and a government Rough Sleepers Unit. In 2000, the unit estimated that around 1,200 people sleep on the streets on any one night.

Heating

The vast majority of homes in the UK have central heating, but about 9.5 million people in Britain (nearly 20 per cent of households) could not afford to heat their homes adequately, or keep them free from damp or in a decent state of decoration (Gordon et al, 2000). The government considers any household which has to spend more than 10 per cent of its income to provide adequate heating and energy to be in 'fuel poverty'. On this criterion, one household in five – nearly five million people – is 'fuel poor'; and one in 20 households suffer severe fuel poverty, as they require to spend more than 20 per cent of their income to stay warm (Howard et al, 2001). As stated above, such conditions result in an unacceptably high rate of 'excess deaths'.

Poor housing conditions

Much of the UK housing stock is obsolete or deficient. In 1996, an official review found that two fifth of public homes and nearly a third of private housing failed to meet official standards of decency. Around 2.7 million families and individuals lived in poor housing conditions, including 750,000 families; and 1.45 million of these households lived in homes officially classified as 'unfit for human habitation' (Revell and Leather, 2000). In 2000, a government white paper was devoted to improving the standard of housing in England and Wales, backed up by additional investment of £1.8 billion. Poor people are especially vulnerable to living in overcrowded conditions. Official figures show that ethnic minorities are eight times more likely to live in overcrowded conditions than white people (the figures are 13 and 2 per cent respectively).

Local authorities have a duty to provide sites for travellers, but these sites are usually badly sited in isolated environments that adversely affect their health. Local communities are often hostile to local authority attempts to place sites in more congenial neighbourhoods.

4.3. How far are wage levels and social security benefits sufficient for people's needs, without discrimination?

Poverty runs deeper in the UK than in any comparable major EU state. In 1997, nearly a quarter (22 per cent) of the UK population lived on incomes below the official EU poverty line of 60 per cent of median incomes. The corresponding figures for France and Germany were 17 and 14 per cent (the EU average was 18 per cent). Only Portugal had a higher poverty rate than the UK. The UK was also markedly more unequal. The ratio between the income shares of the top and bottom 20 per cent of the population in the UK was 7.4 compared with 5 and 4.7 in France and Germany; and while poor people took a larger share of total national income between 1994-95 and 1999-2000, the richest people became even richer. The UK figures suggest that there are links between greater poverty and a more unequal society. Historically also the UK has spent less on social protection than countries like France and Germany. 27.3 per cent of GDP in 1997, as against 29.5 and 30.8 per cent in Germany and France and slightly less than the EU average (28.1 per cent).

In Labour's first four years in office, the overall number of people living below the EU poverty line scarcely changed (see Table 1).[3] In 1997-98, some 13.5 million people (or 24 per cent of the population) lived below the EU poverty line; in 1999-2000, 13.3 million people lived in poverty (23.4 per cent). Of these, some five million lived in working-age households with at least one person in work.

1. People in Great Britain living below the poverty line (1997-98 and 1999-2000)

Year	No of individuals below 60% median income
1997-98	3.5 million
1999-00	3.3 million

Note: These figures include the self-employed

Sources: DSS, *Households Below Average Income 1999/00* (2001) and DSS, *Households Below Average Income 1998/99* (2000)

The fact is that the recent strength of the UK economy has not been mirrored by significant improvements in public welfare. Wealth creation has not been translated into significant wealth redistribution. On the one hand, the UK's GDP is the fourth highest internationally, and has grown at an average annual growth rate of 2.2 per cent over the last decade. Yet the average wealth per head of population is US$21,410, placing the UK behind most other West European countries and in thirteenth place internationally. The UK is ranked fourteenth internationally on the UN Human Development Index.

The government disowns any interest in reducing the large and growing inequalities in income and wealth in this country. At the lowest levels of earnings the minimum wage, introduced in April 1999, has raised the living standards of some 1.5 million workers; and the earnings of working families with children have been augmented by benefits related to work and income. But the government has largely neglected basic income support, the state's safety net, in its strategy of encouraging work as the main route out of poverty (though young children's rates have been surreptitiously raised). As a result, income support leaves workless families well below the EU poverty line. For example, in 1999-2000, a workless family with two children, aged four and eight, were entitled to £134.95 weekly – a 65.4 per cent shortfall. A single parent with a six-year-old child fell £24 weekly below the EU level (a 78.5 per cent shortfall).

Child poverty

A UNICEF league table for child poverty in June 2000 showed that the UK has the fourth worst record on child poverty among 23 of the world's wealthiest countries (Innocenti Research Centre, UNICEF). The inadequacy of benefits for parents out of work was a principal cause; 2.2 million children lived in workless families or homes in 2000, and 800,000 were growing up in families living on out of work benefits for more than five years. However, in keeping with his doing good by stealth strategy, Gordon Brown has more or less doubled the weekly rates for children under 11 in families on income support.

The government is pledged to eradicate child poverty in the UK; and in 2001 the Treasury announced that the government's tax and benefit reforms in its first term of office (1997-2001) would lift 1.2 million children out of poverty. But official figures released in April 2002 showed that, on the Treasury's own definition, only about 500,000 fewer children lived in poverty, leaving 3.9 million children in the year 2001-02 below the EU poverty line (Brewer et al, 2002).

Among the poorest families, it is estimated that 50,000 of children aged eight to ten have nothing to eat or drink before going to school in the morning. Children in single-parent families are more likely to be deprived of necessities, like three meals a day, and almost twice as likely as children in two-parent families to go without. In 1995, researchers at the London School of Hygiene and Tropical Medicine found that, no matter how carefully the poorest lone parent budgeted and shopped, their families' diets were bound to be less healthy than those of higher income families across a range of indicators (adequacy of nutrient intake, good dietary variety, etc).

Pensioners

In 1997, 2.6 million pensioners were living below the EU poverty line. To lift them out of poverty, Chancellor Gordon Brown introduced the Minimum Income Guarantee (MIG) in April 2000, and boosted the initiative a year later by linking the new means-tested benefit to earnings. We estimate that although MIG will significantly raise old people's pensions this year, and should lift single pensioners out of poverty, but it is not yet enough on its own to take most old couples above the EU poverty line. And these estimates depend on old people applying for it (see below).

Ethnic difference

Two thirds of people of Pakistani or Bangladeshi origin live in poverty, compared to one in five white people. Over 80 per cent of Pakistani and Bangladeshi households have incomes that are less than half the national average, compared with of 28 per cent of white households. People of ethnic minority backgrounds are more likely to live in poor areas: over half live in 29 local authority areas which are among the 44 most deprived areas in the country (Modood et al, 1997).

Women

The poverty statistics reveal a marked differential between the proportions of men and women who live below the EU poverty line. In 1997, one in four women (25 per cent) lived below the poverty line, as against one in five men (20 per cent). The gender gap grows with age: over a third of women aged 65 or more lived in poverty while just 22 per cent of men did.

Disabled people

After allowing for the costs of disability, half of all disabled people have incomes below half the average for the general population. A study of the economic exclusion of disabled people found that 60 per cent of disabled adults in families with children fell below the poverty line. Overall the study concluded that the 1999 disability benefit reforms left benefit levels still too low to raise the living standards of workless disabled people above the poverty level. Although those in work benefited, the transitory nature of employment for disabled people (with one in three losing their new job within a year) leaves them vulnerable to poverty (Burchardt, 2000).

Falling through the safety net

The government's targeted strategy for the relief of poverty relies on people claiming the means-tested benefits that they are entitled to. But thousands of people do not get these benefits, whether out of ignorance, shame or official inefficiencies or disdain. In 1998-99 it is estimated that a third of the 670,000 old people entitled to income support did not receive it. But the estimates of non-take-up are notably imprecise. Table 2 shows the wide variations in the estimates for the potential pool of people who may go unprotected. For example, some 1.75 million people entitled to council tax benefit may not receive it.

2. Take-up of means-tested benefits, 1998-99

Benefit	Take-up estimates (all) %	Non take-up by families with Children (No.)	All non-recipients (No.)
Income support	79 – 89	330-670,000	430-940,000
Housing benefit	91 – 97	10-70,000	130-430,000
Council tax benefit	75 – 81	60-190,000	1.25-1.75 million
Jobseeker's allowance	68 – 82	–	200-440,000
Family credit*	66 – 70	280-340,000	280-340,000

* Family Credit was replaced in October 1999 by the Working Families Tax Credit (WFTC)

Source: DSS, 2000, *Income Related Benefits: Estimates of Take-Up in 1998-99*

4.4. How far are poor people able to participate in the wider British society?

The causes of individual poverty – unemployment, illness, racial discrimination, etc – create and are involved with wider deprivations, like bad housing, environmental degradation, inadequate private services, poor transport, low educational attainment. This wider impact of poverty is known as social exclusion. Demographic data show that social exclusion is often concentrated in small neighbourhoods (even though more people live outside such areas than within them).

Individual distress in these neighbourhoods, often with a high proportion of ethnic minority people, is compounded by the shared experience of poverty, unemployment, lone parenthood, crime, racial harassment, poor housing, bad environmental conditions, vandalism, etc. At least one in five of all the wards in England – and possibly 30 per cent – could be described as deprived. For example, rates of child poverty and household worklessness in one in five wards are double the national average (Social Exclusion Unit, 2000).

Further analysis reveals that the difficulties of these deprived neighbourhoods on the margins of mainstream society range wider still. Their inhabitants are known to be cut off from basic services such as shops, telephones and banks, and are more exposed to crime, drugs and racism. While there is no firm statistical evidence, there is also plenty of evidence of examples of very limited access to the public transport on which poor people on large, isolated housing estates and in many other urban areas must rely. Moreover, the Social Exclusion Unit's policy action teams have found that:

- fewer than half the homes on some deprived housing estates have a telephone, compared with a national average of 90 per cent
- unemployment rates in the 100 most deprived wards are six times the national average
- most of the 488 secondary schools with more than a third of pupils entitled to free school meals are in deprived areas; only 11 per cent of these schools obtained national average levels of GCSE passes in 1998
- 1.5 million households (7 per cent) have no bank account or insurance cover. Most live on deprived council estates and are out of work (SEU, 2000).

Even at larger district level, the Social Exclusion Unit analysis of the 44 most deprived local authority areas reveals that, compared with the rest of England, they had:

- nearly two thirds more unemployment
- mortality rates 30 per cent higher
- a quarter more adults with poor literacy and numeracy
- a quarter more children who did not get a single GCSE
- two to three times the levels of poor housing, vandalism and dereliction.

The 44 areas also contain four times as many people from ethnic minority backgrounds than other areas; and over half all people from ethnic minorities live in just 29 of these most deprived areas.

Additionally, the SEU has assembled data showing (SEU, 2000) that:

- burglary rates in the most deprived basic police areas were three times the national average
- teenage conception and birth rates in the poorest areas of England were six times those in the most affluent areas
- non-participation rates for 16-18 year olds in education, employment or training in the most deprived areas, like Knowsley and Salford, were as high as 40 per cent. This compares with a national average of 9 per cent
- The Acheson report on health inequalities provided examples of health differences between places: e.g., compared with Surrey, Manchester has six years lower life expectancy among men and four years fewer for women; 11 years fewer years of good health among men (nine among women); and treble the death rate from coronary heart disease in people aged under 65.

Isolation among the elderly

Basic deprivations make the elderly particularly vulnerable to social isolation. A Mori survey for Help the Aged and British Gas found that one million pensioners live in isolation and feel trapped in their homes and another 630,000 feel that nobody knows they exist. Poor mobility and such feelings are twice as common among old people with low incomes or in poor health than among their better-off counterparts.

A wider view of social exclusion

But how best to measure social exclusion in the UK? Clearly a developed nation with the fourth largest economy in the world ought to be able to ensure that none of its citizens lives in the kinds of poverty and exclusion that we describe above. But what are the appropriate bench-marks for such a nation? We use the official European poverty line – 60 per cent of median incomes – above (see 4.3). But we need to go further if we are to judge how far British citizens experience a standard of living adequate to share in the society around them and, if they so choose, to exercise their rights as citizens. This relative measure is very hard to establish. Should, for example, every citizen be able to have a bank account or access to credit on reasonable terms? Should everyone be able to afford run a car or possess a home computer with Internet access? Part of the problem here is that developments such as home computing are constantly re-defining the parameters of active citizenship and creating potentially important new areas of social exclusion.

The Poverty and Social Exclusion (PSE) Survey of Britain 2000 tried to measure how many people were excluded from the opportunities of citizenship. A first survey among the general public established a set of 'socially perceived necessities'; a follow-up survey then asked a sample of people which of these social necessities they wanted and could or could not afford. On this basis, the survey found that some 14.5 million people – 25.6 per cent of the population – were poor by contemporary British standards. That is, they could not afford two basic necessities, as defined by their fellow citizens. Such necessities extended beyond items such as a damp-free home, two meals a day, beds and bedding, and a fridge, to 'visiting friends or family in hospital', 'celebrations on special occasions', school visits, and enough money to keep a home in a decent state of decoration. Another 10.3 per cent of the population were on incomes low enough to make them 'vulnerable to poverty'. Alarmingly, a third of all children were poor by society's reckoning.

The PSE research team also measured the effects of poverty on this scale on social exclusion and civic involvement. They found that three quarters of the poor people in their sample felt 'isolated' and almost as many 'depressed'. They tended to be dissatisfied with their neighbourhood and felt unsafe walking out on their own and in their homes at night. Some 43 per cent of them did not participate in civic life and only 18 per cent saw themselves as 'highly participative' (PSE survey, 2000).

4.5. To what extent is the health of the population protected in all spheres and stages of life?

The UK relies more heavily on public spending on healththan most comparable EU and Commonwealth countries, but spends less public money on health as a share of GDP than any of them (Wanless, 2001). Health outcomes are poor in comparison to these countries: for example,

- women in the UK had a shorter life expectancy than in all the other countries and were more likely to die prematurely in all but New Zealand;
- cancer is the biggest killer in Britain. Cancer survival rates lagged behind all the other European countries and accounted for one in four deaths;
- children were more likely to die in their first year of life than in any other of these countries, except New Zealand
- waiting times for treatment were longer in the UK and more patients experienced difficulties in seeing specialists when they needed to. In March 2001, 41,000 people had waited more than a year for in-patient treatment; 284,000 were still waiting to see a consultant more than 13 weeks after referral by their GP; and 82,000 of them waited more than 26 weeks.

Poverty and ill-health
Various studies from the Black report in 1980 to a recent report from the Chief Medical Officer and the PSE 2000 poverty survey have established the basic truth that poverty causes ill-health among the poor: it is linked with inadequate incomes, unemployment, smoking, and poor diet. The PSE 2000 study also found that the link is more significant in the UK than in comparable countries. Research for the Joseph Rowntree Foundation also shows that poor people die earlier than they should, estimating that poverty causes some 10,000 premature deaths annually. The study concludes that even a modest redistribution of wealth would prevent some three quarters of these people dying before they reach the age of 65; and the eradication of child poverty could save the lives of 1,400 young people (Independent, 26 September 2000).

There are also racial inequalities in health. People of Pakistani and Bangladeshi origin are one and a half times more likely to suffer ill-health than white people, and black Caribbean people a third more likely (Nazroo, 1997). Travellers die early (their life expectancy is just 55 years; the average for the UK is well over 70). Among the causes for this massive gap are the stresses and physical hazards of their lives and poor environment. In addition, there is evidence of institutional discrimination in the NHS. GPs often refuse to register or treat travellers.

Care of the elderly
The 1999 report of the Royal Commission on the Long Term Care of the Elderly found provision biased

towards residential care 'irrespective of the appropriateness or value for individuals'. The report high-lighted the scale of current and potential abuse of the vulnerable older people in the care system – now some 475,000 old people. Most care homes for the elderly and physically disabled are now privately run. Local authority fees are insufficient to fund care homes and are also often directly discriminatory. The low rates of profit reduce the quality of services private homes provide and are decimating their number. In the past year alone, 750 care homes have closed.

The existing system of care for the elderly is only available free to old people on low incomes and with very limited capital assets: it is largely the poor and the poorest old people who have to rely on residential care and people with moderate means are impoverished before they can get any help. The Royal Commission proposed that personal care should be available free once someone's need was assessed and established. Means testing should apply to living and housing costs only.

The government has established a National Care Standards Committee to monitor the state of the market in residential and nursing care and set benchmarks for the future. It accepted the view that nursing care should be free in all settings, but rejected the proposal that personal care should also be free and paid out of general taxation. In contrast, the Scottish Parliament has adopted the principle of free personal care.

4.6. How extensive and inclusive is the right to education, including education in the rights and responsibilities of citizenship?

Children in the UK have no right to schooling or further education, although in practice this is assured for children up to age 18 or 19. Compulsory school education ends at age 16. Between the ages of 16 and 19 young people are obliged to be in work or training under the government's New Deal employment scheme. But equality in education fractures largely along fault lines of class, race and income.

The impact of class and poverty

The skills and levels of knowledge of 15-year-old children in the UK are among the highest in the world, according to a major OECD survey conducted in 2000 in 31 developed countries. In reading, maths and science, their performance was well above the OECD average. Such findings confirm that educational attainment is rising at all stages in state schools under an intensive testing and examination regime. The DfEE's youth cohort study shows an increase in basic pass rates at GCSE over the past decade, and also in the proportion of pupils obtaining two or more A levels (or their equivalent).

But here class raises its disabling head, as it does throughout children's educational progress in the UK. The OECD found that there is a closer link in Britain between high achievement and social background than in most other countries: for example, the gap between the reading skills of children of the 25 per cent highest-ranking parental occupations and the lowest 25 per cent was the sixth largest in the survey. Thus one in eight British 15-year-olds show serious deficiencies in the basic reading skills needed for further learning.

Analysis of the government's own review of GCSE results in 2001 confirms the disabling effect of class and poverty on children's education. The *Guardian* found that in secondary schools with fewer than 5 per cent of pupils on free school meals three-quarters of the children achieved at least five Cs at

GCSE; but in schools with half the pupils on free school meals only a quarter of the children reached the same level (22 November 2001). Wealthy councils dominate the top of the scale and poor urban councils cluster at the bottom. In 1999, the UN Special Rapporteur on Education, Katarina Tomasevski, warned:

> This gap is likely to expand with time into an abyss unless there is a comprehensive, sustained and well-resourced strategy to equalise opportunities and – in a long-time perspective – educational attainment (see her report, E/CN.4/2000/6/Add.2, United Nations, Geneva, 1999).

From the earliest age, class tends to determine children's educational progress. A Treasury-backed study found that infants just 22 months old already show quite different class-based life chances: the educational progress of those from the highest social class is already 14 per cent better than those from the lowest class (Treasury, 1999). By the statutory school-leaving age, tracking surveys of people born in 1958 and 1970 showed that the children of professional parents were already far higher up the educational ladder than those of unskilled parents (*Guardian*, 12 July 2000).

The impact of race

In 1999, an Office for Standards in Education (Ofsted) report found that many British schools were 'institutionally racist'. Ethnic minority children perform as well as their white counterparts at primary school, but they fall behind at secondary level. The results of GCSE examinations, taken at age 16 in all schools, reveal discrepancies among the performance of different ethnic groups. Table 3 shows the big differences between boys and girls who pass one or more GCSEs by ethnic origin. Schools fail to collect accurate data to monitor progress, teachers promote racial stereotyping through the use of out-of-date teaching materials, few education authorities have a clear strategy for improving the performance of ethnic minority groups.

3. Success at school (by ethnic origin and gender)

	5-plus GCSEs(A*-C) (%)	1-4 GCSEs (A*-C) (%)
Young men		
White	43	25
Black	23	24
Indian	52	23
Pakistani/Bangladeshi	29	29
Others	37	28
All males	47	25

	5-plus GCSEs(A*-C) (%)	1-4 GCSEs (A*-C) (%)
Young women		
White	51	25
Black	35	42
Indian	55	28
Pakistani/Bangladeshi	32	45
Others	52	31
All females	51	26

Source: Youth Cohort Study, Department for Education and Employment, 1998

One significant sign of racial bias is the unequal exclusion rate from schools. The overall rate is unhealthily high – though it has fallen (from a peak of 12,700 in 1996-97 to 10,400 in 1998-99).[4] The government aims to reduce exclusions by a third by the end of this year. However, the exclusion rate for black Caribbean children was four times higher than average in 1998-99. Among the causes, Ofsted recognises that 'racism, perceived or actual, in the areas if not the school' is significant.

Other disadvantaged children

Two other groups suffer from excessive exclusion rates, namely children in local authority care and those with special educational needs (SEN). It is estimated that there are some 58,000 children in care, of whom some 6,500 are looked after in children's homes. The numbers of children in care is increasing and the pressures on the finances and specialist resources of local social services are becoming intense. These children often come from families suffering from generations of social deprivation, bad housing, poor education, ill-health and often substance abuse. Traumatic separations and the uncertain search for placements compound the severe damage from which they already suffer. Not surprisingly, the educational standards for these children are low: just half of them are supposed to gain one graded GCSE pass by the age of 16. But three quarters of them leave school with no qualification at all. They are also eight times more likely than other school children to have a statement of special needs.

An education officer has alleged that SEN has been 'used to exclude those who are just difficult to accommodate, rather than those who are genuinely prejudicial to the education of other children' (*Guardian Education*, 12 December 2000). Children with special education needs generally have inadequate resources devoted to them. The government is however seeking to improve the educational opportunities of children in care and young disabled and SEN pupils (through the Special Education Needs and Disability Act 2001). The Act requires schools, colleges and universities not to treat young disabled people less favourably than non-disabled peers and to adapt their procedures and buildings to ensure they are not substantially disadvantaged. The Act also strengthens the ability of parents to ask that their children be taught in ordinary schools, subject to protecting the education of other children.

Children from traveller families have the same right of access to schools as other children, but in practice access is often denied. Official policies suppressing illegal camping necessarily disrupt their school attendance. They are often bullied at school – and as a report for the Scottish Parliament showed, schools often back the bully and exclude the traveller child. Schools do not always accommodate their life-styles; as the UN Special Rapporteur observed, 'inadequate emphasis has been placed on the attitudes of the majority, both teachers and learners'. The cumulative impact is that traveller children do not want to attend school and then as parents don't want to put their own children through similar experiences. Though the government has allocated special funds to meet the needs of traveller and refugee children, she also concluded that the government had to demonstrate a 'political and financial commitment to ensuring that education is available, accessible, acceptable and adaptable'.

Higher education

The demand for higher education now exceeds the capacity of British universities and other education institutions. The student body expanded six-fold between 1970 and 1998 to 1.2 million students. The class divide is striking. More than half all young people going to university come from the two highest two socio-economic groups. As Table 4 shows, the participation rates across socio-economic groups in 1998-99 were grossly unequal; the rate for young people from professional homes was six times higher than for that for those from unskilled homes.

4. Participation rates in higher education (by class)

Social class	Participation rate %
Professional	72
Intermediate	45
Skilled non-manual	29
Skilled manual	18
Partly skilled	17
Unskilled	13
All socialclasses	31

Source: *Social Trends* 30, Table 3.13

The introduction of tuition fees, albeit means-tested, and the withdrawal of maintenance grants for all but the very poorest has reduced working class participation still further. The decrease in enrolments from working class homes is more than twice as high as that from professional homes. Generally, students must now rely on loans, parental contributions, savings and part-time work to get through their courses. However, the Scottish Parliament has abolished fees for young Scots at Scottish universities. In 1999, the UN Special Rapporteur on Education, Katarina Tomasevski, argued that tuition fees and the withdrawal of public funding for higher education violated the UK's obligation under Article 13 of the International Covenant to give access to higher education on the basis of academic ability and not on ability to pay (see her report, E/CN.4/2000/6/Add.2, 18-22 October 1999). The UN oversight committee has also just condemned the new policy (see page 61).

Students from ethnic minorities are over-represented in higher education as a whole. But while

Indian and Chinese students are more likely to go to university, young Bangladeshi and Pakistani women and young black and Caribbean men and women are under-represented.

Education in human rights

The Crick report in 1998 recommended that citizenship education should form at least a statutory 5 per cent share of the school curriculum. Education in citizenship entered the curriculum in September 2000 and should become compulsory from autumn 2002, although how much specific attention will be given to human rights within the limited time available remains to be seen.

4.7. How far are workers' rights to fair rates of pay, just and safe working conditions and effective representation guaranteed in law and practice?

The European Social Charter guarantees just conditions of work; protection of workers' health and safety; fair pay; maternity benefits for women workers; equal treatment and opportunities for women; and 'dignity at work'. The supremacy of EU law in the UK gives legal protection to these rights. But not necessarily *de facto* recognition. A series of EU directives, for example, have been issued to establish a maximum 48-hour average working week. But one in five British workers work over the maximum. The TUC reports that one in ten men work more than 55 hours a week, and one in 25 more than 60. Four out of five workplaces require their employees to work over their standard hours, half of them without extra pay. Such expectations are not compatible with the International Covenant (that recognises the right to rest, leisure, reasonable limitation of working hours and paid holidays). The effects of this 'work-home' imbalance are damaging to family life and children's upbringing.

Employment tribunals have proved an effective means of securing workers' rights and giving them remedies for their violation, largely because they often have the backing of EU law. In response to employers' complaints, the government aims to cut their caseload by 40,000. The Employment Act 2002 will jeopardise the promotion and protection of workers' rights to just working conditions by giving employers the right to insist, as a condition of employment, that their workers give up their rights to sue them. In the House of Lords, Lord Wedderburn said the Act 'crosses a Rubicon into the new territory of management prerogative, which will enable employers to keep workers from enforcing their rights in tribunals'.

Health and safety at work

About 360 people are killed at work every year in Britain (a rate of two persons per 100,000 workers; the EU average is five per 100,000); and 1,550 people were involved in accidents requiring more than three days' absence from work. The Health and Safety Executive, the quango charged with protecting people at work, is under-resourced and unwilling to prosecute companies for failing to comply with safety standards. In 1996, it instructed its inspectors to reduce prosecutions of companies that were in breach of safety rules, which is incompatible with international rights to safe and healthy conditions or work. In 1999, the Centre for Corporate Accountability informed the Environmental Select Committee that only one in ten of 47,000 major accidents at work reported between 1996–98 resulted in a prosecution (Monbiot, 2000).

Women

Britain's gender pay gap has been halved since 1970, but it remains the worst in the EU. Full-time women workers are paid just 82 per cent of the pay of equivalent men, and part-time women workers receive less than two-thirds full-time male rates (the EU average is three-quarters). Over a lifetime, the EOC estimates, discrimination in earnings would cost a 'middle-skilled' childless woman £241,000, and the same woman with two children £140,000. Bonuses, performance-related pay and pension entitlements widen the gap between men and women still further, raising the 18 per cent gap in hourly earnings to some 26 per cent a year. One in ten large employers illegally exclude part-time workers, mainly women, from pension schemes.

Family rights

Under the influence of the EU, the Employment Relations Act 1999 introduced parental leave after one year's service for both men and women who have a baby or adopt a child; extended maternity leave; preserved workers' employment contracts throughout parental and additional maternity leave; gave employees with children a right to take reasonable time off work to deal with a family emergency; and protected workers who exercise these rights against dismissal or detrimental treatment. But British mothers only receive the equivalent of eight weeks' full salary in maternity pay – less than half the EU average.

Some 70 per cent of mothers return to work before their 18 weeks entitlement are over. Childcare then becomes important. In 1998 the government launched a national childcare strategy to provide places for one million children by 2003 and free nursery care for all three-year-olds by 2004. But childcare is increasingly expensive and free or affordable childcare for poor parents with children under three is still rare: in 2001, there were only 42,740 free or subsidised places for 600,000 under-threes living in families in poverty.

Trade union rights

The Conservative administrations of 1979-1997 passed a series of acts restricting and then outlawing trade-unions rights and reforming trade union procedures. New laws created new criminal offences for pickets; enabled employers to dismiss workers selectively for taking part in unofficial industrial action; repealed statutory recognition procedures; gave individuals the ability to seek injunctions against unlawful action; and encouraged the shift towards individual contracts.

Labour has kept much of the previous government's trade union legislation since 1997; it has also signed up to the EU Social Chapter, which is supportive of trade unionism. In 1999, the government passed the 1999 Employment Relations Act, which:

- re-established the right of individual trade union members to take action for unfair dismissal if they had been dismissed for taking part in official industrial action;
- prohibited blacklisting or other discrimination against trade union members;
- gave employees a new right to be accompanied by a fellow worker or trade union representative during disciplinary and grievance proceedings; and
- gave trade unionists a statutory right for the first time to seek recognition in the workplace.

However, in 2000, the European Committee of Social Rights found that the UK was failing to fulfil its obligations under nearly a third of the EU Charter's articles and raised several concerns, particularly the ability of an employer to dismiss all employees who participate in industrial action. This in effect violates the right to strike. Employers are also able to award preferential remuneration to employees to persuade them to relinquish trade union representation. The Committee also challenged the narrow scope of lawful industrial action. Further, the Trade Unions and Labour Relations Act 1992 encourages voluntary negotiation at the expense of the right to collective bargaining; and still unduly restricts the ability of trade unionists to organise.

4.8 How rigorous and transparent are the rules on corporate governance; and how effectively are corporations regulated in the public interest?

The power of global business in the modern world is universally recognised. Major foreign-based as well as British corporations own and run companies in the UK and around the world; these corporations can locate their activities, move capital and shift and vary their investments, open new enterprises and close or move existing projects, and increase, cut or dismiss workforces as they see fit. A decisive ideological shift away from state regulation and the public sphere towards neo-liberal ideas and the primacy of the private market has accompanied their rise. Major corporations and trade associations exert considerable power on and through the state in this country, and on most aspects of civil society, work and culture. One conse-quence of the shift in attitude at government level has, for example, been the moves to contain worker and trade union powers and to lessen the impact of state regulation of employers' activities. How effectively, then, are major corporations and the smaller firms and enterprises regulated in the public interest?

The rules on corporate governance are framed to protect the interests of shareholders, other enter-prises and the customers of private companies, large or small; to guard against fraud and insolvency; and so on. Rather than being governed in the wider public interest, 'the corporation,' as George Monbiot writes in *Captive State*, is more accurately understood as 'an ingenious device for acquiring rights and shedding responsibilities'. The rules do not provide for extensive transparency. Freedom of Information laws apply only to those firms that are carrying out public functions; and imperfectly even then (see Section 7.7). The DTI advises companies to avoid potentially damaging information being released by protecting sensitive information, insisting on confidentiality clauses for staff and routinely destroying all sensitive documents. Even employees have only limited rights to information on their employers. For several years, Tony Blair has blocked a mild EU information and consultation directive, to the anger of the TUC. Meanwhile General Motors closed the Vauxhall plant without any warning; BMW sold off most of the Rover group; the steel company Corus pushed through huge redundancies. In December 2001, John Monks, the TUC general secretary, condemned Blair's 'inexplicable blocking of the European directive . . . given the unacceptable conduct of General Motors, Coats Viyella and BMW'.

A small host of public bodies, regulators and tribunals exist to try and safeguard the public interest. For example, the Financial Services Authority acts as a public watchdog over financial institutions and the City of London. The Health and Safety Executive oversees safety regulations and has powers to prosecute firms that fail to observe them. Regulatory bodies seek to hold the balance between the priva-tised utilities and their customers over investment, profits and prices. EU directives and influence have raised the standards of the working environment in the UK, but much remains to be done; the government tends only to aspire to the minimum standards set by the EU.

But it is very hard for such bodies to police major corporations that operate in secrecy, often from headquarters outside this country. Further, the prevailing tendency among supervisory bodies is for a 'softly, softly' approach with an emphasis on persuasion and voluntary compliance. They nowadays work in a climate that is hostile to regulation. The government machinery for reviewing regulation is tasked to ensure that it is 'necessary, fair and affordable' and takes special account of the needs of small businesses. Lord Haskins, who heads the Better Regulation Task Force, is a businessman who is against more regulation of business and the task force is dominated by business interests. Thus there is now less government regulation and more self-regulation. In April 1999, a new Regulatory Impact Unit emerged with the aim of reducing 'the cumulative burden of regulation'. The then DTI Secretary, Stephen Byers, announced in June 1999 that any enforcement action would be 'business friendly'.

Business influence

Business interests have exercised a long-standing influence on policy-making within the corridors of Whitehall (see also Section 12.1). The CBI, drug, processed foods, aerospace and arms industries, oil companies, major brewers, farmers and other private business interests often participate in a parallel and often more decisive system of representation to that of the people through Parliament. It is argued that though they are self-interested participants, they can bring special knowledge and experience to bear upon the policy process. Representatives of industrial interests also sit at the core of advisory government committees which take crucial decisions, for example, on the safety of drugs and food, or the dangers of BSE, even the quality of the air people breathe. In the aftermath of the 1997 election, ministers set up some 318 advisory task forces to review and advise on a wide range of government policies. A Democratic Audit analysis of their composition found that more than a third of their members were drawn from private industry (Barker et al, 1999).

The Blair government has adopted a 'business friendly' stance since taking office and the trade unions, once part of a tripartite corporate state, have less access then business interests to government. For example, John Cridland, the CBI director-general, found Blair 'very receptive to business arguments' (Taylor, 2001), while the trade union leader Bill Morris complained that TUC delegations might walk in the front door of 10 Downing Street, but the CBI could get in the back way. Democratic government in a capitalist economy inevitably involves a compromise between the rule of the people, by way of their elected representatives, and established private powers. While the balance of advantage has moved towards the private sphere since the 1970s, it is a reasonable conclusion that it has moved even further in the current government's relationship with private industry.

1   The section summarises Democratic Audit evidence to the UN Committee for Economic, Social and Cultural Rights in May 2002. Restrictions of space make it necessary to deal very briefly with most issues and to exclude others. We are preparing a fuller free-standing report, Unequal Britain, for publication later this year.

2   Employment tribunals, however, hear disputes between employers and employees – over 130,000 in the past year – and they are obliged to apply EU law within their parliamentary-given jurisdiction. They are so popular that the government plans to restrict access to them (see Section 4.7 below).

3   The statistics in this Audit will be updated in the Unequal Britain report, to be published later this year.

4   Figures released as we go to press show a rise again in 2000-01 in England and Wales (but not Scotland). Most worrying are the differences in exclusion rates for Asian, white and Afro-Caribbean pupils: three, 13 and 38 respectively in every 10,000.

Section two: representative and accountable government

Five: free and fair elections

The other national lottery

Do elections give the people control over governments and their policies?

We always come up against the problem of the current electoral system in which the gambling, betting and sporting instincts of the nation seem to have found their characteristic political expression.
Egon Wertheimer, historian, 1929

Introduction

Free, fair and regular elections stand at the very heart of representative democracy. They are the chief means by which the two basic principles of the Democratic Audit are realised – popular control of government and political equality in the exercise of that control. It is through the ability of citizens, at regular elections, to retain or dismiss their elected representatives and the political parties they stand for, that the principle of popular control is made flesh. Section 5 examines how well elections in Britain conform with these two principles and related issues of government formation and representation.

In the UK, the role of elections is particularly significant since constitutional accountability is based primarily on the electorate's ability to choose, recall and dismiss governments as well as their representatives; and on the ability of an opposition party to gain sufficient electoral clout to be able to oppose the government in Parliament between elections and to pick up the reins of government at subsequent elections. Previous Democratic Audit studies have shown that the system for elections to Westminster does not give every vote equal value, an idea that is central to the principles of popular control and political equality, whereas systems of PR would (see Weir and Beetham, 1999; Dunleavy et al, 1996, 1997 and 1998).

Put at its simplest, every elector's vote should count for one, and none for more than one. It is possible to measure how far an electoral system deviates from this goal, known as the Deviation from Proportionality index and we use this index in this Section.[1] It is also important that electors should have a range of choice at elections which broadly reflects the most significant political preferences and needs of the whole electorate – and that the choices they make are effective.

The House of Commons, the elected chamber in Parliament, is supposed to represent the electorate and make government accountable on its behalf. There are three ways in which the House of Commons could be made representative of the electorate:

- according to each party's share of the votes cast;
- according to geographical distribution; and
- according to its social characteristics.

The three modes of representation are all important for Democratic Audit. The first, because elections are nowadays primarily about choosing a party or parties to form a government; votes should not be more or less effective according to which party people vote for, or in which constituency they vote. The second because voters should not be privileged or disadvantaged just because they live, say, in the country rather than the city, or in the south-east of England rather than the north; nor should the House of Commons be weighted disproportionately towards one set of geographical interests than others. The third because a popular chamber biased towards one social group or groups, or gender, will be limited in experience and focus and more likely to lose trust or even legitimacy – especially among people who are excluded. We consider the nature of representation in the UK below in Sections 5.1, 5.4 and 5.5; and then in a brief conclusion.

As regards fairness in the conduct of elections, the Electoral Commission was established in November 2000 to oversee new laws on party and election finance and the conduct of elections. Its remit is wide. The Commission is charged with registering political parties and 'third parties', enforcing electoral regulations, supervising the use of advertising, modernising election laws and procedures, promoting public awareness and overseeing electoral boundaries. For the first time, the 2001 election came under official invigilation. We consider the Commission's role in Sections 5.2 and 5.3 below.

5.1. How far is appointment to government and legislative office determined by popular competitive election, and how frequently do elections lead to change in the governing parties or personnel?

General elections in the UK are the prime agents for determining both the composition of the popular chamber in Parliament and selecting the governing party.

But much of the governing structure in the UK is now being determined not by election, but by appointment (often directly by the executive). The House of Lords, the second chamber of Parliament, is an unelected body and its democratic illegitimacy weakens Parliament as a whole (see Section 7.5). Under Blair, more ministers are not themselves elected, but, like lords Falconer and Macdonald have been made peers by Blair so that he can appoint them to his government. A whole host of unelected official bodies and officials – executive agencies, quangos, public corporations, regulators, czars, ad hoc plenipotentiaries, etc – also act as 'miniature governments' in their own sphere, for the most part mostly or wholly independent of government control (see Section 7.1).

General elections now centre a great deal on the party leaders, so the electorate's votes in effect choose or at least endorse a party candidate for Prime Minister. The prevailing theory of British government is that we live in a two-party system in which power alternates between two major parties, the Conservatives and Labour. The fact is that the celebrated 'swing of the pendulum' often gets stuck with a single party in power over several elections. The Conservative party dominated inter-war politics between 1918 and 1939; and in the postwar period, from 1951-64 and 1979-97. Labour held power in two minority inter-war governments; two postwar periods of majority government (1945-51; 1964-70); and very shakily from 1974-79. Until 2001, Labour was unable to secure majorities large enough to win consecutive full terms in office.

Incumbency has generally proved to be a major advantage for the party in power; and at many postwar elections, the swing required to overturn the governing party has been quite outside the grasp of the main opposition party.

At the same time, both major parties have been protected from challenges from third parties. The effects of plurality-rule (or 'first-past-the post') elections and party political culture have combined to exclude the Liberal Democrats from the role in Parliament and government that their share of the votes should give them. In the 1983 and 1987 elections, the Social Democratic Alliance won almost a quarter of the nation's votes, but the plurality-rule electoral system rewarded both the Conservatives and Labour disproportionately and denied the Alliance the share of seats its vote justified. Thus the two-party domination of Parliament, British politics and the media was preserved.

The system's lack of responsiveness has now swung in Labour's favour. Pollsters John Curtice and Michael Steed, who have analysed the election results for 1997 and 2001 in detail, have noted a growing electoral bias towards Labour that could mean that the Conservatives cannot hope to win an election for a decade (Curtice and Steed, 2002). This bias is structural rather than political. It is simply that Labour's vote becomes more strongly concentrated in smaller constituencies between elections than the Conservatives'; its vote is 'more efficiently distributed' than theirs; and the differential effects of the Lib-Dem presence in constituencies held by Labour and the Conservatives subtly improves Labour's electoral strength, quite apart from the impact of tactical voting. Even if the Conservatives were to win the same share of the vote as Labour at the next election, they would win no fewer than 140 seats less than Labour – 60 more than the disadvantage they suffered in 1997. Second, according to Curtice and Steed, the Conservatives would have to be ahead of Labour by 11.5 per cent simply to win an overall majority of one, whereas Labour could be 3.7 per cent behind the Tories and still come out with an overall majority. In 1997, the equivalent figures were 10.1 and 1.5 per cent. The adoption of proportional representation would end such biases either way at a stroke.

There is also the local incumbency effect – the 'personal vote' that a sitting MP can build up through effective local politics and promotion technique. The incumbency vote slows down any swing from party to party at constituency level and thus favours the party with most sitting MPs who are standing again. This factor clearly favours the Labour party, which has most MPs in the House (45 per cent of whom are aged under 50).

5.2. How inclusive and accessible for all citizens are the registration and voting procedures, how independent are they of government and party control, and how fair are procedures for the registration of candidates and parties?

In principle, every adult over the age of 18 normally resident in the UK is eligible to vote in elections to Parliament, the European Parliament and local authority. To exercise the vote they must register on the electoral roll for the area in which they live. The electoral law, now amended by the Representation of the People Act 2000, sets out the rules for eligibility. To be able to vote a person must:

- be a citizen of a Commonwealth country (which includes all types of British nationals, except British protected persons) or of the Republic of Ireland; and
- have an address in the UK at which they have lived for up to a month (in Northern Ireland, someone can only register to vote only if they have been resident in Northern Ireland for a period of three months); or for a British citizen living abroad, must have been registered on the electoral roll of a constituency at any time within the last 20 years.

Aliens, members of the House of Lords, convicted prisoners serving a prison sentence, offenders detained in a mental hospital and people convicted of a corrupt election practice during the last five years, may not legally vote.

Causes for concern
The formal processes of registration and voting are well-organised and independent of government and party control; both processes are organised and supervised by local registration and returning officers (usually chief executives of the relevant local authority area). Parties encourage people they have identified as 'their' voters to make use locally of postal ballots, proxy votes, etc, and to vote on polling day. Party workers often stand at the approaches to polling stations, but there are strict rules about who can actually enter a polling station. The police supervise all polling stations. There are however several wider causes for concern:

- The UN Human Rights Commitee in 2001 condemned the ancient bar on prisoners voting as a human rights violation. The Committee could see no justification for maintaining the old law in modern times and argued that it amounted to 'an additional punishment' that did not contribute towards the reformation and social rehabilitation of prisoners;
- All people aged under 18 are excluded from the direct democratic leverage of the vote, even though 16 and 17 year olds are subject to certain rights, duties and obligations; must usually be in employment, education or training or suffer penalties; are liable for taxes if in work; may leave home and

(with parental consent) get married; may raise children; may join the army; may serve prison sentences or buy cigarettes and tobacco;

● People who are without British nationality or Commonwealth citizenship are denied the right to vote however long they have resided in the UK. Voting rights depend on nationality, not directly on immigration status, so Commonwealth-country citizens living here, on whatever basis, may register to vote and do so. Non-Commonwealth citizens may not (with the exception of EU nationals who may vote in elections to the devolved representative bodies, local elections in England, Scotland, Northern Ireland or Wales, and in European Parliament elections).

Rules for candidates

Any British, Commonwealth or Irish citizen aged 21 or over who is resident in the UK may stand for election to Parliament, except for those in politically-sensitive positions, such as civil servants, some office-holders in local government, members of the armed forces and police, judges and so on. Prisoners sentenced to a year or more in jail and bankrupts are disqualified, and anyone convicted of an offence under electoral law may be disqualified for five to ten years. All candidates must be nominated by local electors and lodge a £500 deposit (£1,000 for European elections) which is refunded if they win 5 per cent or more of the vote. It is hard to justify preventing anyone under the age of 21 from standing for office when people over 18 are considered adult enough to vote. All parties must now register with the Electoral Commission if they wish to use a party name on ballot papers for an election. In 2001, the new regulatory framework caused some difficulties for some very small parties, but these should be evened out in time for the next election.

Recent reforms

The government's Representation of the People Act 2000 has righted some wrongs that Democratic Audit noted in 1996 and 1999. Homeless people, travellers and others with a transitory life-style now possess an effective right to vote for the first time. Anyone who has no permanent address of their own can now register to vote, giving an address near a place in the UK where they 'commonly spend' their time. So homeless people can, for example, register to vote giving a community centre or hostel as their residence. Patients suffering from a mental disorder in hospital can also now vote, registering either from the hospital or another residence with which they are connected. People with physical disabilities, the blind or partially sighted and those who cannot read may now take advantage of additional facilities at polling stations, enabling them to vote with the assistance of a nominated companion. Prisoners held on remand have always been formally entitled to vote, but could not do so as they were not allowed to register from a penal institution. That obstacle has now been removed. Under the Disability Discrimination Act 1995, registration and returning officers are bound to make 'reasonable adjustments' to make their services and polling stations accessible to disabled electors.

Making voting easier

Our previous Audit critically reviewed the obsolete registration and voting procedures that survived still in the 1990s; people were registered only once a year in an increasingly mobile and pluralistic society. Over the years the cumbersome process was gradually disenfranchising people; in 1983, the rates for people registered were falling (from 97.8 per cent in 1983 to 94.5 per cent in 1998 – that is, more than 2.5 million people). Certain groups of people – young adults, people living in insecure rented accommodation, etc – were disadvantaged, with knock-on effects among inner-city, and especially young black, populations. Thus the process itself contributed to structural inequalities in the population that was registered to vote. The 2000 Act has introduced 'rolling' registration that updates the electoral register every month. But registration is not as instant as it needs to be in the run-up to an election. To be able to vote in 2001, a citizen had to register to be on the electoral roll by 5 April – so on 7 May, when the election was announced, it was already too late to register. It is clearly important to make it possible for people to register when they learn that the next election is about to be held.

The Act also simplified postal voting and made it more or less available on demand by widening the criteria of eligibility. Local authority experiments in new voting processes – for example, allowing people to vote by e-mail, placing polling booths in supermarkets or conducting wholly postal ballots – showed that postal voting did raise turnout. For example, turnout rose by about half in seven local elections in May 2000 where postal ballots entirely replaced polling stations (Electoral Commission, 2001). However, for the moment the cut-off point for applying for a postal vote at a general election stands at 11 days before an election, even though computerised polling processes make a shorter deadline possible. Postal voting doubled from over 730,000 postal votes in 1997 to 1.4 million in 2001.

Secrecy of the ballot

The secrecy of the ballot has long been recognised as essential to fair elections free from bribery and intimidation. Most people in the UK vote assuming that their vote is secret. But the authorities can check on how an individual voted. The registration number of everyone voting is recorded on the counterfoil of used ballot papers. After the local count, the counterfoils and ballot papers, bearing each person's vote, are sealed in parcels and despatched to the care of a senior official of the Lord Chancellor's Office and kept at a secure location in London. It is therefore possible to identify for whom particular individuals have voted, or which individuals have voted for any particular candidate. This process is an old safeguard against voter impersonation; but a recent study has pointed out that allegations of voter impersonation in Britain are negligible and 'vote-tracing hardly ever helps in the detection and prevention of any offence in itself' (Blackburn 1995).

The most serious allegation made about vote-tracing is that the intelligence services have in the past gained access to the ballots in order to determine the identity of those who voted for the Communist Party of Great Britain. Here we are obliged to rely on the anecdotal recollections of ex-intelligence operatives (see for instance Winter 1981). But such an investigation is within the capacity of the intelligence services. The retention of retrospective records should be abandoned, since other, alternative methods of preventing voting fraud would actually be more effective. The principle of a secret ballot should take precedence over all other considerations.

Finally, proxy voting (which allows a relative to vote on behalf of an elector who cannot readily go to the poll) also breaches the secrecy of the ballot. At one time, proxy voting may have seemed a reasonable option. But it is clearly open to abuse and is hardly necessary now that postal voting has been made far easier.

Fixing boundaries

We noted in the previous Audit that local government boundaries were open to political manipulation that allowed governments to gerrymander local authority areas and strongly to influence the pattern of subsequent re-drawings of parliamentary boundaries by the four impartial Boundary Commissions (for

England, Scotland, Wales and Northern Ireland). Our review extended back to the Conservative reorganisation of local government in the 1970s. But the most brazenly self-interested, indeed eccentric, example was the government's unilateral re-shaping of local government boundaries for Scotland in 1993, with the exclusive aim of creating councils that would elect Conservative administrations.

Such partisan influence on local boundaries exerts an indirect impact upon national elections, since the Parliamentary Commissions are bound to take local authority boundaries into consideration when redrawing parliamentary boundaries.

Their work has obvious partisan implications for the political parties. The removal or addition of a particular area from or to an existing constituency can and does affect or even change its political affiliation. The Boundary Commissions are therefore guided by formal rules in their redistribution reviews. They are first enjoined to make the size of constituency electorates as near as practicable to a fixed 'electoral quota' that would make them all of equal size and to respect local government and ward boundaries; and are then given considerable discretion to depart from these rules to allow for 'geographical considerations' (i.e., the size, shape and accessibility of a constituency), local ties, recognised communities, etc.

This discretion undermines the equity that the 'electoral quota' is meant to provide. The Commissions hold hearings on their proposals for boundary changes and the political parties and local publics are able to intercede. The parties can exercise considerable influence. It was estimated, for example, that the Labour party entered the 1991-94 reviews, prior to the 1997 election, liable to lose four to 17 seats, due to boundary changes; they emerged with four winnable seats and effectively neutralised the effects of redistribution (Gardner, 1995). The formally neutral process is also subject to unequal political pressures; while the Conservatives played a 'significant role' in 82 hearings and Labour in 77, the less well-resourced Liberal Democrats presented arguments in only 17.

In theory, a plurality-rule election can work fairly and make people's votes equal between constituencies if all constituencies have electorates of the same size. But the four boundary commissions each have a different quota; and none of them stick consistently to their quotas. So no quota is applied uniformly across the UK and constituencies vary considerably in size. There is a five-fold discrepancy between the largest constituency – the Isle of Wight with 106,583 voters– and the smallest, Western Isles (21,691), and all manner of variations in size between.

It is possible that the new Electoral Commission will improve matters. The Commission will absorb the functions of the Parliamentary Boundary Commissions and the Local Government Commissions of England, Scotland and Wales after the forthcoming series of reviews (2003–7). A permanent body such as the Commission, with a continuing degree of impartial authority through its other activities, is likely to govern boundary fixing more consistently and effectively than the current ad-hoc arrangements.

5.3. How fair are the processes of registration for parties and candidates, how far is there fair access to the media and other means of communication with the voters, and how free are they from government and party control, intimidation and abuse?

The new Electoral Commission oversees the new legal framework for the conduct of the political parties and others during elections. The new electoral laws oblige all parties to register with the Electoral Commission. Further, in 2001:

- registered parties were bound by national spending limits, of £15.8 million nationally, or £24,000 per constituency contested;
- registered parties were required to submit weekly reports to the Commission on donations of over £5,000;
- any third party (a trade union, private company, a pressure group, an association, etc) intending to spend more than £10,000 in England (or more than £5,000 in Scotland, Wales or Northern Ireland) on material designed to promote a registered party or category of candidates had also to register with the Commission; and
- registered third parties were subject to a regime of spending limits of up to £988,500 in a year; it was an offence for other third parties to spend more than £10,000 in England (£5,000 in Scotland or Wales).

The Commission can now also prevent parties or candidates adopting misleading party labels, such as the 'Literal Democrat' description that cost the Liberal Democrats a seat in the 1994 Euro-election.

Government and party influence and control

In the main, British electoral and voting procedures are independent of party and government influence and control. The Parliament Act 1911 lays down the maximum life of a Parliament, but does not specify a minimum. In constitutional law, the timing of a general election is supposedly a Royal Prerogative matter – i.e., a matter for the Prime Minister's personal discretion. The Queen formally dissolves Parliament, the Prime Minister makes the decision. There is no law or convention that requires him to consult Parliament, let alone seek its approval.

Thus the government of the day retains a considerable advantage over other parties contesting a general election. The Prime Minister decides the polling date that best suits his own party; and Chancellors can try and time economic cycles to electoral advantage, or manipulate tax and spending decisions to reduce the impact of taxes and raise public spending (especially in key areas) in an election year. For example, Tony Blair performed a spectacular about-turn on the election date in 2001 when he delayed the election for a month to avoid going to the country while some parts were literally ablaze with pyres of animals killed to halt the spread of foot and mouth disease.

Government control of the election date also enables the Prime Minister to set the length of the campaign and gives his own party a head start over the others in terms of preparation and strategic planning. Virtually all other parliamentary democracies fix the timing of elections in law, and indeed every other British election, whether for the Scottish Parliament, Welsh Assembly, European Parliament or local councils, takes place on a fixed date over an agreed timetable. A majority of people in the UK believe that parliamentary elections should also be fixed (Dunleavy et al, 2001).

Government advertising

The most alarming development in this unreformed domain is the blatant manipulation by the Blair government of official advertising for party political gain prior to the 2001 election. For the most part, the Cabinet Secretary and civil service police any use of state facilities, buildings, equipment, etc, by the governing or any other party, by MPs or by others. This protection against abuse derives entirely from convention, rather than law, but it has worked. However, in the year running up to the 2001 election (April 2000–March 2001), government spending on advertising rose to a record £192 million, 70 per cent more than the previous year. In March 2001 alone, the government spent £49 million. In fact, the government even outspent the traditional big spenders on advertising. The campaign was weighted towards the first months in 2001 and was clearly pre-planned. The advertisements, both on television and in the press, were not factual; they were rather designed to promote the government on issues such as nursing, the state of the NHS, benefit fraud and assistance to single parents. Neville Taylor, former head of the Central Office of Information, which runs government advertising campaigns, expressed concern on BBC *Panorama* about the nature, density and timing of the campaigns:

> To concentrate expenditure and impact and message all in a very tight time-scale in the run-up to an election has got to smell, it has to indicate another motive [other than information–giving] for doing it' (26 May 2002).

On the same programme, former senior civil servants, including a former Cabinet Secretary, questioned the propriety of the campaigns. Ironically, Tony Blair several times forcibly condemned the Conservatives for misusing public funds on promoting their policies in the late 1980s. Now his government has outdone them. Such expenditure does not only misuse public money. It also escapes the restrictions on airtime which apply to all political broadcasting; and in future would, if continued, evade the new curbs on national election spending by the political parties.

The Prime Minister's decision to make Alastair Campbell overlord of all government communications will inevitably add to concern about political abuse of government advertising (see Section 7.8). Campbell is of course a party political appointee and the head of the COI reports to him. There are bound to be suspicions, well-founded on the evidence of the 2001 pre-election surge in government advertising, that party political considerations will affect government advertising in the run-up to the next election. There exists no effective constitutional means of preventing such abuse.

Cheap elections

Elections are relatively cheap in the UK since the electoral law forbids paid political advertising on television and radio. Instead parties have free access to the five main terrestrial TV channels for a limited number of party political broadcasts (PPBs). The broadcasting authorities and broadcasters themselves decide the allocation of airtime for these broadcasts, and then by convention they put proposals to the major parties represented in Parliament with a view to reaching consensus. They take into account the number of candidates standing for each party in the election and the number of MPs the party has in the previous Parliament. The precise allocation of PPBs is then decided by ad-hoc negotiations between broadcasters and party representatives. The usual rule of thumb is that the Conservatives and Labour are given equal time, while other parties receive an allocation broadly in proportion to their vote at the previous election. Any party fielding 50 candidates or more receives a minimum five-minute spot on television. For the 2001 election 11 registered parties could present PPBs, six nationwide, the Greens in England and Wales, and the three larger and nationalist parties in Scotland or Wales. Six parties produced broadcasts in Northern Ireland.

There are always disputes over the allocation of broadcasts. The most significant controversy over access to the free PPB slots came in 1997, when broadcasters censored a Pro-Life Alliance film which showed 'shocking' images of abortion. The Alliance took the case to the courts and in March 2002 the Appeal Court upheld its right to show the images. The BBC argued on behalf of the broadcasters that the film was 'grossly offensive' and they were obliged by law not to show material that offended 'good taste or decency'. But the judges ruled that the broadcasters' decision was 'censorship'; the images were not gratuitous, sensational, or untrue; and they were a 'message' that conveyed the human character of the foetus. At the time of writing, the BBC is expected to appeal.

Overall, the decision-making process is typically informal and ought probably to be brought into the remit of the Electoral Commission. However the free access to television and radio has an equalising effect and keeps the costs of elections down. The main parties can of course use their greater resources to produce more researched and effective short advertisements than their opponents, but the differential is much smaller than it would be in a free market.

The role of the media

Most of the public get the majority of their information about politics and elections from the media. Television and radio are the media that most people trust to give them factual and impartial information. Pre-election polling for the Electoral Commission established that 88 per cent of the public used television as their source of information about politics (followed by daily and Sunday newspapers at 74 and 54 per cent respectively). The broadcast media are bound by law and custom to strict rules of impartiality, even to the amount of coverage the main parties receive (see Weir and Beetham, 1999, further). The print media are not obliged by law to report elections or politics impartially.

After the long era in which the Conservatives could count on the support of most of the press, the Loughborough University media research centre found that some 90 per cent (in circulation terms) endorsed the Labour party in 2001. Even the *Daily Mail*, usually ferociously loyal to the Tories, did not explicitly call for a Tory vote, but simply asked its readers to vote against a large Labour victory. Political scientists gave evidence to the Electoral Commission that the broadsheet press initiated more analysis and punditry in 2001 than in the 1992 and 1997 elections. However, the tabloid press remains aggressively partisan. A majority of the press are strongly opposed to further integration into the EU, and thus to Britain's entry into the Euro; and the tabloids are notably right-wing in their focus on themes such as low taxes, asylum-seekers and most things foreign. It is most unlikely that the media had any but a marginal effect on the outcome of the 2001 election. But the media may very well set parameters of behaviour for the parties and the policies they present at elections (see also Section 10).

One welcome reform in television coverage of the election in 2001 came with the relaxation of the rules governing reports from local constituencies. Prior to the 2000 Act candidates could only take part in a local TV report if all the rival candidates took part. The new code agreed under the Act removes the power of veto and requires that the candidates of the three main parties (four in Scotland, Wales and Northern Ireland) should be invited to participate; that there should be participation by significant smaller parties; and that viewers should be given a full list of the candidates standing.

Intimidation and abuse

Occasional cases and allegations of abuse arise in parliamentary elections. In 2001 there were various allegations that people were abusing the new rules widening postal voting, but only one case warranted a police investigation. There are occasional complaints about overspends on local election limits (that are only loosely observed). There were credible allegations from the Ulster Unionists and SDLP in 2001 of electoral malpractice by Sinn Fein in several constituencies. Intimidation is very rare, except in Northern Ireland. In 2001, the intense parliamentary election campaign there spilled into violence, most notably against David Trimble, the Ulster Unionist leader, and his wife. They were assaulted by a loyalist mob before and after his election count and suffered death threats as well as the intimidation, kicks and punches that left her bruised and cut. Trimble accused the DUP of fomenting the mob violence. He said that loyalist terrorists tracked him on the stump and 'were responsible for harassing and beating up my party workers during the campaign'; and that they were 'hanging about their [DUP] entourage throughout the campaign and during the count' (*Observer*, 10 June 2001).

5.4. How effective a range of choice does the electoral and party system allow the voters, how equally do their votes count, and how closely does the composition of the legislature and the selection of the government reflect the choices they made?

As indicated in Section 5.1 above, elections to the House of Commons give priority to the task of electing a party to government with a majority large enough to govern effectively and to make it clearly accountable to the public. Britain retains the medieval plurality-vote electoral system on the grounds that it achieves 'strong government' (though this assumption is open to question; see Section 7.1). However, it has long been recognised that the system produces a clear result at the expense of the representativeness both of the government and the legislature. Indeed, the use of the plurality-rule vote has traditionally been justified precisely because it distorts the election result by over-representing the two leading parties in the House of Commons. The argument is that this distortion provides both a governing party with a 'working' majority and an opposition government in waiting. By the same token, it fails to represent the electorate's votes for parties in Parliament and significantly reduces the value of some people's votes in comparison with others.

But plurality-rule is also a notoriously unstable electoral system; and especially in the current era of 'tactical voting' (see below) now fails convincingly to establish the capacity of the second largest party to assume government at the subsequent election. The formal title of 'Her Majesty's Opposition', created to institutionalise the two-party system, rings hollow today.

Voter choice

In any democracy, the electoral system in use will either restrict or enlarge the choice between different parties that voters are given. Britain's plurality-rule voting system is biased against smaller parties and keeps them in the shade of the larger parties. In the heyday of the 'two-party system' – that is, between 1945 and 1979 – the Conservative and Labour dominance of parliamentary elections was regarded as the natural order of things. Now plurality-rule produces a 'lumpy' two-and-a-half party system in England, with the Conservatives, Labour and Liberal Democrats in contention. Scotland and Wales have had four-party systems since the 1980s; though the eclipse of the Tories in both nations now produces a three-party system for elections to Westminster. In Northern Ireland, the overall contest between Unionist and Republican parties splits also into parallel contests in which the Unionist and Republican parties battle between themselves to represent their communities. The small non-sectarian Alliance party is squeezed out. Voters there are denied the opportunity to vote for a party that can win or share power at Westminster.

One way of measuring the way in which plurality-rule elections squeeze out smaller parties is known among political scientists as the 'Relative Reduction in Parties' (RRP). The RRP figure for Britain expresses the difference between the representation of parties in the House and their presence in the election as a percentage. The RRP figure of 34 per cent in 1997 is very high by European standards and set a postwar record in the UK (Dunleavy and Margetts, 1997); the figure of 35 per cent in 2001 just surpassed it. In less technical terms, such figures mean that plurality-rule elections in the UK deny voters a full and effective choice among political parties; and that their votes for smaller parties are usually 'wasted'.

These are national figures only which mask even higher figures at sub-national and regional level – even twice as high in Scotland and Wales. Only two regions – the north and south west of England – had scores of below 10 per cent that would be the norm in PR elections around Europe. But at the regional level in Britain, even voters for the larger parties can find that they live in one of the 'electoral deserts' created by plurality-rule elections and are denied a meaningful vote for their chosen party of government. For the Independent Commission on the Voting System under Lord Jenkins (hence the 'Jenkins report'), these 'electoral deserts' represented a major democratic deficit. In 1997 and 2001, the Tories gained no seats at all in Scotland, Wales and some English regions or urban areas; and in the 1980s, Labour suffered a similar fate of exclusion from the rapidly growing and prosperous southern half of the UK. The Jenkins report commented:

> Such apartheid in electoral outcome is a heavy count against the [plurality-rule] system which produces it. It is a new form of Disraeli's two nations (the Jenkins report, 1996)

Equality of votes

The value of an individual citizen's vote varies according to the party he or she chooses to vote for, the region and local area in which he or she lives, and the political circumstances in the actual constituency. Table 1 shows the national deviation from proportionality (DV) in recent elections to Parliament in Great Britain – that is, how large the gap was between the votes that the parties won and their seats in the House of Commons (see foot-note 1 on page 105 for a fuller explanation). The national deviation figure of 22.4 per cent means that more than one in five seats in the House of Commons is occupied by the wrong party. Table 2 compares deviation from proportionality across a selection of European nations: the figures for the United Kingdom are by far the worst. The table also shows how closely the shares of seats held by the governing parties, or coalitions, correspond to their shares of the popular vote. In all cases governments have benefited from a premium in seats, usually quite small. No other nation gives a single party such power over the legislature as the UK. The Labour party is also the beneficiary of the most dramatic over-representation of them all.

1. The unrepresentative results of recent Westminster elections (Great Britain)
The 2001 general election

Party	Votes (%)	Seats (%)	Deviation from proportionality (DV) (%)
Conservative	32.7	25.9	6.8
Labour	42.0	64.4	22.4
Lib Dem	18.8	8.1	10.7
SNP/PC	2.6	1.4	1.2
UKIP	1.5	0	1.5
Green	0.7	0	0.7
Other	1.7	0	1.7
Total	100.0	100.0	22.4

Deviation from Proportionality in 1997: 21.1

Deviation from Proportionality in 1992: 17.4

2. How European elections represent the people's votes at government level

European state	Voting system*	Governing party/ coalition's share of popular vote %	Seats under governing party/ coalition control %	Deviation (Seats to votes figure)** %
Finland	L PR	67.2(5-party coalition)	69.5 (139 of 200)	6.9
France	DB	52.8(centre-right coalition)	69.2(399 of 577)	14.1
Germany	AMS	47.8%(SPD/Green coalition)	51.6%(345 of 669)	4.5
Norway	LPR	35(minority gov't)	39.4(65 of 165)	7.0
Romania	LPR	36.6(minority govt.)	44.8(155 of 346)	16.6
Scotland	AMS	49.5(Labour/ Lib-Dem coalition)	56.6(73 of 129)	7.6
Slovakia	LPR	58.1(4-party coalition)	62(93 of 150)	5.0
Spain	LPR	46.6 (People's Party)	52.3(183 of 350)	6.5
United Kingdom	P-R	40.7(Labour)	62.7(413 of 658)	21.8***

Sources: Derksen, W [website] , except Scotland: Scottish Politics Pages [website]

Notes: * The four types of voting system are: P-R: Plurality-rule, often known as 'first-past- the-post', the electoral system in use for parliamentary elections in the UK; LPR: List PR is a proportional system commonly used in Europe (and now in use for UK elections to the European Parliament). Under most such systems, electors vote for party candidates from lists supplied by the parties, rather than for individuals. Under 'closed' List PR systems electors must accept the parties' candidates in the order set out in the party list; the UK system for the Euro-elections is closed. Under 'open' systems, electors can choose between candidates listed by their parties; AMS: The Additional Member System combines direct constituency elections under a plurality-rule system, with an additional List PR element to make the elections results more proportional between the parties. Typically, the Parliament then consists of a tranche of directly-elected members and a tranche of 'top-up' party members. The nearer the division is to 50-50, the more proportional the system becomes; Double Ballot: Under this two-round voting system, candidates first stand against each other in plurality-rule elections in individual constituencies. If no candidate gains an absolute victory in the first round, the two leading candidates alone stand again in a play-off ballot to produce an outright winner.**. For explanation of Deviation from Proportionality(Seats to votes), see footnote 1, page 105. *** This figure for deviation is for the UK (including NI); the figure in the text is for Great Britain (exc NI)

The experience of voting at regional level

The deviation figures that we give above are averages only. But they mask astonishing variations between regions and seats across the country. We calculated the level of deviation down to the level of 18 regions across the nation in the 2001 election. We found that 12 of 18 regional figures surpassed the national average figure for deviation. The large regional variations range from 45 per cent in central Scotland to a low of 5.7 per cent in south-west England. But what do such figures mean? Well, the 45 per cent figure for Scotland shows that the election there was nearly wholly disproportional. Labour won nearly every seat (97 per cent of them all) on less than half the popular vote (45 per cent). The Conservatives (12.5 per cent of votes), Liberal Democrats (13 per cent) and the SNP (18 per cent) only gained one seat between them. For voters, this means that people who voted for one of the three other parties were effectively disenfranchised. Central Scotland is one of Jenkins's 'electoral deserts' (see above).

Thus an aggregate of regional scores is a more accurate reflection of the experience of voting in Britain than the national average DV figure. The aggregate scores in the last three elections are as follows:

Election	DV: National average	DV: Regional aggregate
1992	17.4	29.2
1997	21.1	23.8
2001	22.4	26.1

The Jenkins scheme

The principal contender for reform of the current electoral system is the scheme advocated by the Independent Commission on the Voting System in October 1998. Lord Jenkins, the Liberal Democrat peer, chaired the Commission and wrote its report after close consultation with Tony Blair and the then Liberal Democrat leader, Paddy Ashdown (see Section 1.5 further). Jenkins recommended a complex two-vote mixed electoral system, known as 'AV-Plus' (see Dunleavy et al, 1998, for a full analysis). The reality is that Jenkins designed the scheme to reconcile the political objectives of Blair, Ashdown and their closest advisers, but formally he had also to meet four principles declared in advance: that the recommended system should offer greater voter choice; deliver stable government; maintain the link between MPs and local constituencies; and produce broadly proportional results.

The Jenkins scheme is a version of the proportional AMS systems used in Germany and also for elections to the Scottish Parliament and Welsh Assembly (see Tables 1 and 2). But Jenkins severely modified the system to suit his masters (Blair, Ashdown and others) and the dominant British political culture. In particular, Blair required him to make it possible for the two larger parties still to win a working majority in the House of Commons on a minority of the popular vote. This goal was dictated in part by the significant aversion to coalition government among Britain's political culture; and the Jenkins report specifically stated that it did not want to impose a 'coalition habit' on the country.

Basically, under the Jenkins scheme people would vote twice in larger constituencies than now, first for a candidate under the Alternative Vote (AV) system; and secondly for a 'party'. (AV is a more disproportionate version of plurality-rule.) Thus it is partially proportional. Jenkins gave three 'schemes', or options, for the proportion of top-up MPs to directly-elected members. We calculated how Jenkins would have worked in Great Britain in the 1997 election, under his three schemes, and using both AV (the Jenkins scheme) and first-past-the-post (AMS) for the direct constituency vote.[2] The deviation from proportionality in each case is shown in the last column of Table 3. All versions of Jenkins are substantially fairer in terms of the votes:seats ratio than the actual 1997 result; but the AMS alternatives are fairer still than the Jenkins scheme's outcomes. This is because AV is less proportional than plurality-rule. Jenkins justifies its use on the grounds that it produces a clear 'winner' in every constituency, since every candidate elected has to gain more than 50 per cent of votes and preferences. But this clarity is won at the expense of proportionality and simplicity in voting.

3. The 1997 election re-run under the Jenkins scheme and an AMS alternative (Great Britain)

Scheme	Con	Lab	LD	Nat	Other	DV*
Jenkins						
Scheme B	175	359	91	15	1	11.6%
Scheme A	167	367	92	14	1	12.9%
Scheme C	160	378	89	13	1	14.6%
*AMS***						
Scheme A	198	345	82	15	1	9.4%
Scheme B	194	354	77	15	1	10.8%
Scheme C	191	363	71	15	1	12.2%
Actual result in 1997	165	419	46	10	1	21.0%

Source: The Politico's Guide to Electoral Reform in Britain, Dunleavy et al, 1997. This book gives full details of how the calculations were made.

Notes: * DV= Deviation from Proportionality. * * For these simulations, the percentage of top-up seats for Scheme A was 19.8%; for Scheme B, 17.6% ; and for Scheme C, 15.6%.

For the 2001 general election, Helen Margetts re-calculated the actual result using the middle option, Scheme B, under which there are 113 top-up seats, or 17.5 per cent of the total. The Jenkins result, compared with the actual general election result under first-past-the-post, would have cut the deviation from proportionality (DV) by nearly half – from the 22.4 per cent to 11.6 per cent. This figure is still on the high side by comparison with results in European PR elections, but is far more respectable than the distorted results our system churns out from one election to another.

5.5. What proportion of the electorate votes, and how far are the election results accepted by all political forces in the country?

Turnout may be viewed as the ultimate judge of whether citizens really 'feel' that they are offered an effective range of choice at election time; and that the party political executive that comes into power reflects the choices that they make. Turnout in the UK over time has exhibited a kind of trend-less fluctuation with peaks of 84 per cent in 1950 and 82 per cent in 1951; a pre-1990s low of 72 per cent in 1970; and otherwise relatively high levels over 75 per cent between 1955 and 1992.

These figures are low for the time, however, compared with other European countries. Turnout in Germany has never fallen below 78 per cent since 1945 and regularly achieves figures in the high 80s. Italy regularly recorded levels in the 90s until the end of the 1970s and since then has not fallen below 83 per cent. In the 1990s, Britain comes nineteenth out of 25 European countries, well below Malta (96.2 per cent), Belgium (91.5 per cent), Italy (85.5 per cent), Sweden (85.4 per cent), Turkey (85.4 per cent) and others; Table 4 shows the registration and turnout figures for the same selection of European countries as in Table 2.

4. Electoral participation

Europeancountry	Adults registered to vote %	Turnout at most recent election%
Finland	99(1999)	65.3(1999)
France	88.1(1997)	60.3(Second round,2002)
Germany	91.6(1998)	82.2(1998)
Norway	98.5(1997)	78(1997)
Poland	52.1(1993)	47.9(1997)
Romania	95.2(2000)	56.5(2000)
Scotland	100–plus* (2000)	58(1999)
Slovakia	93.6(1998)	84.2(1998)
Spain	100–plus(2000)	70.6(2000)
United Kingdom	96.9(2001)	59.4(2001)

Sources: International IDEA 2001; Office for National Statistics 2001

Notes: *this figure reflects the discrepancy between the estimated adult population in mid-2000 and the number of voters registered at the time. The explanation may be that people not normally resident in Scotland registered to vote there, but the low turnout at the election would appear to contradict this hypothesis.

The figures for parliamentary elections in the UK indicate a relatively poor performance, but turnout levels in elections at all levels of government around the new millennium have plummeted. In 1999, turnout in the Euro-elections in this country fell to less than a third. Even the widely publicised elections for the new London Mayor and London Assembly in May 2000 attracted only a third of voters. Then, in the 2001 general election turnout fell to well below two-thirds (59 per cent), almost as low as the turnout in 1918 that was severely depressed by wide-scale movement of populations after the war and by the fact that 40 per cent of men (as well as some women) had the vote for the first time.

The full damage this result inflicted upon the legitimacy of the Blair 'landslide' and party politics in general may be gauged by adopting David McKie's concept of the 'non-voting party'. In 2001, the NVP 'won' over 40.6 per cent of the electorate, while the Labour Party secured the votes of just 24.2 per cent of the electorate (see Glover, 2001; and Nairn, 2001).

Politicians and the media tend to blame falling turnouts on 'apathy'. But pollster Nick Sparrow, head of ICM Research, believes that they do not reflect apathy among electors. For Sparrow, the low turnout in 2001 was a consequence of 'unfulfilled Labour promises', the feeling that the Conservatives did not offer a credible alternative, and the large margin of victory for Labour predicted in the polls.

Our own experience of studying and working in democracies around the world (see Beetham et al, 2001 and 2002) does also suggest to us that it is disillusionment with governments and politics rather than apathy that contributes to public alienation and falling turnout elsewhere.

5.6. How far does Parliament reflect the social composition of the electorate?

Parliaments around the world rarely reflect the composition of their society and the United Kingdom is no exception. Both the House of Lords, now an almost exclusively appointed chamber, and the House of Commons, are essentially white, male, middle-aged, well-educated and comparatively wealthy assemblies.[?] In this Section, we concentrate upon the composition of the Commons as it stands after the 2001 general election. (We present a brief analysis of the composition of the Lords on page 142.)

Age, education and background
The House is dominated by members in their forties and fifties, as is true of the leading figures in most professions and walks of life. But the age-profile of the elected political elite – which has stayed more or less constant for 50 years – may contribute to the dramatic fall-off in voting among young people qualified to vote. Most MPs are well-educated: three quarters of them hold degrees and another 15 per cent have benefited from some form of tertiary education. There are significant differences in the educational profiles of Labour and Conservative MPs. Public schools and Oxbridge still dominate the Conservative ranks – with nearly two thirds having attended public school and then Oxbridge; whereas most Labour MPs studied at new or redbrick universities.

Over time, the representation of working people within the parliamentary Labour party has greatly diminished (though many of its graduates have qualified via the trade unions). In 1945, one in four Labour MPs had manual working backgrounds. In 2001, only 44 Labour MPs had been manual workers (10.7 per cent); 37 were former trade union officials; and marginally more – 46 – had business backgrounds. Otherwise, Labour MPs are largely professionals – lawyers, lecturers, teachers, social workers, civil servants, journalists, political researchers, etc. The smaller parliamentary Conservative party has largely business, professional and white-collar roots; the Liberal Democrats have the largest proportion of professionals. One Tory MP was once a miner; the Liberal Democrats have no working class member.

Finally, local government provides local political experience to some two thirds of Labour and Lib-Dem MPs (295 MPs in all) and a third of Tory MPs (51). Overall 367 MPs have at least local roots (57 per cent of the House).

Women MPs

Members are predominantly men. As Table 5 shows, progress towards gender equality has been slow and a partial breakthrough in 1997 has not been built on:

5. Women's representation in the House of Commons, 1979-2001

Election (year)	No. of women elected
1979	19
1983	23
1987	41
1992	60
1997	120
2001	118

The House of Commons performs badly in comparison with the Nordic countries and other major EU members, other than France and Italy. None of them have achieved parity, but the three Nordic countries each have more than twice the proportion of women than the UK at 17.9 per cent in the House of Commons – Sweden's figure is 42.7 per cent, Denmark's 37.4 per cent and Finland's 36.5 per cent. Overall the UK comes tenth out of the 15 EU member states.

The partial breakthrough in 1997 – when women's representation in the Commons doubled – was the result of Labour's then policy of reserving some winnable seats for 'all-women shortlists' up to 1996 (when an employment tribunal ruled that the practice breached sex discrimination laws). In 2001, the breakthrough was reversed, since none of the parties had adopted positive discrimination measures to put women into 'winnable seats'. The Labour party, which adopted 'twinning' – that is, paired neighbouring constituencies, one of which chose a woman candidate and the other a man – for elections to the Scottish Parliament and Welsh Assembly – opted only for 50:50 shortlists for the parliamentary election (see further Lovenduski, 2001). The government's Sexual Discrimination (Election Candidates) Act 2002 has removed any legal bar to positive discrimination, but it is a permissive measure only. The Act allows political parties to take special measures to increase their parliamentary representation of women.

The discrimination against women evident at Westminster is largely due to the way the existing plurality-rule electoral system and the practices of the main parties interact. Joni Lovenduski, a specialist on women's role in politics, has recently pointed out that plurality-rule, while in theory legally neutral, sets a high threshold of representation that greatly reduces the available options for women (Lovenduski, 2002). Women are better represented through PR elections, but as the Scottish and Welsh elections have shown, the parties must also take political action to raise women's representation. (In Scotland and Wales, the absence of incumbent members made this easier.) At Westminster however the only channel of entry is in practice through one of the few parties that can secure seats in the House of Commons (and plurality-rule reduces their number; see Section 5.4. above); and incumbent male MPs inevitably block progress.

The representation of women in the Commons depends therefore on the parties' rules, customs and procedures that determine who the candidates (and therefore the MPs) will be. Party choices are subject to very little external regulation. Each party has its own system of selection and differing sets of barriers to aspirant candidates. Historically fewer women than men have tried to become elected politicians in the UK. However, women are not selected in proportion to the numbers who come forward. Table 6 shows that choosing more women as candidates does not normally lead to more women being elected because the parties are reluctant to nominate women for winnable seats.

6. Women candidates and MPs, 1987–2001

	Conservative		Labour		Lib Dem		PC/SNP			
	Candidates	MPs	Candidates	MPs	Candidates	MPs	Candidates	MPs	Candidates	MPs
1987	46	17	92	21	105	2	15	1		
1992	63	20	138	37	143	2	22	1		
1997	67	13	159	102	142	3	23	2		
2001	94	14	149	95	132	5	22	1		

In 2001, only five women were chosen to stand in the 75 seats where an incumbent MP was retiring (i.e., in the seats that a party is normally most likely to win). See Table 7:

7. Men and women chosen to succeed retiring MPs in 2001

	Total	Men	Women	Women as % of party selections
Conservative	23	23	0	0%
Labour	37	33	4	11%
Lib Dem	7	7	0	0%
SNP	6	5	1	17%
PC	2	2	0	0%
Total	75	70	5	7%

A similar pattern was apparent in seats a party had the best chance of capturing. As Table 8 shows, 117 women and 503 men were selected in seats where the relevant party came second in the previous general election:

8. Men and women chosen for 2001 for seats where their party came second in 1997

	Total selected	Men	Women	Women as % of party selections
Labour	99	78	21	21.21%
Conservative	370	310	60	16.22%
Lib Dem	103	76	27	26.21%
PC	4	3	1	18.18%
SNP	44	36	8	25.00%
Total	620	503	117	18.87%

The low proportion of women in the House of Commons can therefore be explained quite simply. Political parties have been less likely to select women than men for their winnable seats. There are clearly still problems of supply, but where supply has been increased, political parties have not seen a proportionate rise in women elected to Parliament. The key problem is therefore one of demand – women do not get selected where it matters.

Women's prospects depend on the electoral fortunes of their party and the measures that the party adopts to assist women. The partial breakthrough in 1997, as we have observed, was achieved by Labour's use of quotas. The evidence that quotas work is overwhelming. They were in use or had been in use in 56 west European parties by 1998. The three countries with the highest levels of women's representation – Norway, Sweden and Denmark – have all used quotas of some kind (Lovenduski, 2002). The new Act makes it legal for the parties to adopt quotas or other measures of positive discrimination. But what are they likely to do? The Liberal Democrats have voted against positive discrimination at their party conference. To say the least, the Conservatives remain to be convinced of the need for it. Labour is likely to agree to nominate women in half its vacant and winnable seats until parity is reached. But on current rates of MPs retiring, it would take until 2033 before women reached parity with men in the Parliamentary Labour Party (and that assumes party shares of seats are stable). Without positive action there is no reason to expect current trends in the other parties to change. Thus the Liberal Democrats could take until 2101 to reach parity while the Conservatives may not reach it before 2301.

Ethnic minority representation

In 1987, the first four MPs with ethnic minority origins were elected in the modern era to the House of Commons; in 2001, 12 minority candidates out of 64 candidates in all were elected. All stood for Labour. One Conservative candidate, Shailesh Vara, stood in one of the party's potentially winnable seats – Northampton South, a marginal seat narrowly won by Labour for the first time in 1997. The incumbent

Labour MP just held onto the seat. The fear that minority candidates are an electoral liability seems to be coming to an end; and in the Labour party the arguments centre on the question of whether the party should aim to put forward minority candidates in constituencies where at least 25 per cent of the electorate in Asian or black (as recommended in the Parekh report, 2000). Shamit Saggar, an academic authority on race and politics, suggests that the 'basic calculus of racial and electoral politics' is being revised, if not fundamentally altered (Saggar, 2001). Yet under-representation continues: the ethnic minorities comprise 6.7 per cent of the population, whereas 12 MPs comprise only 1.8 per cent of all MPs. Such figures contribute to a degree of voter alienation from politics which is illustrated by the fact that a quarter of the black community are not registered to vote, compared to 6 per cent of the white community (Anwar 1994). A Fawcett Society report on selection processes in the Labour and Conservative parties shows that ethnic minority women suffer from both race and sex discrimination.

The 1999 Euro election

A List PR system was introduced in 1998 for the regional elections to the European Parliament. There were strong demands in Parliament for an 'open list' system, which would have allowed voters to choose between the candidates for the parties instead of just between party lists. Instead, the government chose a 'closed list' system that denied voters such a choice and gave party chiefs the ability to choose between candidates, by placing favoured candidates high on the lists (making them more likely to be elected) and less important or out-of-favour candidates lower. Jack Straw at the Home Office accepted the case for open lists, but he was overruled at the last minute by Downing Street. The 12 standard government regions were used as the constituencies for the elections in 1999, with between four and 11 members in each.

Historically, the turnouts in Euro elections have been low, at about a third of the electorate. But the unpopularity of 'Europe', the low profile of MEPs and the European Parliament and a deliberately subdued Labour campaign saw turnout plunge to 23 per cent in 1999. Labour used their lists to reward loyalists, while the Conservatives placed pro-Europeans low on theirs. The election was turned by the Tories into a quasi-referendum on EU membership. There was also a more pluralist tinge to the election, with small parties gaining more votes and seats than usual (the Greens, on 6 per cent of the vote, won three seats and the UK Independence Party took another three). In July 1999, Labour's national executive voted to drop closed list voting and explore a version of AMS for the next Euro election in 2004.

---

1   The Deviation from Proportionality (DV) index measures how far an election result deviates from perfect proportionality. We have used it to measure deviation from the principle of one person, one vote, since 1992; and we quote the results in this Section and its tables. The scores on the DV index range between 0 and 50 per cent; the lower the score, the greater the proportionality; the higher the figure, the nearer it is to being utterly distorted. The European norm is around 4–8 per cent. , For further discussion, see Dunleavy, Margetts, O'Duffy and Weir, 1997; or Taagepera and Shugart, 1989, Seats and Votes, Yale University Press.

2   In fact, the calculations in 1997 and for 2001 were made on the basis of the Supplementary Vote system, a close cousin of AV which produces almost identical results.

3   Further data that substantiate these conclusions will be found on the Democratic Audit website.

New deal for parties

Does the party system assist the working of democracy?

Of all political institutions, the two-party system since the war has received least attention and discussion, despite the fact that its rigidities and the legends that support them have at least as much to do with the current political malaise as have the alleged failings in all the other institutions thought ripe for reform.
Alan Beattie, historian, 1975

Introduction

Political parties are unpopular institutions and their memberships are falling fast. But if they did not exist, we should be compelled to invent them. In a large society, people can exercise little public influence as individuals, but can do so if they act in association with others. Political parties bring together like-minded people to frame programmes for political office and to campaign for influence and office. In doing so, they perform several essential functions:

- for the electorate, they simplify the choices that people make at elections by offering them broad policies and different sets of politicians to choose between; they also make clear who is responsible when policies or politicians fail;
- for governments, they provide a reasonably stable following of political supporters in Parliament to enable them to achieve their programmes, if elected; and
- for the more politically active, they provide an opportunity to be involved in public affairs and a channel for influencing public polices.

Political parties are in these ways one of the sinews of representative democracy; however imperfectly, they provide a political link between citizens and the state alongside the media, pressure groups and citizen's associations, and opinion polling. But they are unpopular because their own interests can come to take precedence over their representative functions and party loyalties over the public interest.

They also raise problems for democracy which are the reverse side of the coin to their positive features. Simplifying electoral choice can readily lead to a loss of genuine pluralism: significant voices within and outside the main parties can be denied full hearing and new parties can find it impossible to gain a foothold. This loss of pluralism is exacerbated by the cost of elections which gives an incentive to parties to subordinate themselves to the special interests of wealth donors. The reverse side of their loyalty in Parliament is that it comes to take precedence over independence of view, even when a government's policy is widely recognised as misconceived. Finally, the increasing tendency of their leaders to tailor policies to public opinion, as relayed through focus groups, opinion polling and the mass media, has marginalised the role of party members in public debate and policy-making. These are tensions that are evident in all mature democracies. How they currently play out in the UK is examined in the questions below.

There have been two major changes to party politics recently, one highly visible, the other obscured. The first change is the sudden introduction of regulation of the political parties, and especially of their financing – a major reform for which the current government is responsible. Secondly, huge shifts in the party structures over the past 30 years or so in the United Kingdom effectively amount to a huge, but almost unseen, constitutional change. Even today the Labour and the Conservative parties dominate the political landscape and most debate. But they no longer command the public's electoral allegiance. Between 1931 and 1970, they won between them some 85-90 per cent of all the votes cast in ten general elections; at the eight elections held since February 1970, they have never won 85 per cent of the total vote at all, and at six of the eight elections they have won less than 75 per cent of a falling overall vote. Up to 1970, both parties were also recognised as national parties and so it seemed natural enough for the leader of the party with the most votes and seats (and even on the one occasion when a party with fewer votes won most seats) to assume government of the UK, even though neither party ever won 50 per cent or more of the popular vote.

Labour and the Tories still largely govern entry to the House of Commons between them and their grasp on central power is unchanged. But the legitimacy of their dominance of the legislature and government is under popular and party challenge. The Conservatives can only just claim to be a 'national party' in Scotland and Wales by virtue of their showing in elections to the devolved assemblies; and these elections under a proportional system are encouraging the growth of small parties that rival the two former giants. Neither the Conservatives nor Labour have any real electoral standing in Northern Ireland. In addition, the rise of single-issue politics throws alternative, and arguably more influential, political forces into the arena – environmental concern, anti-abortion groups, antipathy to EU membership. Worse still, politicians of both the main parties in particular generate hardly any respect or trust among most of the people.

Yet at the same time the major parties enjoy a close cohabitation with political and state power at Westminster and Whitehall through custom, convention and invention (like, for example, state funding for policy research ('Short money') by parties represented in the Commons; the growing cadre of state-funded special advisers at the centre of government, etc). They determine issues such as reform of the electoral system in their own party interests (see Section 1.5); and manage the rules and procedures of Parliament through the 'usual channels', the discreet phrase for the operations of the party whips, and through the Parliamentary Commission, another inter-party body under the tutelage of the Speaker (a party man, though neutral).

6.1 How freely are parties able to form, recruit members and engage with the public?

Until 1998, the political parties have had no formal state or statutory recognition: they were simply 'unincorporated private bodies', or associations. They evolved in a typically informal way into more disciplined bodies. They had the 'negative' political freedom that most associations and individuals enjoyed – that is, they were unsupervised and could do largely what they liked as long as it was not against the law. This freedom did not amount to a constitutionally-guaranteed liberty. Rather it reflected the basic political realities that the first two great 'mass' parties – the Tories and Liberals – had evolved out of trusted aristocratic and middle-class bodies; and that the growing Labour party could gradually be schooled in the proprieties of parliamentary and political life (not least in coalition government during the second world war). Moreover, the plurality-rule electoral system for parliamentary elections provided a safe bulwark against unpredictable political parties. It still does.

In fact, as we show in Section 5.4, plurality-rule elections for the House of Commons inhibit the pluralist representation of the public's political preferences following the breakdown of the two major parties' claims on their near exclusive allegiance. The ability of other parties to form, develop and engage with the public at local level is also stultified by the dominance that the same electoral system gives the main party duopoly – though breakthroughs do occur as politics becomes more diversified. Thus the campaign in Kettering against a PFI hospital scheme finally broke the Labour party hold on the local council and then propelled a doctor, Richard Taylor, into Parliament as MP for Wyre Forest. At the same time, the proportional European elections, have for the first time, allowed the Green Party to gain an electoral foothold; and proportional elections in Scotland and Wales have broadened the base of the nationalist parties and given the Greens and Scottish Socialist Party representation in the Scottish Parliament.

Beyond the pale

But parties beyond the pale cannot necessarily count on official tolerance. The government considered proscribing the Communist party in 1941 following the short-lived Stalin-Hitler pact, but ministers finally held back from so drastic a measure, contenting themselves with a ban on the party's newspaper, *The Daily Worker*, and communist pamphlets (Branson 1985) that proved to be as temporary as the Soviet-German alliance. During the cold war, the Communist party contested elections, but the government banned its party members from working in areas relating to state security and kept civil servants and government scientists under strict surveillance. By 1956, about 150 officials and scientists had either been sacked, resigned or transferred to other jobs (Branson 1997). It is also alleged that the security forces checked who voted for the Communist party in the cold war era (see Section 5.2).

In more recent times, the government did not ban Sinn Fein, the political arm of the IRA, but in 1998 the then Home Secretary, Douglas Hurd, introduced a broadcasting ban preventing any representative of the party from speaking on TV or radio in order to deprive Sinn Fein 'of the oxygen of publicity'. The move misfired and the ban was eventually dropped when peace negotiations began. Of wider concern is the question of the oath of allegiance to the Queen. Tony Benn has described how he subverted his own oath-giving ceremony. But Sinn Fein MPs have refused on principle to swear allegiance to the Queen and so cannot take their seats to represent their constituencies at Westminster. For a time they were also as a consequence refused access to an office and facilities in the House. Many other MPs and MSPs take their oaths under protest – the entire SNP group, some Labour MSPs and Tommy Sheridan, the Scottish Socialist MSP, did so in the Scottish Parliament. This is not a healthy phenomenon. Why cannot a more neutral induction into participating in Parliament or the devolved assemblies be introduced?

The advent of state regulation

The Euro-elections made it necessary to create a register of political parties for the new party list electoral system. The Electoral Commission has since taken on the responsibility for the registration of political parties; and the parties must now register to contest any elections in the UK with the exception of parish or community council elections. Under the Political Parties, Elections and Referendums Act 2000 the Commission has a wide-ranging remit over party finances, donations, elections, and the ballot. However, the Act's major purpose was at last to control and make transparent the existing processes by which the parties funded themselves and to set limits on election spending (see page 109). The last measure of this sort – in 1883 – has been rendered almost wholly obsolete by modern conditions. The public had long wanted reform. Polls in 1991 – before all of the scandals came to light involving both the Conservatives and Labour – found that 81 per cent of those surveyed supported set limits on the amount of money that political parties could spend on general election campaigns. There was also significant support for suggestions to ban contributions from trade unions (46 per cent) and companies (44 per cent) (see Dunleavy et al, 2001). The new system has yet to bed down, and the parties have undoubtedly found it a strain complying with the detailed rules governing the transparency and propriety of party finances and accounts. The rules are particularly onerous for smaller parties. But the new regulatory regime does not entail any interference with internal party affairs, and should not over time inhibit the ability of parties to form and engage with the public. The big question is whether it actually works by allaying public and media suspicions. (See also Section 6.6 below.)

6.2 How effective is the party system in forming and sustaining governments in office?

In spite of its waning popularity, the two-party system remains formidably effective at forming and sustaining governments in office. Ever since 1945, stable one-party government by one or the other main party has been and remains the norm, with only occasional periods of instability in the 1970s and the tail end of the Major government in 1996-97 (though that government still wielded considerable power). In fact, the flawed and biased system is too effective at forming governments, since a single-party executive at the head of a parliamentary majority is usually very strong, but also remarkably unaccountable and not necessarily effective (see Section 7.3). Moreover, the duopoly in power by definition excludes coalition government and more pluralist and consensual politics.

Political Parties, Elections and Referendums Act 2000

- Public disclosure of sources and amounts of donations of £5,000 and above to a party at the national level and donations of £1,000 and above to a party at the local level (such as local associations or regional organisations)
- Disclosure to the Electoral Commission of donations of £200 or more
- Ban on foreign and anonymous donations to parties
- Company donations over £5,000 require shareholder authorisation
- Prohibition on use of blind trusts as mechanism for funding parties or politicians
- No cap on the size of political donations
- Limits on campaign spending for elections: generally around £20 million in the year leading up to a general election
- Introduction of controls over the amounts which other organisations or persons can spend during national elections
- Only parties which receive more than 30 per cent of the vote are allowed to spend the maximum amount of £5 million on referendum campaigns
- Parties required to submit an annual statement of accounts which is open for public inspection
- Revised registration requirements for parties
- Creation of Electoral Commission to police the new rules

6.3   How free are opposition or non-governing parties to organise within the legislature, and how effectively do they contribute to government accountability?

The British tradition relies on political checks and balances through the parties in Parliament to make government accountable. Thus the role of the main opposition and other opposition parties is crucial, the more so as a government can usually depend on the disciplined loyalty of the majority party. The prime duty of the second largest party in the Commons, dignified by the title of Her Majesty's Loyal Opposition, is therefore to act as a 'government in waiting'. But it has to be a credible alternative government. The trouble is that this credibility is often absent, even over several elections, as it was during Mrs Thatcher's long rule from 1979 to 1990 (when her own party brought her down), and is now while Tony Blair is in power. The less the governing party has to fear, the more ineffective the opposition party becomes.

The opposition parties have traditionally worked within 'a culture of contestation', as the political commentator Anthony King describes it:

If disagreements did not exist they should be invented. If they did exist, as they usually did, they should be exploited (King 2001).

But the fierce opposition that ensues is a form of displacement activity that disguises the almost total powerlessness of the opposition. We describe the weakness of both Houses of Parliament in Section 7.4. No amount of partisan huffing and puffing in the chamber and on the media will blow the government down. Only if the governing party is split, can the opposition hope to make it accountable. And anyway, that is not the object of the opposition parties. They use Parliament as a forum for convincing the public that they and their policies are superior, or closer to the electorate's views, than those of the government. They get scant opportunity to subject government actions, policies or draft laws to remorseless scrutiny; but if they did, they would almost certainly neglect it. The trouble is that the sound and fury has become increasingly ritualistic; and the 'yah boo' atmosphere of the Commons does not enhance the reputation either of Parliament or politicians. The engines of accountability in Parliament are the all-party select committees that work through a non-partisan ethos so far as they can.

The opposition parties are able to organise with relative freedom in the House. The main opposition party can choose a limited number of topics for debate; can initiate debates and has rights of response; it has various procedural devices to embarrass ministers at its disposal (used to advantage for example, by the Tories in their hounding of Stephen Byers into resignation in 2002). Individual members of all opposition parties are able also to participate in debates at the discretion of the Speaker; and have the right to ask both oral and written questions (but they cannot rely upon a serious or informative reply). However, the practices of the House of Commons, being based on the prevailing views and needs of the two largest parties, tend to restrict the contribution that the Lib-Dems and other parties can make. The Lib-Dem leader now has a recognised place in the pecking order. But the parliamentary timetable is organised around the wishes of the two larger parties and thus deprives the Lib-Dems and other parties of opportunities to vote for a distinctive policy platform of their own. They are instead often forced to vote aye or no on propositions determined mostly by the two largest parties (Cowley et al, 2001).

Inequalities of resources
The weakness of opposition parties is not simply a question of ineptitude. Opposition parties are expected to produce alternatives to government policies and draft legislation, but even the main opposition party is hopelessly outgunned by a governing party that commands the Whitehall machine; has the advantage of all the consultation work that has gone into official policy-making; and can marshal the resources of the state behind its programme. By contrast, the opposition parties must produce alternative policies on a shoestring. The inequality in resources was recognised by the introduction of state funding for opposition parties, 'Short money', in 1975, specifically for developing policy. The Committee on Standards in Public Life recently secured an increase in Short monies, but the resources allocated to opposition parties are a fraction of those that are at the disposal of ministers.

6.4. How fair and effective are the rules governing party discipline in the legislature?

There is inevitably a tension between the need for governing parties in parliamentary democracies to give their government stability, and on the other hand for government backbenchers to check the government when it breaks with the party manifesto or they believe it is deviating from its basic political position. In the UK the main fear is that government backbenchers will be too loyal; and for example the 'rock-hard discipline' (*Guardian*, 16 July 2001) of Labour MPs since 1997 has been regarded as a major cause of Parliament's inability to control the executive. There is no doubt that Labour MPs since 1997 have shown remarkable self-discipline, but their cohesion is a natural response to the damage rebellions have in the past inflicted on their party, and the perception that the previous Conservative government had been irretrievably damaged by the split over Europe. Yet the parliamentary party's loyalty is a subtler phenomenon than it appears; and indeed, as the political scientist Philip (Lord) Norton has shown repeatedly, MPs have been increasingly prone to express their dissent from the party line over the last 30 years (see Norton 1975, 1978, 1980, 1994). Governing parties are not poodles that will roll over at the whips' every command.

Take the parliamentary Labour party (PLP) conduct since 1997. At first sight, discipline has been 'rock hard'. The government was undefeated in the division lobbies for the whole Parliament from 1997-2001, the first time that a government has survived without defeat since Labour in 1966-70 (Cowley and Stuart, 2002). Yet a third of the PLP – that is, a half of all backbenchers – voted against the government at least once during that Parliament; and the average size of the rebellions was the third highest of any Parliament since 1945. The rebellions were infrequent; but when they did rebel, Labour MPs 'rebelled in numbers and across a wide range of issues' (Cowley, 2002; Cowley and Stuart, 2002). The first 44 votes of the post-2001 Parliament saw ten backbench rebellions by Labour MPs against the whips; the comparable figure for the previous Parliament was zero. Obviously, outright rebellion is not the only way in which MPs from the governing party can influence and even change a government's policies. The government was usually also prepared to give ground and negotiate behind the scenes on issues where it feared that it might lose (for example, in 1999, Jack Straw made concessions on government plans for asylum-seekers). The most striking example from the current Parliament is the government's retreat on its plans to re-shape the House of Lords as a largely appointed House when it became clear that the parliamentary party would not accept this solution.

However, the over-arching desire of Labour's leadership to impose effective discipline on the PLP does have undesirable consequences. The pressures they apply are not necessarily designed to ensure the PLP's adherence to the election mandates endorsed at a general election; often the reverse is the case. Party managers distort selection procedures to block potential rebels before they gain the platform of elected office in the first pleace. They demand uncritical loyalty as a pre-condition for government office.

Party hopping

Few MPs cross the floor in the House of Commons. The only notable example in recent years was the defection of 25 Labour MPs to the newly-formed SDP in 1981 (along with a solitary Tory). Lately a handful of Conservative MPs have defected to Labour and the Liberal Democrats. The former Tory MP, Shaun Woodward, like Alan Howarth before him, was promised a Labour seat in return for his apostasy. This in itself makes for an undesirable interference in the party's internal democracy. But since such MPs were largely elected as representatives of their party (and not for their personal qualities), they essentially disenfranchised their electors. But in practice only three defectors have stood for re-election after switching parties since 1945. Such contempt for party and voters should no longer be tolerated: MPs who switch parties should be obliged to stand for re-selection.

6.5. How far are parties effective membership organisations, and how far are members able to influence party policy and candidate selection?

British political parties are small by comparison with those in other European countries. They enrol the third lowest proportion of the population (only France and Poland have fewer members of political parties). In all, around 840 000 people or under 2 per cent of the British population are members of a party. The European mean is 5 per cent. The exact figures are unreliable, as the parties don't like owning up to their shrinking memberships, but broadly the total membership of the British parties has fallen by half (or over 850,000 people) in the last 20 years (Mair and Van Biezen 2001). Quite why British parties cannot match their counterparts in Europe in recruiting members and managing party decline is not clear, since they are confronted by similar far-reaching sociological changes. Plainly the fall in ideological or partisan alignment, evident in the electorate at large, also affects party membership. So probably does the weak performance of governing parties in the UK, especially from the perspective of the committed: you only join and work for a political party if it delivers (or tries very hard to do so) the policies in which you believe. Yet the Conservative party membership fell sharply under Mrs Thatcher's fiercely ideological period in office. It may be that she offended many party members while pleasing many others. But the party organisation must surely shoulder some of the blame since it made little effort to invigorate the party at the grassroots. Until William Hague's attempts to raise membership to one million, there was no ongoing effort to recruit or retain members and the prized autonomy of local Conservative associations even stopped the party from creating a central membership list. Hague linked his membership drive to internal reforms in the party structures, wider participation in leadership elections, and postal ballots on the manifesto and the Euro. The party which in its heyday had been primarily a social organisation now began to offer politics to its members (Willetts, 1998).

1. Falling party membership in Britain's three largest parties since 1964

ElectionYear	Labour	Conservative	Liberal/Lib-Dem
1964	830,115	2.150 million	278,690
1966	775,695	2.150 million	234,345
1970	680,190	2.150 million	234,345
1974	691,890	1.500 million	190,000
1979	666,090	1.350 million	145,000
1983	295,345	1.200 million	145,260
1987	288, 830	1 million	137,500
1992	279,530	500,000	100,000
1997	405,000	400,000	100,000
2001	360,000	325,000	80,000

NB. These figures are unreliable as the parties always inflate them. For example, in 1982, the party's National Agent swore the Labour NEC to secrecy and informed them that the true membership was only 124,000.

Sources: Webb, 2000; *Guardian*, 6 June 2001 (Labour); *The Times*, 13 March 2001 (Conservatives); private interview (Liberal Democrats).

In this sense, Hague and his lieutenant, David Willetts, were seeking to recreate the Conservatives as an effective membership organisation, in which members could influence policy and candidate selection. The reformed leadership election processes did widen the role of the members. But the convoluted new structures carefully guarded the autonomy of the party hierarchy from challenge; and other apparently democratic reforms, such as the ballot on the party manifesto, were stage-managed exercises rather than genuine ventures in member participation. The party's finances remain obscure and the party's treasurer is appointed, not elected.

Labour too has historically been complacent about its membership. The party's identification with the trade unions, their direct involvement in party affairs and their contributions to party finances allowed party managers to bask in the myth of 'this great [labour] movement of ours' (or 'Moo', as the columnist Alan Watkins mocked). Thus Labour, of all the traditional 'mass' membership parties, took recruitment least seriously. Tony Blair as party leader immediately set out to turn the party's faltering membership figures around and he succeeded, but only briefly. The rise to about 400,000 members did not survive the experience of Labour in office after 1997.

The consequence of lower memberships is that local party organisations are often moribund and fail to engage with local populations, except fitfully at election time. A survey of 340 Tory constituency parties by *The Times* in 1997 found they hardly existed at all. One in five had fewer than 100 members, with marginal constituencies weakest of all (6 June 1997). Labour has shown more awareness of such failures and the weaknesses of introverted, often bureaucratic, parties (Labour Party 1999). The central party has tried to encourage local parties to focus on political discussion at all-member meetings and take a more active role in their local community. By contrast, the Conservatives have shown far less interest in reviving local parties.

The future of members

British political parties are not likely to increase in size ever again. As a result some observers suggest that they should not persist single-mindedly with the model of fee-paying membership. Instead they should become more fluid organisations and recruit registered supporters with a looser role – though they could still contribute towards its activities and perhaps even have a say, for example, in choosing candidates for political office (perhaps through primaries on the US model). The Internet, it is argued, could provide wider forums in which the parties could involve sympathetic people. But there is a lot to be said for fee-paying members. They alone can supply a reliable core for a form of internal democracy in the parties; they form a credible base for fund-raising; and there is some evidence to suggest that they can make a contribution to party campaigning that is significant enough to make a tangible difference to electoral outcomes (see Seyd and Whiteley, 1992; Whiteley, Richardson and Seyd, 1994). Supporters are unlikely to show the same commitment.

But there is no necessary contradiction between having paying members and registered supporters, who could clearly provide additional assistance and build bridges between committed party members and the wider society from which the parties seem to be increasingly estranged. Just as American Express attaches different levels of rights and obligations to Gold and regular credit cards, it cannot be beyond the wit of the parties to recognise and value different levels of commitment (see further Richards, 2000).

Internal democracy

Political parties in democracies tend to be oligarchies, even if they have adopted apparently democratic structures. But the way the major parties organise core functions, such as candidate selection and policy-making, has caused controversy outside as well as within the parties themselves. As a result, both Labour and the Tories have carried out wide-ranging internal reforms since the 1980s that have widened the roles of all their members – and narrowed the differences that previously existed between them. (Here we should apologise for being obliged to study only the internal arrangements of the two main parties, and the Lib-Dems to a lesser degree.) Previously, Labour relied on the traditional trade-union model of internal representation with its layers of bodies, affiliations, and voting conventions. The Conservative Party, by contrast, was a loose, improvisatory body with few rules in writing, but rather a willingness to respond to the needs of the leader. The Conservatives have shifted towards more formal structures and Labour has eased the influence of its still large body of trade-union affiliates. Both have also moved towards giving their whole memberships a larger, if largely symbolic, role – partly in deference to public opinion.

The rhetoric in both parties is designed to create an impression of commitment to democratic principles (see further Peele, 1998; Seyd, 1999). Paradoxically, while ordinary party members now possess more formal rights within the parties than they have enjoyed before, the public still believe them to be dominated by small and exploitative elites. This may be partly because both parties have widened participation in their parties the better to control them. Within Labour, in particular, individual members were empowered as a check on the activists who tried during the 1980s to seize control of the party through its representative structures. The 1997 *Labour into Power* document made the goals of being 'properly representative of all our members and affiliates at every level of the Party' and making 'our membership as fully representative of the people in general as possible' two of the party's priorities. Blair himself loathed the 'culture' of the party he had taken over.

It was additionally felt that a more wide-based party would avoid the kinds of conflicts that had arisen in the past between Labour governments and party activists, especially at party conferences. Party managers like Tom Sawyer, the former trade union officials, genuinely sought to create a party more representative of the country that would adopt a more constructive relationship with a future Labour government. But they were also experienced enough to seek the safeguard of strong internal controls hidden in a reform process apparently designed only to widen internal party participation (see further, Mair 2000).

The Conservatives were moved by similar thinking. The diffusion of authority, real and symbolic, among an atomised party membership rather than locating it, say, in the party conference would reduce the ability of organised groups working through intermediate representative bodies to challenge the leadership. They viewed their ordinary members as more loyal and less ideological than their own activists. All-member democracy also presents formidable logistical barriers to groups seeking to challenge the leadership. Without regular meetings or conferences, it is more difficult for them to communicate, organise, conduct debates and share information (see Mair 1997).

Hague's reorganisation fused the three existing, and separate, sections of the party – the parliamentary party, Central Office and the local Conservative associations – into a single whole under a unified constitution. But while he carried out his reform under the banner of democratisation, he made it virtually impossible for any ordinary party member to initiate any constitutional change within the party.

Party elites can propose any change they wish, through resolutions of the Party Board or the Executive of the 1922 Committee. But ordinary members must collect 10,000 signatures for a petition if they want to alter the constitution; and voting on any change takes place in an exclusive electoral college, consisting of MPs, MEPs, selected senior peers and the members of the National Conservative Convention (essentially the constituency chairs). Even then, any substantial change must win over two-thirds of the parliamentary party, thus ensuring that MPs possess an effective lock upon the constitution.

Policy-making

The diffusion of power to the memberships includes an element of consultation in both the bigger parties; but its more significant outcome has been to reduce the participation of party activists in policy-making. Policy-making raises issues of the balance between free and open internal debate, electorally popular policy-making and party unity. The parties argue that activists should not be allowed to usurp policy-making at the expense of the wider constituencies of support. They are convinced that bitter internal arguments about policy are electoral poison. In addition, policy formation is often thought to require a level of knowledge and technical expertise that party members and activists alike do not possess. Thus party leaders take the view that democracy is best served sharing their own policy role with experts, often within associated think-tanks like the Labour and trade union creation, the Institute for Public Policy Research. At the same time, party leaders pay lip service to democratic norms and encourage ordinary members to believe that they play a key role in shaping party policy and influencing their leaders.

The Conservative Party keeps control of policy in the shadow cabinet while in opposition and consults members only modestly under the aegis of the Conservative Policy Forum (CPF), the replacement for the old Conservative Political Centre. But no formal structures exist to give members any opportunity to initiate or shape policy. Party conference is a media showcase rather than a forum for debate. Ballots of members are used on occasion to ratify policies (e.g., on party policy on the Euro in 1998 and for approval of a 'pre-manifesto' document from the leadership in 2000). Both ballots were arguably introduced as devices of party management and public relations rather than channels for democratic participation, but the Euro ballot at least offered a rare example of a party allowing its members to determine its position on a fairly specific policy issue. The 'pre-manifesto' vote was worthless, since it offered a simple yes or no choice on a whole package of policy proposals, with no possibility of the members offering amendments.

By contrast, the Labour Party has developed a rule-based structure for policy-making which explicitly sets out to enable members to participate in developing party policy. The avowed aim is to create a deliberative and inclusive process in place of the confrontational public battles of past conferences. An elected National Policy Forum guides a rolling programme of consultative documents on specific policy areas, eventually culminating in a final document that is discussed and voted on at Labour party conference. All constituency parties receive consultative documents for discussion at local policy forums of party members. But party press staff assured the media at the opening of this new structure that the leadership was in command of what was in effect a charade. It is more than that since many members take the process very seriously. However, party officials exert considerable influence over proceedings: they draft the documents that form the parameters of discussion and tightly control the responses received from local parties. At the central forum, amendments are discussed in workshops at which small groups consider the amendments without the benefit of hearing proposers explain the reasoning behind them. Senior party officials facilitate the workshops and summarise their views. The national forum then simply votes for or against the amendments without debate. This leaves considerable interpretive powers to the facilitator (see Seyd, 1999).

The documents that emerge are bland and unchallenging. As the political journalist Patrick Wintour has observed, they 'offer little insight into new directions. Instead, they glowingly render the Blair government's achievements to date ... Rarely have so many platitudes been gathered in one place' (*Guardian*, 31 May 2000). The simple fact is that actual party policies are determined at elite level; and the National Policy Forum essentially exists as window-dressing with a small degree of influence at the margins. Charles Clarke, the new party chairman, has acknowledged that there needs to be more genuine debates and votes at future party conferences.

The Liberal Democrats allow greater membership involvement in policy formation than either of the two larger parties and do not try to manage or stifle internal debate. Their reward is adverse media coverage of their party conferences. The party's Federal Policy Committee guides policy-making, appointing working groups on specific subjects. These groups take submissions from interested parties and then produce consultative reports for debate throughout the party. These papers typically offer policy options rather than prescriptive solutions. Final drafts are then put to the party's federal conference, where local parties can propose amendments for genuine debate and the media ridicule the participants

Selecting parliamentary candidates

The three major British parties, and both nationalist parties, now run selection schemes with a nationally approved lists of candidates, overseen by a representative and independent panel of senior party figures, from which local parties are free to select a candidate after interviews.

But the Labour party alone comes in for intense criticism for manipulating the choice of parliamentary candidates. There is a case for most of its safeguards. Parliamentary candidates should be of a high enough calibre to represent their constituencies well. They should be loyal party members who broadly share the party's ethos. There is also a case for cherry-picking candidates who will come across well in the media at by-elections, or who will make outstanding MPs and ministers. Moreover, central dominance is not the only undesirable feature of selection processes. Insider mafias or entrenched trade unions can exert too much power locally, sometimes with sectarian or partial interests.

But it is not acceptable for party leaderships to exploit the safeguards to which they are entitled to impose conformity on the party or to advance their own favourites or own narrow interests. However, since 1997 such improper interference in selections has been a mark of New Labour; and though it is justified as being in the interests of party unity and the party's image, it has often harmed both party morale and unity and damaged the party's reputation with the public as well as in the media. The party was probably not guilty of excluding two sitting MPs, Dennis Canavan and Ian Davidson, from the approved list for the elections to the Scottish Parliament because they were not the stuff of New Labour. For the supervisory panel was seeking to freshen its range of approved candidates and to boost women's representation; and also prominent on the approved list were two MPs who had recently resigned from Labour's front bench at Westminster on grounds of principle and at least 15 identifiably left candidates who were chosen for safe seats (*Guardian*, 2 March 1999). But there was convincing evidence that the national panel for selecting prospective MEPs was more obviously ideological in its design (Wring et al, 2000).

It is also widely accepted that the Labour party leadership ruthlessly manipulated the processes for choosing candidates for the London mayoral elections and leadership of the Welsh Labour party, deviating from the official rule-book and adopting procedures against the wishes of outraged party members to prevent them from choosing Ken Livingstone and Rhodri Morgan. Party managers even took a partisan part in elections when they should properly have played a wholly neutral role (*Guardian*, 13 December 1999, 17 December 1999; and see Flynn, 1999). This is a clear breach of the elementary rule that party officials should not intervene in intra-party selections. The Labour party NEC has conceded that it must introduce consistent democratic processes for internal elections (see Labour Party 2000).

Tony Blair was clearly involved in these manoeuvres, just as he was in questionable interventions in the run-up to the 2001 election. Several MPs in safe seats delayed standing down until it was too late for their parties to initiate open selection processes; and Millbank (the Labour party's HQ) was able to impose its own shortlists on the local constituencies. There were allegations that sitting MPs had been bribed by the offer of peerages. Two beneficiaries of this manoeuvre were David Miliband, the former No.10 policy adviser (and now a junior minister) and the Blairite commentator, Siôn Simon. Most shameless of all, the former Tory MP Shaun Woodward was placed on the shortlist for St Helens South, while strong local contenders for the seat were conspicuously excluded. Those left off the list included the popular female leader of the local council. Woodward was duly selected (after much arm-twisting). The cynicism of the Labour leadership fails any democratic test and exposes the shallowness of its commitment to introduce more women and minority candidates into Parliament.

Democracy in the balance

It is important not to measure current practice against some golden age of party democracy, or even against some golden mean of democratic practice. Parties in Britain have never been particularly democratic and not unnaturally are reluctant to take the risks of entryism and extremism inherent in a fully open internal democracy, as the recent history of the Labour party demonstrates. The parties must be allowed to protect their integrity. They must strike a balance between robust democratic process and the projection of a unified, competent party to the wider public. It is fair to say that none of the major parties in Britain has been successful in balancing these two commitments, with the Liberal Democrats coming closest.

However, we should also recognise that recent reforms have significantly enhanced the power of party members in the Labour and Conservative parties. In both parties, all members can now participate in elections for their party leaders, albeit in conditioned circumstances in both cases. There is wider consultation in both parties on policies and genuine participation in the Liberal Democratic party. There are internal rules governing party procedures in the two larger parties. The least that a democratic audit can ask is that party managers and officials should observe the rules or due process. In the case of Labour, that minimum condition is evaded.

6.6. How far does the system of party financing prevent the subordination of parties to special interests?

Across Europe, political parties of all complexions have been beset by funding scandals, as the costs of elections have spiralled and party memberships have fallen. We deal in detail with the issue of corruption and improper influences on government in Section 9 (and especially 9.4). Here we ask whether the Electoral Commission and the new statutory rule-book can protect the parties from special interests and funding scandals. The purpose of the rules is to make the funding of political parties transparent and to limit the costs of election campaigning (and thus to relieve the pressures on the parties to raise very high donations that might make them vulnerable to special interests).

These rules enact most of the recommendations of the report by the Committee on Standards in Public Life (otherwise known then as the Neill Committee), published in October 1998. The Neill Committee did not recommend state funding of the parties and the parties all remain unduly reliant on big donors. As a result, the new era of openness has fostered more suspicions, rather than dispelling them, since the media question most large donations and link them to government decisions or policies seen as being in the interests of the donors (see Section 9.4). But the reliance on big donors is corrupting in a wider sense: it demeans leading politicians, their offices and parties, to make themselves available for fund-raising dinners and events and otherwise to sell access and their time. As Henry Drucker, once Labour's fund-raising adviser, has said, such fund-raising involves 'access to the great man, the implied promises of favours, and in this country, honours' (*Sunday Times*, 16 November 1997). To his credit, Tony Blair makes evident his distaste for the whole process, although remains content enough to accept large donations.

Further, though the Commission can impose a cap on election spending, elections and party politics remain expensive. In 2001, the Conservatives spent £12.8 million, Labour £11.1 million and the Liberal Democrats £1.36 million. The Commission's first quarterly report into party funding under the new disclosure regime (covering the election period of April–June 2001) showed an increasing reliance on large individual donations. For the first time, donations from the three top Labour donors exceeded £6 million and the Conservatives received £11 million from their top three (out of £12.4 million in total over the period). Lord Ashcroft, who currently serves as the Tories' appointed party treasurer, is said to give the party about £80,000 monthly. Obviously, no donors are likely to admit to giving a party money to influence its policies in or out of government. Stuart Wheeler, the spread-betting millionaire, who gave the Conservatives £5 million, has come nearest to doing so; he insisted that his was a 'no-strings-attached' donation, but then said that if Kenneth Clarke became party leader after the 2001 election and changed party policy on the Euro, he would withdraw his support (*Guardian*, 22 January 2001).

To avoid becoming subordinate either to big donors or the trade unions, Labour seeks to achieve a balanced policy based on differing sources of income. Its aim is to accumulate 40 per cent of its income from membership fees and small donations (less than £1,000), 30 per cent from trade union affiliations and donations, 20 per cent from large donors and 10 per cent from commercial activities. Broadly speaking, the party manages to maintain this balance. Its reliance on the trade unions has fallen substantially; in 1983, almost all its income (96 per cent) came from trade union affiliation fees and contributions. The influence that the 'trade union barons' actually had over Labour party policy was always exaggerated. Lewis Minkin's meticulous and scholarly studies of past Labour party-trade union links shows how limited trade union influence over Labour's policies was even in their heyday (Minkin, 1978, 1991). It is clearly very limited now under New Labour. Several larger unions are making or considering reductions in their financial contributions to Labour for this very reason.

The Conservatives do not pursue a policy of balance. In 1999, for example, members of the party's Board of Treasurers (numbering seven people) gave the party donations worth a third of its total income.

Because the electoral system obstructs their ability to compete with the two larger parties and to share in national government, the Liberal Democrats operate in a lesser financial league from the two larger parties and are greatly disadvantaged as a result. Over two-thirds of their total annual income of around £3 million can be traced back to party members (Webb 2000).

How far the new regime of openness and regulation prevents the subordination of parties to special interests cannot be determined. It is certainly the case that the transparency has failed to remove the public suspicions of party sleaze. It is likely that failure of the new regime to create greater trust will have to be reviewed. Such a review would have to re-consider the possible introduction of state funding, along with other measures such as, say, a £5,000 annual limit for individual donations, a far lower cap on election spending and incentives for smaller donations from more people (as other party political regimes abroad already do).

Meanwhile, British parties are under-funded by comparison with political parties elsewhere. For example, the total income of the three main UK parties in 1997 was only just over half of the income of Germany's Social Democratic Party in 1990 (Webb 2000). The main British parties are constantly struggling to manage their debts and avoid cuts in staff and services. Thus the Neill Committee sweetened the proposal for a new financial regime for the parties with another proposal for an increase in the state funding, 'Short money', paid to opposition parties for policy development. The Lib-Dems and the Tories now share around £4 million in Short money at Westminster. We further estimate that public funding, in the shape of Short money, allowances for political staff and office costs for party politicians at Westminster, Holyrood, Cardiff, the GLA and local councils, is worth at least £50 million a year to the political parties.

The rationale for this large subvention is that it is paid to improve the quality of service that the elected politicians deliver to the public. But it is surely time for public debate on the rising issue of more open state funding. The argument for this is that the political parties are essential to the workings of representative democracy – and there is no obvious substitute for them – and so it makes sense to ensure that they are adequately and consistently resourced without relying on major donors, or subventions from business or the trade unions. State funding could be given a new and wider rationale than now by gearing it to the public support the parties receive individually (as it is in other democracies); and possibly by relating each party's share to their own fund-raising. Major politicians like Tony Blair may then be freed to act with dignity

But as we recognise in Section 9, state funding does not guarantee an end either to corrupt practice or the undue influence of wealthy individuals and corporate interests. But it is hard to see any alternative that will at least give political parties the means to resist temptation and create a fairer distribution of funding to them all. It is also argued that it is undesirable for the political parties to rely for their existence on the state; and that the public are hostile to the idea. Perhaps the three separate reviews on party funding, being conducted simultaneously by the Electoral Commission, the think-tank IPPR and the Local Government Select Committee, will stimulate public interest and debate on state funding.

6.7 To what extent do parties cross ethnic, religious and linguistic divisions?

Party politics in the United Kingdom are not dominated by differences that reflect major and divisive cleavages in society at large, except in Northern Ireland and to a lesser degree in Scotland and Wales. The divide is sharpest in Northern Ireland, where the main British parties abandon the attempt to act as 'national' parties and do not contest elections. There the Catholic communities support the SDLP and Sinn Fein, while Protestants give their support to the UUP, DUP and other unionist and loyalist parties; the memberships and representatives of these parties all reflect the sectarian divide. Attempts by the Alliance party and others to bridge the sectarian divide have proven ineffective. It is clear that these divisions in political alignment will persist for as long as the underlying polarity between the two communities structures public affairs in the province; and while the main UK political parties fail in their duty to offer a voice in the UK government and Parliament to the people of the province.

Other religious divisions between Anglicans and Nonconformists, and then Protestants and Catholics, once played a significant part in shaping the political parties. But these divisions are now less significant in British society, although a Catholic mafia is still very influential in some places in the west of Scotland, like Monklands. But racial divisions are significant. The racial mix in all parties fails to reflect the composition of the population as a whole: in the 1990s, only 3 per cent of Labour members were Afro-Caribbean or Asian, and 1 per cent 'other'; Asians formed a 1 per cent bridgehead among the Tories (Seyd and Whiteley, 1992; Seyd et al, 1994). However, Asians in particular play a major and often commanding role in local Labour parties in a few inner-city areas. Their role creates resentments where their presence is felt to be artificially swollen. The Lib-Dems fielded more black and Asian parliamentary candidates (25) than the Conservatives and Labour (16 each) in 2001, but only Labour put ethnic minority candidates in seats that were won (see 5.4 further). Attempts by Tory party leaderships to adopt a more positive and pluralist image are frequently undermined by the racist views and attitudes of some party members and a handful of MPs.

In Scotland and Wales, the nationalist parties reflect the popularity of nationalist sentiments and have created distinct party systems in both nations, now further encouraged by devolution. It is worth observing that to suppose that Scottish or Welsh nationalism is confined to the ranks of the SNP or Plaid Cymru alone would be to misunderstand the breadth and nature of their nationalist movements. The domination of the UK government by the Conservatives during the 1980s precipitated a radical shift in opinion inside the other major opposition parties, with both Labour and the Liberal Democrats adopting nationalist sentiment and policies in response to the popular perception of the Conservatives as an exclusively English party (see Marr 1995b). The Conservative parties in Scotland and Wales have suffered as a result. The SNP and Plaid Cymru have emerged as the principal opposition parties in both nations. People occasionally suggest that this political expression of nationalist aspirations could encourage tensions and even hatreds damaging to the harmony of British society. But the parties represent perfectly legitimate aspirations; and the important issue is how inclusive they are within their own territories.

Seven: government accountability and effectiveness

Servants of the people?

Is government accountable to the people and their representatives?

We are not the masters now. The people are the masters. We are the servants of the people
Tony Blair to Labour MPs, Church House, 1997

The central issue in British politics has not been how to curb the elective dictatorship but how to capture it... Regardless of whether it is called a 'top-down' model or an elective dictatorship, the formal concentration of political authority in Britain is remarkable.
Dennis Kavanagh, political analyst, 1986

Introduction

'Tony wants' may be the two most compelling words in Whitehall. But they are a poor guide to the complexities of modern government in this country. The United Kingdom is governed by a duopoly: at supra-national and intergovernmental level through the institutions of the European Union in Brussels and Strasbourg; and at national level by the political executive and Parliament in Whitehall and Westminster.

Two goals – accountability and effectiveness – are the two sides of the coinage of government, which is why Section 7 examines both together. A government must be organised and resourced to carry out (or at least begin to do so) the pledges in its election platform and to act in the public interest. In this sense, the British tradition of 'strong' government has democratic value. But in the modern world, it is now a truism that practically no government has the power or resources to exercise control over all the matters that affect the lives of its people. So we must consider how far a British government is constrained by globalisation and external forces (see Section 14), and also internally by domestic interests, the power of private business, other limits on government action, and so on.

It is equally important that government should be accountable; and accountable between elections as well as at them. Accountability is vital to satisfying the basic democratic principle of popular control of government. For it means that government, ministers and state officials are required directly or indirectly to 'render an account' to citizens and their representatives about their conduct and performance in government. Citizens and their representatives are then in a position to judge not only how well government has performed, but also its honesty and other qualities. Secondly, making government accountable is vital to making government work. Policies and decisions are all the better for being made transparent, and subject to checks and balances, through Parliament, the media, interest groups, public audit and the like.

In this Section, we consider how far government at the national level is effective and accountable. The primary means of securing accountability is through fair and regular elections (see Section 5). Here we review the role and scope of the political executive in Britain; and then the principal political means by which it is held accountable. Parliament itself is or should be the main instrument of political accountability. But over the years additional institutions, agencies and processes have evolved to secure accountability and to try and match the growing power and diversity of government and the state. We assess the contributions that freedom of information law, public audit, the Ombudsman service, and rules of conduct for ministers make. We also consider the role of the judiciary and the rule of law. The part that the media play is considered separately in Section 10.

At the same time, we seek to appraise those parts of the British political system that affect the democratic qualities of EU decisions. Behind this distinction lies an important, though often neglected, insight: when a country joins the EU, it accepts that democratic standards in matters delegated to the Union are largely determined by the EU's political system (see Section 14.1); yet, it also retains significant control over the democratic implications of its own membership.[1] Choice remains in three areas: in how national parliaments bring their governments to account for use of the rights and powers assigned to member states under the Union's decision rules; in how changes to EU treaties are put to national publics or parliaments for ratification; and in how national electoral and party systems connect voters to EU decision-making. In Section 14, we consider the issue of the effect of EU membership on British sovereignty separately.

7.1. How far is government able to influence or control those matters that are important to the lives of its people, and how well is it organised, informed and resourced to do so?

The United Kingdom is a very rich country with extensive and varied resources, not least in its human capital. The British economy is the fourth largest in the world and the second largest in Europe. There is therefore no question about the country being sufficiently resourced to deal with issues that are important to the lives of its people.

There is no doubt also about the power that an elected government has at its disposal, thanks to the fusion of executive and legislative power in its hands, and the fusion between the Prime Minister and ministers and the senior civil service. Academic analysts describe the political executive as the 'core executive', a label that seeks to convey the complex mesh of actors and institutions that, with the Prime Minister, cabinet ministers and senior civil service at the centre, governs this country (see Rhodes and Dunleavy, 1995; Smith, 1999). No one political figure or official – not even the Prime Minister – has absolute power within the core executive; it is the site of an inter-active and shifting process of decision-making. Yet the Prime Minister and Chancellor are invariably dominant figures; and the Treasury and, to an increasing degree under Blair's regime, the PM's office and the Cabinet Office, are the key institutions.

The Prime Minister, ministers and senior civil servants within this core share a remarkable degree of executive flexibility. First, they possess wide discretionary 'prerogative' powers, inherited from the monarchy, which remain almost wholly outside political or judicial scrutiny. Though formally these powers belong to ministers, they are in practice at the disposal of senior civil servants. Prerogative powers, for example, allow Prime Ministers constantly to re-shape government and the civil service without having to resort to Parliament. They give the Prime Minister and ministers extraordinary freedom in foreign affairs. Ministers augment their prerogative discretion through statutory instruments (or delegated legislation) in Parliament. British ministers only rarely fail to secure the legislation they propose to Parliament – a notable contrast to other systems, both parliamentary and presidential – and the additional powers they seek through that legislation. There has been a phenomenal increase in the accretion of ministerial power though statutory instruments. The absence of a written constitution, and with it a developed body of public or administrative law, leaves substantial areas of government activity open to the operation of this executive discretion. Finally, the executive's activities are protected by excessive secrecy (see Section 7.7).

This concentration of power at the centre usually raises public concern under a 'strong' Prime Minister with a large parliamentary majority, like Mrs Thatcher or Tony Blair. But even a 'weak' government, like that of John Major, can be very powerful. Troubled as his government was by vicious divisions over Europe and a receding parliamentary majority, John Major got all his business through Parliament more or less unscathed, including highly controversial policies like rail privatisation. Public opinion, the opposition, many Conservative MPs and peers saw that the government's scheme was wholly misconceived and its defects were fully revealed in parliamentary debates. Yet Major thrashed the Railways Act through Parliament, even though it was thoroughly discredited long before it staggered into law in late 1993.

Government under Blair

Blair came to power in 1997 determined to assert the power of the Prime Minister at the centre over departments and their ministers – 'expect a change,' Jonathan Powell, his chief of staff, warned civil servants, 'from a feudal system of barons to a more Napoleonic system' (Rawnsley, 2000). The outside world has long worried about the presidential ambitions of Prime Ministers – and reasonably so. But from within Downing Street, the problem has always been how hard it is for a Prime Minister with fewer resources and formal powers than his or her cabinet colleagues to impose his or her will on government policies. Blair intended to remedy the ill-coordinated world of Whitehall by asserting political control over his government's activities. Thus the pursuit of 'joined-up' policy-making. A more coordinated approach to cross-cutting and intractable problems like social exclusion could resolve and focus departmental responsibilities over a range of issues, concentrate on his party's election pledges and make government more effective overall.

Blair moved fast to strengthen his formal position through the PM's office and the Cabinet Office. He has been accused of creating a new Prime Minister's Department by fusing the new departments (Burch and Holliday, 1999). The *Times* columnist, Peter Riddell, described the shift from co-ordination to central control as 'the biggest centralisation of power seen in Whitehall in peacetime' (20 May 1997). However the need to strengthen the Prime Minister's position has long been recognised, and Blair's changes (or step-changes) are in fact part of a trend that began under Harold Wilson in the 1960s. Meanwhile government since 1997 has tended to revolve around the working duopoly of Prime Minister and Chancellor of the Exchequer that has long been the norm (Deakin and Parry, 2000). The Treasury remains the most powerful department in Whitehall and under Gordon Brown, a powerful political figure in his own right, it has become more powerful in two significant respects: first, its influence over the strategic direction of government has grown; and secondly, the system of Public Service Agreements (PSAs) developed under the Treasury's rolling programme of three-year comprehensive spending reviews has substantially increased its influence over the affairs of spending departments.

The Treasury has reduced the social security department to a satrapy; and become overlord over most domestic policies through the PSAs – agreements negotiated by the Treasury with departments that link their objectives and targets to their spending allocations. The Treasury select committee concluded that the Treasury had 'too much influence over policy areas which are properly the business of other departments' (Treasury committee, 2001). Further, through Brown, the Treasury has so far maintained its position as 'guardian' of the conditions for UK membership of the Euro (Gordon Brown speech in the City of London, 15 June 2000).

Ultimately, however, Blair is the boss. Some academic analysts challenge the idea of the 'presidential' Prime Minister, arguing that he or she is simply a more powerful inter-dependent actor in the political executive. It is also the case that Blair does not possess the executive powers of a president. However, the idea should be taken seriously, since the British system does not offer the constitutional protections against the concentration of powers in a single individual's hands that exist in presidential democracies.

The sinews of the body politic

By 1997, the cabinet had long since ceased to be the 'efficient secret' of government. It remained formally part of the core executive, but it was far from being the hub of government. It was generally a sleeping dog (though it could awaken and bite, as Lady Thatcher discovered to her cost in 1990). Blair continued to diminish its role in government. For example, the first major decision of the government – handing over control of monetary policy to the Bank of England – was taken without consulting the cabinet. Sir Robin Butler, the Cabinet Secretary, suggested that cabinet ministers should be involved or at least be informed, but Blair was unmoved. The cabinet was also excluded from the great debate of the first Blair term – the decision on joining the Euro. Blair publicly rejected the idea that the cabinet was the right place in which to take important decisions, openly deriding 'the old days of Labour governments where meetings occasionally went on for two days and you had a show of hands at the end' (*What Makes Tony Tick?* BBC2, 20 January 2000).

However, below the cabinet the 'efficient secret' of postwar government in the UK – the interlocking and highly-developed structure of cabinet committees – still acts as the government's main coordinating mechanism. These committees are powerful decision and policy making bodies in their own right; John Major's advisers described them as 'the unseen sinews of the body politic' (Hogg and Hill, 1995). Here the Cabinet Secretary and Cabinet Office officials come into the reckoning – linking departmental interests and inputs, preparing agendas, recording decisions; and Treasury ministers occupy significant places on the major committees. It is possible to trace shifts in power within government on the places ministers hold on which committees; after 2001, for example, Blair promoted John Prescott's position in the committee structure to offset Brown's pre-eminence. The committees are formally part of the cabinet and their decisions are normally binding on the whole cabinet. Central policies are made in committee. Thus, for example, Derry Irvine, the Lord Chancellor, was the unseen chief architect of devolution as chairman of the devolution committee, not Donald Dewar nor Ron Davies.

The role of the civil service

Even in the era of 'hollowed-out government' and public-private partnership, the civil service, greatly reduced in size since 1988, remains the main instrument of state policy and decision making. Even the Treasury, Whitehall's power-house, is a surprisingly small department. Blair has retained Mrs Thatcher's vision of a policy-making core in Whitehall with a new 'can-do' managerial drive, overseeing delivery rather than being immediately responsible for it. In March 2001, the Public Administration Select Committee (PASC) published an interim report, *Making Government Work*, which recognised the civil service as 'a resource of immense value to government' (PASC, 2001f). But the committee also cited criticisms of some key shortcomings in terms of information, skills and resources – slow reactions, poor policy advice, inattention to policy delivery, bad project management, and inadequate understanding of 'risk management issues'. Senior officials argue that its traditional generalism is 'in itself a form of professionalism'; others, like Patrick Dunleavy, then adviser to PASC, point out that very few civil servants hold the higher, more specialised qualifications that are common in comparable public bureaucracies abroad, leaving top civil servants with 'fewer resources of expertise or developed analytic capacities'. Outside observers have also argued that the thinning of the ranks of the senior civil service over the past 20 years has reduced its capacity to give good policy advice. Overall, there are doubts about the capacity of the civil service core in Whitehall to improve and deliver the public services that are at the heart of the government's electoral mandate.

Can government deliver?

What can be said about the present position is that

- the resources exist within Britain to provide for a secure and decent standard of life for the great majority;
- past neglect of the public infrastructure demands a vast injection of public funds into public services, whether publicly or privately owned; and
- the Blair government is engaged in the most concerted attempt in peacetime to create a central government sufficiently well informed and organised to improve the quality of public services and bring about a more equal society.

At the same time, there are quite proper fears that its emphasis on central control and its 'command and control' strategies are damaging for the future long-term balance of power within the UK and counter-productive in the immediate future. In an influential paper on 'policy disasters' during the Thatcher era – such as the poll tax, the costly Trident programme, the first years of the Child Support Agency – the political scientist Patrick Dunleavy tentatively identified five main causes. At their centre were the arrogance of Whitehall, failings of managerial grasp and 'ineffective core executive checks and balances'(Dunleavy 1995). A study of the poll tax fiasco by another political scientist, David Butler and others, reached a similar conclusion: 'An ingenious but flawed initiative . . . was allowed to go ahead unchecked, despite all the supposed safeguards and filters of the policy-making and legislative processes' (Butler et al, 1994).

Policy disasters and fiascos have since occurred under both the Major and Blair governments – for example, the costly scramble out of the European monetary system, rail privatisation, the BSE epidemic, the SERPS debacle, the Millennium Dome, the foot-and-mouth epidemic, in most of which the central executive's virtually unbound strength has figured. The questions for the future – and much of the rest of this audit – must be: how far has the Blair government gone in building in stronger checks and balances on the power of the central executive? And what will the lasting impact of a stronger central executive be on government in the UK and the relationships between its various parts?

7. 2. How much public confidence is there in the effectiveness of government and its political leadership?

The most consistent measure of public confidence in the governing system is to track over time a partic-ular question first asked in a survey for the Kilbrandon Commission on the Constitution in 1970 (see Table 1). The Kilbrandon survey found even then a 'diffuse feeling of dissatisfaction' with the British governing system (Crowther-Hunt and Peacock, 1973). Yet there was a sharp fall in confidence up to the mid-1990s when the prospect of the Blair government raised people's expectations and they still remain higher. Even so, nearly two thirds of people now believe that the system needs to be considerably improved, as against just under a half in 1973. However, an ICM poll for Democratic Audit in June 2002 also found that 55 per cent of people had either a 'great deal' or 'a fair amount' of confidence in the ability of government, irrespective of party, to 'solve the main problems that confront society'. A third had only a little confidence in government and one in ten none at all.

Over broadly the same time-span as the Kilbrandon polls (1974-96), British Social Attitudes found a strong downward trend in people's belief that political leaders would govern in the national rather than party interest; and a growing belief that they wouldn't. Three quarters of respondents think that governments would generally put their party interest first (see Table 1).

1. Public confidence in the way Britain is governed

The system of governing Britain

	1973	1977	1991	1995	1996	2002
'Could not be improved' or 'could be improved in small ways'	48	34	33	22	35	36
'Could be improved quite a lot' or 'a great deal'	49	62	63	76	63	62

How much do you trust British governments of any party to place the needs of the nation above the interests of their own political party?

	1974	1986	1987	1991	1994	1996
'Just about always' or 'most of the time'	39	38	37	33	24	22
'Only some of the time' or 'almost never'	57	57	60	63	73	75

Sources: Dunleavy et al, 2001; ICM poll for Democratic Audit, June 2002; and Jowell et al, 1997

Finally, if we assume that low turnout at the general election in 2001 is dissatisfaction either with the governing system or with its ability to respond to people's aspirations and needs, then it seems that public confidence in government is especially low in urban areas of social deprivation. Less than half the people entitled to vote turned out in 67 constituencies – that is, in one in ten of all constituencies – and turnout was lowest of all in inner Liverpool, Glasgow, Manchester, east London, etc.

7.3. How far is the executive subject to the rule of law and transparent rules governing the use of its powers?

In contrast to the position in most comparable countries, the political executive is not bound by a written constitution. Nor is the state bureaucracy governed by statute or by a developed system of public or administrative law. Instead the constitutional structure is founded on the principle of parliamentary sovereignty under which the UK Parliament is the highest court in the land and the supreme institution of the state. This principle limits the capacity of the judiciary to review legislation and the acts and decisions of the central executive.

The Human Rights Act 1998, introduced largely to protect civil and political rights in the UK (see Sections 2 and 3), has, however, also strengthened the law of judicial review over government decision-making. Prior to the Act, the courts could review the acts of the central executive or any public body on limited grounds only: that the decision-making procedure broke rules of fairness; that the body taking the decision was acting beyond its powers; or that the decision itself was utterly irrational. While the courts were able gradually from the 1980s to check some arbitrary government actions, the inadequacy of these grounds was illustrated in 1995 when the courts were obliged reluctantly to uphold the MOD ban on gays and lesbians in the armed services since they could not conclude that it was irrational. The 1998 Act will require a more searching review of the quality of public policies and actions and will measure them against more than a minimum standard of rationality. It is also likely that the authorities will over time be obliged by law to give reasons for their decisions.

However, the courts are generally reluctant to 'usurp the functions of government' (in one judge's phrase), and appear to defer to ministers when they exercise prerogative powers (see also Section 2.2). Moreover the courts have shown remarkable restraint during the vast and continuous programmes of public service reforms since the 1980s and it seems likely that they will continue to respect the administrative needs of the executive. Thus the executive will generally retain its freedom to act as it sees fit in its direction of the civil service.

Control of the central executive

Outside the courts, there is a growing shift towards legal controls in government away from the traditional reliance on political control of the executive and rule by conventions (the non-legal understandings that govern political conduct in the UK). Ministerial and parliamentary codes, civil service and recruitment codes, and numerous handbooks and booklets, some produced by external watch-dogs, are examples of official efforts to establish or maintain standards. Thus the conduct of the executive and civil service is nowadays governed by a mixture of codes and regulatory bodies, including the seven ethical principles for public life established by the Nolan Committee (Committee on Standards in Public Life, 1995, 1996 and 1997), alongside the conventions and understandings of the old regime.

The Whitehall watcher, Martin Smith, argues that the rules that govern civil servants are largely carried in their heads, asserting that the constitution, to a large degree, 'is what officials do' (Smith, 1999). Kate Jenkins, the key architect of the executive agency reforms in 1987-88, argues strongly for more clarity in the rules. 'In my 20 years in the civil service,' she informed the Public Administration Select Committee, 'I do not think anybody could ever tell me what my professional and constitutional role was – even though everybody assumed that I knew it and had acquired it by osmosis on entering the civil service'. Recent changes had made the position even less clear. 'My sense, talking to a lot of civil servants, is that they have rather lost the sense of what their professionalism is' (PASC, 2001f). The government is now committed to introduce a Civil Service Act to give statutory weight to these codes and conventions. But they are unclear, largely concern ethical standards and do not add much to the public accountability of the central executive.

Rules of conduct for ministers

As the Scott report on arms-related exports to Iraq revealed, the absence of strict rules of accountability for ministers and officials alike makes serious abuses and evasions possible. Scott found himself obliged to turn to John Major's ministerial code, a curious mixture of rules of propriety and housekeeping matters, as the only set of published rules for executive conduct on which he could base his recommendations. This code, actually confidential until 1992, was hardly a robust base for reform, especially as it is the property of each incumbent Prime Minister and much of its content is up to his or her discretion. Tony Blair has strengthened the code, re-named *The Ministerial Code* (see Section 9), which seeks to give some substance to the doctrine of ministerial accountability to Parliament. It insists, as did Scott and the parliamentary resolution of March 1997 following the publication of his report, that ministers do not simply have a duty to Parliament to account, and be held to account, for their departments' policies, decisions and actions, but also that:

> iii. it is of paramount importance that Ministers give accurate and truthful information to Parliament, correcting any inadvertent error at the earliest opportunity. Ministers who knowingly mislead Parliament will be expected to offer their resignation to the Prime Minister;

> iv. Ministers should be as open as possible with Parliament and the public, refusing to provide information only when disclosure would not be in the public interest which should be decided in accordance with the relevant statutes and the Government's Code of Practice on Access to Government Information;

> v. Ministers should similarly require civil servants who give evidence before Parliamentary Committees on their behalf and under their direction to be as helpful as possible in providing accurate, truthful and full information in accordance with the duties and responsibilities of civil servants as set out in the Civil Service Code . . . ;

> ix. Ministers must . . . uphold the political impartiality of the Civil Service and not ask civil servants to act in any way which would conflict with the Civil Service Code.

However, the code specifically rejects the status of being a 'rule-book' rather than just guidance; and it leaves a vacuum where independent arbitration and scrutiny of the actions of ministers and senior civil servants is essential. The Prime Minister remains the sole and ultimate judge of the conduct of ministers. His primary consideration is bound always to be the protection of the viability of his government rather than the proper conduct of government business. Thus, for example, Blair has kept several ministers in government when they had clearly transgressed his own rules of conduct.

If *The Ministerial Code* has any force, it is the force of non-legal convention. These conventions lie at the heart of the celebrated flexibility of Britain's political system; and that flexibility in the conduct of the executive and in wider constitutional arrangements enhances the power of the executive. In the past constitutional theorists have believed that the flexibility of British constitutional arrangements was a great strength that enabled governments to govern effectively 'without allowing them to rule for long in an arbitrary and irresponsible fashion' (Moodie, 1964). Mrs Thatcher and her ministers showed a flagrant disregard for conventions and undermined their continuing force. The hallmarks of the UK executive are still flexibility and informality; and executive self-restraint remains one of the essential underpinnings of democratic government and the rule of law (Daintith and Page, 1999).

The idea that senior officials could individually or collectively enforce proper standards on the part of ministers is often floated. Yet the idea is utterly unrealistic. Such a role is simply at odds with Whitehall's culture and the symbiotic relationship between officials and ministers. If the conduct of minister is to be supervised, it must be by an official or authority outside government – some kind of Public Standards Commissioner. MPs raised the idea of the Cabinet Secretary taking a supervisory role over ministers with Sir Richard Scott when he gave evidence to the former Public Service Committee in 1996. Scott replied, 'The Cabinet Secretary is a very important figure *within* government' (Public Service Committee, 1996). Further, as various holders of the office have shown, a Cabinet Secretary is just as likely to join or cover up an improper plot or conduct as to rule against it. Take for example Sir Robert Armstrong's role in the Westland affair in 1987 or Butler's part in schemes to belittle the Scott inquiry and report in 1996 (Weir and Beetham, 1999; Norton-Taylor et al, 1996). Butler at one point refused to give Scott documents from the Cabinet Office; and Scott had to warn him that he would send in the police to seize them before Butler gave way. The conflicts of interests for a Cabinet Secretary as the impartial head of the civil service and a Prime Minister's confidant and fixer are profound.

7.4. How effective and open to scrutiny is the control exercised by elected leaders and ministers over Whitehall, executive agencies and other public bodies?

Ministerial control of the civil service is vital to the traditional structure of public accountability in the UK. Under the British system, civil servants are not directly accountable to Parliament. They are servants of the Crown and owe their loyalty to the government of the day. It is only through ministers, therefore, that they are made publicly accountable; they are in this sense politically invisible and protected from political controversy. As the Civil Service Code makes clear, civil servants must be politically impartial and serve ministers of all parties with equal loyalty and diligence. They must conduct themselves in such as way as to deserve and retain the confidence of ministers; honestly and impartially to assist and advise ministers, without fear or favour; to make all information relevant to a decisions available to ministers; and conscientiously to carry out their policies. After 18 years of Conservative government, there were fears that the civil service might not readily re-adjust to Labour rule after 1997. But the transition was well prepared and accomplished smoothly. Ministers like Gordon Brown seized control and at once imposed their views (and often their special advisers) on their departments. Not all ministers, however, could count on official loyalty. For example, it took Robin Cook some time to establish himself at the Foreign Office, and his first year there was subtly undermined by officials, who were sceptical about his 'ethical foreign policy' and did not take to him personally.

It is true of course that ministers can be at a disadvantage in their dealings with officials, being transient beings with a limited capacity to deal with issues while their officials are permanent and can share out responsibilities. Officials also have the authority of their expertise, knowledge and command of information; and they control the bureaucratic machinery. But these are resources that they can and usually do put at the disposal of ministers. Indeed, our major concern about the relationship between ministers and departments is the fusion of their interests and the willingness of officials to provide political advice and assistance; as a senior official put it to us:

> Civil servants support their ministers in their adversarial role in Parliament and the media. They do not prepare them for a reasoned debate on whether the policies are actually right ot wrong; they see their job as making sure that ministers are not embarrassed and can answer the attacks on them. People don't realise that you have to regard ministers and senior civil servants together, as a unity (Weir and Beetham, 1999)

In other words, officials may be politically impartial; but they are partisan in government. The problem with this concept of 'unity' is that the allegiance of official is to their partisan political bosses, and not to the public; that they are formally responsible to the public only through ministers with the interests of those ministers foremost in their minds; they act together in a secrecy that the current FOI act will continue to protect; and their support to ministers in Parliament makes the balance between them and their 'adversaries' – i.e., opposition spokespeople and MPs who are recognised representatives of the public – very unequal.

But ministers do not necessarily get their own way. Most departments have their own, often long-standing, policy agendas and interests, plus networks of organised interest groups, professional associations and other bodies which have influence within them (see Section 12.1). These interests affect the policy advice that officials give to ministers as well as the policies they follow out of the minister's current spheres of concern. Even with the huge ministerial contingents of the day, ministers cannot hope to control the vast expanse of decision-making for which they are formally accountable. It is for this reason that the central doctrine of ministerial accountability has been revised. Ministers are now officially said to be accountable for the policies of their department, for the policy framework and resource allocation, but not for operational or other actions of which they are unaware. This is an understandable response to the difficulties, but it is hardly satisfactory. The distinction between 'accountability' and 'responsibility' means that there are occasions when Parliament cannot determine who is actually responsible when something goes wrong and more importantly why it has gone wrong. Ministers may deny personal responsibility while civil servants are shielded by the convention of ministerial responsibility.

Miniature governments

It has long been recognised that the doctrine of ministerial responsibility to Parliament is a fiction (see, for example, Marr 1995a; Woodhouse 1994; Wright 1994). But the sheer institutional diversity of government makes the doctrine obsolete and its complexity obscures who is accountable to whom for what. A whole host of official bodies and officials exercise a great variety of powers over the spectrum of government – executive agencies, quangos, public corporations, regulators, czars, ad hoc plenipotentiaries, and inspectors. Many of these are 'miniature governments' in their own sphere. The 138 executive agencies (like the Benefits Agency and Customs & Excise) are still formally part of their parent government departments. There are 187 national executive quangos – semi-autonomous public bodies like the Housing Corporation and Learning and Skills Council. The Cabinet Office has acknowledged that ministers exercise scarcely any direct control over them. The regulators are independent of government, but take major public policy decisions. There are 414 advisory quangos and over 300 task forces; some of these committees effectively make policy on the safety of drugs, foods, air pollution, etc.

The Liberal Democrat peer, Lord Smith of Clifton, has applied Walter Bagehot's twin categories of 'efficient' and 'dignified' parts of the constitution to modern Britain, asserting that both Parliament and the cabinet belong to the 'dignified' realm and this host of public bodies in the *demi-monde* of government are virtually unseen members of the 'efficient' brigade (HL Deb, 18 July 2001). They are, he warned, beyond the capacity of Parliament to monitor. Research by Democratic Audit has found that their accountability to agencies like the Ombudsman and their openness to the public are also very patchy at best (see PASC, 2001d).

The central executive under Blair is probably more unitary and focused than any of its predecessors. Yet it is far from capable of coordinating and directing this vast and complex machinery of government. 'Much still slips through the net for one reason or another,' writes Ian Holliday, a professional Whitehall watcher. 'Indeed, the present government has generated a degree of executive fragmentation . . that could actually make imposing any sense of central direction on government policy harder than easier. Beyond that, there is plenty of resistance in the wider executive to control mechanisms launched from the centre' (Holliday, 2000).

7.5. How extensive and effective are Parliament's powers to scrutinise the executive and hold it to account, and to initiate, scrutinise and amend legislation?

The need to redress the balance of power between the central executive and Parliament has long been recognised. Some 25 years ago, the Procedure Committee in the House of Commons admitted:

> The balance of advantage between Parliament and the government in the day-to-day working of the constitution is now weighted in the favour of government to a degree which arouses widespread anxiety and is inimical to the proper working of our Parliamentary democracy.

The position has since worsened. Parliament has become a virtual cipher under 'can-do' governments that are impatient with the conventions of self-restraint that once governed executive conduct and its relationship with both Houses. The Prime Minister and ministers hardly bother to conceal their indifference to the House of Commons.

Parliament's ability to subject the executive to scrutiny and to hold it to account is fatally weakened by a variety of associated factors:

- government usually commands a party majority in the Commons, swelled by an electoral system that gives it more seats than its votes justify; in most circumstances, government MPs support its policies, actions and legislation out of loyalty and self-interest;
- the House of Commons is more a partisan cockpit for party and electoral campaigning than a forum for deliberative debate and dispassionate scrutiny; its fiercely political nature reinforces party loyalties on all sides;
- the key doctrine of ministerial responsibility to Parliament, the king-pin of accountability within parliamentary democracy in the UK, is, as we have explained above, an obsolete fiction;
- government whips maintain strict and normally unchallenged control over the disposal of the activities and time of the Commons, directing most debates and allowing the opposition and individual MPs only marginal space for their own debates and initiatives;
- government whips work continuously to enforce party loyalty, intimidating and bullying governing party MPs, if need be, or bribing them with a mixture of perks and patronage; the MPs for their part are generally anxious not to forfeit the prospect of political advancement;
- select committees, the main instruments of non-partisan scrutiny of the government, all too often split on party lines when they examine issues where the reputation of the government is at stake;
- the ad-hoc 'standing' committees that scrutinise legislation in the Commons are purely partisan bodies on which the governing party majority sit simply to assist the fast passage of government bills;
- the non-elected House of Lords, even with most hereditary peers now removed, does not have the representative legitimacy fully to employ its limited powers to require a government to think again; unless pressed for time, the government can usually insist on reversing Lords' amendments in the Commons to get their legislation through intact;
- both Houses lack the powers and resources to make the central executive accountable. The Treasury Committee stated in 2001, 'Parliament lacks the resources necessary to hold the Treasury fully to account'; similarly, the Procedure Committee declared in 2000 that 'Parliament does not have time to give comprehensive scrutiny to all legislative proposals';
- equally, MPs unambiguously acknowledge that Parliament fails properly to scrutinise the activities of utility regulators, executive agencies and quangos (Hansard Society 2001); the National Audit Office called for agencies to provide greater assurance to Parliament about their reported performance by arranging for the performance information in their annual reports to be externally validated. But the executive has not yet conceded the principle of independent validation, merely requiring performance information to be independently validated 'wherever possible' (Daintith and Page, 1999).

Parliament's capacity to subject the executive to scrutiny is further hampered by the government's refusal to recognise that this is its legitimate role. Blair believes that he and his government have a virtually direct compact with the electorate rather than through the people's representatives in Parliament. In constitutional terms, Labour MPs are asked to fulfil conflicting roles: they must first sustain their government in power; they must act as guardians of the manifesto on which they were elected; and they must make government accountable. But Blair believes that Labour MPs should act neither as the government's conscience nor as watch-dogs for the public, but rather as the government's ambassadors (Rawnsley 2000).

The Labour party promised to 'modernise' Parliament after 1997, but its first-term modernisation programme had nothing to do with creating a new balance between the executive and Parliament, nor with improving Parliament's ability to secure its accountability. True, there were modest reforms, like making Westminster Hall an additional debating chamber. But its real purpose was to clear obstacles out of path of government legislation and business. Its new process for 'time-tabling' scrutiny of draft legislation, for example, seriously tilted the balance against proper scrutiny (see below).

Parliamentary and public concern about the weakness of Parliament is rising. MPs are in assertive mood and have created a 'Parliament First' group to lobby for reforms. The Liaison Committee (2000) in the Commons, and the Hansard Society (2001) and the Conservative Norton Commission (2000) outside, have between them produced an agenda for change. Such was the concern in the Commons that MPs overturned an attempt after the 2001 election by the government whips to evict two active, and critical, select committee chairs, Gwyneth Dunwoody and Donald Anderson, from their posts. MPs voted to reinstate them – it was the first Commons defeat for the Blair government. Robin Cook, Leader of the House since 2001, responded to the demands for reform by strengthening select committees (see below), but the government whips informally persuaded Labour MPs to vote down the lynch-pin of his reform package – the proposal for a new committee to take the job of appointing MPs to select committees away from the party whips. This reform would have made select committees more independent of government and party patronage.

Ministerial responsibility to Parliament
Ministerial responsibility is still in theory the democratic 'buckle' that connects the executive to Parliament and, ultimately, the people (Weir and Beetham 1999: 336). Sir Richard Scott, appalled by the mendacity of ministers and officials during the 'arms to Iraq' affair, sought to give it more force by insisting on the duty of ministers under the then ministerial code to give honest and open account of their policies and actions to Parliament and the public.

Thus Parliament insists strongly on the rule that ministers should be honest in their dealings with the two Houses (though it is clearly impossible to demand openness within current structures). This is why Stephen Byers had ultimately to resign in 2002. There has no other obvious breach of ministers' honesty in their dealings with Parliament, although Gordon Brown and Stephen Byers (inside the House) and Jack Straw and Alan Milburn (outside) have all indulged in 'creative' accountancy – double and treble counting of resources devoted to spending figures, police and doctor numbers, etc. And a select committee admonished Byers for his 'regrettable habit' of giving 'potentially misleading' information to MPs.

However ministers often avoid the House and tend to announce significant decisions outside, very often through leaks. Gordon Brown has for example made nonsense of the old convention that details of the budget must be laid first before the Commons. Home Secretary David Blunkett spoke in the media of the 'public emergency' that terrorism posed in November 2001 and then laid the parliamentary order before the Commons for the derogation from the European Convention on Human Rights to allow detention without trial. Several MPs attempted to persuade the Speaker that the Home Secretary should appear in person to discuss the 'public emergency'. Richard Shepherd MP asked if there were no rules to insist that when 'a public emergency of such extraordinary dimension as to require legislation and an instrument of this nature the House Secretary should come to the House?' The Speaker replied: 'There are no rules' (HC Deb, 12 November 2001).

The fact is that decisions and debates that once centred on the Commons chamber now take place in the media, in European institutions, in the devolved assemblies and in the courts. Ministers frequently announce policies on the *Today* programme or in a television studio rather than in the House, and are almost as frequently rebuked by the Speaker. As the former MP and minister Tony Benn said in the Commons:

> We must face the fact that we are, to a large extent, an impotent House of Commons....We have been in recess since July, and during that time there has been a fuel crisis, a Danish no vote, the collapse of the euro and a war in the middle east, but what is our business tomorrow? The Insolvency Bill [Lords]. It ought to be called the Bankruptcy Bill [Commons], because we play no role (HC Deb, 23 October 2000).

The value of rules of honesty and openness in ministers' dealing with Parliament is therefore weakened when so many contested issues, such as say the Bernie Ecclestone affair (see Section 9.3), are primarily debated outside either House. Peter Mandelson was said to have resigned on the second occasion over a misleading answer to questions from the *Observer*. In fact, he had to go because colleagues, notably Alastair Campbell, lost faith in his veracity. The House has less purchase on ministers' lies outside Parliament since the convention that they should resign applies only to misleading Parliament. Taking the Ecclestone affair as an example, it is clear that both Gordon Brown (on the *Today* programme) and Tony Blair (in a crucial BBC television interview with John Humphrys) both lied (Rawnsley 2000; *Guardian*, 31 January 2001). They did so with impunity.

The House must of course meet to play a role. As we write, a furious debate is being waged about the legality, morality and practicability of war against Iraq. The Archbishop of Canterbury and other church leaders have presented a petition to 10 Downing Street. Individual MPs and peers have joined the debate, but the House of Commons cannot because Tony Blair refuses to recall Parliament. There are credible reports that preparations are being made for military action; and there are fears that by the time Blair does allow parliamentary debate, it will be too late to influence his decision. Blair explains that no decision is 'imminent' and that it would be premature to hold a debate at Westminster. Yet the debate is now joined and Parliament, which is supposed to be the forum for national debate on profoundly significant issues of this kind, cannot take part.

Under Standing Orders, the Speaker decides whether Parliament should be recalled, but only after ministers have made representations to him that the public interest requires it. Thus the trigger for recall lies with the executive rather than Parliament. It is clearly undesirable that such a decision should rest only with the executive. The Hansard Society has suggested that an individual MP should be able to instigate a recall in a national emergency and the Speaker would adjudicate upon the request after consulting party leaders. This is a sound proposal as far as it goes. But new Standing Orders should not give the party leaders an implicit power of veto as they may block reasonable requests in their joint interests. Better still to require cross–party support from a substantial number of MPs. But now a recall depends upon the say-so of Tony Blair who doesn't think it is in the public interest for the people's representatives to debate the issue of a war against Iraq. The last time he asked for a recall was in April 2002 to enable Parliament to pay its respects to the Queen Mother on her death.

Parliamentary Questions

Parliamentary Questions are basic tools by which MPs can hold ministers to account. One major advance here has been Tony Blair's decision to subject himself to two–and-half hours of questioning twice a year by select committee chairs on the Liaison Committee. The first of these sessions in July 2002 had a deliberative quality that oral question times in the House have entirely lost. As with the parallel decision to hold media question times in person, Blair is clearly seeking to restore a degree of public confidence in a Prime Minister and government tarnished in the public mind by 'spin'. But the decision is all to the good; as Blair said before the Liaison Committee, 'there is no point in me coming before a gathering like this unless I am to open up more than I would if I was doing the normal knock-about'.

Oral questions have been devalued, first by the 'knockabout' partisan culture in which they are asked and answered. The former Tory leader William Hague described his role in Prime Ministers Questions as 'fun' and 'wholly unproductive in every sense' (HC Deb, 18 July 2001). Secondly, the government whips plant toadying questions with compliant party backbenchers and even supply supplementary questions. The aim is to give ministers an easy ride. It is hard to see how the original purpose of oral PQs – i.e., making ministers answerable to Parliament for their actions – can be restored.

Written questions are a more useful means of obtaining solid information from ministers. The Scott report laid great stress on their significance for accountability; condemned inaccurate official replies in 1989 to some written questions as 'deliberate'; and insisted that they should be answered openly and honestly. More than half of MPs value them. But PASC has found in successive reports that ministers too often evade or block them, often on grounds of 'disproportionate cost'. In July 2002, PASC published a detailed analysis of answers to MPs' written questions that exposed widespread evasion by government departments of their duty to answer them (PASC, 2000d). For example, Downing Street, DCMS and the former DTLR systematically refused to answer PQs on the Millennium Dome, Lord Irvine withheld information on complaints about judges, the Home Office kept secret settlements of racial discrimination cases. The Department of Health was the worst offender and PASC has summoned Health Secretary Alan Milburn to explain why. The department admitted that in March that it was involved in 'systematic falsification in recording the handling of PQS' and ran a system that was open to abuse. At one point, the department had a backlog of over 400 unanswered PQs and it took ten months for it to respond to PASC's inquiries. Further, it seems that guidance to civil servants at the Department for Work and Pensions asked them to consider whether the motives of the MP asking a PQ were 'friendly' – a breach of the long-standing convention that MPs' questions should be answered on a simple basis of fact, regardless of who was asking it (*Guardian*, 12 June 2002).

Select committees

Select committees are the workhorses of parliamentary scrutiny. Most of them shadow departments and provide the only real opportunities in Parliament to question ministers and officials closely about their policies and actions. They also act as forums for pressure groups, organised interests and academic and other specialists to contribute to policy thinking. They have on occasion brought to light policy and administrative failures, as in the case of the Child Support Agency and Serps (the state earnings related pension scheme). In both these cases, they were able to draw on the complaints from constituents to their MPs – a strength of the parliamentary system. Both cases also absorbed MPs' time, resources and effort in inquiries that could not be sustained across the whole range of government activity. Other committees, like the Transport Committee under Gwyneth Dunwoody, have proved themselves effective critics of government policy. But there is little concrete evidence of select committee findings directly influencing government policies. Very few of their reports are debated in the House.

Nominally, select committees are empowered to send for 'persons, papers and records'. Yet committees continually run into problems getting the information they need (Liaison Committee 2001). Departments refuse to supply the records they seek and can also refuse requests to give evidence. Ministers too refuse requests to appear. In theory, a select committee can appeal to the whole House to enforce a request to appear; in practice, such an appeal would be futile since the government would determine the vote. Select committees also operate on inadequate resources – about £7.7 million annually, or 0.002 per cent of central government spending.

Moreover while members attempt to pursue a non-partisan approach to their inquiries, the party whips still control the composition of the committees; and when an issue that affects the reputation of the government arises, majority members tend at least to soft-pedal the findings. It is not just the whips who might intervene either. For example, a junior minister recently warned the chair of a select committee that their prospects of advancement into government would be damaged if the committee continued with one of its current investigations.

In 2002, Robin Cook put a modest reform package to strengthen select committees through a Modernisation Committee report. Proposals to pay committee chairs (to help establish an alternative career structure in the Commons); to re-name select committees as 'scrutiny' committees and to focus their work more clearly; to review their powers to require witnesses to give evidence; and to fund a central unit of specialist support staff for select committees and additional staffing for committee chairs were all approved. But the central idea of a new Committee of Nomination of senior MPs to decide committee membership – designed to remove select committees from the shadow of the whips – was defeated through the machinations of the government whips.

Legislative scrutiny

The government has a virtual monopoly over legislation. MPs are entitled to introduce their own measures, but their chances of doing so are very limited. First, they must first win a high place in the ballots for backbench legislation, and must then get government support, either overt or covert, to get a bill through. Even then, more contentious bills are liable to be ambushed by only one or two opponents without proper debate about their merits.

Ideally, to discharge its law-making role, Parliament needs to obtain information and explanation from the government; to consider the merits of policy in the light of alternatives; to identify obscurities, ambiguities and other drafting problems; and the time and resources to necessary to fulfil these tasks. But governments of all colours are impatient and press large and ill-prepared bills through Parliament that require hundreds of last-minute amendments in the Lords that do not necessarily succeed in making them workable. Government MPs are expected to acquiesce, regardless of concerns they may have about particular pieces of legislation.

The standing committees that we criticise above are at the heart of the inability of the Commons to subject legislation to effective scrutiny. The whips control these ad-hoc bodies, which replicate the relative strengths of the parties in the Commons, throughout. The government whips generally choose MPs with no knowledge of the background to the draft bill they are supposed to examine and actively discourage them from participating in or even showing any interest in the proceedings. The point is to get the bill through as fast as possible. In return, opposition MPs try and drag the proceedings out to slow down the government's business. The net effect is first to duplicate the adversarial politics of the chamber; and secondly, to oblige the government to cut debate short, so large parts of a bill are not considered at all.

At first, there were signs that the Labour government recognised the fundamental weaknesses of legislative scrutiny in the Commons. The Modernisation Committee identified changes that could improve the process. First, government had to be sure it would get legislation through in reasonable time. Secondly, MPs should have a full opportunity to discuss and seek to amend key issues and to consider all parts of a bill. Later on the committee added a proviso that bills should be properly prepared in advance to avoid adding a mass of government amendments as they proceeded. A few reforms were introduced, such as the publication of a handful of bills in draft for pre-legislative scrutiny. Such reforms were useful, as far as they went. But the most useful – publishing bills in draft – has always been marginal and the practice is falling away (though the Prime Minister himself expressed surprise that this should be so before the Liaison Committee in July 2002; HC 1095). Further, the government is not above exercising influence over whether an existing select committee or a special ad-hoc committee considers a draft bill, or in seeking to co-opt the process of scrutiny. On the other hand, PASC and the Lords' Freedom of Information Committee gave the government a bloody nose over its draft FOI bill. Their analysis of its faults subsequently informed both Houses' deliberations on the bill, and flagged up concerns that the government later gave some ground on. However, Tony Wright, the PASC chairman, believes that the government has since been reluctant to subject other bills to pre-legislative scrutiny; and Blair informed the Liaison Committee that some bills like its anti-terrorism legislation were so pressing and important to the government that they could not go through a pre-legislative phase. Yet these bills are among those that require scrupulous scrutiny.

Programming bills
The government is now committed to 'programming', or time-tabling, legislation compulsorily. Since 1992, governments have negotiated the amount of time that should be given to their legislative programmes with opposition parties through 'the usual channels', i.e., the party whips. After a trial period, the Modernisation Committee decided in 2000 that certain bills should in the future be 'programmed', arguing that this process would benefit both the government (giving ministers the certainty of knowing when bills would be approved) and the opposition parties (giving them a recog-

nised role in deciding the structure and focus of debate) (Modernisation Committee 2000: para. 13). Opposition MPs on the committee objected strongly, largely because programming deprives them of their main weapon – pressure of time on the government. The trouble is that this weapon depends upon 'filibustering', or time-wasting, that itself cuts short debate on issues that require to be examined.

However, programming is simply 'guillotining' in another subtler guise. It does at least give advance notice, whereas the guillotine chops off debate without warning. But the ultimate effect is the same: both limit the time available for debate. In fact, the government still resorts to the guillotine anyway. Its impatience to get its legislation through by such means is alarming. Almost every government bill in the 2000-01 session was subject to a guillotine or programme motion – indeed, all programme motions were in effect guillotine motions, as none of them had cross-party support. The effect has been to restrict full scrutiny of the government's legislative proposals, which is particularly worrying since much of it is controversial. For example, the Criminal Justice and Police Bill in the 2000-01 session was twice programmed unilaterally by the government. When the guillotine fell on the Bill in committee, it had only reached clause 90 out of 132 (and some earlier clauses went unexamined) and amendments were yet to be discussed. The government sought to cover up the guillotine by introducing an emergency motion in March 2001 that required MPs to 'deem' that the standing committee had finished its scrutiny of the Bill when in fact the government had prevented it from doing so. Labour MPs voted the motion through.

Other legislative safeguards

One major advance in legislative scrutiny has been introduced by the Labour government. The Joint Committee on Human Rights, formed from both Houses, monitors every Bill passing through Parliament for compliance with the Human Rights Act 1998. This committee was set up with an expert adviser, Professor David Feldman, by the government (rather than a free-standing Human Rights Commission) to give early warning of Bills that might infringe the 1998 Act. It has published 22 reports in the 2001-02 session and has expressed concerns about Bills on hunting, the private security industry, regulatory reform, social security fraud, etc. Several of these reports have been very influential inside and outside Parliament, among them two reports on the Anti-Terrorism, Crime and Security Bill (Hugo Young in the *Guardian* spoke of their 'devastating sobriety'). In every case the committee specifies its human rights concerns and demands a substantive response from the government.

A Constitution Committee has also been set up in the Lords, as recommended by the Wakeham Commission on reform of the second House. The Committee, chaired by Lord Norton, the Tory peer and political scientist, has adopted scrutiny of Bills for their constitutional implications as part of its remit, but it looks as though it will concentrate more on investigating constitutional issues.

Delegated legislation

Parliament passes a mass of rules, order and regulations every year by means of statutory instruments. Most Acts of Parliament give ministers the power to make rules or regulations for their future operation and these are known as secondary, or delegated legislation. They have the same force of law as the parent Act. Most delegated legislation deals with detailed issues that make government workable and flexible. But some new rules or orders are controversial and even unconstitutional. The trouble is that Parliament can examine only a handful of the huge volume of statutory instruments (SIs) that pour out from

Whitehall – now about 3,000 a year. Roughly half of these are only important locally and simply become law on a specified date; of the others, some go before Parliament for information only; some (about 1,300) go through a 'negative' procedure and come into force on a specified date unless either House objects; and some require Parliament's approval before they become law.

A substantial amount of this law-making goes through Parliament with no or scarcely any scrutiny at all. A joint Commons/Lords committee checks that SIs conform to the powers set out in the original Act, but it does not examine their merits. Even so, ministers often ignore its conclusions. Most SIs that require express approval are debated in a standing Commons committee unless the government accepts that they should go to the full House. In 1998-99, 150 of 178 such 'affirmative' instruments were considered in committee, 21 were debated in the chamber and seven were withdrawn. Of 1,266 'negative' SIs in the same session, only 28 came before the committee and just one before the full House. Worse still, the committee itself has no power to object to a statutory instrument and may neither reject nor amend one. The House of Lords can reject SIs, but until February 2000 peers observed a convention that it would not do so. It then however rejected two orders governing the London mayoralty and assembly elections to mark its increased legitimacy under its half-reformed status. But peers will generally remain reluctant to use this power for fear of offending the executive. The Wakeham commission proposed that the Lords should possess only a power to delay an SI for three months, to give a government time to reflect.

There is one beacon of thorough investigation of the more alarming kinds of secondary regulation – the Delegated Powers and Regulatory Reform Committee in the Lords. Its main task is to identify Bills that give ministers too much delegated law-making powers or avoid adequate parliamentary scrutiny. This committee was formed in 1992 after law lords had expressed concern about ministers taking too much unchecked legislative power. Its watching brief catches both 'Henry VIII' clauses 'that enable ministers to amend or repeal primary legislation by orders rather than through Parliament'; and 'skeleton' Bills that leave full government policy to later SIs rather than setting it out for debate on the Bill. For example, the Pollution Prevention and Control Bill in 1998-99 would have given ministers almost unlimited powers to make policy on pollution control by regulations. But the signs are that both these executive excesses are on the wane. The committee has identified only four 'skeleton' Bills since 1992 that gave it concern.

The House of Lords
The removal of most hereditary peers since 1997 has given the Lords a greater legitimacy that has encouraged peers to be more assertive. Party loyalties exist and play a part in the Lords, but the second chamber is distinguished from the Commons first, by the absence of fiercely partisan party politics and strict party discipline; and secondly by the fact that no single party has a majority in the House. The Lords' role in legislative scrutiny is circumscribed by statute and convention. Under the Parliament Acts 1911 and 1949, the Lords cannot amend or delay a financial measure or 'money bill' beyond one month, and can only delay most other legislation by a year. Delay is not an insignificant weapon, since it often forces ministers to think again about their proposed measures. The Lords can veto bills that would extend the life of a Parliament, delegated legislation (see above) and private bills concerning local issues and construction projects. There is also a convention (the Salisbury convention) that the Lords do not reject bills that derive from manifesto commitments.

In practice, government has used and uses the Lords as a revising chamber in which its own amendments that cannot be introduced in the Commons are added in profusion to make bills workable (Shell 1993). However, the Lords is nowadays more likely to press its own amendments and to shake off its previous timidity. For example, in the 1999-2000 parliamentary session, the Lords inflicted 36 defeats on the government while considering 14 bills. Some of these defeats were high-profile. For example the Lords protected trial by jury by twice quashing the Criminal Justice (Mode of Trial) Bill that sought to restrict the right to jury trial in certain cases; the government is still considering how to proceed without being blocked again by the Lords. The Lords also stopped the repeal of 'Section 28', which supposedly prohibits the promotion of homosexuality in schools. The Lords also confronted the government over the sale of the National Air Traffic Services (NATS) and lowering the age of consent for homosexual sex (see further, Cowley and Stuart 2001).

There is a tendency to welcome the reinvigorated Lords' activity. But the fact is that the House as presently constituted is entirely illegitimate and unrepresentative, being unelected in the first place and biased in its composition. Democratic Audit analysis has shown that representatives of the private sector and professions far outnumber those from the public sector; and the privileged position of Church of England bishops and senior judges has attracted widespread criticism (Democratic Audit, 2002). The government's plans to continue its reform programme by creating a huge chamber of nominees have been blocked by the weight of parliamentary and popular hostility. But were the government to succeed in re-creating the Lords as a nominated chamber, it would be a wholly illegitimate body, able to exercise its own views and prejudices from within the legislature rather than representing the general public. Moreover, both the Wakeham report and government white paper assume that future members would not be properly paid but would continue to receive allowances only. This may well be suitable for a body consisting of comfortably-off individuals performing a part-time public service. But it assumes that such service would remain socially exclusive and would ensure that it did.

In part, the government's goal of a part-time nominated House of Lords is also framed to ensure that the political parties would for the foreseeable future be able between them to shape a second chamber that was sympathetic to the needs of the central executive of the day; and would never possess the legitimacy or powers necessary to make it an effective partner in Parliament's central tasks of making government accountable and subject to scrutiny.

7.6. How effective are Parliament's powers to subject European legislation and policies to scrutiny ?

The UK is bound by treaty to accept European Union laws that take direct effect and over-ride British law (which is therefore exposed to being declared incompatible with European law). The result is to create a problem of national parliamentary control, both directly over the flow of EU legislation, and indirectly, insofar as national legislation may end up by having different consequences to those originally intended by Parliament.

Parliament has, since 1972, placed an emphasis on the scrutiny of EU decisions before they are made. Proposals for EU legislation, common positions or joint actions and most other EU documents are forwarded to a European Scrutiny Committee chaired by an opposition MP. These documents must be accompanied by explanatory memoranda prepared by Whitehall. The Scrutiny Committee then decides whether the proposal is of sufficient 'political or legal' standing to be reported to the House, and whether it should be debated either in one of three standing committees on EU affairs or on the floor of the Commons itself. MPs in committee can question ministers in depth without prior notice of what they will ask. Debate in the chamber allows all MPs to participate, but it is only possible with the government's agreement. The government is expected to enter a 'scrutiny reserve and not to agree a proposal in the Council of Ministers' until the Commons scrutiny is completed; but it may make an agreement to avoid legal uncertainty or if it is in the 'national interest' to take advantage of an opportunity to reach quick agreement with partners. Under such circumstances, though, the government must explain itself to the committee.

This scrutiny procedure is comprehensive as it covers not only legislation and regulation, but also the Common Foreign and Security Policy and Justice and Home Affairs. The Commons can also pursue questions associated with monetary union in anticipation of possible UK membership of the single currency and react to European Parliamentary (EP) amendments. This is important, since scrutiny of initial proposals is inadequate where complex multi-stage bargaining between Commission, Council and European Parliament produces outcomes that drift significantly from early drafts.

But how much control does this wide procedure offer the House of Commons over EU decisions? Here it is useful to distinguish between decisions that can be changed neither by the Commons nor by the British government on its own, and those that can. These include the decision rules of the EU, the prescriptive nature of Union measures and the transparency of its procedures. Where decisions are subject to Westminster influence, we must assess the Commons' capacity to take on the workload of tracking another political arena, and the character of executive-legislature relations in the UK. We examine each of these in turn:

Decision rules employed at Union level

Unanimity continues to be used for most significant Union decisions, foreign and security policies, justice, home affairs, and new forms of macroeconomic co-ordination associated with Monetary Union. In such areas, it should in principle be possible for Parliament to hold the executive responsible for each EU decision as if it were its own action. But where Qualified Majority Voting (QMV) applies, a government may loyally reflect the concerns of its parliament only to find itself outvoted. Even so, the UK government only needs to gain backing from three other member states on the Council of Ministers to block a proposal (though it takes a much larger coalition to promote one). Thus the Commons has significant potential to exercise indirect leverage against a proposal, especially as the Council only resorts to formal votes where efforts to reach unanimous decisions have been exhausted (Hayes et al, 1997). How effectively does it exercise this leverage?

The capacity of the House of Commons

A 1999 report estimated that the European scrutiny committee considered about 1,350 documents in a year; reported fully on 450 it felt to be of political or legal importance; recommended about 60 documents for debate in European Standing Committees, and about a dozen for full Commons debate.

This is twice the load in the 1980s before the Single European Act and Single Market programme transformed the European community; and with the rising load, the scrutiny committee recommends proportionately fewer measures for further debate. But the constraints are not of time only. The EU is a highly specialised polity that tends to accumulate much technocratic expertise. Few MPs can afford to engage fully with such a process when British domestic politics is already a full-time occupation for them. On the other hand, fitful attention to Union matters affects the quality of MPs' interventions, especially in the ill-attended Commons debates that are dominated by MPs with views on European integration in general rather than on the legislation to be scrutinised (Giddings and Drewry, 1996).

The character of UK executive-legislature relations

The realities of single-party control of the Commons affect the operation of the scrutiny procedure. The bar on a British government from approving a measure still under scrutiny in the Council is a power of delay, and reflection, only. It does not stop the proposal from being carried by a vote of other members of the Council, nor does it prevent the government from using its Commons majority to unlock the scrutiny reserve. Even the 5 per cent of proposals that reach the final stage of scrutiny can be debated at short notice by a government that is determined to expedite its EU business. The party balance on the scrutiny committee and EU standing committees reflects the partisan balance of the House itself and is therefore open to government control. Under the current electoral system, the most propitious conditions for scrutiny are probably where a British government has a small majority and its European policy is contested by its own supporters. These conditions have only twice existed since Britain joined the EC (1974-79 and 1992-97).

Single-party majoritarianism further constrains the ability of the House of Commons to embrace other modes of parliamentary control available in other member states. The European Affairs Committee (EAC) of the Danish Folketing is the best known alternative approach. The Folketing mandates the position that its government takes in the Council of Ministers. Danish ministers must troop in front of the EAC weekly to explain the positions they intend to take on issues on the next week's Council agenda. The committee then announces the mandates it has given ministers to the media. If the government feels unable to keep to the mandate in subsequent negotiations, it must return to the committee for fresh instructions. In sum, the Folketing has a legislative partnership with its national government at every stage of Council decision-making, and not just a right of pre-legislative scrutiny (Arter 1996).

European integration has also reinforced executive domination, in large part because the Council automatically co-ordinates national governments at European level, while national parliaments have had little contact with one another. A twice-yearly Conference of the European Affairs Committees (COSAC) convenes representatives of both national parliaments and the European Parliament, but only handfuls of parliamentarians attend. Its ability to organise a common front between EU parliaments in the interests of strengthening control of their respective executives is limited by the diversity in executive-legislature relationships across the EU; and institutional jealousies and competitive jurisdictions between national parliaments and the European Parliament.

The EU and the devolved authorities

A more speculative question is what implications devolution should and will have for how the Westminster government represents 'British' society in the European arena. The Scottish and Northern Irish Assemblies are among 51 regional bodies in the EU whose legislative powers are at risk of being pre-empted in some areas of competence by national governments in the Council of Ministers. In other words, EU institutions could conceivably reverse decentralising tendencies within the UK, as the German Länder claim has tended to happen in Germany. On the other hand, devolved authorities within the UK are themselves able to mobilise and build alliances in the EU. It is also up to each member state to decide how to it is to going to be represented in the Council. No country is entitled to split its allocation of votes, but several member states allow regional bodies to attend, and sometimes even represent, their country in Council meetings.

Ratifying changes to EU Treaties
One view of the EU is that its powers are delegated to it by Treaties that cannot in the long run drift too far from an underlying consensus of democratic actors in member states. A functioning Union requires frequent changes to the Treaties. Four Treaty changes have been negotiated in quick succession since the mid-1980s: the Single European Act (1986), the Treaty on European Union Maastricht (1992), Amsterdam (1997), and Nice (2000). A fifth round is scheduled for 2004. Each Treaty change requires ratification either by a national parliament or public; and parliaments have learnt to link assent to increased rights of supervision of Union questions (Norton, 1996). In the past the UK has chosen to ratify all Treaty changes by Act of Parliament, though a referendum has been promised if the government proposes to enter the single currency.

Present arrangements for ratifying Treaty changes are open to criticism. First, there is little public debate at the agenda-setting stage of Treaty change. This is important, since packages of Treaty changes cannot be amended or accepted piecemeal. They constitute a 'take it or leave it' choice. The only opportunities for detailed influence are during negotiations or even earlier. Secondly, governments here anticipating domestic opinion when bargaining changes tend to consider the views only of elite actors within their own majority, and not voters.

Connecting with voters on EU issues
British citizens are doubly represented in the EU's political system, indirectly through the Council of Ministers, and directly through the European Parliament. These are interdependent and complementary pillars of representation. In a polity whose main business is the making of rules, rather than the redistribution of resources, most Union laws now require co-decision between the Council and European Parliament. This introduces a potential for more balanced representation in the Union. For while the UK's ten votes (out of 87) on the Council are exclusively exercised by the government of the day, the 87 (out of 626) seats assigned to the UK in the European Parliament are held by representatives of all parties, with a bias towards opposition parties (since European elections tend to register mid-term swings against governments). We deal with European elections in Section 5.4.

7.7 How rigorous are the procedures for parliamentary approval and supervision of taxation and public expenditure?

On the historic 'no taxation without representation' principle, Parliament formally holds the central role in approving taxation and public expenditure. In theory Parliament's powers extend to being able to refuse or reduce expenditure, though it cannot increase spending levels (outright refusal would of course bring down a government). In reality, Parliament has virtually no power to question the government's tax and spending plans. The government tightly controls the budgetary process to the extent that Parliament's role is reduced to one of passive acquiescence. In 1998, the Procedure Committee described the Commons' powers over expenditure as akin to a 'constitutional myth'.

The Chancellor announces the government's tax and expenditure plans in the annual budget statement to the Commons, it is debated for several days, and votes are taken on individual resolutions that approve changes to each tax or duty. The tax measures in the budget are then given permanent legal effect by the Finance Bill. The Finance Bill undergoes broadly the same parliamentary process as other bills, except that the Lords cannot amend it. Limits on the financial powers of the Lords have their basis in the ancient 'rights and privileges' of the House of Commons and are enshrined in the Parliament Acts 1911 and 1949.

The Labour government introduced a new framework for determining public spending in 1998 through three-year spending plans produced with departments under the Comprehensive Spending Review. So departmental funding is settled several years in advance, but still requires parliamentary authority annually through approval of the 'supply estimates'. Approval for additional expenditure through the year may be sought via 'supplementary estimates'. After debate, a series of Consolidated Funds Bills give the Treasury formal authority to release the funds. These bills are typically approved without a vote in the Commons. Proceedings in the Lords are also restricted in practice to formal approval.

In effect, parliamentary approval of tax and expenditure proposals is a ritual. Governmental control over the budgetary process is so strict that Parliament's role is limited to assent, not scrutiny. Neither the Commons nor its select committees have proved effective at subjecting departmental expenditure estimates to detailed examination, partly because the resources aren't there, partly because few MPs are interested in the fine detail. But the processes of approval marginalise scrutiny. Spending plans go to Parliament late in the process when all the negotiations between the Treasury and departments are over; the government, which after all controls the House, is not then willing to make changes. Just three days are allotted to debate on the supply estimates, but the debates focus on issues rather than figures. Departmental select committees are not required to look at the relevant estimates or departmental annual reports. In 1999 the government rejected out-of-hand a Procedure Committee proposal that they should be charged with the duty to report on estimates; and that the government should normally have to wait for a committee's report before the estimates could be voted on. However, under Robin Cook's reform proposals, financial scrutiny is to be one of the 'core tasks' for departmental select committees.

Scrutiny of public expenditure

Parliamentary auditing of past government expenditure is generally considered to be better. It is relatively well-resourced. The Comptroller and Auditor General (C&AG), the head of the National Audit Office, is an independent officer of the House of Commons. It is his duty to report to the House on the NAO's audits and investigations into the economy, efficiency and effectiveness with which government departments and other bodies use their resources. His reports go to the Public Accounts Committee, the most powerful and busiest select committee. The PAC in turn examines officials and then issues its own reports – about 50 a year. The NAO's independence from the executive, won in

1983, is crucial (though there is valuable collusion between the Treasury and the NAO). Through the C&AG, the NAO officers possess statutory rights of access to all relevant official documents and powers to compel officials to provide information. The NAO is debarred from examining or questioning a department's policies, but has recently flowered, concluding hard-hitting analyses for example of the Millennium Dome and Passport Agency fiascos. The NAO estimates that it saved the government about £1.3 billion between 1997 and 2000. Its partnership with the PAC works well and the government adopts practically all the PAC's recommendations (387 in 1999-2000).

Nonetheless, the ban on investigating policy (which extends to the PAC) is a serious weakness. The NAO must discuss and agree its reports with the department concerned before they go to the PAC and they are often watered-down. Further, the basic principle of effective audit – and the goal of the 1983 Act that freed the NAO from the executive – that Parliament should be able to chase public money wherever it goes is not fully observed. A third of executive quangos and many other public bodies are outside its remit. They are often monitored by auditors who report instead to ministers. For example, the Environment Agency and English Heritage are two weighty quangos that have so far escaped parliamentary audit. Responsibility for public audit is also split. The Audit Commission audits the police, local authority, NHS and other local bodies; but professional as it is, the commission is itself a quango and may (as a select committee recently warned) be vulnerable to executive pressure.

The overall principle that Parliament should have the right to follow public money wherever it goes also applies to private bodies receiving public money for public functions and services. But the way is far from clear. For example, the Sharman inquiry into public audit found that the then DETR blocked the NAO's right of access to the books of registered social landlords on the grounds that they were regulated by the Housing Corporation, one of the DETR's executive quangos. Instead the department insisted that NAO access must be governed by informal agreement; access to one social landlord took six months to negotiate (Sharman 2001). The Sharman report proposed that in future all quangos should be audited by the NAO on behalf of Parliament. Sharman also suggested that the NAO should strengthen the ability of select committees to scrutinise their departments' accounts and supply estimates by giving them annual financial briefings.

7.8 How comprehensive and effective is legislation giving citizens the right of access to government information?

Access to official information is a potentially powerful instrument for accountability, obtaining redress and influencing policy, both for Parliament and the people. Sir Richard Scott in 1996 made statutory access to official information (FOI) a central recommendation in his report on arms exports to Iraq with the purpose of improving executive accountability to Parliament; and in the same year Tony Blair himself recognised its significance, saying that Labour wanted to end government's 'obsessive and unnecessary secrecy':

> Information is power and any government's attitude about sharing information with the people actually says a great deal about how it views power itself and . . . the relationship between itself and the people . . . The crucial point is, does the government regard

people's involvement in politics as being restricted to periodic elections? Or does it regard itself as in some sense in a genuine partnership with people?

The Freedom of Information Act 2000 makes it clear where his government stands. The long-delayed Act, which need not come into force until 2005, introduced a statutory right to information for the first time, but it is a moot point whether it is more or less liberal than John Major's code of practice for access to government information which was in force in 1996 (and still is). The Act creates a statutory right of access, but also sets strict limits on access: 23 clauses in the Act specify 36 separate exceptions to disclosure, some more stringent (or 'absolute') than others. Other Acts, such as the Data Protection Act 1998, and more than 300 other Acts, orders and statutory instruments prohibit disclosure. All in all, ministers and officials retain hundreds of reasons to keep official information secret.

The FOI Act's birth was long-drawn out and painful. In 1997, David Clark, then at the Cabinet Office, published relatively liberal proposals in a white paper that were as short-lived as his ministerial career. The then Home Secretary Jack Straw took over responsibility at the Home Office and he and his officials published a draft FOI Bill in 1999 that was markedly more illiberal and defensive in character. Straw was obliged to abandon a few of the most restrictive provisions, but its main bones survived a highly critical passage through Parliament to become law in 2000.

Restricting access to information

The Act's 36 exemptions may be categorised as follows:

- they either apply to a whole class of information, or are subject to a 'prejudice test'. The prejudice test requires government and public bodies to assess whether disclosure would prejudice the interest or activities to which the exemption applied: e.g., would disclosure of commercial information (which falls under a prejudice-based exemption) prejudice the commercial interests of the private or public body involved?. Officials can keep secret any documents in the 'catch-all' class categories without having to discriminate or formally to consider whether disclosure would prejudice a particular interest or activity; and;
- the exemptions may be 'absolute' or subject to a public interest test. With 'absolute' exemptions, the authorities are under no duty to consider whether disclosure of official information would be in the wider public interest than secrecy or not. In other cases, class-based or prejudice-based, an authority must consider whether the exemption should stand or information should be disclosed in the public interest. 'Absolute' exemptions are specified in the Act; are always class-based as well; and no prejudice test applies to them.

Thus, there are in all three types of exemptions:

i.   ten class-based and absolute exemptions ('absolute class exemption');
ii. 15 class-based exemptions subject to public interest test ('qualified class exemption'); and
iii. 11 exemptions subject to prejudice and public interest tests ('prejudice-based exemption').

It is of course ministers and officials who classify the information and apply prejudice and harm tests.

The Act therefore creates the new post of Information Commissioner who can re-consider the executive views of what exemptions apply to information and whether they have applied tests properly and rightly withheld information. The Commissioner can even challenge decisions to place information in an absolute category. Either the person who wants the information or the public authority refusing it may appeal to the Information Tribunal (and on into the courts) against the Commissioner's decisions. (Most nations' FOI laws typically only give the applicant a right of appeal.) But the public authority can also trump any Commissioner decision that information should be released by way of a signed certificate from an 'accountable person' – e.g., a cabinet minister – that prevents the decision from taking effect. This executive veto may be subject to judicial review.

Table 2 attempts to supply an Ariadne's thread through this maze of complex procedure:

2. Categories of information that may be kept secret

Source: adapted from information supplied by the Campaign for Freedom of Information

Categories of information that may be withheld	Process for refusal or disclosure	Types of activity protected from disclosure	Role of the Information Commissioner	Can a cabinet minister reverse the Commissioner's decision?
Absolute class (10 exemptions)	The whole class of information is kept secret. Documents are not considered separately. No prejudice test; no public interest test.	The security services (MI5, MI6, the SAS, special branch, etc). Court and tribunal business. Breach of confidence Personal information	The Information Commissioner (IC) may on appeal review the public authority's decision that the information requested is covered by the blanket exemptions in this category.	Usually no need. But *yes* if the Commissioner rules that information is wrongly classified.
Qualified class (15)	The whole class of information is kept secret. No prejudice test. But the test of public interest applies. Information may be disclosed if in an official's view the public interest in disclosure is greater than the public interest in withholding the information	All material relating to government policy making, including officials' advice to Ministers and connected factual information. Ministers' communications. Official investigations The conduct of 'public affairs'. Trade secrets. Legal & professional privilege.	The IC can (i) assess that the blanket exemption applies to information requested; and (ii) the official view of where the public interest lies and reverse or uphold the official decision.	*Yes* (in both cases)
Prejudice-based (11)	Both the prejudice and public interest tests apply. First, officials will release information unless they decide that its release would 'prejudice' the public activity involved. The public interest test then applies (see above).	Defence. International relations. Economic affairs. Law enforcement. Commercial interests	The IC can assess (i) whether one of the 11 exemptions really applies; (ii) the official view of the prejudice likely to be caused; and (iii) where the public interest lies. In each case the IC can reverse or uphold the official decision.	*Yes* (in all three cases)

Flaws in the FOI regime

The Freedom of Information Act contains fundamental flaws, many of which the government explicitly refused to get rid of during the Act's passage. These flaws include:

● the Act has no clear purpose clause signifying the government's intention to be as open and accessible as possible; this omission leaves it unclear how the public interest in disclosure is to be determined

- the test of prejudice is notably weak by international and even UK standards
- 25 'catch-all' class exemptions apply – almost half of which are 'absolute' in the sense that officials are not required to consider tests of harm or public interest
- absolute exemptions build a firewall around the activities of the security services (which may be breached when it suits officialdom)
- all official investigations, including those by the police and safety authorities, are protected from disclosure; class protection even applies to investigations that have ended
- virtually all policy-making information and material feeding into the policy process are kept secret, except statistical information
- the executive is the sole determinant of which disclosures would prejudice policy making interests
- a minister's or official's opinion as to what causes prejudice to policy making interests is given legal weight
- private firms that have dealings with government or perform public services can usually rely on such dealings being kept strictly confidential, either on a 'qualified class' or 'prejudice-based' basis;
- the government can refuse to disclose whether certain information exists
- the executive can exercise a veto over decisions by the independent Information Commissioner that the public interest requires disclosure.

There are a number of recent high profile cases of non-disclosure of information which would still be valid under the new Act. These include failings in the police investigation into the Stephen Lawrence murder; police refusal to release full information about the circumstances leading to the death of Roger Sylvester in police custody; government suppression of information during the BSE crisis and the arms to Iraq affair; Foreign Office refusal to disclose information about its advice on the Ilusu dam project in Turkey; and many more.

The protection of executive interests under the FOI Act contrasts markedly with the equivalent US FOI regime.[1] In the USA exemptions from disclosure are permissive rather than mandatory, and are subject to a justiciable test of harm on a case by case basis. British journalists have long exploited the USA's greater openness to extract documents relevant to the UK which would be withheld by their own government departments, including documents relating to company malpractice, purchase of military equipment, drug enforcement, and so on. The long list of class exemptions from disclosure in the UK's FOI also contrasts markedly with the much more limited exemptions proposed in Scottish draft legislation and legislation already in force in the Irish Republic.

The secrecy net over government policy

The secrecy net cast over all aspects of policy-making is far more restrictive than the 1994 openness code introduced by John Major. The code requires information on policy discussions to be disclosed unless this would 'harm the frankness and candour of internal discussion' – i.e., the code requires harm to be shown before information is kept secret. But there is hard evidence that disproves the FOI Act's a priori assumption that disclosure of policy deliberations is harmful. In Wales cabinet minutes are published without damaging the devolved administration's work; the Bank of England publishes minutes of its Monetary Policy Committee meetings to reinforce business and public confidence in its decisions. The scope of secrecy about the government's policies is wide, undesirable and harmful to its interest as well as to the public interest. And once government information is withheld, most of it goes into the shredder; the small quantity of information that survives goes into the archives and will not necessarily be released for 30 years or more (if then).

7.9 How independent is public information about government policies and actions and their effects from the government's own information machine?

More information, both in print and electronic form, about the government's policies and actions is available to the public than ever before. There is almost an official information glut. But there are severe limits on what information may be divulged (see above). The rules both of the current code and 2000 Act give ministers strict control over information about government policies and actions – not simply control of what is suppressed, but also over the content and manner in which policy information is released. In other words, they are free to promote their policies safe in the knowledge that MPs, the public and media are denied access to information that could put their policies in perspective.

There is no recognition in government of the principled need for information that is impartial in respect of a government's policies and actions. Thus the current government has rolled up presentation and policymaking into the same process and the information released is designed to justify and promote government policies. The only boundary drawn is a purely party political one, and even that is continually breached and compromised; no effective sanctions exist to prevent or punish such breaches.

The chief channel of daily information about government activities for the media is the Government Information Service (GIS), with information officers in all departments. This service has traditionally been confined by constitutional convention to a neutral and objective presentation of the government's business; as civil servants, information officers are supposed to be non–party political. In 1953, Viscount Swinton, the Conservative minister responsible, set out the classical definition of the GIS's role: that its duty was to give

> prompt and accurate information and give it objectively about government action and government policy. It is quite definitely not the job of the GIS to try to boost the government or try to persuade the press to.

The fact is that the GIS, the government's information machine, has never (at least in our time) been entirely neutral. But its work was progressively compromised in the 1980s under Mrs Thatcher and her press secretary Bernard Ingham; and has been further politicised under the Labour government since 1997 (see Jones, 1999 and 2001). The Labour government has also centralised the government's information and marketing service under Alastair Campbell, Blair's press secretary and a political appointee; and ministers have appointed as special advisers 'spin doctors' who often present unabashedly partisan information to the media. The dangers of centralising official information-giving have long been recognised. In 1952, when Lord Swinton urged Winston Churchill to re-establish a press office at 10 Downing Street, he conceded that 'a centralised information agency of this character might, in the hands of an unscrupulous extremist government, prove both a powerful and dangerous weapon of propaganda' (Harris, 1994).

Campbell became Director of Communications and Strategy in Whitehall in 2001. He remains the Prime Minister's chief spokesman, but he also controls the Government Information Service (GIS) in Whitehall, three 10 Downing Street departments (the press office; the strategic communications unit; and the research and information unit), and even the Central Office of Information. He is the government's unacknowledged Minister of Information. He has direct authority over the whole of government's information machine from 10 Downing Street, with official license as an unelected party political adviser to present the government's affairs 'in a political context' and to give orders to civil servants.

Under Campbell's guidance, Blair and ministers have imposed a 'hard-sell' ideology on the Government Information Service. Within a year ministers had eased out nine of the 17 departmental heads of information and directors of communications; a year later all but two had either been removed or had left government. Campbell also persuaded Sir Robin Mountfield, then permanent secretary in the Office of Public Service, to re-write the rule book for government information officers in November 1997 and endorse Campbell's New Labour strategy. The Mountfield reforms also gave ministers' spin doctors more influence over the flow of information from their departments. The deeper significance of Jo Moore's activities at the former DTLR was that she was in a position to advise GIS officials to 'bury' bad news on 11 September 2001 in the first place. She had also previously instructed them to brief against Bob Kiley, London's transport commissioner (see also Section 10.2). She of course exceeded her authority and provoked a rebellion among the DTLR's information officers, but other special advisers do so without suffering the same fate.

Campbell consolidated New Labour's grasp of the GIS through his influence over recruitment to the higher posts. Career civil servants were repeatedly passed over as senior positions went to journalists and external media professionals, seven of them at least from newspapers and broadcasting organisations with known sympathies for the Blair administration. Three senior posts went to former Labour Party press officers; two to journalists from Campbell's former newspaper, the *Daily Mirror*. Of course, the formal rules for such appointments continued to apply. But they were not proof against the determination of Campbell and his master, Tony Blair, to recruit like-minded and sympathetic media professionals (see Jones and Weir, *New Statesman*, 25 September 2002).

At first, the Cabinet Office lied about how many special advisers were spin doctors. In evidence to PASC in June 1998, Campbell said, 'The vast majority [of special advisers] do not have any contact with the press whatever'. In December 2001, the Cabinet Office told PASC that only eleven of the 81 special advisers in Whitehall were 'employed primarily in the area of communications'. But only after the *New Statesman* article by Nicholas Jones and Stuart Weir had identified at least 37 special advisers throughout Whitehall – ironically eleven of them in Downing Street alone – who were either primarily employed to promote the image of the government and their minister in the media, or anyway did so, the government was obliged to admit that some half of special advisers performed media roles (see PASC 2002a; and section 10.2).

We discuss the aggressively partisan approach that Campbell adopted towards the media in Section 10.4. Here we draw attention to the fact that an unashamedly party political special adviser, accountable only to the Prime Minister, has the power to re-shape and direct the traditionally impartial Government Information Service and all government marketing and advertising activities? And that special advisers were able from within Whitehall to practice the 'black arts' of New Labour spin – 'the flying of kites, the softening up of victims, the bouncing of colleagues, the massaging of expectations' (Rawnsley 2000).

What baffles many observers is that Sir Richard Wilson, the Cabinet Secretary, seemed powerless to stop the process of politicisation; and, indeed, that he and other senior bureaucrats often seemed to collude at least in obscuring the spread of spin throughout government. The roots of official weakness lie in the long-established tradition of secrecy that has long given the senior bureaucracy and ministers monopoly control over government information and thus the power to manage its release. Thus, for senior bureaucrats like Wilson and Mountfield, the Campbell revolution was not unwelcome insofar as it 'raised the game' of the official information service. Effective presentation of the government's business benefits the civil service as well as their party masters. Spin relies on restricting independent access to official information. The lies and half-truths of the government's *shlok* troops are to be protected by an FOI Act that limits access to information on government policies and commercial dealings for a generation or more.

Campbell derides the constitutional issues that his presence, powers and conduct, the swarm of spin doctors throughout Whitehall and the infiltration of the GIS undoubtedly raise as unworldly concerns with mere 'process'. He argues forcibly that it is government policies that have substance in the real world; and that his task is simply to ensure that those policies are presented to the public undistorted by spin from the media. But 'process' is the very substance of democracy and the rule of law in this country. In the absence of a written constitution, proper process and procedures matters even more – 'they are all the poor Englishman has,' as a former mandarin once said. They are in fact all we have to protect us from arbitrary and deceitful rule.

There are signs of a change of heart. Ministers have expressed regret at the excesses of spin since 1997. Tony Blair has embarked on a programme of regular and open press conferences and scrutiny meetings with the Liaison Committee in the House of Commons. But the structures of control and manipulation remain in place; and there is no effective mechanism to prevent their abuse now or under a later government. This is yet another worrying aspect of the unruled informality of government at the centre.

---

1   We do not attempt here a 'democratic audit' of the European Union's constitutional structures, accountability and transparency. An EU Constitutional Convention opened in February 2002 and is due to report next spring. This Constitutional Convention is partially open to European civil society and offers an opportunity to improve the EU's democratic workings.

2   We have carried out a detailed comparison of the UK Act and law and practice in the USA, which will shortly be placed on the Democratic Audit website.

Eight: civil control of the military and police

The force with us

Are the military and police under civil control?

The insidious process of military indoctrination, a deadly mixture of pomp and secrecy to which most politicians involved in defence are susceptible, tend to blunt one's normal sensitivity. One can easily become a part of the very military machine that one is supposed to control.
Lord Owen, formerly a Labour naval minister, 1972

The first duties of the state are to defend the realm against foreign aggression and other external dangers, and to maintain law and order within its boundaries, so that citizens are protected as far as possible against physical dangers and criminal activities. The United Kingdom must therefore maintain armed forces to deter potential enemies and organised terrorism from abroad; security and intelligence agencies to keep watch over and counter potential aggressors, terrorists, criminals and other threats, from outside and within its territories; and police forces to maintain order and investigate crimes. These coercive forces and agencies are vital to the well-being of the country and its inhabitants. But it is equally vital to democracy that they should be kept under strict civil control and surveillance to ensure that they do not take charge of the state, as the military and police do either openly or covertly in many states; that the security forces should be kept under democratic scrutiny; and that the police should be open and accountable to their local communities. They must also be as representative as possible of all sections of society: first, to ensure that they bed well down into society and are capable of understanding the differing needs and customs of its differing sections; and secondly, to prevent any one section of society from dominating the force in question and thus possibly the nation or locality.

8.1 How effective is civil control over the armed forces, and how free is political life from military involvement?

In general, the military are under formal parliamentary control and political life is wholly free of direct military involvement. However, in practice, it is the executive that runs the military through its command of Parliament (see Section 7); and the executive generally confines their role in Great Britain to preserving essential public services (e.g., during industrial disputes) and intervening in national emergencies (e.g. culling sheep and cattle during the 2001 foot-and-mouth epidemic), though they have been mobilised in Northern Ireland to keep order in and for counter-insurgency operations, as well as in specific crises (e.g., the Libyan embassy siege).

This is not to say that Parliament is powerless. Article VI of the Bill of Rights 1689 states:

> That the raising or keeping of a standing army within the kingdom in time of peace unless it be with the consent of Parliament is against the law.

To satisfy this rule, Parliament must continually give authority for the existence of the armed forces in times of peace. It does so each spring by approving defence expenditure in the form of Defence Votes. Parliament must also regularly renew the three service discipline acts: the Army Act 1955, the Air Force Act 1955 and the Naval Discipline Act 1957. These acts are renewable annually by orders in council for a maximum of five years; and every five years Parliament must pass primary legislation re-enacting them. The most recent Armed Service Bill was passed in 2001. The bill goes to a specially-constituted select committee, which acts as a standing committee with the ability to take evidence and make visits (Armed Forces Bill Committee 2001: para. 1).

The five-yearly renewal of the service discipline acts gives the government and Parliament the chance to review military law at regular intervals. At times this has proved controversial (as with the government's increase in the scope and powers of the Ministry of Defence Police in 2002; see 8.2). In addition, Armed Forces Bill select committees have often taken advantage of the procedure to consider broader issues than those raised in the bills before them. For example, the 1996 Committee investigated the issue of racial discrimination in the armed forces. Of course, the government (or Parliament) has the ability to amend legislation governing the armed forces at any time, and did so in 2000 with the Armed Forces Discipline Act which reformed military discipline to comply with the European Convention on Human Rights after an adverse finding in the European Court.

Generally, Britain's armed forces take pride in a tradition of keeping out of political controversy, and observe a formal deference to their political masters. Senior military officers, notably the heads of the three branches of the armed forces and the chiefs of defence staff, are politically neutral, like senior civil servants. However, in no way are they political eunuchs; they are acutely aware of current political sensitivities and controversies. The Chiefs of Staff Committee regularly draws up reports for cabinet ministers. The Chief of the Defence Staff attends cabinet committee meetings, particularly during crises involving the armed forces. General Sir Charles Guthrie, then chief of the defence staff, developed a close relationship with an inexperienced prime minister, Tony Blair, during a series of controversial military interventions – the bombing of Iraq in operation Desert Fox in December 1998, the 1999 Kosovo war, and the British military presence in Sierra Leone in 2000.

By convention, the heads of the three armed forces and the chief of defence staff have the right of direct access to the prime minister. They frequently let it be known when they deploy this right, usually when they are seeking to curb budget cuts or demanding budget increases, through leaks to the media. Indeed, judicious leaking is a powerful political weapon in the armoury of the chiefs of the three armed forces branches (who at times have also leaked against each other).

In 1980, General Sir Edwin Bramall, now a field marshal and peer, then head of the army, gave a seminal lecture to the Royal Society of Arts in London on the armed forces' role in keeping order. They would only play such a role, he said, if disorder was on such a scale that the police could not cope and parliamentary government was threatened, or if 'a minority, by violent means and armed force, was attempting to challenge the very authority of government with a view to changing or overthrowing it'. The armed forces have been involved in civilian life, through intervening in industrial disputes, combating terrorism and keeping public order (particularly in Northern Ireland). Among the formally established schemes for their intervention are:

- *Military Aid to the Civil Community* allows the armed forces to intervene without ministerial approval – for example, when lives are at risk. Soldiers helped during the floods in 2000, in boating accidents and other rescue operations. The military receive up to 100 such requests a year.
- *Military Aid to Other Government Departments* usually takes place during industrial disputes, often when the emergency services are on strike (e.g., during the fire service strikes in Essex in 1977-78 and in Merseyside in 2001, soldiers and airmen drove 'green goddesses' – service fire engines). Some 2,000 service personnel were trained to drive fuel tankers following the picketing of petrol terminals in 2000. The army was brought in to cope with the foot and mouth outbreaks in 2001.
- *Counter Drugs Operations* can involve the forces, notably the navy in the Caribbean.
- *Military Aid to the Civil Power* covers assisting police during party conferences, for example, but has been used to justify political intervention by the forces (e.g., during the 1926 general strike). It forms the basis for the army's intervention in Northern Ireland.

Northern Ireland

The army's role in Northern Ireland has been fraught with controversy. The Ministry of Defence was reluctant to send troops when ordered to do so by the Labour government at the start of 'The Troubles' in 1969. The government was deeply critical of the 'B-Specials' of the Protestant-dominated Royal Ulster Constabulary and believed that the army would provide a neutral barrier between the two communities. Indeed, the Catholic community initially welcomed British troops. However, the polarised politics and escalating violence soon transformed the troops into an army of occupation in some districts, directly combating the IRA, keeping public order, mounting check points, surveillance and secret operations, armed patrols and house searches; and led to the killings of civilians on Bloody Sunday on 30 January 1972, and internal guerrilla warfare. For many republicans and nationalists, the British authorities and soldiers seemed to act as if this were a colonial dispute, and too often with a casual brutality (Clarke, 1983).

Soldiers are in principle bound by the same broad rules governing the use of force as the police and civilians. The army manual, *Counter-Revolutionary Operations*, states that: 'A person, whether soldier or civilian, may lawfully use such force as is reasonable in the circumstances in the prevention of crime and in making lawful arrests'. Soldiers in Northern Ireland are issued with Yellow Cards emphasising that firearms 'must only be used as a last resort'. Soldiers are told to challenge somebody unless doing so would increase the risk of death or grave injury to the soldier or another person. Opening fire is allowed only if someone 'is committing or about to commit an act likely to endanger life and there is no other way to prevent the danger'. The notion of minimum force also applies to the police.

These rules did not offer sufficient protection to civilians under the exigencies of the Northern Ireland conflict. British soldiers were involved in several incidents when unarmed and innocent civilians were shot and killed; and a 'shoot-to-kill' policy (i.e., deliberately killing suspects rather than arresting them) was adopted (though the UK authorities deny this). The courts and authorities took an indulgent view of the legality of such fatal shootings. But the 1996 Audit volume found that the test of 'reasonableness' in the British courts fell short of the European Convention's requirement that the use of force was permissible only if 'absolutely necessary' – a distinction that was critical in the European Court's ruling that the killing of three unarmed IRA members by the SAS in March 1988 in Gibraltar violated their right to life (see 3.1; and Klug et al, 1996). The Human Rights Act ought now to remedy the weaknesses in the British position.

Northern Ireland became a testing ground for what Brigadier Frank Kitson, a senior army commander there, called 'low intensity operations', i.e., urban warfare and counter-terrorist activities (Kitson 1971). The government introduced a policy of 'police primacy', but the army soon became involved in undercover special operations, recruiting informers and colluding with loyalist paramilitary groups. An inquiry under Sir John Stevens, later appointed Metropolitan Police Commissioner, is, as we write, still gathering evidence to examine how far the security and other military forces, including the SAS and a covert unit given the euphemistic name of the Force Research Unit, were out of control; and into claims of collusion with the loyalist terrorist group, the Ulster Defence Association, over murders of IRA personnel and others, like the human rights lawyer, Pat Finucane, in 1989 (see Section 8.4 below; and also Section 2.6).

The Ministry of Defence did not tell the police about the covert army operations, let alone ministers. Military commanders and senior police officers exercise operational freedom. The prime minister's approval is supposed to be required before an operation is conducted – for example, the SAS surveillance and shooting down of the three unarmed IRA members in Gibraltar or the mission to rescue British army hostages in Sierra Leone in 2000 – but the way operations are conducted is up to those involved on the spot.

8.2   How publicly accountable are the police and security services for their activities?

Police accountability

The police exercise powers – including the use of 'legitimate force' – which profoundly affect the lives of all citizens and can lead to their incarceration, injury or death. The police possess these powers to enforce the laws of the state and to secure its internal security. The police must be accountable for the exercise of their unique powers, yet how? It is argued both that the police should be subject to political control and that they should not be. At the level of individual policing decisions, the principle of independence from political involvement is clearly right, but the role and performance of the police service as a whole – and of individual forces – must be subject to political scrutiny and decision.

At heart, policing bears on the regulation of social conduct and conflicts and of individual people's lives on critical matters involving their liberty and protection – and hence is profoundly political, with all that involves in establishing and choosing the laws that they enforce, their discretion in enforcing those laws, the policies they adopt and determining how they should be made accountable. The problem in the UK is the dominance of the political executive over the representative process and the absence of adequate checks and balances over its policies. But effective accountability is vital for several reasons:

- to engender public confidence in the police service; it is increasingly recognised that effective policing depends on community trust and cooperation;
- To provide against abuse by police forces now more powerful than ever through the additional powers that bear upon the privacy of individuals and organisations under the Terrorism Act 2000, the Criminal Justice and Police Act 2001 and the Anti-Terrorism, Crime and Security Act 2001 (see Section 3); and
- to restore confidence among ethnic minority communities. The findings of the Macpherson inquiry into the death of black teenager Stephen Lawrence indicate that the police service cannot assure ethnic minority communities that it is accountable and responsive to their needs.

The Freedom of Information Act is unlikely to promote greater police accountability, since sensitive information held by the police is protected from disclosure under the Act; information relating to investigations can be withheld even if its release would not prejudice legal proceedings (see section 7.8).

The formal structure for police accountability involves three main parties: chief constables, police authorities and the Home Secretary. This tripartite structure of governance and accountability was first set out in 1964 and was recently consolidated in the Police Act 1996. Accountability to the local community has been an important tenet of police governance from the origin of locally-based police forces in the nineteenth century – the idea being that local accountability prevents the emergence of a national police force under central direction. But policing has steadily become more centrally regulated and standardised and a Home Secretary exercises strong control over police finances, policies and ultimately discipline (as David Blunkett demonstrated when he insisted on the sacking of the chief constable of Sussex in 2001).

Yet police authorities remain the nominal focus of accountability for all police forces (including the Metropolitan Police who are now responsible to a Metropolitan Police Authority). Chief constables, who are in charge of the 44 local forces in the UK, are accountable to these authorities; and they in turn are charged with the responsibility for securing the maintenance of an efficient and effective police force in their area. The chief constable must have regard to the local policing plan, developed by the police authority, which contains national and local policing objectives and performance targets. Yet chief constables retain significant operational autonomy, can establish their own policies, and can and do defy the wishes of their police authorities. The courts have upheld the operational independence of chief constables and their discretionary powers to decide how to carry out individual operations. In 1968, Lord Denning laid down the prevailing view:

> No Minister of the Crown can tell him [a chief constable] that he must or must not keep observation on this place or that; or that he must or must not prosecute this man or that one. Nor can any Police Authority tell him so. The responsibility of law enforcement lies on him. He is answerable to the law alone (R v Commissioner of Police *ex parte* Blackburn; see Oliver 1997).

However, police authorities are supposed to hold their chief constables to account for the performance of local police forces through policing plans and their annual report on policing in their area. They appoint the chief constable for their area and can also require the chief constable to retire 'in the interests of efficiency or effectiveness'; the exercise of both powers, however, is subject to the Home Secretary's approval. The chief constable is required to report annually to his or her police authority and the authority can demand additional reports on any policing matter in the area. However, the chief constable can object to a specific demand on the grounds that it is not in the public interest.

Police authorities are in fact the weakest link in the tripartite structure. The Home Secretary has much greater influence over the operation of individual police forces. Continuing reforms from 1994 to the Police Reform Act 2002 have changed the structure of control from one of partnership to the Home Secretary's dominance over policing in England and Wales. The once independent police services, chief constables and police authorities of the past are now largely subordinate to the political executive (see Oliver 1997). The Home Secretary

- now issues a statutory National Policing Plan setting out strategic policing plans for England and Wales for the next three years and requires police authorities to issues their own three-year plans under his guidance;
- decides police objectives and performance targets, circulars and guidance and so sets the operational framework for all police forces;
- has powers to issue codes of practice for chief officers;
- may direct HM Inspectorate of Constabulary to inspect any police force, police division or unit (the NI Secretary has similar powers in Northern Ireland) and may order forces found to be ineffective or inefficient to adopt reforms of his choosing, or he may demand a remedial 'action plan' from the force;
- decides the overall financial settlement for policing every year, and the level of grant to each individual police authority; and
- may specify what equipment – vehicles, IT systems, batons, incapacitant sprays, etc – police forces should use.

The police should be accountable on three levels: for overall national policy, for appropriate regional policies, and for the actions of individual officers. Hopefully the 2002 reforms of the complaints commission will tackle the last of these. But David Blunkett is taking unprecedented powers over policing in the 2002 Act and his plans create an imbalance in police accountability towards the centre at the expense of local control. The structures of policing did and do require reform – but rather to reduce the power and influence of government and to increase that of local communities. As John Wadham, of Liberty, argued when the Police Reform Bill was published, 'Local policing and local accountability are precious constitutional safeguards' (*Daily Telegraph*, 2 March 2002).

Police authorities

Police authorities are appointed, not elected, bodies. Prior to 1994, two-thirds of police authority members had at least to be elected councillors for the areas covered by the relevant police force, while the remaining third were magistrates. This set-up was supposed to reflect the desire for local democratic legitimacy in the accountability arrangements for local forces. Since 1994, most police authorities now have 17 members: nine are councillors; three are magistrates; and five 'independent' members (as they are called in the Police Act) are appointed by a three-member selection panel. The Home Secretary (usually through Home Office officials) appoints one panel member; there is a representative of police authorities; and these two panel members then have an equal share in appointing the third member. The panel then submits nominations for 'independent' authority members from which the Home Secretary draws up shortlists for each area. In other words, the Home Secretary now has a significant say in the composition of all police authorities.

The new Metropolitan Police Authority consists of a mix of elected representatives, magistrates and independent members, though it has 23 members to reflect the task of overseeing the biggest police force in the country. The 12 elected members of the MPA are chosen by the London mayor from those elected to the London Assembly, and must include the deputy mayor.

Meanwhile, under the Anti-Terrorism, Crime and Security Act 2001, the Ministry of Defence Police (known in some circles as ModPlod) now has the same powers as other police forces to act outside the military bases they guard. There are roughly 3,700 MOD police officers, making it around the tenth largest police force in the country. The MOD Police is a Ministry of Defence agency answerable only to the Defence Secretary (with day-to-day responsibility delegated to a senior MOD official). Thus it lacks local accountability to the communities in which it can now be deployed.

Police complaints

How people's complaints about the way the police behave are dealt with is an important aspect of their accountability. Complaints procedures should deliver effective and fast remedies to citizens whom the police have ill-treated or failed; and should be monitored to ensure that failures or ill-treatment are not repeated. Yet the police complaints system in Britain has for many years been dogged by concerns about its perceived lack of openness and independence ('the police investigate their own,' it is said). In December 2000, the government announced plans to overhaul the current system and to inject more independence into complaints investigations.

In England and Wales, the police investigate most complaints themselves under the oversight of the Police Complaints Authority (PCA). The Authority conducts very few independent investigations directly and instead supervises investigation of the most serious complaints against the police. A chief constable who receives a complaint must decide whether to resolve it informally, start an investigation or refer it to the PCA. In serious cases, e.g., if it is claimed that a police officer's conduct has led to death or serious injury, the chief constable must refer a complaint to the PCA. The PCA may also decide to 'call in' a complaint that has not been referred to them. Most complaints are investigated by police within the force concerned, but for serious complaints an investigating officer is drafted in from another police force and is likely to be independently supervised by the PCA. In 2000–01, the PCA chose to supervise 586 complaints out of almost a thousand referrals.

The system is generally neither independent nor transparent; and is always open to the suspicion that police officers will tend to protect fellow officers when investigating complaints. The PCA hasn't the resources or time to carry out detailed supervision of every case it takes on, so there is simply not enough independent oversight of the investigations conducted. The lack of independence, rigour and transparency taints public confidence in complaints investigations. This is particularly so among ethnic minority communities, as the findings of the Stephen Lawrence inquiry made clear. Subsequent cases seem to confirm the view among many black and Asian people that police-directed complaints investigations are inadequate and unfair. In one case involving the death of a black man in police custody, the victim's mother had this to say about the conduct of the resulting investigation involving Essex Police and the Police Complaints Authority (INQUEST 2000–01):

> The investigation has not centred on the behaviour of the eight officers who laid hands on my son that fateful night. Their actions were not investigated with the thoroughness and rigour that would have been the case had they been civilians. This is unjust. Instead Essex Police chose to investigate Roger, the victim, in an attempt to blame him for his own death.

There have been many calls for reform, notably from the Home Affairs Select Committee in its 1997 report into police complaints procedures and the 1999 Macpherson report. In December 2000 the government commissioned a report on reform, consulted on its findings and published some proposals. The main plank of the government's proposed reforms is the creation of a new body, the Independent Police Complaints Commission (IPCC), with its own investigating teams independent from the police. The investigating teams will comprise a mix of police and non-police members, and will be headed by civilian investigation managers. Other reforms address issues like complainants' rights to appeal to the new body against a force's decision, and disclosure of information to complainants about complaint investigations.

The IPCC is due to start work in April 2003, following legislation this year. Yet the independence of the process is already under question. Liberty, the civil liberties group, fears that the IPCC's investigating teams won't have enough non-police members for them to act independently – and, just as important, for them to be seen as independent in the public's eyes.

The police also investigate most complaints internally in Scotland where the deputy chief constable in each force is responsible for handling complaints. He or she appoints an investigation officer to examine a complaint. Allegations of criminality on the part of police officers must be referred to the Procurator Fiscal Service (Scotland's equivalent to the Crown Prosecution Service), but in practice are investigated at force level first. Her Majesty's Inspectorate of Constabulary for Scotland has a limited role in reviewing how complaints are investigated. In April 2000 the inspectorate published a complacent report, A Fair Cop?, which concluded that arrangements for investigating police complaints in Scotland were generally satisfactory. Scottish civil rights groups reacted by demanding a wholly independent procedure for investigating complaints; and finally in July 2001, the Scottish Executive initiated a consultation on reforming the system. At the time of writing, the Executive has yet to decide the final shape of its proposed new police complaints body – whether it will be an ombudsman overseeing complaints procedures, or an independent police complaints authority with the power to conduct its own investigations.

One of the options being considered for Scotland already exists in Northern Ireland. The Northern Ireland Police Ombudsman started work in November 2000, after the post was created by the Police (Northern Ireland) Act 1998. Nuala O'Loan, the first Police Ombudsman, exercises total control over the complaints process in Northern Ireland. She independently investigates serious complaints against police officers and directs how others are to be investigated, as well as deciding what type of disciplinary action is appropriate if a complaint is upheld. There is still a role for police officers in complaints investigation, however, as between a third and a half of the investigating officers under the Police Ombudsman's direction are seconded from British police forces.

Mrs O'Loan demonstrated the strength of her independence in December 2001 when she persevered with a highly critical report on the police conduct of the Omagh bomb inquiry. The report was leaked in advance of publication and provoked uproar from the police and Unionist politicians, furious rebuttals from Sir Ronnie Flanagan, the chief constable, and complaints from John Reid, the Secretary of State. Sir Ronnie castigated the report as inaccurate and demanded more time to respond to the report before it was formally published. But Mrs O'Loan rejected his demand because he failed to describe the nature of the 'inaccuracies' he wished to refute.

The security services: quis custodiet custodies?

The UK has three main intelligence and security agencies: the Secret Intelligence Service (SIS, or MI6), the Security Service (MI5) and Government Communications Headquarters (GCHQ). The Defence Intelligence Staff (DIS) in the Ministry of Defence also forms part of the UK's intelligence machinery. Nominally, each of these agencies can be held accountable through its responsible minister – the Home Secretary (MI5), the Foreign Secretary (MI6 and GCHQ) and the Defence Secretary (DIS) – with the Prime Minister retaining overall responsibility for security matters. Only recently were these agencies even placed on a statutory footing under the Security Services Act 1989 (MI5) and the Intelligence Services Act 1994 (MI6 and GCHQ).

The 1994 Act set up an Intelligence and Security Committee that for the first time provided a modicum of scrutiny over these unaccountable agencies. However though it is situated in Parliament, it is not an independent select committee. The committee examines the expenditure, administration and policy of the three intelligence and security agencies, but may not look at operational matters or the agencies' past performance. Its remit extends also to the Defence Intelligence Staff, the Joint Intelligence Committee (the central committee of senior officials within the Cabinet Office) and law enforcement agencies, including the police. The committee reports to the Prime Minister and, only through him, to Parliament.

The committee may be described as a fig-leaf, for it gives a measure of parliamentary respectability while covering up the private parts of the security apparatus. It is certainly not an independent overseer of the security and intelligence agencies. The Prime Minister appoints its members from MPs and peers (after consulting the Leader of the Opposition) and they meet in secret. The Prime Minister vets its reports after consulting the agencies themselves; and the reports are distinguished chiefly by a mass of asterisks denoting passages that have been censored. Even the budgets for each of the individual agencies are withheld by the government, a degree of secrecy the committee itself has criticised. Details of the overall intelligence and security budget are released, but according to the *Economist* (31 March 2001) are grossly underestimated (the official figure is about £900 million a year; the *Economist* estimate is closer to £2.5 billion).

Committee members are chosen for their trustworthiness and are sworn to secrecy on many questions (they operate in what is known in Whitehall parlance as the 'ring of secrecy'). Even so, the Secretary of State and agency chiefs can refuse to give the committee 'sensitive' information. This led Yvette Cooper MP, at that time a committee member, to ask: 'How can we have proper oversight if the very people whom we are supposed to be overseeing are determining what information we get?' (HC Deb, 2 November 1998). Further, the agencies are uniquely protected by draconian criminal sanctions in the Official Secrets Act, which impose an absolute and life-long duty of silence on existing and former members of MI5, MI6 and GCHQ. There is no defence allowing them to argue that information was disclosed in the public interest, even if disclosure was made to Parliament – and even if illegal activities are exposed as a result.

A former legal adviser to the security services has dismissed the Committee's reports as 'anodyne'. He contends that its members simply do not have access to the information they need to inform their work, and anyway lack understanding of the breadth of issues they should be investigating (Home Affairs Committee 1999). The committee is certainly deferential to the powers-that-be, refusing for example to let rogue MI6 agent David Shayler appear before it, despite his insider knowledge and significant claims (e.g., that MI6 was aware of a plot to kill or depose Colonel Gadafy).

In 1999, the Home Affairs Committee argued that the agencies should come under scrutiny from a select committee and Parliament, rather than a statutory committee under the control of the political executive and the agencies themselves. The committee asserted that the current arrangements were merely a staging post on the way to real parliamentary accountability:

> In our view, it is inevitable that the intelligence services will one day become accountable to Parliament . . . We have no doubt that the suggestion of parliamentary scrutiny will meet the stiffest resistance from some within the agencies and from some in Whitehall. We trust that the Government will not succumb. Finally, we repeat our view that the accountability of the security and intelligence services to Parliament ought to be a fundamental principle in a modern democracy.

In 2000, the Liaison Committee (which is made up of the chairs of all of the Commons' select committees) declared that while the Intelligence and Security Committee may be made up of parliamentarians, its dominance by executive interests means that it is 'emphatically not a committee of Parliament' (Liaison Committee 2000). The committee censured the government for its reluctance to provide information about the security and intelligence agencies to select committees, and for preventing members of the agencies from giving evidence.

Complaints against the security forces

The Regulation of Investigatory Powers Act 2000 combined the existing commissioners for MI5, MI6 and GCHQ in a single new post, that of the Intelligence Services Commissioner; established a new Interception Commissioner; and merged previously separate tribunals into an Investigatory Powers Tribunal. Between them, they consider complaints from the public and review the issue of warrants for telecommunications interception, for entry onto premises and interference with property.

As with the Intelligence and Security Committee, the commissioners in the past proved unwilling to challenge the agencies they are supposed to oversee. The commissioners, who have typically been senior appeal court judges, operated in private, paying visits to the agencies to try to ensure that they kept to the formal procedures covering the issue of surveillance and interception warrants. Their annual reports have usually been short and unforthcoming. Likewise, the tribunals that were set up to receive complaints from the public met in private and were forbidden to confirm or deny whether an individual making a complaint was targeted by the agencies. They were able to do so if they found that activities against an individual were undertaken without a warrant – but since they relied on evidence from the agencies themselves, they were unlikely to discover whether an individual had been improperly or illegally targeted. To date no complaint has been upheld by the new tribunal or its predecessors.

It is not possible yet to judge the new regime. The new Intelligence Services Commissioner, Lord Justice Simon Brown, held both the previous commissioner posts prior to their merger and so there is unlikely to be a major shift in policy or operation. However, Liberty states that the reforms have improved the previous system of 'restrained and secretive' tribunals (Liberty 2000).

The need for effective scrutiny of the security and intelligence services is becoming more, not less, essential. Following the terrorist atrocities of 11 September 2001 in the USA, the security and intelligence agencies are being given more resources and greater powers. GCHQ is now empowered, like MI6, to gather intelligence outside Britain. A month after 11 September 11, the government gave MI5, MI6 and GCHQ an extra £15 million (and quite possibly more) on top of their combined annual budget of £876 million, with the likely prospect of additional money to fund their anti-terrorist efforts. Additionally, the growing level of co-operation between security and intelligence agencies among European Union countries, including the EU's Schengen Information System, which holds millions of files on individuals, has the potential to diminish further the accountability of these agencies, nationally and abroad.

8.3 How far does the composition of the armed forces, security services and police reflect the social composition of society at large?

The armed forces
There is genuine concern among the top brass that the armed forces do not sufficiently reflect British society, particularly in terms of ethnic minority and gender representation. Ethnic minorities are now estimated to total about 7 per cent of the British population, and some 9 per cent in the relevant age group (i.e., 16 to 34 years old) – yet they account for around 1.5 per cent of the armed forces' total trained strength. Women comprise a small majority of Britain's total population, but only 8 per cent of all armed forces personnel.

Much of the explanation for this lies with the military's culture. The military has over the years developed as a unique social organism, complete with its own traditions, discipline and social conventions. There is a deeply engrained class system, hinging on the distinctions between officers and 'other ranks', between regiments (cavalry versus infantry, for example), and between services (with the navy seeing itself as the 'senior service'). The armed forces have close links with the royal family, and the military are often conservative with a small 'c' – as well as with a large 'C'. They are old-fashioned and elitist in their culture and not in the least socially representative. One army officer, Major Eric Joyce, publicly said as much in 1997, and was dismissed from the army as a result, subsequently joining the Commission for Racial Equality (CRE) and becoming a Labour MP. He claimed that the army was sexist, racist, snobbish and class-ridden, and that it urgently required to be modernised (*Guardian*, 6 August 1997).

The intake of women

The Equal Opportunities Commission (EOC) has accused the armed services of not putting as much effort into recruiting more women (who nowadays make up 8.8 per cent of officers in the armed forces and 7.8 per cent of other ranks) as it has within the ethnic minorities. There has been only a slow increase in the proportion of women in the military and it was as late as 1998 that the army increased the number of posts open to women from 47 per cent to 70 per cent. Equivalent figures for the Royal Navy and the RAF are 73 and 96 per cent respectively.

The exclusion of women from some front-line combat roles in the three services is an obvious barrier. But this exclusion arguably reflects long-standing and deeply-rooted attitudes which are both overtly and subtly sexist and narrowly macho. It seemed that the old guard may be outflanked when Defence Secretary Geoffrey Hoon hinted in April 2001 that he backed allowing women to fight on the front line, pointing out that the combat ban hampered efforts to recruit and retain women in the forces and prevented them from taking senior posts because they lacked combat experience (*Independent*, 16 April 2001). However in May 2002 Hoon confirmed the status-quo.

Ethnic minorities

Since the late 1990s, the armed forces have put in place several measures to boost the intake of ethnic minority recruits. The MOD has raised its target from 2 per cent in 1998–99 to 5 per cent by mid 2002, with further increases until the proportion rises to the national figure of about 9 per cent for the relevant age group. The catalyst for this change was a (CRE) investigation into recruitment and transfer into the Household Cavalry. Sergeant Jacob Malcolm, a black soldier, was denied a transfer to the regiment in 1993 because of his race. The CRE threatened to take enforcement action and then hammered out a package of equality measures with the MOD, comprising recruitment, complaints handling and racism awareness training initiatives. In 1998, the CRE and MOD entered into a partnership agreement under which the CRE receives regular reports from each of the armed services about progress on improving ethnic minority recruitment and retention.

However, the armed forces are still performing poorly and in 1999 all three services failed to reach the then 3 per cent target for ethnic minority recruitment. In October 2000, the CRE warned in evidence to the Defence Committee that the MOD would not meet its commitments under the agreement unless the department and service chiefs showed firm leadership and radically improved their equal opportunity work.

The ban on gays

The long-standing ban on gays and lesbians in the forces was finally lifted in 2000 following the unequivocal finding by the European Court of Human Rights that the ban was illegal. The change of policy by the MOD does not seem to have harmed either recruitment or the effectiveness of the forces, according to an official assessment of the new policy in each of the armed services (*Observer*, 19 November 2000). Despite the dire warnings of plunging morale from the service chiefs, there appeared to be widespread acceptance of the new policy within the forces themselves.

Disability

On disability, the government has exempted the armed forces from the employment provisions of the Disability Discrimination Act 1995 and in 2000 negotiated an opt-out for the armed forces from a clause in Article 13 of the EU directive on equal employment banning discrimination on the basis of disability or age. The rationale for this policy is that disability is considered incompatible with maintaining combat effectiveness among the armed forces (though service personnel disabled on duty are allowed to continue serving as long as overall operational effectiveness is not impaired). In a speech to the Royal United Services Institute in December 2000, Sir Charles Guthrie, then chief of the defence staff, ridiculed what he saw as the notion that disabled people had a 'right to serve'. In response, Bert Massie, chair of the Disability Rights Commission, accused the military of subscribing to outdated stereotypes about people with disabilities.

The security and intelligence agencies

Few staffing figures are available for the security and intelligence agencies. Out of the three agencies, MI5 releases the most detail about its workforce. In November 2001, MI5 employed roughly 1,900 people, 47 per cent of whom were women. Women occupy nearly half of the senior posts within the organisation, including agent-runners and that of deputy director general. Two director generals have now been women. Since the mid-1990s, MI5 has made greater efforts to recruit from a broader cross-section of society, rather than merely from the Oxbridge graduate pool. It has particularly focused efforts on engaging ethnic minority recruits, even advertising in the ethnic minority press. This broader policy is a result of a clear-out of top management staff in the 1980s, until which time former service-men and colonial officials with deeply conservative attitudes tended to dominate. Nowadays MI5 officers are encouraged to adopt a broader and more contemporary view of British society – though, by definition, they still live a cloistered and secretive existence.

Far less information is publicly available on GCHQ's staff, apart from the specialist skills they require (such as facility in languages, mathematics, computer programming or electronics). The agency's website discloses that it is actively trying to recruit more staff from the ethnic minorities who are under-represented there. MI6 has recently also been seeking to increase its intake from the ethnic minorities, as well as more women. In October 2001, the agency declared that it was looking for staff from 'wider socio-economic and ethnic backgrounds' (*Guardian*, 16 October 2001) to leaven its near 2,000 largely white male staff.

Following the terrorist attacks on the US in 2001 and the war in Afghanistan, the security and intelligence agencies were reported as seeking to recruit Arabic, Pashtu and Farsi speakers. British military and intelligence agencies, along with their American counterparts, were severely criticised for not detecting the extent of the terrorist threat. This was largely attributed to gaps in the agencies' intelligence gathering capabilities, especially in terms of the 'human intelligence' needed to understand and infiltrate diverse movements.

Police

Creating police forces that are representative of the communities they serve has become a high profile cause for government and police authorities in recent years. It is officially recognised that a higher proportion of ethnic minority officers is vital to eradicating institutional racism in the police; and may also go some way to assuaging fears in minority communities that they are more often the target of law enforcement than its beneficiaries. Recent figures illustrate the distance police forces across the country have to go to recruit ethnic minority police officers. In 1999, there were 2,520 ethnic minority officers out of a total overall police strength of 98,520, or 2.56 per cent. Disaggregated figures for the regions reveal that London and the east and west midland forces are failing badly. Nearly 29 per cent of Greater London's population in mid-2000 had ethnic minority backgrounds, but only 3.4 per cent of police officers in 1999 were from ethnic minorities.

One problem that the authorities have to overcome is the perception among young people in the ethnic minorities that they will be isolated among their colleagues and out in the community as well. Cases like that of Gurpal Virdi, the Asian sergeant falsely accused of sending racist hate mail to colleagues and sacked in March 1999, plainly reinforce such perceptions. Virdi was finally exonerated by a police inquiry that found 'institutional racism' in the Metropolitan Police's disciplinary procedures and was awarded £90,000 compensation by the Met. Virdi said that he had been 'set up' by white officers hc had challenged.

According to the British Association of Women Police (BAWP), women are only 16 per cent of police strength. The key barriers to greater recruitment of women police officers identified by BAWP are the macho image of policing, its culture of long hours and poor support for achieving a healthy work–life balance, and the preponderance of male officers in the senior hierarchies.

Northern Ireland

The former Royal Ulster Constabulary in Northern Ireland was notoriously sectarian in composition and conduct. The government has changed the name, crest, oath and uniform of the police force in Northern Ireland following the Patten report on reforming policing after the Good Friday agreement. Progress on reforms has however been slowed by the intense sectarian conflicts over decommissioning, policing and security. For the Protestant community, the RUC was a symbol of security, and over half the population was opposed to the change of name to the Police Service of Northern Ireland. The government has however drawn up a plan for implementing the Patten reforms, though in deference to strongly-held Unionist opinion, its response has not been as radical as the original proposals. Nevertheless, the government has enacted the Police (Northern Ireland) Act 2000; instituted the new office of Police Ombudsman; appointed an Oversight Commissioner; and established a new representative Policing Board (albeit one boycotted by Sinn Fein). Some 1,000 RUC officers have left under a special severance scheme.

However plans to establish community policing through district policing partnerships and to phase out the full-time police reserve are in abeyance as sectarian tensions and violence have increased. The new Police Service of Northern Ireland remains broadly 90 per cent Protestant in composition, and new trainees are being recruited on a 50:50 basis. But incidents such as the near fatal bombing of a new Catholic recruit's car in June 2002 as a warning to Catholic recruits generally are a reminder that breakaway paramilitary groups continue to regard the force as a legitimate target.

8.4   How free is the country from the operation of paramilitary units, private armies, warlordism, and criminal mafias ?

Britain has no national paramilitary force akin to the French gendarmerie or the Italian carabinieri. However, the SAS acts as the armed wing of the security and intelligence agencies. For example, MI5 briefed the SAS before the anti-IRA operation in Gibraltar in 1998 and prior to anti-terrorist ambushes and operations in Northern Ireland. The government also appears to have accepted that private military and security companies are here to stay.

Paramilitary violence continues in Northern Ireland after the IRA ceasefire and peace agreement. The breakaway Real IRA, Continuity IRA and INLA (on the margin) continue the 'armed struggle'; in August 1998, the Real IRA was responsible for the Omagh bombing which killed 29 people in the market town. The Ulster Defence Association, the largest loyalist paramilitary grouping, has disbanded its political wing and is committed to sectarian violence, targeting Roman Catholics who live in predominantly Protestant areas through fire-bomb and other attacks and constant aggravation. In 2001, UDA personnel were active in the picketing and abuse of Catholic parents and children on their way to the Holy Cross School in north Belfast. The previous year the UDA and smaller Ulster Volunteer Force fought a bloody feud, punctuated with shootings, on the Shankill Road. Other loyalist organisations still committed to violence are the Ulster Defence Force and the 'Red Hand Defenders' (the soubriquet under which loyalist groups carry out sectarian killings that they do not want to own up to).

Both the IRA and UDA enforce brutal social control in their own areas through shootings and beatings of people accused of 'anti-social behaviour'. In 1999-2000, some 45 under-18s were beaten by punishment squads, according to Professor Liam Kennedy, of Queen's College, Belfast, the youngest being a boy of 13. In one case, a gang of ten masked men, carrying guns, burst into the home of a disturbed 16-year-old with an IQ of 45 and severely beat him in the bathroom and an alley outside. His mother could hear him screaming and found 'blood everywhere' in the bathroom. The IRA also carries out criminal activities to raise funds; and for example is generally held to have carried out a major cigarette heist in June 2001. The UDA is involved in protection rackets and even drug-dealing. One prominent UDA figure is widely known to be a prosperous drug czar.

It is estimated that paramilitary organisations were responsible for some 22 sectarian murders last year. Though the sizes of the groups responsible are measured only in hundreds, their activities sharpen the sectarian divide in Northern Ireland and contribute to the bitterness on both sides. The level of killings is about the same as in the Basque country where terrorist murders are often accompanied by mass protests by the citizens. No such protests occur in Northern Ireland.

In the rest of the UK, the most worrying phenomenon is the clusters of violent white racist youths who are prepared to raid Asian neighbourhoods and engage in provocative marches under the banner of racist parties. Their invasions sparked off the riots in Oldham and other northern English towns in the summer of 2001 and inspired the violent response of young Asians. Armed drug gangs also infest certain inner-city areas. These gangsters carry guns and use them, usually against each other, but the violence spills over. Football hooliganism is nowadays largely contained by the police, but pitched battles and individual beatings still take place.

The most disturbing aspects of the state's engagement in Northern Ireland have been the unresolved suspicion that the army pursued a 'shoot-to-kill' policy there against IRA suspects; and more recently, the revelations by BBC *Panorama* and in the *Guardian* of RUC Special Branch and army collusion in the murders of prominent Catholics and IRA activists in the 1980s and early 1990s. According to *Panorama*, the army's Force Research Unit ran at least one agent who targeted victims for UDA death squads; and a Special Branch officer colluded directly in and facilitated the murder of lawyer Pat Finucane (June 23, 2002). Special Branch officers knew who the killers were but gave no information to the RUC investigating officers. They also seem to have inspired UDA threats against one RUC officer who 'was treading on toes'. Three inquiries under Sir John Stevens, now the Metropolitan police commissioner, over ten years have been obstructed and sabotaged by the police, but they have exposed the activities of the FRU agent and have found widespread collusion between individual police officers, soldiers and loyalist terrorists (*Guardian*, 24 June 2002). The head of the FRU, Brigadier Gordon Kerr, who denies the charges of his unit's collusion in these murders, has since been promoted to be the British military attaché in Beijing. Both *Panorama* and the *Guardian*, relying on different sources, insist that MI5 had unlimited access to FRU files and knew all about the collusion that took place. Nevertheless, MI5 have only recently given information to the Stevens inquiry.

Nine: minimising corruption

The endless saga of sleaze

Are elected representatives and public officials free from corruption?

People want honest politics and they are going to get it.
Tony Blair, during the 1997 election campaign

Introduction

Corruption – the abuse of public office for private, personal or party gain, on behalf of the office holder or their family or associates – is particularly damaging to a democracy as it undermines the relationship of trust between the people and their elected government. The purpose of democratic government is to serve the public interest, not the private interests of office holders. Confidence in government can be quickly eroded if people know or suspect that politicians or public officials are using their official position, paid for by the taxpayers, to further their own interests.

However, the precise boundaries of what counts as 'corruption' are difficult to define with certainty. In the 1990s, the looser term 'sleaze' was used in the media to cover a range of improper conduct: sexual misdemeanors; receipt of cash for asking parliamentary questions; irregular party funding; financial conflicts of interest, privileged access to ministers and general misconduct in office. Although this term is something of a catch-all, there was a widespread and accurate perception among the public that political standards had fallen over the long period of Conservative rule. This perception contributed in no small manner to their ejection from office in 1997. In this section, we confine ourselves closely to financial and political corruption.

Minimising corruption

Prior to the 1997 election Labour portrayed itself as the 'clean party' in direct contrast to the sleazy politics then associated with the Conservatives. This was despite the fact that it had its own problems of nepotism and sectarian bias in rotten boroughs and hidden traditions of low-level corruption. At the 1996 party conference Tony Blair said that he would be 'tough on sleaze and the causes of sleaze'. Labour's 1997 manifesto pledged that:

> We will clean up politics…The Conservatives are afflicted by sleaze and prosper from secret funds from foreign supporters. There is unquestionably a national crisis of confidence in our political system, to which Labour will respond in a measured and sensible way.

The government has certainly acted on corruption, but not with the resolve that is required. New rules on party funding have introduced a more open regime, including the disclosure of large political donations; but they do not curb the size of donations, thus leaving the parties vulnerable to accusations of undue influence. There has been some movement on modernising and consolidating corruption law, though no updating statute has yet made it onto the legislative agenda. However, the conglomerate Anti-terrorism, Crime and Security Act 2001 now makes the bribery by UK firms or individuals of foreign public officials illegal under British law.

The most significant contribution so far to minimising corruption was John Major's creation of the Committee on Standards in Public Life in October 1994, in part to take the heat out of the sleaze scandals of the 1990s. However, the Committee's remit was not to investigate past events but to examine current concerns about 'standards of conduct of all holders of public office' and to make recommendations for the future. The Nolan Committee (as it was promptly named, after the law lord who was the first chairman) had an almost immediate impact by formulating new principles and rules for the conduct of MPs, with an independent element in the self-regulation on which MPs insisted (see 9.1 below) and new rules and processes for appointments to public bodies. The Committee also set out seven principles for public life, that were designed to provide an ethical framework within which holders of public office should act. The seven sisters were Selflessness, Integrity, Objectivity, Accountability, Openness, Honesty and Leadership (Committee on Standards in Public Life, 1995).

In January 2001 a Cabinet Office review of the Committee's work found that it had contributed to a significant development in standards (see also the Committee's own report, 2000a). The Committee's recommendations have resulted in further reforms, such as a new and more open party funding regime. But it is only a non-departmental body that may be abolished at any time by government and has therefore acted cautiously, and at times too much so, to check potential government abuse or to insist on effective regulation of MPs' conduct. The Committee – now known under its new chairman, Sir Nigel Wicks, as 'the Wicks committee' – has not always applied its own principles consistently and it has no investigatory powers. The very existence of a body that monitors and responds to concerns about standards in public life is of value; its weakness is that it seeks consensus for its remedies within the party political class rather than the general public.

Corruption since 1997

Within a month of the 1997 election, one Labour MP was censured by the House of Commons and another suspended by the party prior to a criminal investigation into bribery.

However, there are far fewer allegations of misconduct by individual MPs than previously. No ministers have been found guilty of corruption, as Jonathan Aitken was, nor have any MPs been accused of accepting bribes to ask Parliamentary Questions, as they were in the mid-1990s.

The Committee on Standards in Public Life concluded in 2000 that there had been a shift in concern from allegations of direct financial reward to accusations of privileged access (2000a: para. 2.20). The Labour party's growing reliance on wealthy donors has also led to concerns that such donors may be rewarded by favourable government or ministerial decisions. From 1997 onwards the long series of high-profile cases – that is, the Ecclestone, Hinduja, Mittal, Drayson and Desmond affairs – has provoked 'cash for favours' allegations from the Conservative opposition and hostile media. If such allegations were true, these would be serious cases of corruption; even unproven, they have already damaged public trust in the current government and politics in general.

The issue of privileged access is closely related to Labour's political fund-raising and 'cash for favours'. Donors to the Labour party, prime ministerial favourites, others close to the party and representatives of big business all find places in the House of Lords, on task forces and quangos, or as policy czars or special advisers, alongside other more conventional appointees. Labour is in a double-bind, since it must raise funds to reduce a £10 million debt and keep the party going; yet when it does so, it exposes itself to suspicions that its simple denials of wrong-doing cannot rebut.

The principal complaint against the Labour government is that it has failed to recognise the seriousness of the new charges and the damage that they are doing to public confidence in politics. Tony Blair and Alastair Campbell have consistently dismissed media reports of corruptions as a distraction from 'real' economic and social issues. They miss the point. Even the wildest allegations about the Hinduja affair, for example, do not show the systemic and often spectacular corruption here that exists in other west European nations where even major leaders like Chancellor Kohl (Germany), Presidents Mitterrand and Chirac (France), and Silvio Berlusconi (Italy) have been involved in major scandals. But they are wrong to argue that the minutiae of propriety and procedure are unimportant compared to bread-and-butter policies that affect the public. Their own code for parish councillors at the lowliest level of government states:

> As well as avoiding actual impropriety, you should avoid any appearance of it. You should not accept gifts or hospitality that might reasonably be thought to influence, or be intended to influence, your judgment.

Good advice which applies equally to the Prime Minister and his colleagues. All that government does depends on its honesty of process and public trust in it.

Labour's conduct since 1997 has been further marred in four significant ways:

- some government decisions, however trivial, are often made behind closed doors in response to influence-peddlers rather than out in the open;
- other government and ministerial decisions and appointments give the appearance of being swayed by party political or public donations that arguably assist the Labour party;
- Labour MPs and ministers have been guilty of using public money for party political purposes and have brow-beaten party members who have complained publicly about their conduct; and
- the Prime Minister and government dismissed or ignored the findings of Mrs Filkin, the public official who thoroughly investigated complaints against ministers and MPs, and colluded in rubbishing and dismissing her.

The media also do democracy a disservice though their own vicious distrust of politicians. Constant coverage of potential wrongdoing or impropriety, however trivial, makes politics seem more sleazy than it is (see also Section 10).

9.1 How effective is the separation of public office, elected and unelected, from party advantage and the personal, business and family interests of office holders?

The last six years have seen significant progress both in developing new codes of conduct for politicians, down to parish council level, and for officials throughout government and public bodies, and also strengthening enforcement mechanisms. They are mainly predicated on self-regulation.

Members of Parliament
The long tradition of self-regulation in the House of Commons has an honourable past, being based on the need for MPs to possess certain rights and immunities to carry out public duties 'without fear or favour, let or hindrance'. Among these rights and immunities is the ability of Parliament to regulate its own affairs and discipline its members. But self-discipline degenerated long ago into an obsolete and self-serving complacency. The scandals of 'cash-for-questions' and MPs acting as paid lobbyists forced change upon the House of Commons. The Nolan Committee recommended new standards of conduct; a stronger and more detailed register of interests; and the appointment of a new Commissioner for Parliamentary Standards.

The Commons appointed its first Commissioner in 1995 and approved a mandatory register of interests, together with a code of conduct for MPs, in 1996. But the MPs' tradition of self-regulation remained paramount. The Commissioner was to investigate allegations of misconduct by MPs, and to report to a newly-constituted Select Committee on Standards and Privileges which would act as the arbiter of all cases of alleged misconduct by MPs.

MPs must now register a wide range of interests that could influence their actions as members of Parliament, namely: directorships; remunerated employment, office or profession; clients; sponsorships; gifts, benefits and hospitality; overseas visits; overseas benefits and gifts; land and property; shareholdings, and a catch-all 'miscellaneous' category. In addition, any 'relevant current, past or expected pecuniary interest' must be declared in any Commons debates or communications with ministers, civil servants or other MPs. The code incorporates Nolan's seven principles of public life and is backed by a 73-paragraph guide to the registration and declaration of interests, rules on advocacy and the complaints procedure. The main rules of conduct for MPs now are as follows:

- The acceptance of a bribe, fee or any reward to influence an MP's conduct, speech or vote is contrary to the law of Parliament;
- MPs are forbidden to act as paid lobbyists in any proceeding of the House (the 'advocacy' rule);
- MPs have a duty to uphold the law and should avoid conflict between their personal interests and the public interest, and declare financial interests in any speech in the House, and even the most marginal financial links with organisations in communications with ministers and officials;
- MPs may not make improper use of official expenses or allowances or break the administrative rules governing such payments; and
- MPs may not use any confidential information they receive in the course of their parliamentary duties for purpose of financial gain or any other purpose unconnected with their parliamentary duties.

Under the advocacy rule, MPs in the pay of an outside organisation are not permitted to initiate any debate or parliamentary proceeding that directly affects the organisation's interests. However, they may take part in any proceedings that relate to the outside body's affairs so long as they register and declare their interest and do not seek to confer benefit exclusively on the organisation.

At first, the House of Lords stood aloof and relied upon a mere voluntary register. They argued they were not professional politicians, but the extent of their interests – the 'lord on the board' syndrome – made change inevitable. In 2001, the House approved the introduction of a mandatory register of interests, following a recommendation of the Committee on Standards in Public Life (2000b). The first full register, in May 2002, showed at once how deficient the voluntary register had been.

Ministers

The rules governing the conduct of ministers belong in the realm of the Prime Minister. The Prime Minister's ministerial code has come to be seen as a rule-book for the prevention of corruption. However, it is concerned just as much to safeguard the political integrity of the government, to enforce the doctrine of collective responsibility, and to organise the government's internal workings and its communications with the outside world (see also Section 7.3). Blair's code of conduct is in parts a high-minded document that is intended to protect the government against corruption and allegations of sleaze within a mix of guidance on procedure, conduct and accountability. Blair distances himself from the difficulties of the Major era, when the Cabinet Secretary was pressed into service to investigate, unfortunately ineptly, allegations of corruption against the Jonathan Aitken, then Chief Secretary to the Treasury. Blair re-states the basic constitutional position of ministers: they only remain in government for as long as they retain his confidence; and he remains the ultimate judge of the whether they meet the standards of behaviour expected of ministers. The Cabinet Secretary and other officials may advise ministers on how to behave and what interests they should declare, but it is not their place to enforce the code or to investigate ministers.

Amidst the general duties of ministers to account openly and honestly to Parliament and the public and to protect the integrity of the civil service, the code sets out rules to protect the government against charges of corruption. Ministers, the code states, must:

1   ensure that no conflict arises, or appears to arise between their public duties and their private interests;
2   avoid accepting any gift of hospitality which may or seem to compromise their judgment or place them under an improper obligations; and
3   not use government resources for party political purposes

Ministers in the House of Commons are also of course bound by the House's own rules of conduct. The code also enjoins them to keep separate their roles as minister and constituency MP. Blair revised the code in 2001 in response to criticisms about gaps in the code's guidance. He introduced a requirement to keep basic records of meetings between ministers and outside interest groups, in response to concerns about ministerial contact with lobbyists.

Civil servants

The civil service code, introduced in January 1996 and revised in May 1999, sets out the framework of ethical values that civil servants are expected to uphold. The code stipulates that civil servants should not misuse their official position or their access to privileged information to further their own private interests. It also warns public officials against accepting benefits from external parties that could be interpreted as compromising their personal judgment or integrity. The code of conduct for special advisers contains identical provisions.

Self-regulation in practice

Any perusal of the register of members' interests (accessible via the internet) reveals the depth and variety of MPs' financial interests. External links were positively encouraged during the Thatcher and Major years as evidence of MPs being in touch with the 'real world'. It is argued, largely by those with financial interests, that the Commons would be duller and less effective if MPs were full-time politicians with no outside interests. However, a survey in 1996 by the academic Donald Shell found that many MPs with wide outside interests hardly contributed to parliamentary business at all; analysis by Peter Bradley MP of MPs' votes in 2001-02, found that MPs with such interests voted in only two-thirds of divisions (against an overall average of 93 per cent).

In opposition, Tony Blair promised that his government would be 'purer than pure'. Peter Mandelson said that the 1997 ministerial code would 'make life harder for ministers'. Yet since 1997 minor and not-so-minor scandals involving ministers and MPs have not only stained the New Labour record, but have not been dealt with rigorously, either by the Prime Minister or parliamentary authorities. Most allegations against MPs that came before the first two Parliamentary Commissioners were small-scale as the idea of registering all financial interests settled in. Table 1 contains the more serious cases of corruption that confronted Blair and the Commissioner, as well as others.

1. Serious accusations of corruption since 1997

Accused	Position	Date	Accusation or Concern	Outcome
Lord Simon	Junior minister	1997-99	Retained £2m holding of BP shares while trade and competition minister; allegations of tax avoidance	Blair stuck by him for 2 years. He was replaced in the 1999 re-shuffle
Geoffrey Robinson	Paymaster-General	1998	Conflict of interest for having investments in off-shore trusts while responsible for offshore tax regulation. Complaints:- 1. Non-declaration of Guernsey-based trust. 2. Previous failure to register company directorship. 3.Undeclared shareholding.	The Committee on Standards and Privileges (CSP) imposed no penalty on items 1 and 2. On third found that he had misled the House and ordered an apology (made in a 54-second speech). He was soon forced to resign, but for his part in the downfall of Peter Mandelson (see below). There was anyway concern to dispel the suspicion that Robinson's conspicuous largesse to Blair, Brown and others could have secured his preferment (see Bower, 2001).
Peter Mandelson	Secretary of State for Trade and Industry	1998-99	Failure to register a £373,000 loan from Geoffrey Robinson to buy a house & to declare it within DTI which was then inquiring into Robinson's business dealings. Mandelson had distanced himself from the inquiry, but had not disclosed the existence of the loan to his Permanent Secretary. The apparent conflict of interest was great. Observers also concluded that Robinson's generosity could have affected Mandelson's advice to Blair on ministerial appointments. Mrs Filkin (PSC) found that Mandelson had breached the code of conduct for MPs by misleading the Britannia building society by not declaring the £373,000 personal loan.	Blair and Mandelson soon realised that they could not ride out the political storm and Mandelson was obliged to resign. Just 2 weeks later, Blair made him his envoy in talks with the German government. Within a year Blair restored him to the cabinet (see below; and 9.4). Though the PSC found Mandelson guilty of breaching the code of conduct, the CSP decided that he hadn't acted with "dishonest intent" and voted to take no action. A committee member told the Wicks Committee that Labour MPs on the CSP decided "to treat him gently because he was such an influential figure in the party and it could affect their careers".
Keith Vaz	Junior minister	2000	Variety of allegations made, 18 to the PSC, including improper use of his ministerial offices; obstructing an internal Labour Party inquiry into alleged irregularities in the affairs of his local council; bullying party members; failure to register payments from businessmen.	Vaz was legally represented and refused to answer Mrs Filkin's questions. So she could not investigate 8 of the 18 charges against him and the CSP had to clear Vaz on most counts. But the CSP found him guilty of recommending a solicitor for an honour without disclosing a financial benefit and criticised Vaz and party members for blocking the inquiries. Blair stood by Vaz (as did Robin Cook, his senior minister), but Blair accepted his resignation on stated grounds of ill-health after the 2001 election.
John Reid and John Maxton	Scottish Secretary & then Northern Ireland Secretary; Labour backbench MP	2000; and 2001	Accused of misusing public money to fund Labour party campaigning. Mrs Filkin concluded that they had misused parliamentary allowances for party political purposes, a clear breach of the code of conduct and (for John Reid) of the ministerial code. She also found that Reid had intimidated witnesses and allegedly urged a Labour party official to give dishonest evidence	The CSP refused to uphold Mrs Filkin's findings, partly in Maxton's case on grounds of insufficient proof. But when she re-opened the case after the election when new evidence became available, Maxton was no longer an MP and the CSP refused to review it.
Peter Mandelson	Northern Ireland Secretary	2001	Accused of improperly using his influence while at the DTI (and responsible for securing funding for New Labour's flagship Millennium Dome project) to press the case with other ministers for the naturalisation of the rich Hinduja brothers in return for a £1m donation to the Dome's Faith Zone.	We discuss this case more fully in Section 9.4 below. Labour's close and complex relationship with the Hindujas went back to before 1997 when party politicians and officials were soliciting party funding from them; and the Blairs were drawn into the Hinduja net. The Hammond inquiry into the case had limited terms of reference and did not inquire too deeply into the facts. Mandelson resigned in confused circumstances over the presentation of the affair; the substance remains unresolved.

Geoffrey Robinson	MP	2000–01	Undeclared receipt of £200,000 cheque from late media tycoon Robert Maxwell. The PSC rejected Robinson's defence that the money had gone not to him, but to his company, since he benefited either way. Robinson gave evasive and dishonest responses to PSC and CSP inquiries, but the Committee gave him 3 months' grace to find the missing cheque at the bottom of the charge.	The CSP's willingness to let Robinson find the disputed cheque delayed their judgment until after the June 2001 election. The Committee found him guilty of failing to declare an interest and suspended him from the House for 3 weeks.
Keith Vaz	MP	2001–02	Eleven new charges of undeclared business interests, including his financial links with the Hinduja brothers (see below and 9.4). Vaz was again uncooperative and tried to intimidate a witness who had given evidence to Mrs Filkin	The PSC and CSP cleared Vaz on most charges. But the Committee found him guilty of "serious breaches" of the code and contempt of Parliament (for failure to register a donation and paid work; giving misleading information; and trying to discredit a witness). Vaz was suspended for a month – a relatively heavy sentence, largely for obstructing the PSC's inquiries.
Henry McLeish	First Minister, Scottish Executive	2001	As a Westminster MP, he sub-let part of his constituency office to 5 organisations while claiming full parliamentary allowances for it. It was said in his defence that he had not benefited personally, but the funds had gone to assist the Labour party in helping the public. McLeish passed the affair over as "a muddle, not a fiddle", and offered to repay the money. But his economy with the facts discredited him.	McLeish resigned in advance of further revelations about the affair in the Scottish media
Nigel Griffiths	DTI minister	2000–02	Nigel Griffiths was one of 3 Scottish MPs who were accused of charges of irregularities, or "muddle", over the use and allowances for constituency offices. The PSC found him guilty of using the office for party political purposes.	The CSP agreed with Mrs Filkin's conclusion, but did not consider that any punishment was warranted for what it described as merely a "technically deficient" claim

Sources: Committee on Standards and Privileges (CSP), 1998a, 1998b, 1998c; CSP, 1999; CSP, 2001; CSP, 2002a; CSP, 2002b

The departure of Mrs Filkin

MPs complained that Elizabeth Filkin took on trivial 'tit-for-tat' and malicious complaints against members. But the major cases that came before her, like a barium meal, revealed the flaws of self-regulation in full colour. The fact that Keith Vaz, for example, could so shamelessly block and obstruct her inquiries without the standards committee intervening on its own discredits the system. As the first Commissioner, Sir Gordon Downey, observed, the system only works if the House of Commons is committed to high standards; and if individual MPs accept that they must observe the code of conduct and cooperate with inquiries. The Commissioner requires the whole-hearted support of the Standards Committee since she does not possess the powers of discipline that are reserved to it (Doig, 2001). Instead,

- senior MPs of all parties united in condemning Mrs Filkin for insisting that they and other MPs should observe the rules that they had framed in the first place; and instigated a whispering campaign against her for being 'over-zealous', even instructing Whitehall officials to brief the media against her;
- ministers (John Reid, Keith Vaz and Geoffrey Robinson) obstructed her inquiries into their conduct, usually with impunity;
- MPs on the standards committee often failed to back up her inquiries against obstructive ministers and MPs;
- Labour MPs on the committee deferred to or colluded with the government in watering down Mrs Filkin's verdicts on ministers; in cases involving John Prescott, Peter Mandelson, John Reid, Keith Vaz and Nigel Griffiths, they ensured that the committee either amended her conclusions or

imposed lenient penalties, or none; Martin Bell MP and Peter Bottomley, the independent-minded Tory MP, who were both members of the standards committee, told the Wicks Committee in 2002 that their colleagues set an impossibly high bar of proof in Reid's case that made it impossible to uphold her verdict 'because he had a ministerial career';

● Elizabeth Filkin herself complains that a minority of MPs under investigation bullied MPs on the standards committee and attempted to 'silence witnesses . . . . a very few witnesses were very fright-ened' (*The Times*, 21 May 2002);

● Blair himself seems to have avoided his responsibilities as 'ultimate judge' of his ministers' conduct, as set out in his own code, acting instead wholly in his political capacity; as Bottomley told the Wicks Committee, 'it does not send a good signal that the PM is backing high standards in Parliament'.

It is a remarkable testimony to the insensitivity of MPs, and the tenacity of members' adherence to ambivalent custom and practice, that ministers' deliberate evasions and obstruction of Mrs Filkin's inquiries aroused concern only outside the Commons. Instead the all-party House of Commons Commission, the highest authority in the House, colluded with the campaign against her; engaged on a process of constructive dismissal; and downgraded the post by reducing the hours and resources available. A major cause of friction was that many MPs believed that they may use public allowances for purposes other than those for which they are allocated so long as there is no personal gain. Labour MPs especially used public monies for party political purposes and resented her verdicts against this conduct.

The Parliamentary Standards Commissioner was supposed to legitimise self-regulation by intro-ducing an element of independence. But Mrs Filkin was too independent-minded for the old boys' culture of MPs and their ambivalent tolerance of what they may regard as 'muddle', but the outside world sees as 'fiddle'. Mrs Filkin may ultimately have destroyed the cosy refuge of self-regulation her post was supposed to safeguard. For the time being a safe establishment figure has been put in place and he will work a three-day week.

Both Elizabeth Filkin and Sir Gordon Downey, her predecessor, have publicly said that the Standards Commissioner needs independent powers and greater resources to do the job properly. Mrs Filkin worked a five-day week instead of the four days for which she was employed. It is also clear that the House of Commons is not an appropriate employer of the Commissioner who must be strong enough to dispel public scepticism about the current arrangements. An ICM poll for the Rowntree Reform Trust in December 2001 found that 85 per cent of respondents wanted a Commissioner who was wholly inde-pendent of MPs; and 79 per cent wanted the rules governing MPs' conduct to be made law, with alleged breaches investigated either by an independent Commissioner (32 per cent) or the police (47 per cent).

Meanwhile, Tony Blair himself cannot escape criticism for his refusal to ensure that the Commissioner's inquiries were taken seriously, or to enforce his code. While Mrs Filkin was battling to investigate the tortuous Robinson case, Blair observed that the case 'was not what the public is interested in' (Bower, 2001). The fact is however that he is probably wrong, with damaging consequences for public faith in British democracy; but right or wrong, it is the public interest, not the public's interest or political self-interest, that should guide him and the House of Commons. Mrs Filkin's view will command greater public resonance in the long run:

> There have been instances where it appears some individuals who hold office have not been treated on the same basis as other people. I do have concerns about why that should

be the case. It looks like more than coincidence. I think it's about how power works in the House of Commons....the process is vulnerable to corruption and some people have not been robust enough to resist that corruption (*The Times*, 16 February 2002).

9.2   How effective are the arrangements for protecting office holders and the public from involvement in bribery?

The current anti-corruption laws – the Public Bodies Corrupt Practices Act 1889, and the Prevention of Corruption Acts 1906 and 1916 – are obsolete, ad-hoc and inconsistent (Law Commission, 1998). Together they make bribery a criminal offence if the offer, acceptance or agreement to accept a bribe takes place within the United Kingdom's jurisdiction. There is also a common law offence of bribery of a public official (Russell on Crime: Turner 1964). Cases of bribery rarely make the courts. In 2001, a team of assessors acting for the Council of Europe conducted a peer review of corruption in the UK. The three experts noted how few convictions for corruption there were in Britain; in 1999, there were just 15 prosecutions and 10 convictions under the two main corruption acts. Results from the International Crime Victim Survey 2000 indicated that public sector corruption was rare; only three people out of 5,500 surveyed claimed that a government official (defined to include police and customs officers) had sought a bribe from them (Groupe d'Etats contre la corruption (GRECO) 2001).

Reform of the corruption laws is on its way. The Law Commission has recommended that they should be re-stated in a single, modern Act that establishes effective criminal jurisdiction over offences of corruption. Further, both the Salmon Commission in 1976 (set up to review the law in the wake of bribery of councillors in the Poulson scandal) and the Nolan Committee in July 1995 said the law relating to the bribery of or receipt of a bribe by an MP should be clarified. There is doubt whether MPs accepting bribes can be dealt with under the statutory framework or the common law – which means that MPs can continue to claim the protection of parliamentary privilege, with punishment for parliamentary contempt resting with the House itself. Following Nolan, the Home Office issued a consultation paper in 1996, giving four options for reform:

i.   to rely solely on parliamentary privilege to deal with accusations of bribery of MPs and peers;
ii. to make MPs and peers fully subject to statutory law;
iii. to distinguish between conduct which should be dealt with by the criminal law and that which should be left to Parliament; and
iv. to make criminal proceedings subject to the approval of the relevant House of Parliament.

Shortly after the 1997 general election, the then Home Secretary Jack Straw issued a consultation paper setting out the groundwork for reform of corruption law. He tentatively suggested a new single offence of corruption; asked if the law should be changed to include the misuse of office; and raised the issues of how enforcement and the role of the courts could be strengthened. But the paper did not specifically address the position of MPs. However, the government also set up a joint committee of both Houses to review the position of MPs and it recommended that MPs should be made subject to the statute law on bribery (Joint Committee on Parliamentary Privilege 1999). The committee said corruption was a serious and 'insidious' crime that was 'particularly damaging if it takes hold in a democratic institution' and could only be dealt with credibly by using the police and the courts.

In June 2000 the Home Office issued a white paper that endorsed the proposals to establish a single offence of corruption for both the public and private sectors to which MPs would also be subject. The new offence would include 'trading in influence' – those situations where an intermediary sought to influence a public official's decision-making on behalf of a person offering the bribe. New legislation would cover cases of corruption committed within the UK and by UK nationals abroad. The new Bill was however delayed by the government's emergency anti-terrorism legislation in 2001.

Finally, a Nolan Committee proposal for a new statutory offence of 'misuse of public office' to cover serious misconduct that does not involve bribery or corruption has not yet been taken up (see Committee on Standards in Public Life, 1997). This new offence would apply to dishonest, oppressive or malicious conduct by a public official, or expenditure incurred unlawfully or as a result of wilful misconduct. The Nolan Committee recommended that the offence should apply to ministers, civil servants, councillors, local government officers, the police, magistrates, and the judiciary.

9.3   How far do the rules and procedures for financing elections, candidates and elected representatives prevent their subordination to improper interests?

Across Europe, political parties of all complexions have been beset by funding scandals, as the costs of elections have spiralled and party memberships have fallen. There are no simple solutions to the problem. Germany has some of the tightest rules on party funding, yet corruption has not stopped. Regulations in Spain, Italy and Japan were all tougher than the regime in the UK prior to the Neill Committee regulations, but these countries arguably had far more serious problems.

We describe the new structures governing party funding that were put in place by the Political Parties, Elections and Referendums Act 2001 in Section 6.6. Prior to the Act the regime was both lax and opaque; large and undisclosed donations were made from abroad to the Conservative party; and there were scandals over donations like that of Asil Nadir, of Polly Peck, and allegations of links between corporate and individual donors, influence over government and the award of honours (see Weir and Beetham). Before 1997, for example, the one in 17 public companies that contributed to Conservative funds scooped up half the knighthoods and peerages that went to directors of companies. The Ecclestone affair (see Table 2) early in the life of the Blair government inspired the extension of the remit of the Committee on Standards in Public Life to inquire into party funding. Lord Neill, the chairman, introduced the committee's reform proposals in a statement that made no bones about its central purpose:

> Many members of the public believe that the policies of the major political parties have been influenced by large donors, while ignorance about the sources of funding has fostered suspicion. We are, therefore, convinced that a fundamentally new framework is needed to provide public confidence for the future, to meet the needs of modern politics and to bring the United Kingdom into line with best practice in other mature democracies.

The new open era
Both the Conservative and Labour parties entered the new era of openness heavily in debt and more reliant than ever on large donors (see Section 6.6). Both Labour and the Conservatives have accepted

large donations from dubious sources that arouse anxieties about undue influence. Paradoxically, the new openness and close media scrutiny of donations and possible pay-offs may well have intensified public distrust. There are further concerns that individuals and private companies are rewarded through the disposition of posts on quangos and similar bodies, seats in the House of Lords and the award of honours. Lords Bragg, Gavron, Haskins and Sainsbury all gave generously to New Labour prior to being ennobled. Blair's appointments of major donors, like Haskins and Sainsbury, able though they are, to influential positions and actual government posts have raised less concern, but also raise issues of patronage and potential conflicts of interest.

2. Cash for favours? Big donors and government actions

Donor	Size of donation	Issues of influence
Bernie Ecclestone, head of Formula One.	£1m in 1997	Labour entered the 1997 election pledged to ban tobacco advertising. In November 1997, the government's plans for the ban exempted Formula One (following the outgoing government's position). The obvious connection between the pre-election donation and policy shift was made worse by the evasive conduct of the Prime Minister, ministers and party officials. Verdict: *Policy inheritance is a strong force. Yet this is a case either of undue influence or unprincipled confusion, made worse by bungled and deceitful cover-up.*
Enron, the US energy giant, notorious for its vast log-rolling political donations in the US and alleged improper influence over US energy policy and key public energy posts.	£38,000	Allegations of Enron's influence over the Bush administration fuelled suspicions of improper in the UK. Ralph Hodge, the former British head of Enron's European operations, revealed that Enron had given Labour around £38,000, saying that "sponsorship and donations are the most efficient ways of getting access" (*Mail on Sunday*, 27 January 2002). However, it had also given £25,000 to the Conservatives. Enron had required government approval for its take-over of Wessex Water, the UK's biggest water operator. Attempts to link then-DTI Secretary Peter Mandelson's grant of approval to Enron sponsorship of a Labour conference reception foundered on the fact that both the water industry regulator and director-general of fair trading had already approved the take-over. Enron also lobbied DTI ministers for a reversal of the moratorium on new gas-fired power stations, which Stephen Byers lifted in 1999. The government insisted that the moratorium had always been temporary and its lifting benefited other energy companies as well as Enron. Later claims that Blair had intervened in the decision and his senior energy adviser had met with Enron officials, did not alter the majority view that Enron's cash might have bought access, but not influence. Verdict: *Not proven.*
Lakshmi Mittal, owner of LNM, the international steel firm	£125,000 in 2001	During 2001, Mittal, an Indian businessman resident in the UK, was negotiating a take-over of an ailing Romanian state steel company with the Romanian government. In July, Blair signed a FCO letter to the Romanian premier in support of Mittal's bid. Blair wrote that he was "particularly pleased" that LNM was a British company. Two days later the deal went through, smoothed according to the Romanian foreign ministry by Blair's letter. But LNM was not a British company and was a competitor of British steel-makers. John Major's government had lobbied against LNM's 1996 take-over of Irish Steel on the grounds that it would harm British steel interests; and Mittal's US steel operations had successfully lobbied President Bush to impose huge tariffs on foreign (and so UK) steel imports. Was Blair's letter therefore a political favour to a big donor rather than the routine support for British business interests that the Prime Minister's office insisted it was? Suspicions were heightened when it transpired that the original draft of Blair's letter referred to Mittal as a "friend" of Tony Blair. Verdict: *Muddy waters, but probably just routine.*
Dr Paul Drayson, of PowderJect	£50,000 in January 2002	PowderJect won a £32 million government contract to provide smallpox vaccine after Drayson donated £50,000 during the secret government negotiations over the contract. Drayson had given a similar sum in 2001. The award of the contract was meant to remain secret. The government contacted five firms about supplying a stockpile of smallpox vaccine as an anti-terrorism precaution and chose Powderject outside the usual tendering process. The DOH disclaimed any knowledge of the second donation and insisted that PowderJect was the only firm that could supply the particular strain of vaccine required. The National Audit Office is investigating the contract. Drayson insisted that this was a personal donation that had nothing to do with his company. Verdict: *The process should have been more transparent, but not guilty.*
Richard Desmond, of Northern & Shell (publisher of pornographic magazines)	£100,000 in 2001	Desmond's Northern & Shell bought Express Newspapers from Labour supporter Lord Hollick's company, United News and Media, in November 2000. The sale was referred to the DTI. In January it is said that there were discussions between Desmond and Blair, Alastair Campbell and Margaret McDonagh, Labour's general secretary, who has gone on to work for Express Newspapers. The prospect of a donation, perhaps "in kind", is said to have been discussed. No 10 denies the meeting occurred. In February 2001, the then DTI Secretary Stephen Byers approved the take-over after consulting John Vickers, Director General of Fair Trading, who saw no need for an inquiry by regulators. It is only purchases of newspapers by existing press proprietors that require a competition inquiry under the Fair Trading Act 1973. Desmond was a magazine publisher only. The donation was made soon afterwards and was designated to pay for advertising in Express titles. The case aroused controversy because Desmond publishes pornographic magazines and runs a pornographic website. Verdict: *Not guilty, but Blair and his ministers did turn a blind eye to Desmond's porn empire so that they could benefit from being on good relations with Express Newspapers.*

Table 2 summarises several high-profile 'cash for favours'cases, and is by means exhaustive of the concerns that arise out of Labour's connections with business. There is for example the Hinduja case which brought down Peter Mandelson. The official Hammond inquiry into this affair leaves various important issues unresolved (Hammond 2001). Would the correspondence between the brothers and 10 Downing Street have revealed, if examined, 'a much more intricate relationship with the Hindujas than the Prime Minister wanted to disclose', as Andrew Rawnsley believes (Rawnsley, 2000)? Why would a major cabinet minister deal personally with passport applications that had no relevance either to his ministerial or constituency duties – unless perhaps prompted by 10 Downing Street? Why was official caution about the brothers' integrity set aside so readily? How come the whole process took only five months instead of the usual 20? Then there are various worrying cases that have not made a large political stir, but still raise considerable doubts about the current rules of the game. For example, there are the cases of:

- Anji Hunter, Blair's gate-keeper and closest confidante, who left Downing Street to join BP, the energy company with close links to New Labour, at an annual salary of £180,000;
- the £100,000 retainer paid to Lord Levy, Blair's special envoy to the Middle East and fund-raiser in chief, by the Westfield, the giant Australian retail developer, which wants to build shopping malls in the UK; and
- Paul Corrigan, a special adviser at the Department of Health and a member of the New Local Government Network, a private company that promotes private sector involvement in the delivery of public services and relies on business sponsors with an interest in securing footholds in the public sector. Corrigan is married to Hilary Armstrong, the government chief whip.

The short-term political fallout of such affairs does not appear to harm Labour (or Blair). But four fifths of the public agree that the current mix of party political funding makes 'people suspicious of politics and politicians' (ICM poll for BBC Radio *Today*, May 2002). Blair himself is now acutely aware of Labour's dilemma: the party needs to court major donors but the deals cumulatively hurt the party. He would like, he told Jeremy Paxman on BBC2 *Newsnight* in May 2002, 'to get shot of ever raising a penny for the Labour party', but appears hostile to state funding, as does the public.

Labour and the unions

Public concern about the influence of the trade unions over Labour polices has fallen sharply, as the political affinity between the party and unions has weakened and their contribution to party funds has diminished as a proportion of the whole. The sharp divisions over policy, especially the use of the private sector in public services, have put paid to fears about the special relationship between the two. Trade union influence over party policy was always exaggerated (see Minkin, 1978 and 1991), but the diversity in the funding that Labour now commands has freed the government from opposition canards about its strength (see also Section 6.6).

9.4 How far is the influence of powerful corporations and business interests over public policy kept in check, and how free are they from involvement in corruption, including overseas?

Big business has long exerted a powerful influence over public policy in Whitehall, as the first Democratic Audit made clear, through policy communities and networks that bind senior civil servants and business people together to develop and agree policies. Given New Labour's enthusiasm for big business, and ministers' willingness to listen to their representatives (see Section 4.8), it hardly seems necessary for corporate chiefs to spend their resources on bribing politicians or civil servants. But the close links between ministers and business figures and firms give grounds for concern about privileged access, influence over policy and 'favours'.

There is a fair amount of formal guidance for ministers and officials in ministerial and civil service codes, but it is mostly designed to ensure that they keep their own private interests in check. After the 'Lobbygate' scandal (see below), however, the code at least requires ministers and officials to record the 'basic facts' of meetings with external interests, but not for public consumption except in a crisis. More extensive and open records of such meetings, and even telephone and other communications, as in the USA, are necessary. The best prophylactic against undue influence is open and transparent policy-making and 'sunlight' on government's dealings with private business. But Labour's FOI law will deliberately cloak policy-making in secrecy and mount excessive safeguards over 'commercial confidentiality' (see Section 7.8 for fuller analysis). The whistle-blower's act – the Public Interest Disclosure Act 1998 – encourages employees to reveal corrupt practice by offering statutory protection against the sack, but still some four out of five whistle-blowers lose their jobs (*Observer*, 8 July 2001)

Official guidance and measures, then, offer only a marginal check on private influence on public policy. The hard part is distinguishing between legitimate corporate interest in government policy-making and excessive influence. The Labour's government's promotion of public-private partnerships blurs the line still more. Even the body which oversees the government's PPP policy and practice – UK Partnerships – has itself been privatised in the hands of City business and Treasury mandarins; and the Treasury does not even list it now as a 'public body'. The government's commitment to these partnerships, and the confidentiality in which they are engendered, enhances their capacity to hold the government, local councils and quangos to ransom where the delivery of public services is concerned (consider the Railtrack fiasco, the air-traffic transfer, the economics of new hospital schemes).

Lobbygate

Unscrupulous lobbying was one of the scourges of the later Conservative years in office and Major's anti-corruption reforms were supposed to regulate it. But Labour was hit almost immediately in 1998 by the 'Lobbygate' scandal that revealed that a new breed of lobbyists, many with New Labour links, had worked their way into the body politic. Derek Draper, formerly Peter Mandelson's special adviser, soon became the most notorious of them. Draper joined Roger Liddle, a close colleague of Mandelson's, at the PR company, Prima Europe. He was clearly hired on the basis that he could deliver access to the heart of the forthcoming Labour government. However, on 5 July 1998 the *Observer* published a picaresque article by the American investigative journalist, Greg Palast, describing his contacts with several New Labourite lobbying firms in the guise of an American energy boss. They all trumpeted their access to government and knowledge of government policy-making. Draper, then at GPC Market Access, boasted to Palast that he had access to ministers and inside information; and at a GPC reception in Whitehall introduced him to Roger Liddle, now an adviser in Downing Street. Liddle, according to Palast, gave him his card and said, 'Whenever you are ready, just tell me what you want, who you want to meet, and Derek and I will make the call for you.'

Palast did not however tape-record the conversation at the noisy reception and was unable therefore to stand his allegations up, although both Draper and Liddle subsequently resigned. Blair rode out the storm by promising to strengthen the rules governing contacts between special advisers and lobbying firms. Palast alleged that there were other instances of improper access to privileged information and policy-making. For example, he said that Karl Milner, of another lobbying firm, GJW Government Relations, faxed him a copy of a select committee report on energy policy prior to its release; and that Lawson Lucas Mendelsohn, another such firm who advised Tesco on its defeat of government plans for a tax on out-of-town supermarket car parks, persuaded the supermarket firm to sweeten its image with a £12 million donation to the Millennium Dome (Palast, 2002). In Palast's own words: 'At issue here is not Tesco's right to make a case against a tax. The issue is whether laws, taxes and regulations should be negotiated in secret for the benefit of clients of connected lobbyists.'

The Millennium Dome

The handling of the Dome illustrates that corruption need not be solely an issue of personal or simple party political gain. The Dome project was a public venture which had however a symbolic value for New Labour. But its success depended on raising funds from big business alongside subsidies from the National Lottery. In Parliament the Conservatives repeatedly pressed Mandelson when he was DTI Secretary, with responsibility for the Dome, over whether his position would be compromised in dealings with big companies such as Tesco, Boots, British Aerospace and GEC, which had provided finances for the venture.

Mandelson, who fell from office over his dealings with the Hinduja brothers on their sponsorship of the Faith zone, constantly denied being involved in seeking to drum up financial support for the Dome. On November 19, 1998, he told MPs during Trade and Industry Questions:

> My role in relation to the Dome is as shareholder, not as head of sponsorship. Although I received regular reports from the board of the New Millennium Experience Company on its significant progress in raising sponsorship, I have never been, and do not intend to be, involved in procuring or negotiating sponsorship deals, so no conflicts arise.

But on 29 and 31 January, 2001, *The Times* published evidence of his personal involvement which also suggested that 'multi-million-pound sponsorship deals for the Millennium Dome were secured after hints that the government would look more favourably on the companies involved':

● Lord Blyth, former chairman of Boots, told *The Times* that he went to see Mandelson at his request. 'It was made very clear to me by Peter Mandelson that Tony Blair was very interested in Boots sponsoring the Dome. Tony Blair and Peter Mandelson saw us as the logical sponsors for the Body zone.' He said that Mandelson then arranged for him to meet the Prime Minister at Downing

Street, where they discussed a range of issues, including their joint wish for Boots to sponsor the Body zone. Lord Blyth welcomed the chance of a private meeting with the Prime Minister, as Boots was keen to expand its links with the NHS. Boots was also involved in a range of government committees.

- *The Times* also stated on 29 January that they had learnt that Tesco was summoned by Mandelson to a meeting in Whitehall to discuss financial support for the Dome. Tesco had already been lobbied unsuccessfully by Jennie Page, then chief executive of the New Millennium Experience Company (NMEC), which ran the Dome. After senior executives from Tesco met Mandelson at the end of 1997, they agreed to give £12 million to underwrite the Learning zone.

- Camelot, the National Lottery operator, claimed on 31 January that it had been told that sponsoring the Dome might help it to win the renewal of its licence against competition from Sir Richard Branson. Two sources informed the newspaper that Mandelson also took an active interest in the Camelot deal after Labour came to power in 1997. Camelot, which finally won the renewal of its lottery licence after a lengthy legal wrangle, gave NMEC free access to its nationwide ticketing outlets (which was worth around £2 million). In 1997, the NMEC's former operations director suggested the idea to the Camelot chairman, George Russell, saying, 'Your licence will be coming up in 2000, it will be a jolly good thing for you to do.' Lord Falconer, who became minister with responsibility for the Dome, attempted to censor a reference to this conversation in *Regeneration*, a history of the Dome. Robinson explained that he had made the suggestion before he started to work formally. He had never meant to imply the offer of sponsorship would influence the government's licence decision.

- Manpower, the employment agency, decided to sponsor the Dome's Work zone after ministers – thought to include Peter Mandelson – appealed directly to one of the firm's directors, Sir Dennis (now Lord) Stevenson, an archetypal New Labour associate.

However, the NMEC responded that as many of its corporate sponsors were involved in negotiations with the government 'over all kinds of policy', the Dome company ensured that 'there was a complete separation between our fundraising teams and the ministers. We are aware that some elements in the media might suggest that there was a conflict of interest and that is why we made sure there was none.'

Consultancy links

Employees seconded by business to government departments became an issue when ministers at first refused to reveal the names of seconded individuals and the areas they were working on. Following a challenge from the Campaign for Freedom of Information and the *Observer* newspaper under the open government code, the government did, reluctantly, release information about its private sector secondees (*Observer*, 17 June 2001). Yet in spite of increased openness, concerns remain about their activities. Alleged cases of improper relations include the oil companies BP and Esso, which have both provided staff to Gordon Brown – and which have gone on to gain tax concessions from the Treasury. The financial consultancy firms PricewaterhouseCoopers, Ernst and Young and Pannell Kerr Forster all supplied staff to the Treasury, and subsequently secured consultancy contracts from the department.

There is no evidence of 'cause and effect' here. But as the Public Administration Select Committee warned in 2001, business secondments could rebound if they were not handled with care, and could be exploited to try to exert influence over government decisions or to drum up business. It advised the government to monitor potential conflicts of interest at the level of individual secondees, at the overall pattern of secondments within a department or agency, and across central government as a whole (PASC 2001b).

The Arthur Andersen connection has also raised concern, not so much over the firm's hapless role in the Enron collapse, but rather over its close links with the Labour government. The firm provided significant assistance to the Labour opposition before the 1997 election, particularly for Gordon Brown on the windfall tax on the privatised utilities. Another connection was Patricia Hewitt, now a cabinet minister, who had been head of research at Andersen Consulting between 1994–97. After Labour's election in 1997, Andersen's share of government consulting work has skyrocketed. One of the more contentious pieces of work it has undertaken for the government was a Treasury-commissioned report on the private finance initiative, which ministers have used to support their claims about PFI projects. However, union chief John Edmonds pointed out that Andersen was involved in 37 PFI schemes itself, including the proposed partial privatisation of the London Underground. He accused Andersen of producing a favourable report on PFI while standing to make millions of pounds from PFI projects.

Jobs for the boys

The rules for civil servants and ministers taking on lucrative business posts after retiring or leaving office are not demanding. The ministerial code prescribes that ministers leaving office should consult the independent, but sympathetic, Advisory Committee on Business Appointments before accepting a commercial position. The committee may recommend delays of up to two years before former ministers take such appointments as a safeguard against any suspicion that a minister was influenced while still in office by the prospect of generous future employment. The rule is also designed to prevent former ministers from making improper use of official information to which they have had access. Similar rules apply to civil servants seeking to move into business, and a significant number of them each year experience restrictions on their acceptance of private sector jobs. The regime may however be fairly described as sympathetic.

Appointments and co-options

The high profile of business people on quangos and task forces, and the growing use of advisers or czars from business, also occasion concern about conflicts of interest. Tony Blair has actively co-opted business leaders to work for him in various capacities, including the publisher Lord Gavron, Lord Haskins, chair of Northern Foods, and Bob Ayling, former head of British Airways. The first two are also party donors. Among the Prime Minister's unpaid policy advisers from business are former CBI head Adair Turner, Nick Lovegrove of McKinsey management consultants, former Coca-Cola president Penny Hughes, and City fund manager Arnab Banerji. The most controversial of these so-called 'blue-skies' posts was that of Lord Birt, the former BBC director-general, as Blair's transport adviser, not least because he was also working for a company owned by one of Britain's major transport operators, Sir Richard Branson. The Transport Select Committee, reporting on Birt's role, complained that:

> . . . powerful business interests make use of the [Prime Minister's] Central Unit to push their own views in a more favourable environment than they might receive from officials in the Department. It is alleged that the Business Planning Zones (areas where no

planning permission will be required), inserted into the Planning Green Paper, are the result of such pressure (Transport, Local Government and the Regions Committee 2002).

The Committee went on to urge, in no uncertain terms, that advisers in the Prime Minister's office must be made properly accountable to Parliament.

9.5 How much confidence do people have that public officials and public services are free from corruption?

Nearly three quarters of the population in a Mori poll in 1994 agreed that 'we, the public' were right 'to expect MPs to behave according to a higher standard of moral behaviour and financial honesty than ordinary people'. The Labour government's ratings on honesty have plummeted. In April 1997, less than one in five people in a Gallup poll found Labour sleazy, as against some two-thirds who believed that the Conservatives were. By 2001, respondents to a Gallup poll said both parties were equally sleazy; and a *Sunday Times* poll in early 2002 found that 60 per cent of people thought Labour gave the impression of being 'sleazy and disreputable', with 41 per cent thinking the same of the Conservatives. The poll also found that 79 per cent of people think the Prime Minister gives special help to Labour's donors from business (*Sunday Times*, 17 February 2002). Findings from the latest Rowntree State of the Nation poll in 2000 indicate that most people think Labour government is permeated by various forms of corruption. About a half think that the various forms of corruption are 'serious'; and two-thirds of respondents believed that ministers were untruthful (Dunleavy et al, 2001).

The public are against MPs' self-regulation of their conduct, even with a nominally independent Commissioner in place. The majority of people believe that the rules governing MPs' conduct should be made law, and enforced either by an independent commission and the civil courts (34 per cent), or investigated by the police as criminal offences punishable in the criminal courts (29 per cent) (Dunleavy et al, 2001). Less than one in ten people accepted that the Prime Minister should be the sole judge of ministers' conduct; and only 16 per cent were ready to trust the House of Commons with overseeing ministers. Some 70 per cent wanted allegations to be independently investigated and enforced – either by an independent commission (42 per cent), or the police (28 per cent) (Dunleavy et al, 2001).

What's to be done?
In 2001, the Council of Europe's team of assessors noted how few convictions for corruption there were in Britain (see 9.2 above), but they urged caution about interpreting the figures and expressed particular concern about self-regulation in Parliament. They proposed that MPs should no longer be exempt from statutory corruption laws, and should make the 'registration system' more open and effective, e.g., by listing the actual amounts paid to MPs and key persons connected to MPs from outside sources, and also their shareholdings. The GRECO team also

● accused the Commons standards committee of failing to give Mrs Filkin sufficient support;
● suggested that the Standards Commissioner should be put on a statutory basis with powers to compel MPs to produce information and attend hearings;

- proposed a register and Commissioner for the House of Lords and similar measures to strengthen the Commissioner's inquiries;
- proposed a central authority for dealing with the registration of the interests of ministers and civil servants, reviewing whether ministers and officials are complying with their codes of conduct, and for recording and investigating complaints; and
- proposed that the ministerial code should be put on a statutory basis.

Clearly, the House must abandon its effort to maintain self-regulation. A future standards commissioner cannot be a servant of a self-interested and opaque body like the House of Commons Commission; and he or she must have the powers to compel MPs to produce information and attend hearings. Nor can the Prime Minister remain solely responsible for enforcing the ministerial code: political considerations and loyalties will always come first. We need some kind of Public Standards Commissioner who can oversee ministers' conduct and dealings with business.

Section three: civil society and popular participation

Ten: the media in a democratic society

Squeezing out media diversity

Do the media operate in a way that sustains democratic values?

Tickle the public,
Make 'em grin,
The more you tickle,
The more you'll win
Victorian rhyme[1]

Introduction

Television, radio, newspapers and magazines – the main means by which citizens are informed about the issues of the day – seek to satisfy the liberal 'fourth estate' view of their social responsibilities and their democratic role to greatly varying degrees. At their most basic, these liberal arguments can be collapsed into three fundamental roles for the mass media:

● they act as purveyors of information which citizens need in order to make informed judgements about their political leaders and to participate effectively in the proper functioning of a democracy;

- they provide a public sphere in which citizens can come together, debate and discuss issues of importance to the country, and relay their views to elected representatives; and
- they provide a critical check on governments and the political classes to inhibit the abuse of political power and ensure that decisions and the decision-making machinery is open to critical public scrutiny.

In each of these roles, the mass media have a potentially vital contribution to make. Television is central to life in modern Britain. Television stations and channels are regulated to achieve the first two of these political roles in an impartial and balanced way under scrutiny from regulatory bodies (the BBC Board of Governors, the Independent Television Commission, and the Radio Authority). The Broadcasting Standards Commission seeks to uphold 'standards and fairness' in both television and radio. The government plans to merge all these bodies into Ofcom, a single giant regulator for broadcasting. The press are not under a duty to be impartial or balanced in their reporting or comment and are loosely regulated on a voluntary basis by an industry-based Press Complaints Commission.

But the ability of the media to fulfil these roles is being eroded by a number of structural pressures, as the answers to the questions that follow will show.

10.1 How pluralistic is the ownership of the media, how representative are they of different opinions, and how accessible are they to different sections of society?

In general, the media in the United Kingdom are diverse, representative of a wide range of opinions and interests, and widely accessible to most citizens, including those who are poor and isolated. The British public has been brought up on cheap or free forms of television and newspapers. Some 98 per cent of households in the UK own at least one TV set; and on the average weekday, well over half the population aged over 15 read a national morning newspaper. Nearly nine out of ten adults read a regional or local paper every week.

Plurality of ownership

Ownership of the mass media, as in most advanced democracies, is steadily moving into fewer corporate hands in the wake of accelerating technological change. News International, the largest UK media player, is the UK operation of News Corporation, a global conglomerate based in the USA and second only to Time Warner-AOL internationally. As well as BSkyB satellite television, News International owns four national newspapers, publishing firms and magazines in the UK. Its head, Rupert Murdoch, once remarked, 'in the end, technology can get past politicians and regulators' (Hird, 1993). There is considerable cross-ownership in the UK of commercial television channels, national, regional and local newspapers; publishing houses; and radio stations. The BBC, itself a major corporate player, stands apart, providing television and radio (from national to local) as a public service. The press is independently owned and represents different political views and interests.

It is becoming increasingly clear that the market liberal view – that a competitive market-place will naturally produce a pluralism of media voices – is simplistic. Several factors are at work to constrain any such pluralism:

- the accumulation of channels and/or titles in the hands of large conglomerates with enormous market power;
- the use of corporate power in cross-subsidies to under-cut competitors (e.g., Murdoch's under-pricing of *The Times* to damage other broadsheet titles and possibly drive one at least out of the market);
- a slow but progressive decline in newspaper readership as other channels of communication expand; and
- the control exercised by media owners to shape the broad thrust of news and editorial comment.

The problem of proprietorial influence has, to some extent, been mitigated since the days of the old-fashioned press lords by broadcasting, whose strictly regulated rules on impartiality allow no room for blatant propaganda. Even here, however, difficulties have emerged over the last few years which have potentially negative consequences in a plural democracy.

In commercial broadcasting, governments have been under both economic and political pressure to allow progressive de-regulation since the late 1980s. For the first 30 years of its existence, it was an accepted principle that only a firm regulatory framework could secure diversity and plurality in broad-casting. As a result of that principle, the main commercial network had been run as 15 separate regional licences, and the second commercial network – Channel 4 – had been created as a publicly-owned channel with strict public service requirements. In addition, through the Independent Broadcasting Authority, there were strictly enforced restrictions that prevented newspaper proprietors from taking control of ITV franchises.

The Conservative governments relaxed the rules against cross-ownership significantly in the 1990s in the interests of the free market and the promotion of a 'bigger' private media industry. The Broadcasting Act 1990 retained the ban on cross-ownership (and in fact wrote it into statute for the first time), but also allowed an exception for any 'non-domestic satellite channel'. This opening applied to Rupert Murdoch's Sky, which had launched in February 1989 from the Luxembourg-based Astra satellite. Since Sky's operation and target audience was entirely British, this was a specious get-out clause engineered by prime minister Margaret Thatcher entirely for the benefit of her political ally, Rupert Murdoch. John Major was the beneficiary of Murdoch's gratitude in the 1992 general election when all his five national newspapers were ardently pro-Conservative.

In November 1993, the government said companies would be allowed to own two regional ITV licences, thereby beginning the process of consolidation within ITV. The Broadcasting Act 1996 then went considerably further by abandoning for the first time the cross-ownership restrictions and allowing newspaper groups to move into commercial television as long as they controlled less than 20 per cent of the national newspaper market (thus excluding Murdoch's News International and, at the time, Mirror Group Newspapers). It also allowed further consolidation of the ITV companies, as long as no company ended up owning more than 15 per cent of the total television market. As a result, two major corporate players emerged within ITV in the late 1990s: Carlton and Granada. Amongst media owners, much was being made of the need to try to create a British 'world champion' media conglomerate to match Germany's Bertelsmann or France's Vivendi. They argued that the rapid changes in technology leading to 'convergence' in the media industries were rendering regulation irrelevant, and pleaded the case for the great commercial opportunities available to those corporations which were allowed to expand and consolidate without the dead weight of government intervention.

Within this context, the Labour government, committed in its 2001 manifesto to a new Communications Act, launched a draft Communications Bill in May 2002. The drive for scale and economic success does not sit comfortably with equal concerns for more creativity, more pluralism, more quality and more diversity in media content. This conflict of priorities between competitive success on the one hand and creative and democratic enhancement on the other is not new, but has been particularly apparent in the thinking behind the new legislative framework which will dictate the shape and priorities of this sector for at least a decade. Announcing a consultation paper on media ownership in October 2001, Culture Secretary Tessa Jowell explicitly acknowledged the dichotomy on this issue but left no doubt in which direction the government intended to move:

> We have two aims. We need to uphold the interests of our citizens. They must continue to receive a diversity of content from their media. They must also continue to receive that diversity from a plurality of sources. But we also want to encourage competition and to make Britain home to the most dynamic and competitive media market in the world. So we will try to be as deregulatory as possible, and intend to allow what market consolidation we can (speech to the Society of Editors, 22 October 2001).

Yet even the government's staunchest friends were stunned by the scale and speed of deregulation being proposed in the draft bill she published. All foreign ownership restrictions are to be swept away, allowing any of the American giants such as Disney or TimeWarner-AOL to buy up British television companies – despite no reciprocal arrangement with the USA. ITV companies will be allowed to consolidate into a single group (subject only to agreement by the Competition Commission), and there will be no restrictions on Channels 3 and 5 being owned by the same corporation. All restrictions on cross-ownership will be swept away bar one: any newspaper group with more than 20 per cent of the national market will not be able to buy ITV. Channel 5, however, is available for sale to everyone and there are some obvious synergies between Channel 5 and BSkyB which make it the most likely prey for Rupert Murdoch. There was even speculation that this particular relaxation was part of an implicit 'deal' with Murdoch in return for a softer line in his newspapers on the single currency in the run-up to a Euro referendum.

The only concession to pluralism was a recognition by the government that television news required special protection. It will therefore maintain the plural ownership of Independent Television News, or whoever succeeds it as ITV's news provider, allowing any single investor no more than a 40 per cent stake. This clause protects it from becoming a news division of ITV's corporate owner and becoming more vulnerable (as has already happened in the USA) to influence from the corporate centre. Unfortunately the same does not apply to Channel 5 news. There can be little doubt that a Murdoch-owned C5 would waste little time in substituting Sky News for ITN on the channel's news slots while simultaneously driving up the C5 share of the television audience by cross-promoting from News International's newspapers and BSkyB. There is a get-out clause for the government should Channel 5 look like taking a significant market share (in other words, overtaking ITV): the Secretary of State, on advice from the new regulator Ofcom, can take steps to ensure that the channel's news provider is nominated by Ofcom which can in turn 'derecognise' Sky News. The prospect of any government being quite so foolhardy as to confront the UK's most powerful press baron in such stark terms is frankly remote. While Channel 4's special remit is to be preserved, the Channel itself has made it clear that it fears being squeezed between two mighty commercial giants, even to the point at which it may have to seek privatisation. At that point, of course, such luxuries as the Channel 4 News – a serious one hour news bulletin in peak time, with at least half the content devoted to foreign affairs – will vanish.

Although Ofcom will be a very powerful regulator, it will have to balance any commitment to pluralism with an explicit duty to help Britain become the 'most dynamic and competitive communications and media market in the world'. The draft bill makes it clear that, for all its rhetoric about wanting to protect pluralism, the government is committed to an ideological belief that competition will be better for 'consumers'. It is difficult to avoid the conclusion that consolidation in commercial broadcasting will bring with it fewer voices. Moreover, there is no reason to suppose that such consolidation will diminish the number of legislative favours which broadcasters seek from government, thereby adding to the 'chilling' effect which such dependence on government patronage can create. It is unlikely that a broadcaster looking for some kind of regulatory relaxation will be investing scarce resources in programmes that ask difficult questions of government or make politically embarrassing revelations.

10.2 How independent are the media from government, and how free are they and government media policies from subordination to multi-national companies and foreign governments?

The most overt attempt by a recent government to impose its will on the media was Douglas Hurd's use of his powers as Home Secretary to prohibit BBC and ITV from interviewing members and associates of Sinn Fein and other Northern Irish organisations (Klug et al, 1996). The Hurd ban was upheld both by the House of Lords and the European Commission of Human Rights. However, it is unlikely that such a ban would be justified under the Human Rights Act in today's climate, unless compelling national security issues were at stake. We deal with legal and institutional means at the disposal of UK governments for the suppression of information above (see 3.2); here we concentrate on government interference and news management (but see also 7.8 and 7.9).

Independence from government interference and harassment
The broadcast media are governed, as indicated above, by institutions like the BBC, ITA and Radio Authority, which are 'hands-off' public bodies formally designed to avoid direct government or political control or interference. The BBC has a royal charter which is meant to signify its independence. However, there has always been a complex and umbilical relationship between the BBC and governments. Though fiercely guarding its journalistic independence most of the time, there have been instances of BBC self-censorship throughout the BBC's history (though never overt government censorship). The three levers of government power over the BBC – setting the licence fee, appointing governors, and laying down the conditions of the BBC charter and licence – have at various times allowed subtle pressure to be exerted despite the determined professionalism of BBC journalists. Governments can obviously also exert influence over commercial broadcasters through their powers of appointment to the regulators.

Perhaps the most blatant example of political interference in recent broadcasting history was the long campaign against the BBC undertaken by Mrs Thatcher after 1979. The government's own man was installed as chairman of the BBC governors; the Corporation's future as a publicly-funded, public service broadcaster was put in doubt; and the BBC Director-General was sacked in 1987. Under the regime of John Birt, deputy director and then director (1987-2000), the BBC became more deferential. Birt for example stopped *Panorama* from revealing, on the eve of the Gulf war, that lax government controls and collusion had allowed Saddam Hussein to build his Supergun. Birt's defenders argued that, with the BBC Charter at stake, he was being cautiously long-sighted (see Barnett and Curry, 1994; and Weir, 1994). But even when the BBC's future was again secure, programmes other than those on matters of war and conflict were cancelled or delayed for political reasons. But while there have certainly been instances of self-censorship, the BBC and its journalists have fiercely guarded its journalistic independence most of the time.

Regulatory oversight of the BBC

While the commercial sector is to face substantial deregulation, the BBC will be subject to greater regulatory oversight than before. The government's determination to use the BBC to push ahead with a shift from analogue to digital television has led to the Culture Secretary's direct involvement in programming. This policy initiative was to be kick-started by a government inquiry into BBC funding in 1999 that was designed to identify ways in which the BBC could provide additional free-to-air digital services – thereby, it was hoped, fuelling consumer demand for digital televisions and speeding up the switchover. The inquiry, chaired by Labour supporting economist Gavyn Davies, reported in July 1999 and recommended an annual digital charge to be added to the licence fee. But the then Culture Secretary Chris Smith rejected the Davies proposal when he agreed a licence fee settlement in February 2000. He opted for a generous settlement – but the quid pro quo was the development of a digital 'package' of new channels which then had to be approved by the Secretary of State.

This was the first time that a government took on itself the responsibility for approving a major plank of programming strategy, at a time when the rapid expansion of new cable and satellite channels meant the arrival of many serious objectors to new BBC services. (When the BBC published its proposals, Smith's successor, Tessa Jowell, was caught in the middle between the BBC and promoting its digital strategy and a furious backlash and intense lobbying from rival commercial channels trying to prevent the BBC intruding on 'their' patch. Her compromise was to allow all the proposed digital services, bar one – the TV channel aimed at young people.) The intimate government involvement in BBC decision-making was exacerbated by Smith's tendency to pass judgement on BBC programming which provoked the new Director General Greg Dyke to rebuke Smith publicly in 2000.

Meanwhile, a contentious policy debate over whether Ofcom should be responsible for regulating the BBC as well as the commercial sector began in the period of waiting for the draft Communications Bill and will certainly continue as the bill makes its way through Parliament. Superficially, this is an attractive option because it places the BBC outside any immediate influence from government. But it would also remove its scope for independent decision-making and make it far more vulnerable to commercial competitors who wish to limit its spheres of operation. For that reason, commercial broadcasters have been lobbying the government intensively to place the BBC under the Ofcom umbrella. There is more commercial pressure than ever before to restrict severely the areas in which the BBC are operating, and ultimately to reduce the BBC to a public service rump in the same mould as America's PBS.

The draft bill resists this option. But it does for the first time give Ofcom the duty of reporting (every three years) on the state of the whole broadcasting sector, including the BBC. Although it will not have the right to instruct the BBC on whether it should be making more of certain kinds of programmes – a power which remains with the BBC governors – it will certainly be able to make strong recommendations which will put the BBC under strong external pressure. With the BBC's charter and agreement up for renewal in 2006, the door has been opened to some very robust debate about the direction, funding and even existence of the Corporation. Meanwhile, a Communications Act based on the draft bill will become law by the end of 2003 and will set in stone the most radical consolidation of ownership in the British media seen for generations. There will, inevitably, be room for fewer and less diverse voices.

New heights in government media management

New Labour came to power in May 1997 after 18 years of opposition with painful memories of vitriolic attacks by the press and incompetent handling of broadcasters. As the media have proliferated and their perceived power has grown, so has the determination within Labour circles to ensure that they would never again suffer through an inability to deal competently with the mass media. There is nothing new or inherently sinister about a government or political party wanting to manage the way in which its policies and actions are presented. But the sheer scale and professionalism of official news management and the resources which this government as a whole – not just the Prime Minister's office – is prepared to invest in exercising control of the news agenda has transformed the relationship between government and the media; and suborned the impartiality and independence of public information about the activities of government (see also Section 7.9).

New Labour's news strategies now permeate the government information service. They have been largely shaped by two men: Alastair Campbell, the Prime Minister's Press Secretary and Peter Mandelson, Labour's director of communications in the 1980s and subsequently MP and cabinet minister. Campbell, who entered government as the Prime Minister's press secretary, is now in charge of the government's media relations, promotion and advertising activities. Campbell is a party political appointee, but he has special powers to direct and manage civil servants and he has revolutionalised the Government Information Service (GIS) (see further Section 7.8). Some of his overhaul of outdated bureaucratic machinery was quite legitimate, but under his direction there has been a further erosion of the line between efficient communication and government propaganda funded by the tax-payer (but see his evidence to the Public Administration Select Committee in June 1998; HC 770). Campbell presents his revamping of the GIS as a response to the gradual erosion of serious reporting, the media's own spin on public affairs, the rise in trivialisation and cynicism in broadcast coverage of politics, and the 'growing gap between the real agenda and the Medialand agenda' (Campbell, 1999).

These are all valid concerns. But the zeal with which Campbell set about mastering the media and shaping and controlling the news agenda in the interests of the government has damaged both political debate and, as he and various ministers now recognise, the government itself. Journalists became convinced that the government was untrustworthy and the public soon came to resent its attachment to spin (Dunleavy et al, 2001).

Some of Campbell's techniques were familiar enough. Thus, timing policy statements and speeches for maximum media impact; rebutting statements made by the opposition as soon as (and even before) they are made; leaking parts of forthcoming announcements to selected journalists; ensuring that all spokespeople are aware of the party line and stay 'on message'; and, in broadcasting, controlling access to certain programmes so that only favoured speakers appear, have all been part of the political reporting landscape for the last ten years. However, for the public the trouble is that the current government does it more systematically, more ruthlessly, and more autocratically, than ever before. These techniques are damaging enough, even if they are the stuff of modern politics. But they can on occasion override the executive's formal accountability to Parliament. The desire to secure the best possible reception for new policy statements or initiatives leads ministers and their familiars to filter them through pre-selected leaks to favoured journalists rather than through Parliament. See, for example, the 'trailing' of budget news across the press in advance of budget day. Betty Boothroyd, the Speaker of the House of Commons in New Labour's first term, frequently voiced her concerns about such leaks (see for example, the *Guardian*, 9 April 1998) and in April 2000 finally forced a junior minister to apologise in the Commons after warning government departments about their tendency to regard 'the interests of Parliament' as being 'secondary to media presentation'.

The influence of special advisers

The position is complicated by the increase of special advisers within government. Their brief, previously largely confined to policy advice, now frequently extends to media relations. Half of the 81 special advisers in government – all political appointees – undertake media work on behalf of the Prime Minister and ministers. These political appointees exert influence over the media strategies of information officials in their department and augment the flow of official information with their own partisan briefings. The case of Jo Moore (see also Section 7.9) illustrated not only the single-minded devotion to information control that Labour advisers displayed, but over time also revealed the kinds of manipulation for which some of them were hired. It soon transpired that senior GIS officials at the former DTLR resisted pressure from Moore before her notorious 11 September memo to convey negative information to journalists about London's transport commissioner Bob Kiley. Kiley's resolute opposition to the government's funding scheme for London Underground made him a New Labour target for political attack. Journalists like Polly Toynbee confirmed publicly the existence of a whisper campaign against Kiley.

It is not as though Moore, a senior press official who had previously worked for the Labour party, was the proverbial 'bad apple', who could be removed without spoiling the whole barrel. Insiders regarded her as a highly professional operator. Her conduct was not untypical for special advisers. Moreover, political journalists rarely reveal or complain about such conduct because they rely on special advisers for surreptitious leaks and gossip. But the 'bad-mouthing' of opponents (and indeed even colleagues and supporters) is one of New Labour's most damaging innovations that roused the novelist Ken Follett to public complaint. Robert Winston, the ennobled doctor friend of Tony Blair, could not be openly bad-mouthed when he complained in a *New Statesman* interview that the NHS was 'gradually deteriorating' (14 January 2000). However, Campbell and his partner Fiona Millar, who was Cherie Blair's personal media chaperone, performed a double whammy on Winston to avert the political damage to Labour. Winston was at once accused of breaching Cherie Blair's confidentiality (for discussing arrangements for the birth of her baby) and Campbell used this personal mistake to extract a retraction from him (see Rawnsley, 2000).

A few ministers complained early in the government's life about the fixation with news management, spin and the practice of the 'black arts'; and over half the electorate saw media manipulation as a major problem under Labour, and a third more as a minor problem (Dunleavy et al, 2001). But the prominence of Blair's close adviser, Campbell (and once Mandelson and Charlie Whelan, Gordon Brown's fixer), at the heart of government clearly implicates the Prime Minister and Chancellor in their machinations, especially as they have often been the beneficiaries of their arts. It is said that it was Blair who saved Moore from the sack when her email memo became public knowledge. And Campbell used Anji Hunter, when she was Blair's close confidante and gatekeeper in government, to leak controversial stories to newspapers, allowing him then to deny any knowledge of how they became public (*Guardian*, 9 November 2001). There are also charges against the New Labour regime in government of bullying and badgering the press (see Section 10.4 below).

Issues of media influence

The obverse to complaints about government spin is the accusation that some of the media were dictating government policy. Almost from the moment that Tony Blair was elected as party leader in 1995, the determination to bring 'on side' those media owners and press interests believed to be critical to electoral success was evident. It was an almost unchallenged view within the Labour party after 1992 that the support of more newspapers, and in particular Rupert Murdoch's right-wing *Sun*, was going to be crucial to winning an election. Following the *Sun*'s decision to switch sides in 1997 and Labour's subsequent victory, the newly anointed Prime Minister Tony Blair sent a hand-written message to the editor of the *Sun* in which he thanked the paper for its 'magnificent support' and said it 'really did make the difference' (*Guardian 2*, 19 May 1997). For Blair, the *Sun*'s support was the culmination of a courtship that started within months of his election as Labour Party leader with a trip to the Cayman Islands to address senior executives of Murdoch's News Corporation.

Observers and many Labour Party supporters, already suspicious of what appeared to be a distinct rightward shift in party policy, started to wonder whether any of these shifts might be attributed to attempts to appease certain sections of the press: not just the *Sun*, but the equally right-wing *Daily Mail*. Those suspicions were given substantial grounding when two damaging leaks emerged from inside the Prime Minister's office in 2000. One, written by the Prime Minister himself two months before it was leaked, complained of 'a sense that the Government . . . are somehow out of touch with gut British instincts'. He talked about the need for a strategy to combat perceptions of weakness, and focused on five specific areas: asylum, crime, defence, the family, and the criminal law (he saw the need for a review of sentencing in the light of the case of Tony Martin, the farmer who had shot dead an intruder and was sentenced to life after being convicted of murder). On the very day Blair wrote that memo – 29 April – a *Daily Mail* editorial railed against a 'liberal establishment' and specifically mentioned four of the five areas identified in Blair's note. A fearful second memo, written a few days later by Blair's marketing strategist Philip Gould, showed just how far concerns about public perception of the government dominated the prime ministerial agenda, and that the most influential filters of that perception for Downing Street appeared to be the editorial approach of newspapers which were not traditional Labour supporters. This obsession with presentation as reflected through Labour's natural opponents received short shrift from Hugo Young in the *Guardian*:

> In Gould's world, perception, far from being at odds with reality, is reality. And that is exactly Labour's problem. Its substance is not apparent. Its manipulation is too obvious

> . . . Though the *Daily Mail* isn't mentioned in these memos, it is the fountain-head of wisdom (20 July 2000).

Implicit in the Gould approach revealed by those memos is an assumption that somehow the agenda of the *Daily Mail* accurately reflects the agenda of its readers rather than its owners. Moreover, it also assumes an influence exerted on readers which is not open to contrary arguments by politicians.

How far the press influences the view of its readers is almost impossible to determine. But they certainly try. In June 2002, Rupert Murdoch openly declared his intention to use his newspaper to campaign against UK entry into the Euro and he has long used his press to advance his commercial and political interests, and especially his outright hostility towards the Euro and closer UK integration in Europe. The *Telegraph* titles are also virulently anti-EU under their proprietor, Conrad Black (who was ennobled at the request of William Hague while he was Tory leader). The attitude of the press as a whole may or not have influenced the popular anti-EU mood, but the hostility of the New International titles towards Europe has certainly contributed to Blair's cautious approach to joining the Euro. Such passive acceptance of the power of the press confers considerable political influence on media owners. That newspaper proprietors can and do wield political power is scarcely novel; but what appears to have changed since the days of press tycoons like Beaverbrook is the faith that this government at least now places in newspapers as tribunes of the people rather than instruments of personal propaganda.

Foreign influence

Foreign governments do not command direct influence over the mass media in the UK, but the world hegemony of the American entertainment media plainly does exercise a diffuse influence over everyday lives and thinking in this country. Less obviously, the ferocious lobbying of the Israeli embassy and its wider popular lobby does, for example, influence the UK media's reports and comments on the Israeli-Palestinian conflict.

10.3 How far are the media able to fulfil their roles of informing the public, providing a public space for debate on issues of importance, and investigating government and large corporations?

In Britain, a series of factors are combining to produce what is probably the most ferociously competitive period in the history of the country's media. In turn, that has had a knock-on effect on the quality of programming and reporting. Briefly, the factors are as follows:

- the relaxation of the regulatory regime in broadcasting (see 10.1 above) has been part-and-parcel of the new competitive environment. Channels 4 and 5 became rivals to ITV in the advertising market; and the introduction of auctions for ITV licences produced large debt levels;
- recently, the two big ITV companies, Carlton and Granada, suffered huge financial losses (around £20million a month) in their attempt to lift Britain's commercial terrestrial digital TV service beyond one million viewers. As this great digital enterprise finally collapsed under the pressure of mounting debt, inability to attract new subscribers fast enough, dodgy reception and competition

from Sky digital (which is still under investigation by the Office of Fair Trading), Carlton and Granada were forced to walk away from a total investment of £800 million;

● the number of broadcasting and electronic outlets is expanding exponentially. Relatively few people tune into 24-hour news channels or make regular use of the Internet, but the number of available sources of information makes for a surfeit of opportunity; and

● similar commercial pressures and falling advertising revenue within the declining press sector have brought about smaller and more hard-worked journalistic staffs; a growth of (cheaper) freelancing at the expense of dedicated staff reporters; and redundancies at most national newspapers in 2001.

All these pressures have forced both television and the press into a pronounced shift towards a more 'popular' emphasis on entertainment. On television, the result was inevitable: a greater emphasis on high profile, big-rating programmes – particularly in peak-time. The great commercial TV current affairs programmes of the 1970s and 1980s – *This Week*, *World in Action*, *First Tuesday* – were the television vanguard of precisely the kind of critical, scrutinising, interrogative programmes which upset governments and corporations and play a vital role in a vigorous democracy. They could usually expect minimum ratings of three to four million viewers, respectable but unsustainable against the ten million plus peak-time audiences routinely won by quiz shows or soap operas. They were the first victims of the free market. Such programmes were no longer protected by the 'light touch' ITC. The days, just ten years ago, when the old Independent Broadcasting Authority was laying down criteria for the volume of peak-time current affairs on commercial television – expecting a range of political material to be covered and monitoring output to check compliance – have gone.

As market pressures intensified, *News at Ten* was not far behind. Now that the regulatory spell was broken, there were increasingly vocal protests about the anachronism of a 'prescribed' time for TV news on commercial television. The cause of regulation was not helped by the ITC's decision first to allow ITV to move its news to 11 p.m. and then to change its mind when the utterly predictable fall in news audiences followed (predictable simply because large numbers of people go to bed before 11 p.m.). The reinstated *News at Ten* – 20 minutes long, three times a week – was from the outset a pale imitation of its former incarnation and is unlikely to last for long. With a strong BBC news presence, this probably matters less than the demise of ITV's formerly vigorous current affairs culture which had a powerful, independent journalistic ethos and was much less vulnerable to accusations of self-censorship than the BBC. Whatever the aspirations of ITV's one remaining contribution, *Tonight with Trevor McDonald*, it has neither the resources nor reputation to pursue a hard-headed investigative agenda. Nor is there any regulatory will-power to demand higher aspirations.

This is partly because of the pressure on budgets. Even before the worldwide recession started to grip the world's corporate throat, effects of increased competition were having a severe downward impact on expenditure. With more emphasis on efficiency savings and delivering 'more for less', the attraction in television of programmes with high budgets and relatively low ratings diminished rapidly, especially after the collapse of ITV's digital adventure. Suggestions that programme budgets on ITV were going to be drastically cut as a result appeared to be wide of the mark, but the loss of such a huge amount of potential investment in programming could only exacerbate the difficulties of a severe advertising slump.

ITV did achieve one cost-cutting victory in 2001 when renegotiating its contract with ITN to provide

ITV's news. For the first time in its history, ITN faced a serious challenge as ITV news provider from a consortium of five broadcasters which included Murdoch's British Sky Broadcasting. Although the political realities made a change unlikely, the competition forced ITN to revise its budget downwards from £45 million to £36 million – a 20 per cent cut which is likely to have long-term repercussions for the quality of ITN's news-gathering operation.

Despite its relative wealth, the BBC has not been immune from the pressure on budgets. Partly as a reaction to concern in the early 1990s that it might be losing its popular touch, partly in recognition of the more ratings-conscious and populist environment in the commercial sector, and partly to divert some resources into its new digital operations, the BBC has been every bit as rigorous in analysing its bottom lines and looking for programme 'efficiencies' (cuts) in news and current affairs. Producers on *Panorama* insist that programmes are being made for less than they were five years ago, and are concerned about the growing pressures on staff and research time (Barnett and Seymour, 1999). During 1999, there was a spate of incidents on factual programmes where mistakes were made as producers and researchers sought to get material on screen without making the kinds of checks that should have been routine. Although confined to documentary programmes, these and other incidents were symptomatic of a widespread sense of corners being cut and staff being pushed to their limits. The more ratings-conscious BBC has recently shifted *Panorama* from its traditional mid-evening spot on Mondays to late on Sundays. There is also the danger that the BBC's 'public service' values may be swept along by the tabloid instincts that a more ratings-conscious environment encourages. The BBC political journalist Nicholas Jones has commented:

> The constant battle for readers, listeners and viewers has had a profound effect on news-gathering . . . However much broadcasters might try to distance themselves from such influences, the excesses of the tabloids do colour their news judgement and are reflected in their treatment of politics (Jones, 1995).

The role of the press

Newspapers once employed investigative teams of reporters to investigate issues of public concern. The most effective of these teams was probably the *Sunday Times*'s former Insight team which broke several scandals, most notably the Thalidomide drug tragedy in the 1960s. The Insight title still survives. But the quality of reporting has been dissipated. Nowadays, only the *Guardian* and, to a lesser degree, the *Observer* and *Independent* titles invest real resources in investigative journalism. Both the *Guardian* and *Observer* have in recent years exposed political corruption (e.g., the exposure of Jonathan Aitken, the 'Lobbygate' sting) and the *Guardian*, for example, also revealed the carnage in Serbia's concentration camps. Most broadsheet newspapers also continue to employ well-informed and skilled specialist journalists and to invest in substantial political coverage.

However, the end result of an environment where less money is chasing a much wider array of news outlets with fewer obligations to provide serious or informational material is, inevitably, an impoverished public sphere. In the press, it is simply not possible for an on-demand freelance who is paid by the word to invest the same dedication, painstaking and sometimes laborious research in a difficult piece of investigative journalism. Many newspaper professionals have commented on the rise of the confessional column (unflatteringly known as 'me journalism' and immortalised in the two *Private Eye* by-lines of

Phil Space and Polly Filler), where readers are treated to the many tribulations of life on the school run, in the supermarket, waiting in the doctor's surgery or on holiday in Tuscany. Where such columns complement rather than dilute more serious reporting, nothing is lost. The fear is that the number of column inches have – for cost reasons – expanded in inverse proportion to the number of reporters who have the time, commitment and employment security to ferret out information rather than sub-edit press releases or write mini autobiographies.

There has been a growing sense of unease about a creeping process of trivialisation in the broadsheets. The author, Anthony Sampson, a member of the Scott Trust which owns the *Guardian*, has written that 'the frontier between qualities and popular papers has virtually disappeared' and that the root cause is the 'cut-throat contest' in which British national newspapers are engaged. '[H]ow far does this competition provide real variety? In many ways, I believe, it has led to less choice. In particular the high ground of serious reporting, investigating and foreign coverage has been vacated' (Sampson, 1997). The experienced *Guardian* reporter and columnist, Matthew Engel, concluded that 'broadsheet newspapers have changed beyond recognition in the past ten years'. He accused broadsheets of slavishly following the tabloid agenda and attributed the change wholly to new competitive forces in the broadsheet market: among them, the price-cutting tactics of Rupert Murdoch's *The Times*; and the influence of the *Daily Mail*, whose popular mid-market style and flair broadsheet editors were now trying to emulate (Engel, 1996).

The kind of agenda which concerns these and other observers is one based on a mix of show-business personalities, royal family stories, sex scandals, entertainment and 'sleaze' stories. These have always been the staple diet of the popular press. What is new is the front-page coverage given in almost every serious newspaper to stories about the misadventures of Angus Deayton, Sven-Goran Erikson or Hugh Grant. Even the *Sun*'s front-page scoop that the Queen keeps in her bathroom a duck wearing a crown found its way into the *Guardian* (albeit on an inside page). There is a growing fear that this kind of journalism is replacing more serious reporting and analysis of public affairs. These fears were echoed by Peter Riddell, a political columnist for the *The Times* who has written:

> The price war and increased competition among the broadsheets has led to a shift down market on at least the news and feature pages of many papers. The emphasis is on attracting marginal and younger readers who are believed to be less interested in reading about 'heavy' politics – that is policy rather than personality. So while many broadsheets, if not tabloids, still carry plenty of space devoted to politics, the style has changed. An increasing number of stories are about scandal and misconduct rather than policy or procedure (Riddell, 1999).

Media disdain for politicians

British politics is adversarial, and many seasoned politicians have been brought up – and themselves survived – in an environment of robust argumentation. Politics is therefore partly about personal rivalries, back-stabbing and dissent, but is also about the nitty-gritty of creating policy, of trying to create a better understand of social and economic problems and searching for ways of resolving them. The increasing media tendency to concentrate on party splits and personal conflict has consequences both for fostering greater political timidity within parties and creating a more distrustful political culture. The media often seize upon a chance remark and exploit it as a significant political 'gaffe'. Hugo

Young, writing in the *Guardian*, described the fears and caution of party managers as 'understandable' and continued:

> The vultures wait to pounce on every particle of contention with an appetite they never had when Mrs Thatcher was getting the Tory Party ready to rescue Britain from the socialist nightmare. Tabloid values, played swiftly into television, kill off serious policy debate before it starts (18 April 1996).

The problem is that such attitudes are relentlessly negative not just about politics but about politicians. Their roots are in a quite proper and non-deferential determination to hold politicians accountable and to demand that public policy decisions should be undertaken in the public spotlight rather than behind closed doors. The question is how that perfectly proper – indeed democratically essential – process of scrutiny can be conducted with detached scepticism without crossing the line into derision and cynicism; and can penetrate deeper than the surface of personality politics. The political executive deliberately denies the media (and public) access to the substance of policy-making through the Official Secrets Act, secrecy laws, the so-called Freedom of Information Act, and spin (see 3.5 and 7.8). Sadly, most of the media are satisfied with scraps and do nothing to redress the balance.

The notion that politicians are honest, honourable individuals doing their damnedest to make their country a better place seems faintly odd in today's media environment. The political parties themselves bear a great deal of responsibility for their continual media manipulation and bad-mouthing of each other. Yet Andrew Marr, now the BBC's political editor, maintains that the media and journalists desperately trying to get themselves noticed by turning up 'the volume on the vituperation machine' are the main culprits. He fears that the 'culture of abuse':

> . . . is acid. It is eating away at the thoughtful culture of public discourse, burning out nuance, gobbling up detail, dissolving mere facts. And that, in turn, cannot help a struggling democracy. Serious news outlets do care about democracy..... But we need, somehow, to crawl back up the slope to level-headed argument as well (*Observer*, 24 October 1999).

The BBC is the main stage on which the tensions between the culture of abuse – or rather let us say, of scepticism – towards the utterances of politicians and a sense of responsibility for fostering a healthy attitude towards democracy are often played out. Here is an organisation run according to worthier criteria than simply returning dividends to shareholders. The BBC has a huge journalistic staff, a tradition of public service broadcasting and a history and reputation of fair-minded, high quality political coverage. Its journalists are just as immersed in the competitive culture as their professional colleagues in commercial television and the press. But the institution's role in public life gives it a special responsibility towards enhancing a vibrant democratic culture. How does the BBC square the journalistic responsibility to seek after truth with the institutional responsibility to respect the nation's democratically-elected representatives?

The BBC's dilemma was illustrated graphically by a speech delivered by its then Director General John Birt in February 1995. He contrasted two traditions in covering politics, 'disputation' and 'reflection'. While accepting that disputation had 'always been an integral part of British... culture and society', he suggested that the balance had perhaps swung too far and argued the case for a balance between policy and politics in the BBC's coverage:

> The media today resound with acrimony, allegations of incompetence, demands for resignation. Rivalry between politicians or differences within parties are played out as a national soap opera. . . . In the era of the soundbite and the tabloid, a stray remark, a poorly judged phrase on a Sunday morning programme – a repeated evasion, a careful nuance, a finely drawn distinction – can build by Tuesday into a cacophony of disputation and a political crisis . . . Tone in journalism matters. A measure of humility and a little more dispassion – always in alliance with sceptical and rigorous questioning – would be worthier qualities (The Independent Newspapers annual lecture, 3 February 1995).

The effect of the media on public attitudes

But what effect does the quality of media output and news coverage actually have on public understanding and attitudes? Does the combination of higher levels of education in the UK and the spread of the mass media create citizens who are better informed and more understanding about political affairs? Or do the media undermine democracy because they over-simplify, trivialise and sensationalise events? In 1996, British Social Attitudes undertook a survey to determine the effect of the media on viewers and readers. Did they promote political knowledge and understanding; belief in their own political efficacy; trust in officials; and faith in the workings of the British political system and democracy; or did they alienate people and create political cynicism and disillusionment? Analysis of the data employed controls for the possibly strong effects of education, social class and party loyalties (Newton, 1997).

The report found that education was a powerful factor in its own right. The more highly educated people are, the more they know and understand politics, feel a sense of personal efficacy and trust the system. But for any given level of education, people who watch a lot of television news are substantially better informed and positive about politics. This is a significant finding because many people who read the tabloids and watch a lot of general television also watch a lot of television news. Over half the population watch TV for more than three hours a day and a similar proportion watch television news as much as seven days a week. 'Falling into the news' in this way thus creates a wider politically informed and less cynical public than is often imagined. The analysis also found that the broadsheet newspapers (after allowing for education and class) promote a more informed readership with a positive attitude towards politics; the tabloids add very little to their readers' political knowledge or understanding, but (in comparison with non-readers) do not seem to create political cynicism and malaise; and watching television primarily for entertainment is only weakly associated with some measures of political malaise.

10.4. How free are journalists from intimidation, harassment and restrictive laws?

In general, journalists are free from harassment and intimidation, except that those who investigate the security forces and state secrecy are liable to be intimidated and harassed. Police for example raided the home of the journalist Tony Geraghty after he had refused to have his book, *The Irish War*, officially vetted and he was prosecuted under the Official Secrets Act on evidence that would not have stood up in court had the charges not been dropped (see 3.3).

But there are other charges against the New Labour regime that are arguably more damaging for the democratic health of the nation. First, the bullying – or attempted bullying – of political journalists and editors. Partly because of the resources invested in monitoring media output, this bullying is usually accompanied by precise and detailed rebuttals to demonstrate why an offending report was slightly inaccurate, given too much or too little prominence, omitted crucial information, was too favourable to the opposition or somehow fell short of what the government's image managers felt was appropriate. Campbell's bullying may range from a barrage of invective directed at a particular journalist or producer, or public disparagement at a lobby meeting, to actual or threatened approaches to editors, chief executives or proprietors to report incompetence or unprofessional conduct. There are times when even the most hardened political journalists believe that these tactics have crossed the boundary from legitimate pressure to brutal and unacceptable intimidation.

Alan Rusbridger, editor of the *Guardian*, has spoken of the sheer perseverance of Campbell's operation, his blandishments and threats. Campbell subjected Rusbridger to a number of attempts to persuade him to adopt a less sceptical and more benign approach. 'He used to ring up to cajole, plead, shout and horse-trade. Stories would be offered on condition that they went on the front page. I would be told that if I didn't agree they would go the *Independent*. They would withdraw favours, grant favours, exclude us from stories going elsewhere' (Oborne, 1999). Some journalists insist that the only proper reaction is to ignore the approaches, raise their game, and ensure they offer no opportunity for a legitimate complaint. Nicholas Jones, the BBC political journalist, reports on his brushes with Campbell in his books on the New Labour communications regime, with obvious pride and prints an abusive message from Mandelson on the back cover of his latest book, *The Control Freaks* (Jones, 1999 and 2001). But the net result of the mixture of bullying and the dangers of exclusion from Campbell's patronage tends, at best, to make even the most competent practitioner more cautious in making critical comments and, at worst, to create a creeping and democratically damaging self-censorship in which the government is given an easier ride.

10.5 How free are private citizens from intrusion and harassment by the media?

The British press has been drinking in the 'last chance saloon' for decades when it comes to invasions of privacy, intrusion and harassment. It is the famous who suffer most prominently from having their privacy invaded by the press, but the tabloid press also frequently plucks an ordinary person out of obscurity and splashes details of their private life over the front and inside pages. Someone at the centre of the press's interest can expect their house to be besieged; their telephone may be constantly rung; they are often followed and harassed; and relatives often get the same treatment.

The case of Maureen Smith illustrates the distress that people can suffer. She had an affair with Jack McConnell, the Scottish First Minister, ten years ago. When he confessed the affair (without publicly naming her) in November 2001, she was subjected at once to 'intolerable harassment from the media' that forced her to speak out to try and bring it to an end. She was offered 'thousands of pounds' for her story from newspapers. The harassment extended to her friends and family, including the parents of her second husband who had died in a motorcycle accident 18 months previously. She and they were still grieving the death of her husband (*The Times*, 15 November 2001).

We describe the growing development of a law of privacy under the Human Rights Act above in section 3.4. But while celebrities can afford to turn to the judiciary for protection of their privacy on holiday or 'kiss and tell' revelations, ordinary people do not have the resources to do so; and the laws against trespass and stalking are not easily applied against the press in full cry. The Press Council is said to be concerned to protect ordinary citizens as well as royalty and celebrities; its success in doing so needs to be monitored.

1   Resurrected by journalist Matthew Engel as the title of a book on the popular press

Eleven: political participation

Active citizenship

Is there full citizen participation in public life?

A healthy society is made up of people who care about the future. People who willingly reject the 'don't care' culture, who are not always asking, 'What's in it for me?' People who want to be practising citizens.
Lord Irvine, January 1998

Introduction

In this section, we use a broad definition of political participation, which equates it more with the 'public' than simply with the 'governmental'. Thus we include participation in a trade union, a tenants' association or a community organisation in our review as well as more narrowly political activities such as voting, involvement in a political party, or lobbying an MP or councillor. The reason for broadening the concept is that an important aspect of a country's democracy lies in the vitality of citizens' self-organisation in all aspects of their collective life – what has come to be called civil society – as well as their formal relation to government. Civil society is both an important arena within which citizens are empowered in the management of their own affairs, and a key agency for making government accountable and responsive.

As to what counts as 'participation', some people require that it be both voluntary and unpaid. The point of this stipulation lies in the difference from a democratic point of view between a citizen body that is prepared to take responsibility for its own affairs and to act independently in the public interest, and one which is rewarded or dragooned into involvement in public works or party membership (or mass demonstrations of loyalty). Obviously voluntary involvement and action are important to the vitality of civil society and its independence from government. But it would be bizarre, for example, not to count compulsory jury service in the UK as 'political participation' when it is rightly regarded as a key democratic feature of our justice system. Equally, the concern currently expressed about the 'participation rates' of women, ethnic minorities and other social groups in paid public office, elected and non-elected, suggests that a definition of 'participation' which excludes paid offices altogether would be unduly narrow. So we prefer a broad definition, such as: taking part in a not-for-profit activity or group with the potential for affecting public policy, public service delivery, the conditions of community life, or related public opinion. Thus, first, we assess participation in the voluntary associations of civil society, and then participation rates in public office, paid as well as unpaid.

A second question concerns the relation between political participation and democracy: is participation always positive for democracy, or is the relationship more ambiguous than that? Obviously, without citizen participation no democracy is possible. Yet this does not make every example of political participation democratic. There is the pseudo-participation of authorities that go through the motions of consultation without any intention of taking notice of the results; there is participation which involves violence or a threat to the basic rights of citizenship of others; there is the dragooned participation of authoritarian regimes, raised in passing above. None of these is particularly democratic.

There is also the more fundamental issue raised by the frequently repeated antithesis between 'direct' and 'representative' democracy. Some see direct democracy as more democratic because it better fits their ideal model of active citizenship, while others see it as a threat posed by influential or corporate interests or busy-body groups to the authority and competence of elected representatives. We regard the sharp antithesis between direct or participatory democracy and representative democracy as simply mistaken. Rather continuous citizen participation ensures that representative government works more democratically: through government being made aware of citizen views and having to be responsive to them; through the testing of policy against independent sources of information and expertise from outside government; through citizen involvement in the implementation of policy; through the existence of an alert and informed citizen body as a check on government excess. In all these ways citizen participation can contribute to making government more democratic in the long periods between elections.

Thus an active associational life with wide citizen participation helps meet our first democratic criterion of popular control, both over the conditions of collective life and over elected representatives. But does it meet the second democratic principle of political equality? Much citizen participation is open to the criticism that, whether individually or collectively, it is unrepresentative of the relevant populations, and tends to favour those already advantaged and articulate. Even where groups are representative, their success in influencing an elected government may involve the triumph of a sectional interest over the wider public interest that governments supposedly represent. Such considerations should serve to temper an uncritical enthusiasm for public participation, regardless of context. But they do not alter the main point that active citizenship and a vigorous civil society are necessary components of democratic life, and help make government work in a more democratic way.

11.1   How extensive is the range of voluntary associations, citizen groups, social movements, etc, and how independent are they from government?

From at least the nineteenth century onwards, the UK has developed a lively tradition of self-help groups, charitable or philanthropic societies and campaigning groups of all kinds. In addition, public protest, organised and disorganised, has always played a significant role in political life. This activist civic tradition shows no sign of diminishing, even though there has been a marked decline in voting and the membership of political parties over the past decade. How widespread and deep this participation is at the individual level will be more fully explored in Section 11.2. Here the main focus will be on the range of associational life. The following types of association can be distinguished, and will be treated briefly in turn: charities, the 'voluntary sector', producer groups, pressure groups, protest movements and actions (some of these categories also overlap one another).

Charities

Around 300,000 separate charities in the UK are registered with the Charity Commission. The typical charity, excluding educational institutions (see below), comprises a mix of paid staff and unpaid volunteers. A recent survey of the top 200 income-generating charities found that the 156 who replied between them involved over two million volunteers (averaging nearly 13,000 each) and employed over 96,000 paid staff , or around 640 each. Overall, UK charities employ over 500,000 people and raise around £5 billion annually from the public (Gannon 2000, Seely 2001).

Since registered charities enjoy substantial tax advantages, such as exemption from income and capital gains tax and VAT, the legal criteria governing charitable status are of considerable significance. The criteria currently used have evolved through successive court judgements, but ultimately derive from the preamble to the Statute of Charitable Uses of 1601. Valid purposes making an organisation eligible for charitable status are: the relief of poverty, the advancement of education, the advancement of religion and 'other purposes beneficial to the community'. Additional criteria are that a charity should be independent of government (in the sense of government direction) and should not have as a primary purpose campaigning 'to secure or oppose any change in the law or in the policy or decisions of central government or local authorities, whether in this country or abroad'.

These criteria mean, for example, that private schools and public universities in the UK can have charitable status, even though they are wholly staffed by paid employees and charge their beneficiaries for the service, while campaigning groups such as Liberty (formerly the National Council for Civil Liberties) are not eligible. Although the Charity Commissioners are continually reviewing the interpretation of the criteria and the official register of charities itself, they are ultimately bound by legal decisions made in past centuries (Charity Commission 1998a).

The voluntary sector

There is no agreed definition of what 'the voluntary sector' should include, despite a considerable overlap with charitable bodies. If the sector is to be defined as the sum of voluntary organisations, then one set of criteria for such an organisation stipulates that it be independent, self-governing, significantly sustained by voluntary contributions in cash or kind, and run for a wider public benefit than that of its members only. Such a definition excludes educational institutions, but would include campaigning organisations and a host of informal associations not registered as charities. Even within this definition it is impossible to identify a full list of such organisations in the UK; though it is possible to enumerate such bodies within a particular sector where a national register has been compiled. For example, the 1994 register of environmental organisations listed a total of 1,600 organisations. If the 'wider public benefit' criterion is relaxed or abandoned, a more inclusive definition would bring trade unions, trade associations, tenants' groups, cooperatives, housing associations, and a host of others into the category of voluntary organisations (Passey et al, 2000; Tarling, 2000).

A different approach would be to define the sector as the sum of voluntary activities, or 'volunteering', whether carried out for a voluntary organisation or a non-voluntary one such as a school or hospital. This puts the emphasis on the voluntary action, which is usually defined as one that is unpaid and for the benefit of others outside the family, which can be 'formal' voluntary activity undertaken through an organisation or network, or 'informal' activity carried out on a one-to-one basis (e.g., visiting a sick neighbour, etc.). The 'formal' category ties voluntary activity into associational life, and is the one most commonly used to calculate the extent of voluntary activity and its contribution to the economy. People's willingness to contribute time through an organisation is a particularly good indicator of the vitality of a country's associational life.

The 1997 National Survey of Volunteering found that 22 million people – nearly half the adult population in the UK – had undertaken voluntary work, averaging about four hours weekly, through an organisation in the previous year. Sports, education and social welfare were the most common fields of voluntary activity, and fund-raising, organising events and committee work were the most common forms of activity (Davis Smith 1997). The section on voluntary and community activities in the 2000 British Crime Survey of the Home Office (in future to be a self-standing Citizenship Survey), using different criteria, found that 42 per cent of the adult population had undertaken at least one of the following activities once a month or more: attending groups, helping groups or an organisation, serving in a public capacity, attending public meetings or taking part in public consultations, working with other people to tackle local issues. Of these, the first two activities were by far the most widespread (Kershaw et al, 2000). How do such figures compare with those for other countries? There is the usual difficulty of arriving at an agreed definition of voluntary activity or volunteering, and international criteria tend to show the UK participation rate as lower than nationally conducted surveys. However they are a fair guide to the position relative to other countries. A 1995 comparative survey of volunteering in selected European countries showed the following percentages of the adult population as having undertaken voluntary activity during the previous year, with most doing so at least once a month:

Belgium	32%
Denmark	28%
Ireland	25%
Netherlands	38%
Sweden	36%
UK	34%

Source: Gaskin and Davis Smith 1997

Producer associations

There is another important dimension of civic participation – that is, membership of self-organising associations whose primary purpose is the benefit of their members. However exclusively focused they may be on the defence and advancement of their members' interests, such organisations can play a crucial role in debate over public policy, or in its effective implementation. And however minimal the activity involved in membership may be, which for most does not go beyond the payment of dues, most interest groups and associations would simply collapse without such payments. Sports clubs, motoring organisations, tenants' groups, cooperatives, stamp clubs, neighbourhood watch schemes – the list of such associations is potentially endless. Most significant in terms of their weight in public debate and policy are the producer groups, and their range and membership is another index of the vitality of society's self-organising capacity.

Trade unions

For all their decline in membership and influence under successive Conservative governments in the 1980s and 1990s, the Trades Union Congress numbers 76 affiliated unions and professional associations, representing 6.8 million workers. Their role is to advance their members' interests through collective bargaining with employers over pay and conditions and through the provision of individual protection in work, and to represent members in discussions with government over public policy (tuc.org.uk 2001).

Trade associations

The UK Trade Association Forum (run by the Confederation of British Industry) includes 691 trade associations representing 671,754 member companies. It defines the role of a trade association as being 'to create a positive business environment, to form public policy and to support its member companies with appropriate services' (cbi.org.uk 2001).

Chambers of Commerce

These perform a similar role to trade associations, but they are organised on a geographical, cross-sectoral basis, with Chambers in most localities. Current total membership is 135,000 businesses across the UK (britishchambers.org.uk 2001).

Pressure groups

'Pressure groups' do not comprise a separate list of associations additional to those already mentioned in the previous categories. They simply comprise these associations in their roles of campaigning, advocacy and attempts to influence public opinion and government policy and legislation. They are usually divided into 'sectional' groups (trade unions, etc.) and 'cause' groups (e.g.. OXFAM), or, in US terms, 'private interest' and 'public interest' groups. Much of the huge political science literature on them is devoted to explaining their relative success or failure in influencing government, which will be looked at under Section 12.1. They will not be considered further here, as the category does not add to the tally of associations already enumerated above (Coxall 2001).

Protest campaigns and activities

This is a loosely defined but important category of political participation, comprising one-off campaigns against government policy or some social evil by citizens who feel so strongly about it that they are motivated to take direct action against it or to mobilise large numbers in support of their protest, or both.

Public protest

The political significance of public protests, campaigns or actions is not necessarily proportionate to the numbers of those involved. Disagreements about how democratic protests may be are not only a matter of support for, or opposition to, the issue involved, but also relate to different conceptions of democracy. Sceptics will argue that such protests typically involve self-appointed and unrepresentative groups or leaders, whose actions seek to preempt the normal processes of representative democracy and may subvert the rule of law. Defenders will point out that protests represent significant points of view that are otherwise excluded from access to the media or the policy process, and that they form an essential complement to the more usual processes of democratic expression, provided they do not involve violence or the threat of violence to other people.

Below is a list of public protests since 1997 which have had a national impact, either because of the numbers mobilised or the nature of the action, or both, regardless of their success or failure in changing government policy. The list and its categorisation cannot claim to be definitive, but it conveys an idea of the range of such protests in contemporary Britain:

Animal welfare
- disruptions of hunting with hounds
- releasing animals from mink farms
- actions against animal experimentation (e.g.., Huntingdon Life Sciences)
- protests against the policy of destroying livestock in the foot and mouth epidemic

Capitalism and globalisation
- May Day protests against capitalism
- international demonstrations involving UK activists at meetings of international financial organisations
- mass demonstrations in UK cities to demand international debt cancellation

The environment and transport
- actions against road-building and airport extension
- reclaim the streets' protests against motorised traffic and pollution
- blockade of fuel distribution in protest against high fuel duties

Farming and use of the countryside
- Countryside Alliance demonstrations against government neglect of rural needs and proposals to ban hunting
- farmers' blockades of ports and supermarkets in protest at the import of cheap meat
- mass trespasses by walkers demanding open access to the countryside
- destruction of trial GM crops

Racial disadvantage and discrimination
● campaign for public inquiry into police handling of Stephen Lawrence's murder
● mass protests by Asian youth in Oldham, Burnley and Bradford
● protest demonstration in Brixton against the police shooting of a black youth

Social policy and welfare
● demonstrations by the disabled against changes to benefit regulations
● campaigns and demonstrations against hospital closures
● unofficial referendum in Scotland to keep 'clause 28' banning support for homosexuality by local authorities

Vigilantism
● actions to force known or suspected paedophiles from their homes and neighbourhoods
● organised campaign to identify the killers of James Bulger on release from detention

Weapons of destruction
● mass campaign to ban handguns ('Snowdrop' campaign)
● campaign to ban use of landmines
● protest against Trident base in Scotland
● invasion of Menwith Hill communications base in protest against its use in 'Star wars' programme

Independence of associations from government

The contribution of civic associations to the quality of democratic life depends on their independence from government. The self-organising capacity of citizens is an important counterweight to the tendency of government to monopolise societal initiative and expertise; and the ability of associations to represent the plurality of society's opinions and interests to government, as well as act as a check upon it, is conditional upon their having a base of support and income that is separate from the state. The importance of this condition is explicitly recognised by the Charity Commission in its stipulation that charitable status is only granted for associations that are 'independent of the state'.

In the main we can conclude that, with some reservations considered later, voluntary associations in the UK are independent of government and are not subject to its direction or control. This does not mean, however, that government is neutral about their existence or vitality. Public money helps finance voluntary associations in a number of different ways:
● through tax relief to charities worth over £2 billion per year (Seely 2001);
● through direct funding for voluntary organisations and volunteering by central, regional and local government, government agencies and health authorities, totalling about £400 million per year (IVS 1999);
● through the National Lotteries Community Fund, which dispensed £373 million in the year to March 2001 to 9,500 organisations (nationallottery.co.uk 2001);
● through contracting out the delivery of services, especially personal social services, to the voluntary sector by government and its agencies, worth over £2 billion in 1999 (Passey et al, 2000).

New Labour has made it a specific policy priority to encourage the further development of the voluntary and community sector in partnership with government through the idea of 'compacts' between government and the sector. This conforms to its search for a 'third way' or 'third force' between government and private business, e.g.., in the delivery of public services. As Tony Blair wrote in a policy document immediately prior to taking office in 1997, 'We want to restore a proper respect for the independence of the voluntary sector. I do not favour simply a contract relationship with the voluntary sector, I favour something more profound: working together to pursue common objectives in the public interest' (Morison 2000). The Labour government has also sought to encourage individual volunteering as part of its concept of good citizenship. Initiatives include:

- coordination of government support for the voluntary sector through an Active Community Unit in the Home Office, which conducts regular 'citizenship surveys', and has set a target for increasing the numbers engaged in volunteering by a million by 2004;
- a millennium volunteers programme aimed at getting more young people to volunteer;
- the encouragement of voluntary work and participation in schools councils in the new citizenship component of the national curriculum.

This degree of support for the voluntary sector by government, and its increasing use in service delivery, have led to fears that the sector's independence will be compromised. Any organisation which is in receipt of government grants and contracts may come to find that its public advocacy role is blunted, especially where this source forms a sizeable part of its income. An analysis of income to the voluntary sector for 1999 showed that 30 per cent came from government sources (Passey et al, 2000). There is also the issue of how far a voluntary service provider remains free to determine its own priorities and selection of beneficiaries when it is carrying out a government contract. The Charity Commission has been particularly exercised about this problem, since its definition of independence stipulates that a charity 'must exist in order to carry out its charitable purposes, and not for the purpose of implementing the policies of a governmental authority, or of carrying out the directions of a governmental authority' (Charity Commission 1998b). Governments, on the other hand, are accountable to the taxpayer for how, and on whom, their money is spent, and will naturally seek to control its use. How this circle of 'independence' and 'partnership' evident in the quotation from Tony Blair above is to be squared is currently a key issue in the relation of the voluntary sector with government. One respected commentator recently claimed that charities working on government programmes had 'to all intents and purposes been nationalised' and were 'no longer independent of government' (Dahrendorf 2001).

11.2 How extensive is citizen participation in voluntary associations and self-management organisations, and in other voluntary public activity?

The answer to the previous question touched on the extent of individual participation in public life. Here we examine more closely the types of activity involved and its distribution between different social groups.

It is a commonplace of discussions of UK public life to point out that traditional forms of political participation are in decline, and to conclude that the country suffers from a 'democratic deficit', a 'crisis of democracy', and so forth. It is true that membership of political parties has been in secular decline, as it has in most established democracies, currently standing at something over 300,000 each for the two largest parties (see Section 6.5). And proportions of the electorate voting in the UK have declined rapidly, to the point where they are among the lowest in Europe for all levels of election (see Section 5.6). Yet these figures are to be explained more by the failure of political parties to engage with the public, to offer a meaningful choice to voters and a meaningful role to members, than by a withdrawal of citizens from the public arena into a world of privatised concerns. A Mori poll taken after the recent general election turnout of 59 per cent showed that there had been no drop over 30 years in the high level of public interest in politics, but that most of those not voting had been turned off by the campaign (*Guardian*, 4 July, 2001). And the figures for membership of voluntary associations and voluntary activity already mentioned show little decline, though there has been a shift in the focus of issues, e.g., with membership of environmental organisations swelling to a figure of around five million in the 1990s (Jordan and Maloney 1997).

What do such figures mean? What are people actually doing? One view is that they are doing comparatively little, at most paying their dues to an organisation and perhaps voting in a ballot for membership of its national committee. This hardly conforms to the 'active citizenship' model of the literature on participatory democracy or new social movements. Nor are all these organisations themselves run that democratically, with policy made by a narrow elite and handed down to the membership on a 'take it or leave it' basis. Indeed some organisations such as Greenpeace are explicitly organised on a 'vanguardist' model, with dramatic actions planned in secret for maximum effect to help recruit new supporters and confirm existing ones (Jordan 1998); (Jordan and Maloney 1997).

Two points can be made in answer to this sceptical view that all the public's involvement amounts to is 'cheque book participation'. The first is that, for reasons of time, much contemporary politics takes place by proxy, but we should not therefore underestimate the role of attentive and critical 'audience', whereby an organisation's members may cheer on its actions from the armchair, or, alternatively, exercise the option of 'exit' if it seems ineffective or in breach of the purpose for which they joined. As long as organisations depend on membership subscriptions for their survival, they cannot afford to get far out of touch with the expectations of their members. And most can rely on being able to mobilise a wider penumbra of potential activists from their armchairs in support of a major issue or event, even if the numbers do not seem large in relation to the total population.

Secondly, the figures from the surveys of voluntary activity or 'volunteering' already mentioned show a quite remarkable commitment of time by people if we widen our conception of the 'political' in the way we have advocated. The 2000 Home Office survey of citizenship showed that 36 per cent of respondents had attended groups of some sort once a month or more in the previous year, and 13 per cent had helped a group or organisation once a month, whereas only 2 per cent had taken part in the more narrowly defined political activities of serving in a public capacity, attending public meetings or consultations or working with other people to tackle local issues (Kershaw et al. 2000). Similarly, the 1997 survey of volunteering by the Institute for Volunteering Research, which showed that nearly half the adult population had taken part in some voluntary activity with an organisation in the previous 12 months, found that the most common forms of activity were the quite time-consuming ones of fundraising, organising events and committee work (Davis Smith 1997). These figures show a remarkable degree of commitment to collective activity outside the spheres of paid work, family and friends. It is not surprising that economists have tried to estimate the value of all this unpaid work to the national economy, and come up with figures such as £40 billion per year.

Such figures of citizen participation are also borne out in a recent survey by UK political scientists for the Economic and Social Research Council's participation programme. As one criterion of participation they asked respondents whether, in the previous twelve months, they had engaged in any 'political influencing activity', such as signing a petition, contacting a politician or an organisation, boycotting goods, etc. They found that nearly three quarters of respondents had done so, with many involved in more than one activity. The percentages for the different activities were as follows:

Question: 'During the last 12 months have you done any of the following to influence, rules, laws or policies?'

	% saying 'yes'
Signed a petition	41
Boycotted certain products	30
Raised funds for an organisation	28
Bought certain goods/products for political/ethical reasons	27
Contacted a public official	25
Worn/displayed campaign badge/sticker	21
Contacted a solicitor or judicial body	19
Contacted a politician	13
Contacted an organisation	11
Contacted the media	9
Attended a political rally/meeting	5
Taken part in a public demonstration	4
Taken part in a strike	2
Participated in an illegal protest	1

Source: Seyd, Whiteley and Pattie, 2001

Participation in statutory public positions
So far we have concentrated on the public's involvement in associations independent of government, as an index of the vitality of civil society or the density of what is called 'social capital' (the sum of connections individuals have to social institutions). A quite different approach to assessing the significance of political participation is to examine how far the government relies on ordinary citizens to carry out its own functions. We have already seen the government's dependence on the voluntary sector for the delivery of social and welfare services. But it also depends on individual citizens in an unpaid capacity to fulfil a variety of public roles, of which the following is a far from exhaustive list. Numbers are given of those involved in any one year, for the year 2000 unless otherwise stated. Together they represent a huge contribution of time and personnel by the lay public to the work of government:

Participation in statutory public positions

Central and devolved government: board members of non-departmental public bodies (advisory and executive NDPBs, public corporations, etc.)	30,520 (Cabinet Office 2000)
Elected local councillors	22,745 (CSV 2000)
Local public spending bodies: board members of higher and further education institutions, TECs, local enterprise companies, housing associations and registered social landlords	42,682 est. (Cabinet Office, 2000)
Legal sector: lay justices of the peace, England & Wales and Scotland	34,400 approx. (Morgan & Russell 2000 & Secretary of Commissions for Scotland 2001)
Citizens undertaking jury servicec	250,000 (*Guardian* 18 July 2001)
Education sector: members of school governing bodies	345,000 (CSV 2000)
Health sector: members of Community Health Councils	4,140 (CSV 2000)
Police: special constables	13,528 (HC Deb (WA) 17 January 2001,)
Prison service: members of boards of visitors	1,747 (Board of Visitors Secretariat, 2001)

Distribution of participation

A final question concerns the distribution of participation in associational life between different social groups. This will be considered in relation to social class, age, gender and ethnic group.

Class: All surveys of voluntary activity through organisations show that participation rates increase the higher the social class of respondents. The 1990 comparative survey of European countries, which included the UK, showed rates of 'volunteering' twice as high for professional and managerial groups as for manual workers, a proportion that was almost exactly replicated in the 1997 UK survey (Davis Smith 1997, Gaskin and Davis Smith, 1997). Existing membership of an organisation is a key route into voluntary activity on its behalf, and higher social groups are more likely to be members and to live in communities with dense social networks. Professional and managerial workers are also much more likely to be recruited into most of the public functions listed in the previous section, with the possible exception of service as elected local councillor, which is more socially representative, and jury service, which many of those in professional occupations find plausible reason to opt out of.

Age: Those in the 18–25 age group are less likely to vote than other age groups, and express themselves less interested in politics. They are also less likely to be involved in voluntary associations, and they spend least time in their involvement. They are more likely to be attracted to doing so where the instrumental benefits are evident, such as the opportunity to learn new skills, to get a qualification or to achieve a position in the community (Davis Smith 1997). Although the Labour government has sought to encourage participation in voluntary activity by young people through schools and the millennium volunteers programme, the UK compares unfavourably with many other European countries by having no national agency to support and promote the development of local youth councils and in their lack of a statutory basis. While there is clear public support in the UK for the UN childhood rights to protection and provision, there is much less for their right to collective participation and representation on issues that affect them (Matthews et al, 1999).

Gender: Surveys of voluntary activity through organisations show that women are as likely to be involved as men, though in rather different activities. The 1997 UK study concluded that women were three times more likely than men to volunteer in schools, and also more likely to be involved in social welfare groups, while men were twice as likely to be involved in sports groups. Men were more active on committees, women in fund-raising. When we turn to campaigning groups, women are more likely to be involved in public interest groups of all kinds than men, and to be disproportionately more concerned on issues of the environment, nuclear energy and the threat of nuclear war (Jordan and Maloney 1997). And despite the advent of 'post-feminist' politics, there are still many women's groups and organisations devoted to advancing the position of women in the economy, society and public life.

Ethnic group: The evidence about group participation of ethnic minorities is contradictory. A recent study by the National Coalition for Black Volunteering reported minimal involvement of black volunteers in mainstream voluntary organisations, with 40 per cent of these involving none at all (NCBV 2000). On the other hand, the 2000 Home Office citizenship survey reported black and Asian people to be as equally involved as white people in helping groups and organisations, and more involved in attending them. This discrepancy may be simply explained by the fact that ethnic minorities are predominantly involved in their own organisations. A recent survey of black and minority ethnic voluntary and community organisations in England and Wales discovered around 5,500 in existence, providing a range of services to their communities, particularly to people with significant social and economic needs. Of the total number, over half had been in existence for more than ten years, and had an annual income each of between £50,000 and £250,000. A frequent comment from respondents was that these organisations lacked visibility in their own localities as well as support from mainstream agencies, despite their significance in helping combat 'social exclusion' (McLeod et al, 2001).

11.3 How far do women participate in political life and public office at all levels?

Other sections of this audit have examined women's participation in elected national office and the uniformed services (see Sections 5.6, and 8.3). Here we look at government and the public sector more generally. The argument for an equal representation of women in public sector offices can be made on our basic principle of political equality: no section of the population should be systematically discriminated against or disadvantaged in access to office. Historically, of course, women have been both discriminated against and disadvantaged, and most statistics show the effect of this. An important issue to explore, therefore, is whether there is an improvement over time, and the pace of any change.

Women in the House of Lords

As Table 1 shows, the task of improving women's participation in the Westminster Parliament is as relevant to the appointed upper house (the House of Lords) as to the elected lower chamber. Forming 16.5 per cent of the Lords' total membership, there are proportionally marginally fewer women in the Lords than in the House of Commons. There is little apparent sign that this is about to change. Although a quarter of new peers selected by the new Lords' appointment committee in April 2001 were women, the absolute number of appointments (four) is not sufficient to make a difference. This mechanism of selection is perhaps not the most appropriate for creating a more truly representative and democratic upper house.

1. Women in the House of Lords

	Male (% total)	Female(% total)
All members of the Lords(July 2001)	581 (83.5%)	115 (16.5%)
New members appointed in the Dissolution Honours list*(June 2001)	22(91.7%)	2(8.3%)
The People's Peers (April 2001)	11(73.3%)	4(26.7%)

* These members of the Lords' are MPs appointed upon their retirement from the House of Commons at the June 2001 General Election.

Source: House of Lords 2001

Women in government

The picture is somewhat more balanced in the executive, with women occupying almost a third of government offices after the 2001 general election (see Table 2). What is particularly interesting about these figures (apart from the fact that unelected members take up more than one fifth of all posts), is that relative to their total strength of numbers, more women than men enter the government through the House of Lords. In contrast, there are no appointed women in the cabinet.

2. Women in the executive

	Male % cabinet	Female % cabinet	Male % executive	Female % executive	Total %executive
Commons	14(60.9%)	7(30.4%)	64(57.1%)	24(21.4%)	88(78.6%)
Lords	2(8.7%)	0-	15(13.4%)	9(8.0%)	24(21.4%)
Totals	16(69.6%)	7(30.4%)	79(70.5%)	33(29.5%)	112

1. Includes Cabinet; Parliamentary Secretaries and Under Secretaries of State; whips; and law officers

Source: House of Commons 2001

Women in local government

There is a general tendency to assume that it is easier for women to participate in local politics because the pattern of demands is more accommodating of the responsibilities that many women fulfil. Local councils are by definition closer to their constituents, rather than based hundreds of miles away in London, and are generally voluntary, part-time commitments. It is generally true that women are more active in local government than they are in Westminster – at least according to research conducted by the Local Government Association, which estimates that following council elections in 1997 women occupied 27 per cent of all council seats in England and Wales. Wales had the lowest proportion of women councillors of the areas surveyed, at just over 20 per cent in 1997; English unitary authorities averaged almost 30 per cent. These figures are considered in more detail under Section 11.4, where we turn to look at race and other indicators of social representativeness.

3. Women in local government

	England and Wales (elected 1997)		Scotland (elected 1999)	
	No. of councillors (est.)	% (est.)	No. of councillors	%
Male	15,604	72.6	946	77.4
Female	5,873	27.3	276	22.6
Not Known	21	0.1	–	–
Total	21,498		1,222	

Source: Columns 1& 2: Employers' Organisation for Local Government 1997. Columns 3&4 Scottish Local Government Information Unit 2000

Women in the judiciary and legal professions

Women in general occupy few or very few senior judicial positions, but are strongly represented at junior levels and in the unpaid lay judiciary. Starting with the appellate and higher tier courts (Table 4), not one of the UK's law lords is a woman, and only two women judges sit in the Appeal Court, making up 6 per cent of its membership. The single most concerning fact is that it appears unlikely that this situation is going to improve much in the foreseeable future. At the present moment, there are barely more women in the high courts or among circuit judges (who hear the more serious cases referred by magistrates to crown courts) than in the appellate courts, meaning that few women will be present in the next cohort of most senior judges.

4. Judiciary in higher tier courts and the appeal courts (England and Wales)

	Circuit judges	High Court judges	Lord Justices of Appeal	Lords of Appeal in Ordinary (law lords)
Male	521(92.2%)	99(92.5%)	33(94.3%)	12(100.0%)
Female	44(7.8%)	8(7.5%)	2(5.7%)	0–
Totals	565	107	35	12

Source: The Lord Chancellor's Department 2001b

Further down the line (Table 5), women are also weakly represented among newly appointed Queen's Counsel in England (almost 13 per cent) – figures for QCs as a whole are not kept. This proportion is almost double that of women Justices in the High Court, but little more than half of the proportion of women barristers (24.5 per cent). The proportion of women increases further among practising members of the Law Society (the professional body for solicitors in England), and among new entrants to the profession, where women are far and away in the majority.

5. QCs, Solicitors and Advocates (England and Wales)

	The Bar Council of England & Wales (barristers and QCs)			The Law Society (solicitors)	
	New QCs (2000)(% total)	(Oct 2001)(% total)	Practicing Barristers (1999-2000)(% total)	Practicing Members [1]	New Entrants to the profession [2] (July 2000)(% total)
Male	68(87.2%)		7,494(75.5%)	52,724(63.7%)	3,094 approx(39.7%)
Female	10(12.8%)		2,638(24.5%)	30,045(36.3%)	4,699 approx(60.3%)
Total	78		10,132	82,769	7,793

1 Practising members denotes members holding practising certificate

2 Students enrolling with the Law Society in July 2001. Figures for men and women are approximate, worked backwards from the percentages and total number of entrants given in the source.

Sources: General Council of the Bar 2000a & 2000b; The Law Society 2000

The situation in the Scotland is broadly similar to that in England, with proportionally more women active in the profession as we go down the scale of seniority (Table 6). It is not possible, however, to make a direct comparison between the Bar Council of England and Wales and the Scottish Faculty of Advocates because the Bar Council does not keep information on the gender balance of members who joined before the mid-1990s.

6. Women in the Scottish High Court and legal professions

of Justiciary	High Court	Faculty of Advocates [1]		Law Society of Scotland	
		Queen's Counsel	All practicing members	Practicing members	New entrants to the profession (% total)
Male	31(93.9%)	80(92.0%)	260(75.6%)	5,401(62.7%)	164(43.5%)
Female	2(6.1%)	7(8.0%)	84(24.4%)	3,208(37.3%)	213(56.5%)
Total	33	88	344	8,609	377

1 The Faculty of Advocates is the professional body for independent lawyers who are admitted to practice before all Courts in Scotland. Its membership includes Advocates, Queen's Counsellors, Sheriffs and Judges. Both Advocates and QCs are classified as practicing members, but the latter are excluded from the final column of this table for the sake of clarity.

Sources: Column 1: Scottish Courts Website http://www.scotcourts.gov.uk. Column 2: Faculty of Advocates 2001; Column 3: Law Society of Scotland 2000 and *The Scotsman* September 11, 2001

There is clearly a trend towards greater representation of women in the legal profession in the more recent cohorts of entrants and in junior positions. This trend appears to be evident in the judiciary in England and Wales and in the figures for lay magistrates. Lay magistrates play an important role in the adjudication of justice in England and Wales – each person charged with a criminal offence will go before a JP or magistrates' bench, who have the authority to impose fines or custodial sentences, or to refer cases to higher courts. As Table 7 (over) shows, lay magistrates are vastly more representative in terms of their gender balance than other sections of the judiciary, and there are two important reasons for this. First and most importantly, the appointing authorities are required by law to ensure that each bench is representative of the area it is to serve; secondly, JPs are not professionals, do not need to have a legal background, and receive on-the-job training. This makes these positions open to a wider circle of people than say, becoming a barrister, which involves a considerable in training and education. (see also Section 11.4).

In addition to part-time, unpaid Justices of the Peace, each magistrates court has one or more paid district judge (known as stipendiary magistrates before reorganisation in August 2001), who has a professional legal background. District judges perform the same balance of duties as JPs, although they do tend to receive the longer or more complex cases (Morgan and Russell 2000). Equality of outcome in the appointments process for district judges, though briefly seen amongst the lay magistracy, again disappears and is replaced with a familiar discrepancy in favour of male candidates (84 per cent men). Given the parity achieved amongst their lay colleagues, it is surprising that the professional district judiciary is so heavily dominated by men, suggesting that a thoroughgoing reappraisal of employment and working practices in the legal profession as a whole will be required to ensure that new female entrants are given equal opportunities for progression.

7. Women in the lower courts in England & Wales and in Scotland

| | England & Wales | | | Scotland 1 | |
	Justices of the Peace	District judges (and deputies)		Justices of the Peace	Sheriffs Court
Male	51%	215(81.4%)		2,826(72.4%)	103(85.8%)
Female	49%	49(18.6%)		1,080(27.6%)	17(14.2%)
Total	30,400 approx.	264		3,906	120

1 In Scotland, JPs sit in district courts, which have a markedly less extensive jurisdiction, than magistrates' courts in England and Wales (Morgan & Russell). Stipendiary magistrates are the equivalent in Scotland of district judges in England and Wales. They have not been included in the figures because the different legal structure means that there are only two stipendiary magistrates in Scotland. Sheriffs Courts are the next highest tier courts.

Sources: Columns 1: Morgan & Russell 2000. Column 2: Lord Chancellor's Department 2001a. Column 3: Secretary of Commissions for Scotland 2001. Column 4: *The Herald* (Glasgow) December 11, 1999

Women in the machinery of government

Here we present some data on women's presence in the civil service. Again, women typically occupy more junior (and less well-paid) positions than men.

8. Women in the Civil Service

| | AO/AA level 1 | | | Senior Civil Service | |
	1984	1999		1984	1999
Men	90,316(31.7%)	90,700(37.5%)		3,381(94.1%)	2,981(82.8%)
Women	194,304(68.3%)	151,338(62.5%)		212(5.9%)	621(17.2%)
Total	284,620	242,038		3,593	3,602

1 AO/AA: Administrative Officer & Administrative Assistant level
Source: Cabinet Office 2000

Table 8 shows that greater gender balance has been introduced at junior (Administrative) and senior levels in the 15 years to 1999. At administrative level, this has been achieved principally by reducing the number of women workers by 43,000, or one fifth. By contrast, three times more women worked in the senior civil service in 1999 than they did in 1984, the number of men having fallen by 300, or 11 per cent. This rebalancing is potentially more complex than figures alone suggest. The 1980s and 1990s saw considerable organisational change in the civil service. Recruitment and pay were decentralised to individual agencies and compulsory competitive tendering was introduced. Civil servants were replaced with contract agency staff (not included in the official figures). Potentially large numbers of women in clerical and administrative jobs were transferred to insecure re-employment in the same or similar agencies; and a two-tier workforce emerged, divided distinctively between decision makers (senior managers, predominantly men) and the clerical and junior administrative workers (lower grades, predominantly women), which in many respects remain unconnected (Marshall et al, 2001). A corollary of slimming-down and restructuring is the reduction of spending on equal opportunities (Cabinet Office 1994; Council of Civil Service Unions 1996), and 'considerable variability' in the way different government agencies address the issue. It is fair to say that women's experience of work in the civil service has diversified, and that in 1999 women made up almost a fifth of the most senior civil servants. It is equally fair to say that this diversity involved down-grading many more women than men.

Women in public bodies

Finally, Table 9 looks one stage beyond the civil service to the appointed governing boards of the industries and executive and advisory bodies that form the quasi-state. It shows that in contrast to the senior civil service these boards have a more equitable gender balance, suggesting rather predictably that it is easier to create representativeness by ministerial order than it is to create equality of opportunity by reforming institutional practices.

9. Women on the boards of public bodies

	Boards of public bodies
Men	20,521(67.2%)
Women	9,999(32.8%)
Total	30,520

NB. Public bodies are: nationalised industries; public corporations; Non-Departmental Public Bodies; and NHS bodies.
Source: Cabinet Office 2000

11.4 How equal is access for all social groups to public office, and how fairly are they represented within it?

In Section 11.3, we looked at gender balance in various public offices and concluded that women are proportionally under-represented. Here we apply a similar analysis to other social groups, and find a similar story. The reference point 'all social groups"(as defined by our search question) is a broad one, and the focus in this section is mainly on equality of access for people from black or Asian ethnic minorities. The reason is that we must rely principally on existing data for this study; while unofficial information on racial discrimination is frequently available, data relating to people with disabilities and to the socio-economic backgrounds of office holders is far less so. As with the previous question, data on ethnic minority representation in national elected office and the uniformed services has already been given in Sections 5.6 and 8.3.

Ethnic minorities in the House of Lords

Gaining a picture of ethnic diversity in the House of Lords is hampered by the lack of official data on the backgrounds of its members – a problem found in other parts of the British state as we shall see below. Unofficial estimates suggest that approximately 20 peers claim black or Asian descent, an even smaller fraction of its total membership than that found in the Commons. Although the Labour government embarked on a first stage of reform of the House of Lords in its first term, the new appointments mechanisms will not create a proportionately representative upper house for many years yet, nor is appointment necessarily the most appropriate way to create a representative and democratically accountable upper house. As Table 10 below illustrates, although people from ethnic minority backgrounds account for a quarter of new peers created in 2001, the total discrepancy is such this cannot realistically be said to amount to a trend towards better representation.

10. Ethnic minority appointments to the House of Lords

	The Lords	The 'People's Peers' [1]
All members	696	15
Ethnic minority membersApprox	20	4

1 Peers appointed by the newly established House of Lords Commission on Appointments, April 2001.

Sources: House of Lords 2001; Lords' Information Office 2001

Ethnic minorities in government

Given that ethnic minorities are significantly under-represented among the main political parties and in both Houses of Parliament, it is not surprising that levels of appointment to the government at ministerial or junior ministerial rank level are also disappointingly low – only two of the 12 Black or Asian Labour MPs is in the current Labour government, though one (Paul Boateng) now holds a cabinet position (since May 2002).

11. Members of the Cabinet from ethnic minority backgrounds, 2001

	Cabinet		All Executive1	
	Elected	Appointed	Elected	Appointed
Ethnic minority members	1	0	2	2
All members	21	2	88	24

1 Includes cabinet; Parliamentary Secretaries and Under Secretaries of State; whips; and law officers
Source: House of Commons 2001

Ethnic minorities in local government

It is a commonly-held assumption that it is easier for members of minority groups to become engaged in local politics where councillors are generally closer to their electors than MPs and represent smaller, and therefore probably more homogenous areas than do Members of Parliament. However, data based on a survey of local councillors elected in 1997 reveal a similar picture to that at national level – at least 96.7per cent of the 21,498 elected councillors in England and Wales are white (Table 12). Given that another commonly held assumption has it that aspirant MPs often cut their teeth in local politics, low levels of participation here suggest that achieving a more representative mix among the national political elite will be a long time coming.

12. Elected local government

	England and Wales (1997)	Scotland (1999)
	Councillors (percentage known)	Councillors (percentage known)
White	20,782 (96.7%)	(99.5%)
Ethnic minority	662 (3.1%)	(0.5%)
Not known	54	–

Source: Column 1: Employers' Organisation for Local Government 1997; Column 2: Scottish Local Government Information Unit 2000

Looking at the data for each of the main parties in turn (Table 13) reveals a depressing picture for the Conservative Party, which has only 31 councillors from minority ethnic groups in all of England and Wales, or 0.7 per cent of Conservative councillors. Proportionally, the Liberal Democrats do not fare much better, with only 55 or 1.1 per cent of their councillors from ethnic minority backgrounds. As

Table 13 shows, the Labour Party is the only one of the three main parties that has succeeded in attracting, and getting elected, an approximately proportionate number of minority councillors.

13. Councillors by party

	Conservative		Labour		Liberal Democrat	
	Councillors	%	Councillors	%	Councillors	%
White	4,335	99.3	9,367	94.5	4,809	98.9
Ethnic Minority	31	0.7	546	5.5	55	1.1
Not known	30		24		7	

NB. Similar data for Scottish councillors is not available.

Source: Employers' Organisation for Local Government 1997

Ethnic minorities in the judiciary and legal professions
In contrast to the surprisingly low levels of ethnic minority participation in elected local politics, we find relatively high levels of participation in the legal profession, which suggests that current under-representation in the senior ranks of the judiciary may be eroded by the up-coming generation. Tables 14 and 15 illustrate the extent of current problems of under-representation in the higher tier courts in Great Britain. Only six judges from ethnic minority backgrounds are present in the entire judiciary at the level of Crown Court and above in England and Wales; the judiciary in the High Court, Appeal Court and in the House of Lords are exclusively white. The position in Scotland is worse, and at the European Court of Justice in Strasbourg, each of the 15 judges and eight advocates general is of white European origin.

14. Judiciary in higher tier courts (England and Wales) and appeal courts

	Circuit judges	High Court judges	Lord Justices of Appeal	Lords of Appeal in Ordinary (law lords)
Ethnic minority	6(1.1%)	0–	0–	0–
White	559(98.9%)	107(100%)	35(100%)	12(100%)
Total	565	107	35	12

Source: Lord Chancellor's Department 2001a

15. Judiciary in higher tier courts in Scotland

	Court of Session and High Court of Justiciary	Sheriff Court
Ethnic minority	0	1
White	32	119
Total	32	120

Sources: Column 1: Scottish Court Service 2001. Column 2: *The Herald* (Glasgow) December 11, 1999

Figures for the legal profession in general show a fair representation of members of ethnic minorities in the ranks of both barristers and solicitors, and especially among new entrants to the latter (Table 16). These figures are in marked contrast to those for appointment as QCs, the most privileged and highly paid members of the profession, where ethnic representation is at its lowest. In the eight years from 1993 to 2000 only 19 ethnic minority appointments were made at this level out of a total of 559.

16. Ethnic minorities in the legal profession – QCs, barristers and solicitors in England & Wales

	The Bar Council of England (Barristers and QCs)		The Law Society (Solicitors)	
	Practising barristers	Newly appointed QCs	Practising members	New entrants to the profession
White	8,263(81.6%)	75(96.2%)	77,720(93.9%)	6,079(78.0%)
Ethnic minority	784(7.7%)	3(3.8%)	5,049(6.1%)	1,714(22.0%)
Not known	1,085(10.7%)	–	–	–
Total	10,132	78	82,769	7,793

NB. The Law Society of Scotland and the Faculty of Advocates are the parallel professional bodies for the legal sector in Scotland. Inquiries with these organisations has revealed that data on the proportions of Black and Asian members iarenot compiled.
Sources: The General Council of the Bar 2000a & 2000b; The Law Society 2000

Ethnic minorities in the machinery of government
We complete this brief survey by looking at ethnic minority participation in the civil service and on the boards of public bodies. Again ethnic minorities are less well represented in the senior than in the junior ranks of the civil service, though women from these backgrounds are more equally so. Table 18 shows the comparative position for appointment to the boards of public bodies.

17. Ethnic minorities in the civil service

	AO/AA level [1]			Senior Civil Service		
	Total (1999)	Men(1998)	Women(1998)	Total (1999)	Men (1998)	Women (1998)
Ethnic minority	13,884(5.7%)	9,395(10.2%)	4,488(2.9%)	55(1.5%)	46(1.5%)	8(1.3%)
All staff	242,038	91,684	153,626	3,602	3,139	617

1 Administrative Office/ Administrative Assistant

Source: Cabinet Office 1999

18. Ethnic minority background in appointment to the boards of public bodies

	Total(% all appointments)	Men(% total)	Women(% total)
Ethnic minority appointments	1,352(4.4%)	863(63.8%)	490(36.2%)
All appointments	30,520(100%)	20,521(67.2%)	9,999(32.8%)

NB. Public bodies are: nationalised industries; public corporations; Non–Departmental Public Bodies; and NHS bodies.

Source: Cabinet Office 2000

Twelve: government responsiveness

Listen up

Is government responsive to the concerns of its citizens?

The essence of consultation is the communication of a genuine invitation to give advice and a genuine consideration of that advice
Mr Justice Webster, in court, 1986

Introduction

In the tradition of British politics, the governors govern and the people allow themselves to be governed – except at elections usually every four or five years when they go to the polls and exercise their imperfect right to choose their governors. The political class has always assumed that the public are satisfied with this significant, but occasional, role. The majority of people disagree. Broadly three-quarters of people asked in polls over the past eight years how much power they should have between elections say that they should possess 'a great deal' or 'a fair amount' of power, but only 13-19 per cent of them have felt that they possess such power (Dunleavy et al, 2001). In other words, most people want government that is responsive as well as accountable. The ultimate accountability of a government is to the people at election time when they pass judgment on a government's record – that is, after the event. Responsiveness requires government to solicit and listen to the views of the public before policy or legislation is made and take them into account.

Responsiveness to the public is therefore a key virtue of democratic government. It requires systematic and legally-grounded procedures for consultation and participation that ensure that as many interests and views as possible are taken into account when decisions are taken. It also requires more informal mechanisms, especially at local level, to keep elected representatives in touch with their publics. There are also obvious dangers. Governments may give special interests, or well-organised communities, or especially committed or vociferous pressure groups, so much attention that they lose sight of wider public interests. Here systematic and open procedures are of great importance as a safeguard. But the inter-relationship between formal politics and elections and processes of consultation and participation is vital. Electoral politics are a check on consultation and participation, especially on single issues. The mutual health of both strands of politics is intertwined.

The Institute for Public Policy Research (IPPR) conducted focus groups in December 2000 that confirmed the desire of the public for more power between elections. The IPPR identified three broad types of policy issues on which people especially want more of a say:

- 'close to home' policies; i.e., usually on planning and service matters which affect people in their homes or local communities;
- 'national strategic' policies made nationally but which affect people locally: e.g., health, crime and education policies; and
- policies on 'risk issucs' (c.g., on the safety of food, drugs, genetics, air quality, and other issues which again impinge upon people's daily lives).

The IPPR also found that people wanted government, local authorities and agencies to be more proactive in seeking and taking note of people's views and wanted a deeper relationship between public service providers and themselves than that offered by voting alone (Clarke, 2002).

In 1997, Democratic Audit found that government was not very responsive to the views of the public when it consulted on particular policy issues (often of the kind that matter to ordinary people; see above). Most formative consultation on government policy took place (and still does) within policy networks and 'communities' of civil servants and representatives of major interest groups. Some of these policy communities – e,g., on defence and procurement issues – are closed to public scrutiny and may well subvert formal consultation exercises and parliamentary scrutiny and decision. Prior to 1997, we found that responses to formal public consultations were rarely published in their entirety; certain interests took precedence over others, thus blocking political equality in government decision-making (Weir and Beetham, 1999). We reviewed complaints from a variety of bodies, like the Law Society, Consumers Association, the Association of Chief Police Officers, that consultation exercises were too often rushed and gave insufficient time for considered responses.

But under both Major and Blair, government has begun to show genuine interest in consulting and involving people more thoroughly and effectively in debate on legislation, policy and service delivery. Think-tanks such as the IPPR and consultancy firms, like the Office for Public Management, have put forward innovative ideas. In March 2001, the Public Administration Select Committee (PASC) published a report of its investigation into innovations in public involvement (PASC, 2001e). The committee made a series of recommendations, most notably for a Public Participation Unit in Whitehall to provide a focus for consultation and involvement across government. In reply, the government proclaimed:

> Effective participation in central and local government decision-making by the widest possible range of people and organisations is an important part of the government's commitment to democratic renewal, with change coming from the bottom up as much as top down (see PASC, 2001g)

The government has established bodies in Whitehall, such as the Social Exclusion and Active Community Units, and sponsors other organisations like the Community Development Foundation to promote community engagement. It also encourages local authorities through a variety of schemes to consult and involve their publics and to experiment with innovative ways of engaging their interest.

However, the Blair government also remains very executive-minded, as we have shown (Section 7). It is committed to greater and more systematic consultation at national level, but its enthusiasm for consultation is focused on the local level and service delivery. Ministers and the senior civil service are wary of opening central government itself up to increased public consultation. In fact, Blair, Brown and other ministers have strengthened internal direction of policy-making; and secondly, experts from bodies like IPPR sense that ministers fear media ridicule amid charges of being weak, vague on essentials and running 'government by focus group' if they consult too ostentatiously. They are seen to be reluctant to widen consultation at the centre and learn from best practice at the local level. The government's own record is patchy, at times praise-worthy, at others opportunistic or opaque; and when it comes to cases, departments find it hard to identify examples of consultation actually changing outcomes (see PASC, 2001e).

At the same time, the government has pursued other avenues of consultation. The most visible has been the creation of hundreds of task forces to advise ministers on a wide range of policy issues. Another was the 'People's Panel', a four-year exercise through which Mori sounded out a large sample of the public (5,000 people) on policy choices. Another is the co-option of special advisers, not only specialists like Greg Power and Meg Russell, who advise Robin Cook on parliamentary reform, but also high-profile figures, like the former BBC Director General Lord Birt, to engage in 'blue skies' thinking.

12.1 How open and systematic are the procedures for public consultation on government policy and legislation, and how equal is the access for relevant interests to government?

The government has acted to reform and make more systematic Whitehall's procedures for public consultation on government policy and legislation, following the criticisms of the Law Society, Consumers Association, and other bodies that are regularly consulted (see Hansard Society, 1993). After a government evaluative and consultative exercise in early 2000, the government published its Code of Conduct on Written Consultation in November the same year. The new code broadly seeks to improve Whitehall's traditional reliance on written consultative exercises and introduces standard procedures across all departments. While it is hardly innovative, and fails to 'deepen' consultation, the code does fill the previous vacuum in guidance on how departments and agencies should consult the public.

Bodies consulted during the evaluation confirmed previous criticisms – government consultation was inconsistent; consultation 'windows' were often too short; the questions asked were leading; background information was lacking; and the feedback was patchy. The code is centred on seven criteria that address these complaints; insists on simpler consultation documents, a minimum twelve-week consultation period and more comprehensive feedback; and requires departments and agencies to reproduce the code's seven criteria in consultation documents, 'with an explanation of any departure, and confirmation that they have otherwise been applied'. The code also directs departments to appoint a consultation co-ordinator to monitor and regulate all consultations.

The government is also establishing a web-based central register of public consultations to publish all consultation documents with links to the department responsible, updates when consultation periods end, and reports of final decisions.

The government's seven rules for consultation

1. The timing of consultation should be built into policy formulation from the start so that the views of groups have a better prospect of being considered
2. It should be clear who is being consulted about what, in what time-scale and for what purpose
3. Consultation documents should be simple and concise
4. Consultation documents should be made widely available, with the fullest use of electronic means
5. Sufficient time should be left for considered responses. Twelve weeks should be the minimum standard period for consultation
6. Responses should be carefully and open-mindedly analysed and the results made widely available, the views expressed made known, and reasons for decisions given
7. Departments should monitor and evaluate their consultations.

There are however doubts about the ability of the Cabinet Office, the focal point for this activity, to ensure that departments and agencies comply with the new approach. Such doubts are inspired in part by the restless changes in units and responsibilities in the Cabinet Office; but more by the notorious 'unlinked' nature of the central departmental structure and weak relations between ministers and departments and their agencies and quangos. Departments have been slow in appointing consultation co-ordinators and those in post vary between those who see simple compliance with the code as their goal, and others who regard the code as a starting line from which they can develop wider and more effective consultation. And though the code is binding in principle, there are fears that its rules can too easily be evaded. While it was being prepared, several departments successfully lobbied for an escape route – that the code is binding 'unless ministers conclude there are exceptional circumstances leading to departure'.

Reviewing national strategic policy
The Blair government's commitment to consultation is tempered by its strong tendency, identified by Anthony Barker, an academic expert on British government, 'to internalise and control the policy review

progress within the executive' (Barker, 1998). Barker describes this less obvious manifestation of 'control freakery' as an executive-based ambition. There are five trends within government since 1997 that temper or condition the new emphasis on wider public consultation, alongside both positive and negative developments:

Policy networks and communities: Officials in government departments orchestrate these informal groupings through which major organised interests and professional groups play a significant and often dominant role in government policy-making in significant areas of business and national affairs. The process is discussed very fully in the first Democratic Audit (see further Weir and Beetham, 1999). Below the generally unruffled surface of Whitehall, officials in individual departments and external actors have long been engaged through these networks and communities in continuing dialogue and negotiation over making and implementing government policies. The intensity of the process varies across policy domains, but many interest groups perform an intimate policy role through these arrangements. Political scientists define these groupings as follows: 'policy communities' are almost closed to other outsiders and even other government departments; 'policy networks' are more open and consultative forums. The influence of organised interests is not necessarily undying: for example, Tony Blair ended the independent life of the old Agriculture Department after the foot-and-mouth epidemic in 2001 and folded its functions into a larger whole, in part to try to destroy the undue influence that farmers' interests wielded within the department.

Task forces: In their first 18 months, ministers established some 295 task forces, 'short-term groups of experts' (in the government's words), who were conscripted to apply their expertise to particular policy issues. The rate of creation then seemed to slow down, but a PASC census in 2001 found that 303 task forces were actually at work in Great Britain (the Northern Ireland Assembly withheld its figures) – a third of them in Scotland (PASC, 2001d). The sudden eruption of these bodies is comprehensively described and analysed by Anthony Barker in his study for Democratic Audit, *Ruling by Task Force* (Barker et al, 1999). They have undoubtedly played a more inclusive and open advice-gathering process than most previous practice in consulting interested parties (but see further below). However they generally contribute to the strengthening of executive control. The minister controls everything from his or her central position; defines the problems; nominates the task force members; and controls invitations to interested bodies or individuals to offer information, advice or other forms of cooperation. Moreover, the function of many task forces has been not to go off and consider what policy should be, but to consider 'how best to design and deliver an established Labour government policy' (Barker et al).

Policy reviews: The new Labour government also launched 207 internal policy reviews in 20 months after taking power in 1997 alongside the 295 task forces. This significant scale of internal review was overshadowed by the intense interest in task forces. Practitioners and experts from outside the civil service were invited to discuss some reviews (relatively rarely and sometimes secretly), possibly seeing internal papers or being informed of matters which ministers and officials might not wish to discuss in public.

Royal Commissions and departmental committees of inquiry: From Mrs Thatcher onwards, Royal Commissions and departmental committees of inquiry have given ground to governments' own internal inquiries, ad-hoc inquiries, task forces, and special advisers – all manifestations of the executive's desire to exert close control. The Labour government has appointed only two Royal Commissions – the first to study long-term care of the elderly, and the second under Lord Wakeham to make proposals for reform of the second chamber. New Labour nominee Lord Lipsey (as he was entitled to) set out to sabotage a majority view that was uncomfortably too generous for the government on the first of these; the second was carefully selected and fixed from the start (see Section 1.5).

Blair did also establish the Jenkins Committee review of reform of the electoral system for Westminster, a small ministerial inquiry that mimicked the commission process, but also was under strict political control (Section 1.5). Lord Jenkins initially ruled out holding public meetings, but was obliged by the protests to think again. The Strategic Defence Review was another, far grander ministerial inquiry that set a new standard for openness and access on defence policy from which it would be hard for a future government to depart. It was a MOD aim, Barker reports, to make it easier for future Conservative governments to conduct further defence reviews by having made regular review exercises the established norm (Barker, 1998). The review was in a sense an opened-out policy community exercise, which ended with a specialist seminar organised by the Royal United Service Institute and Deloitte Consulting (RUSI, 1998); it was also shadowed by an intense Defence Select Committee series of hearings and final report.

However, it is clearly a loss to democratic debate if disinterested people of weight and specialist knowledge are now less likely to sit in public on Royal Commissions and departmental committees of inquiry; to receive open evidence; to question witnesses in public; and then to retire and consider their findings for a final reasoned report, with findings of fact and recommendations on policy. One especial loss is the stimulus to ongoing debate and accountability from such exercises as the media and Parliament report the conclusions and ask if they are to be accepted, rejected, postponed or ignored. As Barker notes, 'Internal executive reviews usually keep secret the range of inputs and policy options considered or, at best, reveal them in the light of the preferred outcome, with the plain implication that any others were weaker'. Without the high-profile of an external inquiry and its public report, the loss of transparency, consultation and accountability is a serious blow to the plurality of debate.

Public inquiries: Governments have various ways in which they can establish public inquiries into issues of public concern. Some inquiries are provided for by law: for example, the well-established provisions for public inquiries on planning proposals, covering housing, roads, new construction, infrastructural projects, etc. There must be an inquiry when people die in railway and other accidents (like the Kings Cross fire). But ministers have a wide discretion to establish inquiries. The Labour government has been most creative in using public inquiries to open up public debate to people or communities with grievances that have deep policy and communal implications. The Macpherson inquiry, for example, into the murder of Stephen Lawrence has done much to heal the wounds of black communities that are discriminated against and hopefully in the long run to eradicate discrimination in the police and all public services. The Kennedy report in July 2001 on the deaths of children from heart surgery at the Bristol Royal Infirmary at last gave voice to their grieving parents and increased pressure on doctors and NHS administrators to be honest and open in their dealings with patients. The Saville inquiry into the Bloody Sunday killings in Derry is still in session, but even unresolved, it contributes to the peace process by re-examining events hotly contested between the two communities openly and dispassionately for the first time.

There is often criticism of how long such inquiries take – Kennedy sat for nearly three years – but their long-term effects are significant. However, official impatience with the time that statutory inquiries into major planning issues take looks like extinguishing these often important exercises in public debate on national planning issues. In recent history non-statutory inquiries, such as the Roskill Commission on a third London airport, have set new standards of open and thorough research for the statutory process. However, Whitehall has been pressing governments for more than 20 years to limit the impact of statutory inquires on major planning issues; and seized upon the statutory Heathrow inquiry into the proposal to build a new Terminal 5 (T5) to discredit the whole process. This inquiry was a pathological case in that much of its work was simply a repetition of previous inquiries into Stansted and T5 and was five years in the making. Major business interests have also been trying to persuade the current business-friendly government to relax planning rules – for example, on out-of-town supermarkets.

The government is now consulting on taking powers to decide national planning issues of this magnitude simply by parliamentary order and restricting public inquiries into them only to 'local issues'. In other words, government means to pre-empt public discussion by taking powers to be the judge in private sector projects, like T5, as well as its own big development schemes by issuing orders (i.e., secondary legislation) that it can normally force through Parliament (see Section 7.4). Other controversial projects, such as major new trunk roads or Lord Birt's parallel motorway system, could thus be driven through on a minister's say-so. The scale of civil disobedience that such decisions are likely to provoke is huge.

It is easy to understand that ministers and Whitehall officials regret the loss of control, time and policy momentum which these formal and open processes impose on their ambitions. But ministerial orders, whether after internal policy reviews or even possibly consultation exercises undertaken under the government's own direction, can be no substitute for the sometimes elaborate public hearings, open, wide and deliberative debate, and documentary analysis, that the full statutory process brings to public policy – exasperating as it must seem to the executive. It is not as though the inspectors are wholly independent: they are executive appointees and must come to judgment within the government's national policies and local planning rules. The European Court recently upheld the existing system against a complaint that the inspectors were not properly independent.

How equal is access?

By their very nature, consultation processes are directed at the wide range of interest groups that exist in British society and the publics which sustain them. As we pointed out in our first audit, some of these groups are inevitably more equal than others. Certain interests – most especially those of big business generally – have more expertise finance, information, status and access to Whitehall than others. A body such as, for example, the CBI is a well-organised professional organisation that has an impeccably 'respectable' reputation in Whitehall and Downing Street (see also Section 4.6). In some cases, as with the MOD and the defence industry, the relationship between officialdom and interest group is umbilical. As for consultation on legislation, the very process of asking for evidence in writing defines the character of those who are expected to respond. The People's Panel was a prominent example of government seeking the views of the wider public, largely on how public services might be improved. The original goals set for this panel of 5,000 people were ambitious, but few departments used it and only eight of the 18 users identified some contribution to their decision-making. Moreover, the high attrition rate left the panel less representative and more white, middle-class, professional and activist over time (PASC, 2001e). Overall, the panel was a missed opportunity.

The government offered the post-1997 task forces and policy review groups as a major exercise in widening access. Senior civil servants used the phrase 'invited to the party' to symbolise the new openness and inclusivity of the new Labour ministers' attitude towards public policy. Alongside the idea of ministers reaching out to a wider civil society, there was also an emphasis on 'partnership' with non-government interests to solve awkward or difficult problems. The process was undoubtedly more inclusive than anything that had gone before and did not justify the gibes of 'cronyism' with which the hostile media showered it. The first wave of task forces drew on a remarkable range of 2,459 'outsiders' (i.e., non civil servants). But the occasional presence of a Trevor Brooking, Bernard Crick, Julia Neuberger, Richard Rogers or Ridley Scott hardly relieved the domination of the process by conventional private business and public producer interests. Private business interests occupied 35 per cent of the places on the first task forces; public sector producers held 31 per cent. Genuine 'experts' occupied only 8 per cent of the places; and as proxies for a wider public, consumer representatives took 15 per cent of places, and trade unionists just 2 per cent. As temporary bodies, ministers were free to appoint members unconstrained by the 'Nolan' rules for public appointments; but the PASC census identified some 52 task forces that were over two years old (the time-limit proposed by the Neill Committee for the life of these supposedly temporary bodies).

The degree of openness among task forces has varied considerably. The Disability Rights and Lord Haskins's Better Regulation task forces consulted widely and were both very open. Lord Marshall, head of the Energy Task Force, took senior Whitehall mandarins with him to meetings with local interests affected by energy tax ideas, taking them outside London on occasion. Other task forces were essentially closed until they reported.

E-democracy

The Code of Guidance applies largely to written consultation, traditionally a medium that is aimed almost wholly at interest groups and rarely at a wider public. There are no plans at present to broaden the code to cover other forms of consultation on government policy and legislation that are appropriate for engaging ordinary people; and it is far from clear how it will be developed even to involve a wider circle of interest groups. The government aims to make it possible for all the public's transactions with government to be conducted electronically by 2005; and in evidence to the PASC committee, government information officers outlined a plan to give every citizen access to a portal for reaching government services and there is already a project dedicated to simplifying e-access to government services.

But e-government is not the same as e-democracy. A National Audit Office study, *Government on the Net*, showed in 1999 that the government's websites have produced dramatic increases in the numbers of people accessing consultation documents and responding to invitations to comment. But most of the government's e-endeavours are designed to provide information and do not yet, as the PASC report (2001e) noted, 'provide opportunities for the public to communicate with government, councillors or with fellow citizens on matters of common concern'. The committee urged the government to explore how far e-communication could be developed to give access to groups who are hard to reach (or who do not respond to) traditional approaches – like young people, those who are housebound, or widely scattered, perhaps in rural areas, or even just too busy.

Public protest

The ultimate resort for people who are or believe that they are excluded is to turn to protest. For example, a significant number of environmentalists disrupted public inquires and obstructed road schemes under construction after some 30 years of presenting disregarded evidence on roads policy to the Department of Transport and pro-department public inquiries. One protester, 'Swampy', became a national celebrity of sorts. More recently, environmentalists have destroyed GM crops and been exonerated by a jury; local populations have taken the streets to protest against the presence of convicted paedophiles in their neighbourhood, and have even attacked them and their homes; and lorry drivers, farmers and others blocked refineries and petrol depots in protest against rising petrol and diesel costs. About 80 per cent of the public agree that peaceful protests, blockades and demonstrations are justified when 'governments don't listen' (Dunleavy et al, 2001).

Executive control of policy review

The more significant or urgent the policy, the less any government consults. In the case of the Blair government its avoidance of consultation in such cases may partly be because the new consultative graft onto government practice inevitably takes time to seal and ministers prioritise action.

Let us look at the public's interest in being consulted on 'national strategic' policy-making that has a local dimension. The main drivers of policies for public services are the Public Service Agreements (PSAs), produced by unequal partnerships between the Treasury and government departments. These agreements, which form part of the government's spending reviews, set out each department's aims and objectives and give them explicit targets for service delivery. The Treasury has also embarked upon a pilot scheme of service agreements with chosen local authorities. The Treasury is very much the dominant partner in the negotiations with departments and local authorities; Treasury in-house specialists play the leading role in establishing the objectives and targets (see Section 7). There is no space for consulting interest groups or the public at this stage. But PSAs are followed by Service Delivery Agreements (SDAs) which are supposed to give the public an opportunity to comment and to state how service delivery will be tailored to meet the public's needs. The Cabinet Office studied SDAs and its report expressed concern about the variable quality of these documents and their often weak 'consumer focus'.

On some occasions, it seems, the government does mean to involve the public in debate; on others, it is not above launching a spurious and meaningless public consultation process to cloak pre-determined policies. For example, Blair promised 'a national debate about the future of the welfare state from first principles' at a Labour party policy forum in 1999 and actually set out on the road for a series of public meetings. However, the decisive shift in social policy from universalism to targeted benefits under Labour bears the unmistakable imprint of Gordon Brown's intent and Blair's pilgrimage came to nothing. In 2000, the Department of Health, under a notoriously hands-on minister, Alan Milburn, embarked on a vacuous and costly public consultation that was so patently much more a public relations exercise that it was at once, and rightly, pilloried in the press. The NHS National Plan pledged to create a 'patient-centred' NHS. Milburn however insisted on driving through Parliament the abolition of community health councils (CHCs), the one independent element representing patients in the NHS, with less challenging bodies, disregarding considerable protests. In response, he promises wider citizen and patient involvement.

We do not doubt the sincerity of the government's commitment to opening up and improving public consultation. But while we appreciate the pressures of 'events' and demands for instant action on ministers, we are obliged to conclude that their commitment to consulting has been flawed and inconsistent, and does not reach out far enough. The road of executive ambition is paved with good intentions.

12.2 How accessible are elected representatives to their constituents and other members of the public?

Most people agree that representing and being loyal to their constituency interests, and dealing with constituents' problems and grievances, are the most important duty of MPs; and most MPs agree with them (Dunleavy et al, 2001; Hansard Society/Vacher Dod, 2001). Most knowledgeable observers of Parliament agree that the party whip comes first in MPs' loyalties. There is no doubt, however, that most MPs strive strenuously to be accessible to their constituents by way of letter, fax and telephone, and hold regular 'surgeries' in their constituencies, not least for reasons of electoral advantage. They are also accessible to other members of the public, but they do not give much weight to these other representations. More than two thirds of MPs (69 per cent) say they receive 100 to more than 500 letters a week and reply to as many weekly too. Table 1 sets out the rate of hours that MPs say they give on an average week to meeting with constituents and dealing with their affairs. The Public Administration Select Committee received evidence in 2001 on the question of the difference that modern technology was likely to make to the service that MPs gave to their constituents and the public. The MPs on the committee noted wryly that e-mail 'certainly encourages voluminous correspondence' and heard from several witnesses that MPs were simply not equipped to respond. Research has shown that MPs, like US Congressmen, distinguish between 'e mails that do not come from their constituents and those that do' – a practice that may reinforce MPs' sense of themselves as constituency representatives, but which may also filter out wider public concerns and representations on current issues. This aspect of their duties however is somewhat academic for now. Only about 380 MPs have e-mail addresses.

1. MPs' weekly constituency activity

Activity	0-2 hours	3-10 hours	11-plus hours
Meeting constituents at Parliament	72.7	17.9	0.6
Being at constituency surgeries	22.9	63.1	3.4
Helping them with local council issues	16.8	62.6	10.7
Helping them with access to welfare	31.9	49.7	8.4
Responding to their policy concerns	45.3	40.8	4.0
Dealing with Child Support Agency cases	47.4	38.0	4.5
Dealing with immigration cases	63.2	22.9	3.9

Source: Hansard Society Commission on making Government Accountable, Vacher Dod, 2001

The percentages shown do not add up to 100% as there is a No Reply category in the original questionnaire. A few activities are omitted from this table; those shown obviously overlap

12.3 How accessible and reliable are public services for those who need them, and how systematic is consultation with users over service delivery?

It is as hard to judge how accessible and reliable public services are in the UK as it is easy to identify efforts by pollsters to consult the public on their delivery and standards, especially at local level. In general the public express high levels of satisfaction with the quality of public services they receive. For example, a Mori report on public attitudes, drawn from responses from the People's Panel, found broad satisfaction with most public services provided by local authorities (though falling satisfaction with housing services since 1998). In May 2002, a YouGov survey of 10,000 people found high levels of satisfaction with their own most recent experience of the health service. Three out of four patients were either very satisfied or quite satisfied with their last visit to a GP or local hospital. Approval ratings for both nurses and doctors rose above 80 per cent.

But how valuable are such surveys when it comes to the substance of what is provided? It is widely recognised that, as the interim Wanless report said, 'standards of health-care in the UK have fallen behind people's expectations' and 'we are not keeping up with the quality of service provided routinely in many other countries'. The Wanless report goes on to assess how the NHS compared with other health regimes overseas and found (among some real strengths) that, for example, the NHS was among the worst at dealing with heart diseases and breast and lung cancers (Wanless, 2001). It also cites a comparative study of hospital care in Germany, Sweden, Switzerland, the UK and USA in which the UK came second worst on six of seven dimensions of patient care.

Consultation on service delivery

Most people deal most of the time with local councils and other local bodies, such as hospital trusts, housing associations, further education colleges, etc. Thus local consultation and participation are key elements in government that involves the public. A recent British Social Attitudes Survey report found however that eight out of ten people believe that councils should make more of an effort 'to find out what local people want' (Rao and Young, 1999).

The Local Government Acts 1999 and 2000 were intended to meet such demands and to fulfil the promise of the 1998 white paper, *Modernising Local Government*, to create a local government 'characterised by councils which are in touch with local people and get the best for them' (Cm 4014). The 1999 Act introduced the Best Value regime to improve the quality and delivery of local services; at its heart is a duty to consult users and the wider public on service delivery. The 2000 Act requires councils to prepare and consult on community strategies. Local PSAs (see above) are supposed to encourage participating councils to make services more responsive to local needs. Funding under the various regeneration budgets requires that there should be partnerships between the public, private and voluntary sectors and such partnerships must demonstrate that they have consulted local interests. But some government regional offices are impatient with the slowing down of delivery that occurs when local communities fail to respond to government targets.

One of the main aims of the executive/scrutiny split on local councils that the government is promoting (see Section 13.3) is to clarify and highlight executive decisions and to encourage backbench councillors to take on a 'community' role and to broker participation exercises. A variety of individual Acts require local authorities to consult. In planning, for example, they are bound to publicise planning applications and consult affected parties. School closure plans require consultation, as do proposals to transfer local authority housing stock to social landlords, tenant co-ops or other managerial hands. Councils must consult the public on development plans, and business ratepayers on their budgets. The government is considering replacing the multiplicity of these individual requirements to consult with one over-arching framework. There are however also doubts about the efficacy of duties imposed from on high, and fears that local authorities will simply 'go through the motions' of compliance.

Effective consultation by councils and non-elected bodies is patchy. Research at De Montfort University for the government found that two-thirds of all councils did not report clear links between participation and decision-taking. The Audit Commission report, Listen Up, suggested that nearly three quarters of authorities thought that there was a failure to 'link the results of consultation with decision-making processes'. Councillors are wary of ceding their electoral authority to possibly unrepresentative bodies or groups of citizens; and council leaders with majorities swelled by plurality-rule elections are often too entrenched to listen to views other than their own. Councils' traditional relationship with the voluntary sector is one of funding and command; with the private sector, one of suspicion; with the public at large, remote. On the other hand, further research at De Montfort suggests that people are discouraged from becoming involved by their negative view of the local authority; a lack of awareness of the opportunities to participate; a lack of council response to participation exercises; and a perception that is 'is not for the likes of me'. In a sense there has to be a controversial or not-in-my-back-yard element to provoke people into becoming involved (PASC, 2001e).

There are genuine and innovative attempts at local level to consult and involve the public in policies and decision-taking:

- at the last count, three councils are known to have held local referendums to seek citizens' views on raising local budgets and council taxes (Bristol asked local people to decide on investment in education in relation to the rate of council tax);
- Birmingham set up a Democracy Commission to involve non-councillors in deciding the future structure of the local authority; has a local initiative scheme that brings senior managers into direct contact with community wishes on service issues at ward level; and runs tenant liaison boards that not only engage tenants as consumers but also as decision-makers in budgets for which they then take responsibility;
- Bristol and other authorities have set up Citizen's Panels, often jointly with other non-elected authorities, to sound out and monitor the views of local residents on service issues; in Bristol an independent community board, serviced by the council, is presiding over regeneration in the inner-city Barton Hill area. This is a pathfinder project under the government's New Deal for Communities scheme. The council is integrating service delivery locally. In 2001, the turnout in elections to the community board was 54 per cent – just over twice as high as the turnout (26 per cent) in the council elections in the same ward;
- A variety of local authorities and non-elected local bodies have held 'citizen's juries', small deliberative bodies recruited randomly, to consider policy options on a wide range of issues of local importance;
- Islington council convened a day-long conference of about 60 people to discuss adult education in the borough; and

● York council has developed a consultation strategy with a range of 21 techniques for consulting people and a built-in evaluation process.

And what of the public? Various studies and polls have identified a 'latent activism', or reactive interest in politics, among the public which can be sparked off by a particular plan or event; and that a readiness to act and be involved is 'an abiding property of a wide sector of the whole population' (State of the Nation 1991; British Social Attitudes 1994; Parry et al, 1992). However, Birmingham council's experience in participation exercises suggested that while nearly half their residents tell pollsters that they want to know more about the council's activities, only about a quarter were interested in taking more decisions themselves. And who are they? The usual suspects, a government survey found, while young, single parents (particularly women), and ethnic minorities are most likely to be disaffected. If such people are not specially targeted, the Public Administration Committee warned, 'not only will more participation not lead to more democracy, but participation exercises may actually reinforce social exclusion' (PASC, 2001e).

PFI – 'The only game in town'

Meanwhile, there are various examples of Private Finance Initiative (PFI) hospital and other capital projects being driven through ruthlessly at local level, on occasions through manipulated consultation schemes. The School of Public Policy, at University College, London, is publishing a series of reports examining the consultation on such schemes in detail. The first of these analyses the way in which the Birmingham health authority and United Birmingham Hospital Trust drove through a PFI scheme to replace two existing hospitals with a new-build hospital. The local Community Health Council (CHC), the statutory watch-dog, set out to consider the trust's plans in a careful and systematic way, but very soon found that they had ventured into a political minefield. The trust, local health authority and regional NHS executive were outraged by their intention to subject the plans to scrutiny and debate; the Secretary of State, ministers and officials combined with experts and spin doctors to frustrate their scrutiny and attempts to consult the public; and even infiltrated two new members onto the CHC as Secretary of State nominees to try and break their resolve. The CHC's recommendations were entirely ignored by the NHS establishment in Birmingham and London, while the CHC members were publicly portrayed as devious ideologues rather than the broadly representative group of people that they were.

The consultation exercise seemed to observers to be a formality that had to be undertaken; a set of 'options' were released to the public that concealed the course of action that was to be taken. One part of the consultation consisted of pro-forma letters given to second year medical students at the Birmingham University Medical School as they clustered around notice boards to get their examination results. One student reported being asked to sign this letter there and then. He asked if he could take the letter away, but was not allowed to. He recalled seeing students signing it 'in droves', and since he had seen no consultation documents on which to base signing the letter, he assumed other students hadn't either. The letter wholeheartedly endorsed the new hospital option (and thus by implication, the PFI scheme, though it was not specifically mentioned). Finally, the authority set up an avowedly independent and expert panel to examine the PFI project, chaired by Lord Hunt, a former colleague of the authority's then chairman and soon to be a junior health minister in the Lords. Seven members of the panel were known in advance to support the PFI project.

For the trust and health authority, PFI was the 'only game in town' after a considerable period of under-investment in public services from 1973 to 1997. As the Bishop of Birmingham, a non-executive director of the UHBT, explained in the House of Lords in June 2000, health planning in Birmingham had been 'deadlocked' for 20 years. 'Everyone knew that radical changes were needed, but no one could agree on what ought to be done'. Their desire to seize the moment may explain the vehemence with which the authority and trust pursued the PFI opportunity, but it does not excuse the manipulation, vilification, under-handed politicking and obstruction with which they sought to crush the CHC's opposition to the plan or the gerrymandering with which they bulked up support in their own consultation processes (see further McFadyean and Rowland 2002).

12.4 How much confidence do people have in the ability of government to solve the main problems confronting society, and in their own ability to influence it?

There is a barometer of popular faith in British government. Since 1973, pollsters Mori and ICM have asked the same question nine times, usually on behalf of the Rowntree Reform Trust, about the 'present system of governing Britain'. The proportion of people saying that the system could be 'improved quite a lot' or 'needs a great deal of improvement' rose from just under half in 1973 to peaks of 69, 73 and 72 per cent in the mid-1990s. In 1998, under the impact of the New Labour government, the figure for people looking for improvement fell to 54 per cent, but it now stands at 61 per cent (see Table 2). So overall confidence in the way we are governed is not high.

2. Faith in way Britain is governed

Which of these statements best describes your opinion on the present system of governing Britain?

	1973	1977	1994	1998	2002
Works extremely well and could not be improved	5	10	2	4	2
Could be improved in small ways but mainly works well	43	24	26	37	34
Could be improved quite a lot	35	33	39	39	37
Needs a great deal of improvement	14	29	30	15	24
Don't know	4	4	4	5	2

Sources: Dunleavy et al, 2001; and ICM poll for Democratic Audit, 21-23 June 2002

In June 2002, Democratic Audit dug deeper into popular attitudes to test the public's view on Question 12.4 through a special ICM poll. We asked first, 'Irrespective of which political party is actually in power at any other time, how much confidence do you have in the ability of central government at Westminster to solve the main problems that confront the country?' In response, nearly half (48 per cent) said a 'fair amount' and 7 per cent 'a great deal'. A third said 'a little' and 11 per cent 'none at all'. This may fairly be described as a half-hearted expression of public confidence. We then asked, 'To what extent do you feel people like you are able to influence what government does to solve problems and deliver good public services?' The replies were as follows:

A great deal	4 per cent
A fair amount	17 per cent
A little	44 per cent
None at all	35 per cent.

Thus broadly four out of five people in Britain believe that they have no real influence, or only a 'little' influence, over what government does to solve national problems or improve public services. But as we have seen above, most people want more power over government decisions than they have between elections. It is perhaps figures like these that give popular clues to the so-called 'apathy' of the public.

Thirteen: decentralisation

An over-powerful centre

Are decisions taken at the lowest practicable level of government for the people most affected?

We are moving from the old Britain of subjects where people had to look upwards to a Whitehall bureaucracy for their solutions to a Britain of citizens where, region to region, we are ourselves in charge.
Gordon Brown, January 2001

Introduction

The territorial dimension of politics is one where our democratic principles of popular control and political equality stand in some tension with one another. From the one point of view, devolved and local government have many democratic advantages over centralised control: they are closer and more accessible to the people, and can shape policies appropriate to regional and local variations in conditions and political identities. At the same time, differences in policy and priorities between localities can produce unacceptable inequalities in services, which in turn generate demands for more uniformity and central control. Central governments are adept at using these pressures in their own interest to manage the economy, limit the powers and resources of alternative sources of power at regional and local level, and especially to frustrate the policies of political opponents at sub-central level. In practice, democracies have to find an effective balance between equal citizenship throughout their territory and the demands of distinctive regional and local autonomy.

In the twentieth century the UK became one of the most centralised political systems in the western world. Devolution of government to Scotland, Wales and Northern Ireland has begun to change the shape of British government. We need to review these changes; assess the nature of the balance between the responsibilities of the centre and the autonomy and integrity of sub-central government; and examine how effectively the different levels are coordinated. The centre has to act to secure and advance the well-being of the people of the UK as a whole, and to make sure that no parts of the UK are disadvantaged by the unequal distribution of resources between them. At the same time, the centre must allow devolved institutions sufficient autonomy in the exercise of their powers and in the use of resources to meet the needs and aspirations of their separate populations.

13.1 How independent of the centre are the devolved authorities and institutions at national and regional level, and how far do they have the powers and resources to carry out their responsibilities?

The scale of Labour's devolution programme since 1997 is so profound that it is rarely looked at as a whole. Scotland, Wales, and Northern Ireland have been given unequal measures of home rule. Both the Scottish Parliament and Northern Ireland Assembly have primary law-making powers over differing ranges of domestic policy; the NI Assembly is empowered to have dealings with another sovereign power (i.e., the Republic of Ireland); and the National Assembly of Wales can make only subordinate law within the framework of Westminster legislation. All three receive a central block grant from the Treasury, but they are free to set their own spending priorities within this grant. These are major (though flawed) advances in independence over the previous regime when central government dictated both policy and spending priorities. Such major changes, so decisively accomplished, represent a major constitutional and territorial upheaval. Yet the civil service and devolved administrations have absorbed and managed the changes with no obvious strain. A handful of political crises have erupted, but there has been no major political shock wave. Only in Northern Ireland is the stability of the existing settlement in serious doubt (though devolution itself is regarded on all sides as a good).

The current devolution arrangements are acknowledged among the political class to be 'asymmetric'. It is of course not symmetry or the lack of it that determines how effective the new governing arrangements are. But there is complacency in the political embrace of this asymmetric system. The principal feature of this asymmetry is that it has 'a hole in the heart' – otherwise known as England. The people of England do not benefit from representative devolved government at a regional level. Even Greater London, the largest 'region' in the UK in terms of population size and significance, has now been given only a weak strategic local authority rather than regional governance. The other eight English regions are governed from Whitehall and Westminster – through regional government offices, newly-created regional development agencies, the regional offices of major quangos and other public agencies, and various ad-hoc arrangements. The government has just published a white paper which leaves the way open for elected regional assemblies in England (Cabinet Office, 2002). Meanwhile, as the white paper admits, 'England now includes virtually the only regions within the EU which don't have the choice of some form of regional government.' Overall, this means that over 83 per cent of the total UK population – nearly 50 million people – are directly governed from the centre; while just over 16 per cent, or nearly ten million people, live under regional government as well (see Table 1).

1. How many people live under devolved governance in the UK?

Population

The population of the United Kingdom	59,500,900	
People living under devolved institutions		
Scotland	5,119,200	
Wales	2,937,000	
Northern Ireland	1,691,800	
People living under devolved institutions	9,748,000	6.4%
People living in London and the English regions		
London	7,285,000	
South East	8,077,600	
North West	6,880,500	
East	5,418,900	
West Midlands	5,335,600	
Yorkshire and Humberside	5,047,000	
South West	4,935,700	
East Midlands	4,191,200	
North East	2,581,300	
People living under Whitehall's rule	49,752,800	83.6%

Source: ONS Population Estimates (as of 4 April 2001)

The sovereignty of Westminster

The Queen, opening the new Scottish Parliament, presented MSPs with a silver mace that symbolises the rule of the UK 'Crown in Parliament' north of the border. The devolved bodies remain subordinate to Westminster and Whitehall. The Devolution Acts preserve Westminister's right to legislate on devolved matters, but the government has stated that it will not do so in Scotland without the Scottish Parliament's consent. By the same token, laws passed by the Northern Ireland and Scotland legislatures on issues within their devolved competence are not the offspring of a sovereign body. Meanwhile, the Welsh Assembly is more supplicant. The UK Parliament legislates for England and Wales, but the government has pledged to take into account representations from the Welsh Assembly on any legislation affecting Wales. The Assembly has to beg government's legislative managers for time at Westminster for primary legislation on policies for Wales alone; its own law-making capacity is restricted to being able to pass subordinate legislation – that is, statutory instruments that derive their legitimacy from Acts of Parliament.

Under the 1999 British-Irish Agreement, an international treaty, the UK government agreed that the Irish government would enjoy rights of consultation on all matters that were not devolved to the NI assembly. But in February 2000, Peter Mandelson, the then NI Secretary, obtained from the UK Parliament emergency powers through the Northern Ireland Act 1998 to suspend the new NI assembly and executive. He used these powers at once to save the Ulster Unionist First Minister, David Trimble, from resignation over IRA decommissioning. Mandelson's action was arguably unconstitutional as he did not have authority under the treaty to act unilaterally outside the terms of the Agreement; and secondly, because the Agreement required him to consult both the parties in the NI assembly and the Irish government over any such 'remedial action' . Mandelson's recourse to the UK Parliament's sovereign powers to take on the power of suspension shows how deeply entrenched the idea of strong and unchecked executive action remains in government thinking at Westminster. But this is also a gut political instinct. Why else could Tony Blair tell the *Scotsman* during the 1997 election campaign that sovereignty 'rests with me as an English MP and that's the way it will stay' (4 April 1997)? (It would have been more correct to say as a UK MP.)

A UK government could therefore pass laws to abolish or suspend devolved bodies in Edinburgh or Cardiff, or could override devolved legislation or policies. Such a crude course of action may now seem unthinkable in Scotland or Wales. But changed realities, such as strife between, say, Westminster and Edinburgh executives under the control of rival parties, could conceivably trigger the deployment of Westminster's superior force, not to abolish devolved arrangements, but possibly to curb the powers of devolved institutions, or to negate their policies. In any event, the Audit criteria propose stronger guarantees of constitutional independence than the devolved bodies now possess. The Scottish Constitutional Convention, the true begetter of Scottish devolution, came to accept that it was unrealistic politically to press for legal entrenchment of a Scottish Parliament. But it urged the government to make a declaration that it would not repeal or significantly amend the founding Act without the consent either of the Scottish Parliament or people (Boyd 1997). The government could, of course, follow the example of the NI Act 1998 and require its successors to gain public consent for any major change in the constitutional position of devolved assemblies and executives.

Inter-governmental arrangements

The government legislated for devolution in an ad-hoc and unprepared way and inter-governmental relations are developing more informally than formally. The main instrument of coordination, the Joint Ministerial Committee (JMC), was announced late at night in a government amendment in the House of Lords (HL Deb, 28 July, 1998), together with the idea of concordats, formal but non-justiciable agreements between the centre and devolved authorities. Under an inter-governmental Memorandum of Understanding, the JMC is the formal consultative forum for bringing together the Prime Minister and First Secretaries and their deputies from three devolved authorities and the NI First Minister and his deputy. The Judicial Committee of the Privy Council, established by statute in 1833 to exercise the

Crown's ancient jurisdiction in hearing appeals from overseas dependencies, has been pressed into service to hear 'devolution issues' cases and has already heard several Scottish cases.

The JMC process has not developed fast because there has so far little need for it. The main JMC has met only twice, but has spawned 'functional' lower-tier JMCs for health, the economy, poverty, etc, that have met infrequently. Some groups of 'functional' ministers have also met more regularly, though not as JMCs. The North–South Ministerial Council has met four times in plenary session, and the British–Irish Council three times (though it is supposed to meet twice yearly). Generally, relations between the four governments are good; they agree on most issues. Those issues which do arise are being dealt with satisfactorily between officials or ministers and do not need to be discussed in formal arenas. A network of concordats, or formal agreements, between the devolved authorities and UK government departments and public bodies such as the Health and Safety Executive is gradually growing; and the Constitutional Secretariat in the Cabinet Office has produced some dozen Devolution Guidance Notes.

Formally these notes are for the guidance of Whitehall departments, but according to Roger Masterman and James Mitchell, monitors of devolution for the Constitution Unit, they are drafted in conjunction with the devolved authorities and so represent agreed administrative positions. They in fact argue that a growing corpus of secondary legislation, codes and concordats is gradually codifying the workings of devolution, or a union state. They also suggest that the centre, re-modelled by Blair after the 2001 election, is moving from a reactive to a more active response to devolution and 'may prove to be a driving force behind policy on devolution to the nations and regions' (Masterman and Mitchell, 2001).

The former Scottish and Welsh Offices (now the Scotland and Wales Offices) were retained to ease the transition of devolution and inter-governmental relations. The rivalry between the late Donald Dewar, the Scottish First Secretary, and John Reid, the first Scottish Secretary, has been superseded. Though both the Scottish and Welsh Secretaries have intervention powers under the devolution legislation, the Scottish executive has grown so fast and confidently that the Scottish Secretary now performs only a minor role. The Wales Secretary is a more significant player who must plead the Welsh Assembly's case for primary legislation at Westminster and watch over other legislation that affects Wales in the Assembly's interests. The Northern Ireland Secretary and the NI Office play a substantial role in the province, being responsible for major political issues – the peace process, security, policing, etc. The NI Office retains responsibility for nine quangos, including the Parades Commission, in Northern Ireland.

Labour party politics
From the start Labour's ruling elite strained every sinew to maintain political control over the devolved administrations through its command of the party and trade union links. In Scotland, a trusted colleague Donald Dewar was the natural choice for First Secretary. But in Wales and London, the Prime Minister blocked 'off-message' candidates – the able Rhodri Morgan in Wales (after the resignation of Ron Davies) and Ken Livingstone in London – and with the aid of friendly trade union bosses, shooed-in his own candidates, Alun Michael and Frank Dobson, though only after twisting party rules and compromising the selection processes (see Section 6.5). John Prescott tried to dissuade Blair from trying to block Morgan, but Blair responded, 'What do I do if he wins?' Prescott replied, 'Say it's democracy . . . That it's a triumph for democracy' (Rawnsley, 2000).

Blair also tried to persuade Paddy Ashdown and Charles Kennedy, successive Lib Dem leaders, to intervene to save university tuition fees in Scotland and Michael's skin in Wales. Both refused. The question of university tuition fees was an early touchstone for independent thinking in Scotland. Gordon Brown and David Blunkett were furious at the prospect of Scottish deviation from their policy and Tony Blair attempted to get Ashdown to intercede with the Scottish Lib-Dem leader Jim Wallace to back off. Ashdown's diaries (Ashdown, 2001) record the following exchange:

BLAIR TO ASHDOWN: 'You can't have Scotland doing something different from the rest of Britain'.

ASHDOWN: 'Then you shouldn't have given the Scots devolution . . . You put yourself in a ridiculous position if, having produced the legislation to give power to the Scottish Parliament, you then say it is a matter of principle that they can't use it'

BLAIR (LAUGHING): Yes, that is a problem. I am beginning to see the defects in all this devolution stuff'.

Blair's machinations ended in public humiliation. Michael did briefly become First Secretary in Wales, but, after resigning in February 2000 rather than face a no-confidence vote, he was replaced by Rhodri Morgan, who went on to form a coalition with the Lib-Dems later that year. Livingstone stood as an independent after being rejected as the official Labour party candidate and won a resounding victory in the mayoral election (see below).

Powers and policy in Scotland

The Scotland Act 1998 gave the Scottish Parliament primary law-making and executive power over a wide range of domestic policy, and also discretion to vary the rate of income tax up or down to 3p in the £. Central government retains legislative and executive power over 'reserved matters'- European and foreign affairs, taxation, defence, the civil service, the Crown and constitution, immigration and extra-dition, social security, most trade, energy and industrial affairs. There is common agreement on most of this agenda, but it does restrict the Scottish executive's redistributive scope and ability to vary social benefits to deal with specific Scottish problems. There are also demands for a Scottish 'say' in the EU. The Scottish Parliament established a flexible committee structure under which committees took on legislative, scrutiny and policy-making roles. A Labour-led coalition with the Liberal Democrats has been established to provide stable government.

The Scottish Parliament has made a difference. The administration has developed distinctive policies and has passed far more ordinary 'Scottish' legislation than would have been possible at Westminster (though post-devolution Westminster has passed nearly as many Acts for Scotland). These policies have not set the Clyde on fire, but they do meet the goal of subsidiarity across a wide range of issues and so (to use Dewar's words) 'touch on the lives of every man, woman and child in the land'. The Scottish executive has pursued distinctive policies on university tuition fees, teachers' salaries, free care for the elderly, Freedom of Information (see below), etc. The statutory rule prohibiting councils from promoting homosexuality was abolished in Scotland, albeit clumsily, where the UK government failed. The Parliament has begun to assert its own law-making capacity and for example passed the Abolition of Poindings and Warrant Sales Act to abolish forced bailiff's sales of the property of people in debt. The work and status of the Parliament has been significantly enhanced by the presence of representatives of small parties, like Tommy Sheridan, the Scottish Socialist MSP, and Robin Harper, the Green MSP. All in all, in spite of old-style political chicanery and scandals, poor executive strategy (as on decommissioning fishing vessels) and an often vicious press commentary, Scottish devolution has made a steady debut.

The desire for more powers in Wales

The Government of Wales Act 1998 created a 60-member Assembly with no powers to pass primary legislation or to vary taxes. The Assembly may ask the government to pass primary legislation on its behalf, but otherwise has only secondary legislative powers to act within a primary legislative framework set at Westminster. The First Secretary and a cabinet are super-imposed on an Assembly, a body corporate with the characteristics of an unreformed local authority. Thus there is a confused separation between the executive, policy-making and scrutiny roles in Wales. After a rocky opening, the formation of the coalition in October 2000 created a new administration with an assured majority and a programme for government with the backing of a generous three-year settlement under Gordon Brown's Comprehensive Spending Review. The foot-and-mouth epidemic then gave the administration an opportunity to show that the Assembly was more than just a 'talking shop' and to give the sense that Cardiff was increasingly replacing London 'as the main location of political accountability in Wales' (Osmond, 2001).

But the original settlement deprives the Welsh administration from realising the goal of proper subsidiarity. There is cross-party and public recognition of the fact that the Assembly is an elected and broadly representative body, but does not possess the powers to fulfil its functions and create distinctive Welsh policies. Morgan himself has complained that his administration is 'repeatedly hamstrung', or as Noreen Burrows, a professor of European law, has concluded:

> The Assembly has legitimacy but lacks a functional capacity proper to its status whereas prior to devolution the Welsh Office had an extensive functional capacity, yet lacked legitimacy (Burrows, 2000).

NOP polls for BBC Wales have shown that support for an Assembly with law-making powers rose by 10 percentage points in a year to 54 per cent in July 2001.

Relations with central government have been very mixed. In 2000, central government did enact a law to establish a Children's Commissioner for Wales, but failed to get any of only four 'Welsh' bills into the 2001-02 Westminster programme. The Assembly has also been frustrated by the Welsh civil service's inability to develop a more distinct position, 'in tune with the political realities of devolution' and more independent of Whitehall and its traditions. The Presiding Officer was involved in a bitter row with the Permanent Secretary over the Assembly's right to decide the location of the Welsh sustainable development unit.

Power-sharing in Northern Ireland

In Northern Ireland, devolution grew out of the Belfast Agreement of 1998 and remains prey to the bitter communal rivalries and exigencies of troubled post-agreement politics of decommissioning, policing and low intensity paramilitary violence. The agreement created a power-sharing executive with a First Minister and deputy elected by MLAs on a parallel consent process which made David Trimble (Ulster Unionist) First Minister and Seamus Mallon (SDLP), his first deputy. The four-party executive committee is also established on a power-sharing basis under the D'Hondt formula, with three seats each to the UUP and SDLP, and two each to the DUP and Sinn Fein. Some decisions can be taken by a simple majority, but important votes require the backing of both Unionist and nationalist MLAs. Other elements of the new structure were a Human Rights Commission, an Equality Commission and a Police Ombudsman (see Section 8.2).

Power-sharing may have been the only means of creating peace, but, it also strengthens and legitimises the extremes, and makes collective decision-making and 'normal' politics very difficult. Political life for the Executive consists of endless series of negotiations among the three pro-agreement parties, harassed by the semi-detached DUP. The civil service is frustrated by the anarchic politics of the Assembly and was alarmed by requests from a committee 'to see discussion papers at a draft stage' (see also below). Yet the Executive does manage to reach accommodations; the Assembly endorsed the Executive's 'holistic' first programme for government in March 2001 (see above); and some Assembly committees are coming of age.

Resources

The government has made no attempt to strike a balanced and equitable division of responsibility for spending between central and devolved control. The devolved authorities have unprecedented freedom (in a UK perspective) to allocate the moneys they receive in block grant from the Treasury as they see fit and are not subject to the detailed meddling by Treasury officials that Whitehall departments experience.

But that is where their autonomy ends. Thereafter the Treasury rules. The Treasury is determined to control the key macro-economic variables in the UK economy and government debt and denies the devolved authorities significant borrowing powers. They have no discretion to increase the size of the central grant that the Treasury determines. They must fund capital projects either out of current revenue or through the government's PFI initiative. The Scottish Parliament has the power modestly to vary income tax in Scotland, but Wales and Northern Ireland have no independent tax-raising capacity at all. The potential for Treasury interference in their fiscal affairs is great. In Wales, for example, the Treasury's refusal to commit itself in advance to match-funding for the £1.2 billion EU aid package for West Wales and the Valleys (one of the poorest areas in the UK) starkly revealed its continuing power over Wales and in doing so unseated the then Labour First Secretary, Alun Michael. Treasury influence also stretches, for example, even into control of council spending in Scotland. In 1997 the Scottish Office warned that should the Scottish Parliament fail to use its powers to control 'excessive' council spending, the Treasury could penalise Scotland by taking 'the excess into account' in fixing Scotland's grant (Bell and Christie, 2001).

The Treasury controls the grants given over time to the devolved administrations through a mechanism known as the Barnett formula. This formula was created in 1978 at the Treasury as a temporary measure prior to the failed devolution proposals of the time. Barnett recalled, 'At the time, I did not think it would last a year or even 20 minutes' (Treasury Committee, 1997). This mechanism for distribution is outdated, unequal and geared not to current needs, but to relative population sizes.

Barnett himself has disowned it, but not the Treasury which likes the fiscal clarity and the control that the formula brings. The formula determines the changes in resources distributed to the Scottish Parliament and Welsh and NI Assemblies – in other words, not to the bulk of expenditures but only to additional changes. Some major expenditures – e.g., social security – are outside its jurisdiction. Basically the Treasury uses the formula to translate increases (or decreases) it has agreed with English spending departments into the increases (or decreases) to the block grants it allocates to the devolved authorities for spending on comparable programmes. The fact that the devolved bodies have no power to take a policy decision to increase to size of grant restricts their ability to make policy. In Northern Ireland, for example, the ambitious pledges in the Executive programme to tackle poverty and right socio-economic inequalities are still-born because the province's revenue raising capacity is very limited (Wilson and Wilford, 2001).

Across the UK, Scottish economists David Bell and Alex Christie have found that the north English regions came out worst under the formula, on a straight per capita basis, so far as basic needs were concerned; and confirmed the relatively generous treatment of Scotland and Northern Ireland (Bell and Christie, 2001). Their simple but valuable exercise is, however, no substitute for a thorough government needs assessment that covers the whole spectrum of government policies and regional needs and costs. There has been no full needs assessment in Britain for more than 20 years.

The position is further complicated by the 'Barnett squeeze'. For Barnett is a convergence formula designed gradually over time to equalise per capita spending across the UK (see Edmonds 2001, further). The devolved authorities have the highest per capita spending across the UK: in 1999-2000, the broad figures for per capita expenditure were £5,939 million in Northern Ireland; £5,271 million in Scotland; £5,052 million in Wales; and £4,283 in England. The UK average was £4,453 million. Thus the devolved authorities receive lower proportionate rises in spending under Barnett than lower-spending English regions. The 'squeeze' therefore puts in doubt the ability of the devolved administrations to sustain policies that differ from Westminster, such as free personal care for the elderly, the abolition of tuition fees, and higher teachers' salaries in Scotland, and free prescription charges for the under-25s in Wales. Bell and Christie judge that such commitments 'are not sustainable in the long run'. But if the devolved administrations are not sufficiently independent of central control to deliver significantly different policies from Westminster, then the whole object of devolution will be seriously compromised.

The Oxford politics don, Iain McLean, argues that the UK requires a 'fiscal constitution' to make good the absence of significant tax-raising powers in the devolved authorities, the deficiencies of Barnett and the asymmetrical devolution settlement (McLean, 2000).

13.2 How far are national and regional levels of government authorised by free and fair elections?

Devolution proposals for Scotland and Wales were approved in principle by national referendums (though very narrowly in Wales on a 50.1 per cent turnout). In the case of Northern Ireland, the Belfast Agreement, which contained the proposal for a devolved assembly, was approved by 72 per cent of the population. The English were given no say at all, even though their interests are obviously affected by the changes. The referendum on the creation of the new London mayoralty and assembly (that we consider here in our round-up of sub-central electoral arrangements) were also approved by a referendum only of the population directly affected. The elections for the Scottish Parliament, National Assembly of Wales and Greater London Assembly were held under modified versions of the proportional Additional Member System (AMS); the NI elections were conducted under the Single Transferable Vote (STV), the system used in NI since 1972 for all elections apart from to Westminster (as well as in the Irish Republic). The election for the London mayor was held under the Supplementary Vote.[1]

The choice of AMS for electing the Scottish Parliament was a 'done deal' in Scotland, which the Labour government was bound to accept. The parties to the Scottish Constitutional Convention ruled against plurality-rule, or 'first-past-the-post' (FPTP) elections, since they they would have installed the Labour party of the central Scottish belt in permanent power at Edinburgh. The convention compromised by choosing AMS (rather than the Liberal Democrats' option, STV), but with a slight majority of constituency MSPs (73 out of the 129, or 56.6 per cent of the chamber) over 'top-up' MSPs on Labour's insistence. (A 50:50 split produces a near proportional result, as in Germany; the constituency bias was expected to favour Labour.) In Wales, Ron Davies, the Welsh Secretary at the time, insisted on the 'inclusive' AMS rather than FPTP, mostly as a means of persuading the Liberal Democrats and Plaid Cymru to campaign for devolution in a referendum which was far from certain. However, two-thirds of the seats were allocated to constituency AMs; the uneven split was expected to secure a Labour majority. In both Scotland and Wales, and later in London, the size of the chambers and constituencies were kept small, so as to reduce the opportunities for smaller parties. In London, the choice of AMS for the assembly elections was compromised by the decision to impose a 5 per cent threshold for party representation in the chamber. The intention was to stop racist candidates from being elected; the effect was to exclude smaller parties other than the Greens.

The first election results paved the way for more inclusive politics in Scotland and Wales, even though the deviation from proportionality was on the high side by European standards, at over 10 per cent in both nations (see Table 2). But while the shares of seats for the parties in the Scottish Parliament and Welsh Assembly did not fairly reflect the votes they had won, neither assembly was left under the dominion of a single-party majority won on a minority of the popular vote. The deviation in the result of the London assembly was higher – too high – at 15 per cent, thanks partly to the high threshold (see above), partly to the small size of the 25-member assembly. The Northern Ireland election in June 1998 was the most pluralist and proportional of all, with a deviation score of just 3.1 per cent (on first preferences). This score compares well with European norms. The Ulster Unionists were slightly over-represented with over 28 seats (a 25.9 per cent share of the 108 seats) on just 21.3 per cent of first preferences, but the parties broadly won seats in proportion to their share of the vote.

2. Deviation from proportionality (DV) in devolved elections, compared with the deviation in devolved areas at the 2001 general election

Devolved nation or region	Devolved coalition's share of the popular vote %	Coalition seats in the Parliament/Assembly%	DV in devolved election %	DV at 2001 general election %
Scotland	47	56	10.7	33.8
Wales	49	57	10.6	36.4
Northern Ireland	na (1)	na (1)	3.1	12.4
Greater London	45	52	15	26.0

Note 1: The NI executive is a cross-party body, not the product of a political coaltion

The composition of assemblies

The elections were also the most open to the participation of fourth and fifth parties ever held in mainland Britain (Dunleavy and Margetts 2001). In Scotland, Green and socialist party candidates won seats alongside a rebel Labour MP and representatives of the four main parties. In Wales, thanks in part to public revulsion at Labour's fixing of the party's leadership ballot, Labour's electoral dominance was greatly reduced and Plaid Cymru ran a strong second, winning nearly a third share of the vote and assembly seats. Ken Livingstone, a non-party candidate, won the mayoralty election in London and three Greens were elected to the Assembly. In Northern Ireland, the elaborate STV counting process ensured that a wide range of political views were represented in the Assembly. Eight parties, including the Women's Coalition, originally won seats and one then split.

3. Women in Parliament or Assembly

	Westminster (2001)%	Devolved Legislature/ Assembly (1999/2000)%	European Parliament (UK MEPs) (1999)%
England	18.9[1](100 of 529 seats)	na	22.5(16 of 71 seats)
Wales	10(4 of 40 seats)	41.7(25 of 60 seats)	60(3 of 5 seats)
Scotland	15.3(11 of 72 seats)	37.2(48 of 129 seats)	25(2 of 8 seats)
Northern Ireland	16.7(3 of 18 seats)	13.9(15 of 108 seats)	0
Greater London	24.3(18 of 74 seats)	44(11 of 25 seats)	40(4 of 10 seats)
Totals	17.9(118 of 659 seats)	29.6(88 of 297 seats)	24.1(21 of 87 seats)

1 Including Greater London

Sources: Column 1: The United Kingdom Parliament www.parliament.uk. Col 2: The Assembly for Wales www.wales.gov.uk; The Scottish Parliament www.scottish.parliament.uk; The Northern Ireland Assembly www.ni-assembly.gov.uk/index.htm; the Greater London Assembly www.london.gov.uk. Col 3: The UK Office of the European Parliament http://www.europarl.org.uk

The elections also resulted in high proportions of women in the devolved bodies (except for Northern Ireland) by comparison with their representation at Westminster (see Table 3). However, minority representation is poor or non-existent across the board. There is no ethnic minority representation in the Scottish Parliament, or Welsh or NI assemblies; and even the Greater London Assembly has only two minority members though minority communities constitute 29 per cent of the Greater London population. One aspect of the make-up of the Scottish Parliament is the comparatively large intake of younger MSPs – eight were in their 20s, when elected, and 29 in their 30s. The class balance is poor, with just 1.6 per cent having worked in 'blue-collar' occupations (Watson, 2001).

Turnouts in the first elections in Scotland and Wales were relatively low, and very low in Greater London (reflecting its local rather than regional character), but stood up well in Northern Ireland where sectarian influences were intense.

The elections made stable and inclusive government possible in both Scotland and Wales. No party could command a majority: in Scotland, where the Lab-Lib coalition held 56 per cent of the seats in the Parliament, on 47 per cent of the vote; in Wales, the Lab-Lib coalition that emerged in autumn 2000 commands 57 per cent of seats in the assembly on 49 per cent of the vote. The Lib-Lab coalition (with conditional Green backing) in the less significant London Assembly has just over half the seats (52 per cent) on a combined vote share of 45 per cent. Livingstone won the London mayoralty as an independent with 58 per cent of the play-off vote.

Issues of representation

Both Scotland and Wales are over-represented in the Westminster Parliament. If seats were allocated on the basis of their population, Scotland would have 58 rather than 72 seats, as at present, and Wales 33 instead of 40. The unequal distribution of seats and widely varying size of constituencies increases the deviation from proportionality at general elections. Devolution has sharpened the perception of the two nations' over-representation, and in accordance with the recommendations of the Scottish Boundary Commission in February 2002 Scotland's share of seats at Westminster is to be cut to 59.

There are serious unanswered questions about whether and where Westminster ministers are constitutionally and politically answerable for policies and actions that affect devolved territories. The attention that is given to devolved issues at Westminster must strike a balance between interference and indifference to the needs of the devolved territories. Generally, the division between reserved and devolved matters determines what Westminster will consider. For example, in July 1999 parliamentary questions on Welsh tourism, the beef industry and abattoirs were ruled out of order by the Speaker because they belonged in the Welsh Assembly. If an issue is the responsibility of a Secretary of State – that is, a non-devolved matter – the UK Parliament has a legitimate role in holding her or him to account. The House of Commons Scottish Affairs and Welsh Affairs Committees, for instance, have a continued role in scrutinising the activities of their relevant Secretaries of State, as well as the UK government departments responsible for matters affecting Scotland and Wales.

Two issues of representation have surfaced in Scotland. Top-up MSPs from party lists have been assuming a territorial role in the constituencies of directly-elected MSPs. Plainly, they have a democratic right to do so, but Labour MSPs complain that SNP top-up members have been exploiting their position for factional political reasons. There have also been 'turf wars' between MSPs and Westminster

MPs over their respective caseloads and pressures on MPs to confine their activities only to 'reserved' matters.

13.3 How far are do the national and regional levels of government satisfy criteria of openness, accountability, and responsiveness in their operation?

The final report of the Scottish Constitutional Committee in 1995 demanded a distinctively open and responsive Parliament and more consensual politics. The key instruments of accountability are the parliament's 'subject' and 'mandatory' committees that were formed with a double brief to undertake scrutiny of legislation and examine the policies and work of the Scottish administration. The idea was that they would become expert in their policy areas and so examine legislation more effectively than their counterparts at Westminster. They seem to be effective. Dewar confided to journalist John Morrison that a Westminster government with a substantial majority could 'forget about the House [of Commons], within limits'. But the Scottish Parliament was an obstacle course for the executive:

> Enormous power has been given to the committees. I sometimes have great difficulty explaining to people [MSPs] that as backbenchers they have more power than anyone ever dreamt of at Westminster . . . we have constantly on a daily basis to reconcile different points of view (Morrison 2001: 71).

The second main role of committees – acting as revising chambers on bills – has fallen unevenly on the committees, with some at first choked with significant legislation. The BBC journalist Brian Taylor, who has kept an eye on the committees, says that ministers and officials are 'chilled' by the committees' scrutiny of bills. Unlike in the House of Commons, he says, at Holyrood ministers cannot control the committees: 'They must win their case, and that's the importance of the new politics' (Watson 2001).

Petitioning the Scottish Parliament

Citizens have had the right to petition the Westminster parliament since 1571, but the right has deliberately been smothered by protocol and it is hardly ever used. But, as part of attempts to create a more responsive parliament in Holyrood, petitions have been made integral to its life. Petitions can be sent by e-mail rather in a laborious prescribed form, as at Westminster. About half the petitions received come from individuals. A Petitions Committee receives all petitions, places them on the Parliament's website, discusses and assesses them in public, and consults the executive and others. The committee passes on more than half of them to the appropriate subject committee where many are pursued; a few even lead to parliamentary debates.

Accountability and responsiveness in Wales

By its very nature, the National Assembly for Wales is too weak to achieve the same degree of devolved activity on behalf of the Welsh people as its Scottish counterpart; and confusion over the divide between the administration and assembly – and so between executive action and scrutiny – is built into its devolution structure. The coalition has brought about a more open and consensual regime than previously and a clearer division between administration and the Assembly by giving the Assembly's Presiding Officer more independence and resources. Assembly committees have asserted themselves. For example, the Health and Social Services committee persuaded the Health Secretary to overrule her officials and extend free eye tests in Wales. Generally the Assembly and its committees have brought far more public information out into the open than was previously available under London's rule, especially on specifically Welsh aspects of policies. But greater accountability and responsiveness in Welsh government depends on more autonomy from the centre.

Freedom of information

In January 2002 the Scottish Parliament passed its own FOI Act into law with an overwhelming majority. The new FOI regime follows the UK model in structure (see Section 7.8, with a long list of categories of protected information, including internal policymaking. However, the test of harm stipulates that release of information must 'substantially prejudice' protected interests, not the weaker test just of 'prejudice' as in Whitehall. Neither is the list of protections in Scotland as full – for example, background and factual information for policy-making is not specifically protected, as it will be in Whitehall. The Information Commissioner will be stronger than the UK Commissioner, with more power, enforceable in the courts, to order the disclosure of information in the public interest. But the First Secretary can overrule a Commissioner's rulings in certain key areas. Thus the Act gives the political executive the power to be judge in its own cause – a power that can clearly be misused. Scotland is still bound by the Whitehall FOI regime on all 'reserved matters', even where they touch on Scotland, and all the Scottish communications with the centre. Wales, too, is largely bound by the restrictive Westminster regime. Rhodri Morgan is pledged to substitute more open international standards, set by the USA and Ireland, for those of Whitehall (*Guardian*, 15 March 2000). But so far he can make symbolic rather than substantial changes. His boldest move has been to publish Welsh cabinet minutes on the Internet six months after the actual meetings.

There are other aspects of openness. Both Scotland and Wales have instituted wide-ranging consultation processes – as, for example, over Scotland's budget-making processes (Dow and Bell, 2000). The Scottish Parliament has made communications a priority. Every MSP has her or his own e-mail address and many MSPs have their own websites, linked to a very informative Parliament site. The Parliament is also seeking to develop internet access with a full network of computer terminals in community bases; and has established a partner library in each of the 73 Scottish parliamentary constituencies.

The English Problem

The 'English Problem' is in fact two different problems. The first is that there is no separate English authority legislating for specifically English affairs, since the UK Parliament carries out this function. This means that MPs from Scotland and Northern Ireland have the right to vote on domestic English (and Welsh) legislation, and have done so, whereas there is no reciprocal right for English MPs to vote on domestic legislation for Scotland or Northern Ireland. There have been half-hearted calls for an 'English Parliament', but they have no resonance with the English electorate. The government's response has been to argue that all MPs are in principle representatives of the union as a whole with the right to vote on every aspect of a UK government's programme; and to emphasise the practical difficulties of classifying bills that apply solely to England (and Wales).

The issue could become acute after a close general election in which the Conservatives win a majority of English seats and Scots MPs give Labour the balance of power at Westminster. If the Labour Scots MPs were disbarred from voting on domestic English issues, then a Labour government with a UK majority only would not be able to carry the bulk of its domestic legislative programme. (The dilemma is likely to affect only Labour governments, given Labour's dominance in Scotland and the electoral rout of the Tories there.)

The Essex constitutional lawyer, Brigid Hadfield, has argued that this first problem can only be resolved by the creation of a specifically English law-making dimension (Hadfield, 2002). However, it tends to be obscured by a second, different, problem, which is that of regional devolution within England, whose regions are more comparable in terms of population to Scotland, Wales and Northern Ireland than is England as a whole. The English regions are largely ruled as they were in 1997, except that new regional quangos, the Regional Development Agencies (RDAs), now share command of regional policies with the regional government offices in England, alongside the regional offices of longer-established national quangos and new regional arts and culture bodies. Appointed regional chambers, representing local authorities and business interests, have an ill-defined oversight role, but few powers and inadequate funding. The 2002 white paper, *Your Regions, Your Choice*, now promises to give English regions the possibility of opting by a referendum for directly-elected regional assemblies, which will assume a range of largely strategic coordinating functions, with modest budgets and tightly controlled tax-raising powers to match.

The white paper fails to set out a coherent blueprint for representative or effective politics at regional level. It scarcely tries to justify the bundle of powers in which the government plans to swaddle the new assemblies that seem to owe as much to Whitehall haggling as to any coherent idea of regional democracy. The underlying concept is one of regional government, akin to local government (see below), as an agency for delivering on central government's priorities, and subject to rewards or penalties as it succeeds or fails in satisfying ministers' and Whitehall's demands. However the English regions evolve, they will not solve the first major 'English Problem' – that of the absence of a clear English law-making dimension and the elision of English and UK (and Welsh) policy and legislation (see further Hadfield, 2002).

13.4 How independent is local government from the centre, and how far do local authorities have the powers and resources to carry out their responsibilities?

Central government has the power of life or death over local government. Local authorities have no constitutional being other than by the grace of Parliament. They are creatures of statute law and a single Act of Parliament could lawfully abolish them all. (In Scotland, the statutory sword held over the heads of local authorities has been devolved to the Scottish Parliament.) Councils are supposedly protected by 'a corpus of custom and convention', as the Widdicombe inquiry, charged with finding ways to strengthen local government, put it in 1986. But constitutional convention has provided poor shelter against the relentless pressure of central government over the past quarter of a century.

Governments since the mid–1970s have continually re-organised, abolished, re-made and dismembered local government in the UK. Local authorities are also in pawn to central government: they raise only about a quarter of their spending and government provides or sanctions the rest. Their independence – boasted of in Bagehot's day – has shrunk as a result. In effect, local government has been reduced to a system of local administration, subject to a central regime of legal restraint, policy rules, spending controls, inspection and audit. There have been two damaging results: the status and stability of local government has fallen very low, and consequently the quality of people standing for local office and the local people's interest in voting have both diminished considerably. The constitutional weakness of local government leads onto three other major structural issues:

1. their role in local governance and service delivery is partial. Territorially, 467 elected local authorities cover the whole of Britain. But the large and diverse local quango state – an unco-ordinated mixture of over 5,200 unelected bodies, statutory and non-statutory, public, private and voluntary – exists alongside them, delivering services and performing public functions within their boundaries (see PASC, 2001d). These bodies are answerable upwards, to central or devolved government, to national or regional quangos, or to regional government offices, not sideways or downwards. Less than one in five is required to consult or report on their activities to local government (PASC, 2001d);

2. governance in the local sphere is more crowded yet. Central government shares its powers over local government and quangos with a wide range of national public bodies, its regional offices, executive agencies, regulators and inspection regimes, and specialist units such as the Social Exclusion Unit. In Scotland, Wales and Northern Ireland, devolved administrations are in charge of local affairs. The NHS and social security are kept separate, but new relationships between the NHS and social services are being created; and

3. councils also face a major legal restraint on their freedom to meet local needs and aspirations –the ultra vires rule that prohibits them from undertaking actions and policies which are not expressly allowed for by legislation. Most local authorities in mainland Europe possess either a constitutional right of 'general competence' which does not bind them with legislative chains, or they have entrenched rights to perform defined functions that cannot be removed by a simple parliamentary majority. The Labour government moved very cautiously in 2000 to give councils a limited power of general competence: to do anything that they consider 'is likely to achieve the promotion or improvement of the economic, social or environmental well-being of their area'.

The current government wants to reinvigorate local government. Its aims have been to reinvent local authorities as effective and visible community leaders; to make their leaderships more accountable; to promote partnership between local authorities and local voluntary bodies and private business; to make councils more consultative and to raise turnout in local elections; and to improve their service delivery. But ministers still intervene heavily in the conduct of local councils; maintain strict financial controls over their budgets; and continue to remove functions and powers from them.

The new executive reforms

The government is transforming the traditional corporate structure of English and Welsh local authorities to prepare them for greater operational freedom. Councils were generally given a choice between a directly-elected mayor (after a local referendum), or a new cabinet structure under a leader. The aim is to clarify council executive decision-making to make them more effective; and also to strength the scrutiny and 'community' roles of backbench councillors. The full council remains responsible for setting the local council tax, making overall policy, and overseeing planning and regulatory activities. The new executives are legally responsible for major services and functions and take decisions within the council's policy framework. New overview and scrutiny committees advise on policy-making, review executive decisions and seek to make the executive accountable.

The inspection and audit regime

Yet local authorities are heavily regulated by government inspectorates of various sorts. The most conspicuous regulatory regime is the 'best value' programme, which is designed to improve services by obliging councils to consult the public over re-designed services, to compare the costs and quality of different providers, and to choose that which offers best value. But the Audit Commission, not local publics, is the driving force behind the programme. There are other external inspection regimes, including:

- district auditors;
- the Ofsted regime in local education authorities, schools and nurseries;
- the Local Government Ombudsman;
- various commissions – e.g., the EOC, CRE and Disability Rights Commission – and bodies like the Health and Safety Executive;
- new standards regimes for England, Wales and Scotland, with ethical standards officers possessing investigatory powers (in Scotland, the standards regime applies to quangos as well as to councils); and
- various official inspectorates check, for example, social services, benefit fraud, housing, fire service, and 'best value', etc.

We recognise the value of such ancillary means of accountability and openness. Some directly involve local inhabitants (for example, local people trigger the intervention of the local Ombudsman service). But the overall level, diversity and intensity of interference is both intrusive and excessive.

The government now plans to expand its performance regime through a new Corporate Performance Assessment framework under the remit of the Audit Commission. The Commission is to place local authorities in four categories – high, good, fair and poor – within the next two years. High performers will be allowed more autonomy, including a reduction in ring-fenced grants, as a reward. Fair and poor-performing councils will be required to agree a prescriptive improvement action plan. At worst, a designated poor performer could lose functions to another provider, have its management transferred to another council or public body, or be put into administration.

Financial controls

The Treasury's writ runs in local as in national affairs. The Treasury treats all local authority expenditure as part of total public expenditure. So its agenda, needs and priorities take precedence over local agendas, and the resources that government is willing to make available to local authorities depend far more on its view of the country's needs and priorities than any local view. Its grasp of local spending is expanding as a pilot project for local authority Public Service Agreements (PSAs) gains ground. The deal between the Treasury, Local Government Association, government departments and pilot local authorities is that in return for more freedom and more money, the pilot authorities will raise the standards for a dozen key services and functions above best value levels. The LGA hopes the deal will lead to more relaxed central control as local PSAs are extended to all authorities over the next few years. For the Treasury, these PSAs represent yet further expansion of its power.

The government has promised to relax its detailed financial control over local authorities. The general revenue grant for meeting assessed local needs will be simplified and councils will be given greater freedom to borrow, invest, trade, charge and spend. But though the capital finance regime is to be relaxed, the Treasury will still force local authorities into the Private Finance Initiative for major building schemes, or semi-privatisations such as transfers of their housing stock (which are often very unpopular with their tenants). Councils are denied a real choice between direct borrowing and PFI for major new-build schemes and are not even able to raise capital to improve their homes on the same, more favourable terms as registered social landlords.

But the government has no plans to correct local government's major handicap – the imbalance of funding between revenue raised locally and government grant. The financial weakness of councils makes them over-dependent on the centre. Local authorities raise only about a quarter of their expenditure them-selves, largely through the council tax. The government has relaxed the severe 'rate-capping' regime imposed by its Conservative predecessors, but retains powers to set a maximum expenditure level for indi-vidual authorities and to penalise them for spending above it. They hardly need these powers because the huge disparity between central government grant and local tax revenue creates a 'gearing' mechanism that makes even small increases in spending disproportionately costly to rate-payers. Until the mid-1980s, they also collected a local business rate, but the Conservative government appropriated that to the centre. In deference to the business lobby, the current government refuses to return it to local councils.

Local affairs in devolved areas

In Scotland, the Scottish Parliament and Executive have introduced a 'lighter touch' regime, encour-aging local authorities to reform through guidance rather than legislation. Councils were encouraged to review their political structures, but change was not forced upon them. Local authorities have adopted best value regimes, but voluntarily. The Scottish Parliament has an active committee for local govern-ment. Westminster legislation applies to Wales, but the National Assembly of Wales makes its own secondary legislation under Westminster enactments and issues its own guidance. The Welsh improve-ment programme, for example, relies more on self-improvement than external intervention. In Northern Ireland, local authorities have fewer responsibilities and powers; quangos run social housing, education and social services.

European standards of independence

In conclusion, the central controls over policy and finance, and absence of adequate tax-raising powers, contravene the standards of the European Charter for Local Self-Government that the government itself has accepted:

Compliance with the European Charter:
Are British councils as independent as European local authorities?

Article 2:   The principle of local self-government shall be recognised in domestic law and, where practicable, in the constitution – **No**

Article 3:
- Local authorities shall within the law regulate and manage a substantial share of public affairs under their own responsibility and in the interests of the local population – **No**
- These authorities shall be elected though they may possess executive agencies – **Yes and No (local quangos are unelected)**

Article 4:
- The basic powers and responsibilities of local authorities shall be prescribed by the constitution or statute law – **Only in statute law**
- Local authorities shall have general competence – **Partial yes**
- Powers given to local authorities shall normally be full and exclusive and not undermined or limited by a national or regional authority – **No**

Article 5:   Changes in local authority boundaries shall not be made without prior consultation of the local communities involved, possibly by means of a referendum – **By constitutional convention, commissions should consult the public, but government have broken with or by-passed this convention. No referendums.**

Article 6:   Local authorities shall be able to determine their own internal administrative structures so they can adapt them to local needs – **No**

Article 8:   Administrative supervision of local authorities shall be proportionate and should normally aim only at ensuring compliance with the law or constitutional principle – **No**

Article 9:
- Local authorities shall be entitled, within national economic policy, to adequate financial resources which they may freely dispose of within the framework of their powers – **No**
- These resources shall be sufficient to meet their responsibilities and diverse and buoyant enough to keep pace with the cost of carrying out their tasks – **No**
- Local authorities shall have the power to determine the rate of local taxes and charges – **No; their financial autonomy is strictly constrained**
- As far as possible, grants to local authorities shall not be earmarked to finance specific projects – **Not fully**

Source: European Charter of Local Self-Government, Council of Europe, Strasbourg. Only major provisions of the charter are listed here.

13.5. How far are local authorities authorised by free and fair elections?

The Labour party's hostility to reform of local elections – and especially that of John Prescott, the grand panjandrum set in place over regional and local affairs – has been a major obstacle to representative and responsive local government in Britain since 1997. While elections to local authorities in Great Britain are free and fair, the use of plurality-rule, or 'first-past-the-post' (FPTP) elections too often produce nearly unchallengeable single-party oligarchies and less pluralistic local politics than would be possible under proportional electoral systems. In Northern Ireland elections under STV are more representative.

The coalition governments in both Scotland and Wales have commissioned reports on electoral reform in local government, both of which have recommended a switch to STV for local elections. But powerful forces, especially in Labour's local council strongholds, want to keep plurality-rule since it protects their local power from effective challenge. This hostility to PR is far less justifiable than at the level of Westminster, since the need at local level is for wide and pluralist representation rather than 'strong' single-party rule. The distorting effect of FPTP is made worse at local elections because people vote in wards, which exaggerates the deviation from proportionality inherent in FPTP voting. Voting in wards benefits parties with more concentrated vote bases (especially Labour and the Conservatives) and discriminates against those with more even support.

One-party domination has long been a prominent feature of British local government. It tends to make voters for the dominant party complacent and to discourage voters for other parties. In 1997-98, one in five councils were controlled by a party that held 80 per cent or more of the seats, typically with a proportion of the vote of little more than 50 per cent. In 1998, 33 councils either had no opposition at all or a token opposition of between one and three council members. Thus, political parties with artificial majorities can control local councils from one term to another with no prospect of a viable opposition able to replace them in power.

However, more sophisticated voting patterns, including a measure of tactical voting, have kicked in and by the end of the decade about a third of all councils were 'pluralist' – that is, no single party had an overall majority.[2] Such councils were increasingly run by coalitions – usually Labour-Lib Dem – and were by definition more representative and pluralist in their make-up. If local elections were conducted under proportional representation, it is estimated that more than a half and perhaps two-thirds of councils would be pluralist (Leach and Game, 2000). As things stand, local elections continued to produce distorted results in 2002:

- the three main parties won clear majorities in councils on a minority of the popular vote, (e.g., in Camden, Labour won 71 per cent of the seats on 35 per cent of the vote);
- they won nearly exclusive control of councils on majority votes far lower than their reward in seats (e.g., Labour won 59 out of 60 seats in Newham on two-thirds of the vote; the Lib-Dems polled half the vote in Sutton and took 80 per cent of the seats on the council); and
- won control of councils even though they won fewer votes than their opponents (e.g., Labour took control in Hammersmith and Fulham with 60 per cent of the seats after polling lower than the Conservatives) (see further Electoral Reform Society briefing, June 2002).

Turnout

Another weakness in local representativeness is the chronic low turnout at local elections in the UK. In a few local authority wards, turnout has been as low as 10 per cent; and the typical overall turnout of 35 per cent since 1995 in the UK is about half the two-thirds mean in the rest of the EU, even though falling turnout is a common phenomenon there as well. Such figures put the electoral authority of local councils in Great Britain in doubt, and have also alarmed the government that fears the consequences of the apparent disenchantment with electoral politics.

The government has encouraged local authorities to pilot ways of improving turnout (postal ballots on demand, electronic voting, longer hours for voting, mobile polling stations, weekend voting, etc). One pilot scheme, allowing for a longer voting period, seems to have made a modest impact on turnout. But the government has refused to consider testing whether proportional representation might raise turnout (even though PR elections in Europe produce higher turnout); and while it is reasonable to assume that the unequal balance of power between central and local government inhibits voting in local elections, the government is unwilling to create local authorities stronger and more able to respond to local wishes.

Appointing the local quango magistracy

The local 'authorities' of the quango state have no electoral authority whatever. There are partial electorates for a few users – on school governing bodies and some social landlord boards – but most quango boards are made up of appointed or self-appointing members, professionals and other providers. The sheer size of the 'new magistracy' of more than 60,000 appointed and self-appointing quango board members is staggering. Their appointment does not fall under the scrutiny of the Commissioner for Public Appointments (except for NHS trusts and health authorities), nor are they subject to ministerial or departmental oversight. Most local quangos are wholly or largely self-appointing bodies and most appointments are by way of 'word-of-mouth' – i.e., they are made via board chairpersons and members and senior managers, 'with a consequent lack of transparency about the criteria for selection' (Skelcher and Davis, 1996). Business men were over-represented and women were under-represented. Nearly a third of board members did not even live in the areas their bodies served.

13.6 How far are local authorities subject to criteria of openness, accountability and responsiveness in their operations?

The UK has the largest local authorities in western Europe, most of which lack clear historic or geographic identity and do not command strong popular loyalty. Local councils and their members are thus more remote from their publics than their counterparts in Europe, as well as being weaker. People see their councils as being remote and find the distances they may have to travel in county areas too great for ease of access. Parish and community councils are too weak and separate from local government to make up the gap in representation. Table 4 shows the size of the gap between councillors and their electorates in the UK by comparison with mainland Europe. British councillors have between two and 20 times more inhabitants on their patches than local representatives in nine other European states. This representation gap is a serious weakness.

4: How remote are UK councils?

	People per elected councillor	Average population per council
France	116	1,580
Germany	250	4,925
Italy	397	7,130
Norway	515	9,000
Spain	597	4,930
Sweden	667	30,040
Belgium	783	16,960
Denmark	1,084	18,760
Portugal	1,125	32,300
UK	2,605	118,400

Original source: Council of Europe, Local and Regional Authorities in Europe, No. 56, 1996; plus Game and Wilson 1998.

Note: to enable realistic comparison with other countries' local and commune councillors, these figures exclude members of parish, town and community councils. They are not found in every area and have very limited powers and responsibilities.

First-past-the-post elections also severely weaken the quality of accountabilility on many councils. Some councils with an overwhelming party majority can be effective and responsive. But there are great dangers in the insulation from genuine electoral competition and effective scrutiny that electoral security can engender. Long-term party political oligarchies are very often arrogant in office and pursue partisan and unpopular policies. Even in 'pluralist' councils – i.e., in which no single party holds a majority – the political position of these parties is still disproportionately protected. A 1995 survey of pluralist authorities reported that over 40 per cent of party leaders and chief executives said policy and decision making had improved, twice as many as those who reported worse conditions; and other academic evidence since 1981 has shown most pluralist councils operate as effectively as their majority-controlled counterparts, with the added benefits of a more representative and pluralist make-up; a greater openness of decision-making; and more genuine debate about decisions. At worst, they can be fragmented, slow, inconsistent, fractious and difficult to manage. But such problems are not unknown among majority-controlled authorities.

Central government's dominion over nearly every aspect of local authority finance and activity, and the existence of the parallel local quango state, also confuses the issue of local accountability. Who is properly to be held to account when the centre so closely controls policies and resources? Who will vote or seek to influence local government when the real masters of local affairs sit in Westminster and Whitehall, in a regional government office, or in a national quango HQ? Local elections that are too often proxies for the 'real thing' further diminish the accountability of local government along with its legitimacy. Such considerations also diminish the pool of ability and commitment from which potential councillors are drawn – unless their eyes are fixed further up the greasy pole of politics.

The government's new models for local authorities are designed to improve visibility and transparency. However, executive decision-making may be made obscure through delegated powers to individual councillors in the executive ('executive members'), or officers, or contracted-out services. There are also different rules of public access to information for some executive actions (see below).

Public access to information

Formally speaking, local authorities are the most open and transparent of all British governmental institutions. Since 1985, access to information legislation has provided that the public and media have the right to attend council and committee meetings; public notice must be given for meetings; their agendas and reports must be available in advance; and minutes of meetings must be published and kept available for public inspection. Councils can only exclude the public from meetings when specified confidential affairs are discussed. But few people or even journalists know enough to make use of these rules and councils can manipulate the exemptions, for example by placing commercially confidential information in a report and thus avoiding the duty to disclose.

The new executive-led councils in England and Wales will operate under different rules. Originally the government drafted legislation to allow them to meet and take decisions in secret, with the consequence that the public would lose their right to know in advance what decisions may be taken and would be informed only after decisions were taken. However, the bill provoked outrage in Parliament, and was amended to require such authorities in England to publish and publicise 'forward plans' with details of key executive decisions on the way. Further, mayors and council leaders must now hold executive meetings in public if they know, or 'reasonably believe', that a meeting will take or discuss a key decision. In Wales, cabinet, council and committee meetings are all subject to the same access to information rules, thanks to a Lib-Lab deal in the National Assembly.

However, there are still weaknesses in both England and Wales. Under the new constitutions, areas of decision-making can be delegated to the mayor, leader or an individual member of the executive, or to council officials. Thus individual politicians can take decisions outside formal meetings. In England, executive-led councils must publish in advance the paperwork for key decisions to be taken by elected mayors or politicians, but council managers and delegated officials are not required to publish advance information for decisions they may take. In Wales, the regulations fail to make any provision for access to information before individuals take decisions, whether they are elected members or council officers. So overall openness on most councils will depend on who takes the decisions and who is present when they are taken.

Out-sourcing services

The government's insistence on 'outsourcing', or privatising, basic services raises issues of accountability and openness. Control of services and facilities already increasingly rests on legal contracts with private or voluntary-sector contractors of all shapes and sizes. The contractors are not accountable to local communities or service-users who must rely on local authorities, official inspectors and ultimately lawyers to enforce the standards set out. The costs in human misery can be very high when the private firms fail to give a good service, for example, to people on housing benefits (as several private companies have). Moreover, private contractors can deny local authorities, communities and users the information they may require to exert control, on the grounds of 'commercial confidentiality'. Local councils or executives may themselves shelter behind commercial confidentiality to avoid political embarrassment. And while council officials are required to give evidence to the new council scrutiny committees, managers and staff of private firms providing services to a council can refuse to appear.

Local quangos

Local quangos are only fitfully accountable and open. At the last count, only 30 per cent of these bodies, for example, were subject to the writ of a public service ombudsman. (The figure for public access to official information is lower still, but is likely to rise considerably under the new Freedom of Information Act.) The general public have access to the meetings, papers, agendas and minutes of less than half these local quangos; and if you remove health bodies from the roster, access is virtually non-existent. The scarcity of measures for public accountability, openness and access compare very badly with the position in local government and yet they should be stronger, given the absence of electoral accountability.

Some quangos consult the public seriously and have experimented with new ways of involving local communities. But most confine their contacts with the public simply to informing rather than involving people. Board members tend to take the view that they are implementing national policies locally, rather than varying such policies to suit local needs and aspirations (Weir and Beetham 1999). They are also more managerially oriented and have far less contact with members of the public than councillors do:

Hours in the week spent on:	Contacts with the public	Meetings withmanagers
Local quango chairs	4	11
Leading councillors	17	8
Ordinary quango members	3	4
Ordinary councillors	15	4

Sources: adapted from Skelcher and Davis 1996; Young and Rao 1994

This gulf in public contact between council and quango members with the public is easily explained. Local councils are more visible and accessible than quangos. Most quango board members are unknown and relatively unknowable. Their addresses are rarely available to the general public and they do not hold surgeries as many local councillors do. Quango board members tend to take the view that they need not be accountable locally, as they are not initiating policies of their own, but simply carrying out central government's policies. But policies are re-made and modified at every level of management; and local quangos have to be responsive and accountable locally, as well as upwards, if they are to deliver local services effectively (Flinders and McConnel 1998).

13.7 How far does government at the most local level co-operate with relevant partners, associations and communities in forming and carrying out policies and delivering services; and how far are local publics enabled to participate?

Most people deal most of the time with local government and local agencies, especially NHS trusts and authorities, rather than with the central state. It is at local level that most decisions that affect individuals and their communities are taken and basic services delivered. So effective arrangements for co-operation between local authorities and quangos, local organisations and communities, and their participation in framing policies and delivering services, are important to local democracy. The government now makes public consultation one of the conditions for local partnerships, but it is probably fair to say that overall local councils have a superior track record on consultation than central government (see Section 12 further). However, standards vary greatly in local government; and some local authorities are unskilled in and unused to effective exercises in consultation and participation. Council members often fear that consultation exercises may usurp their own position as representatives of the people. Professional, managerial and other producer power bases can block consultation or acting on its results. As the case of Birmingham suggests, councils often lack the resources to pursue effective consultation (see Section 12 further).

Partnership

The government has sponsored a bewildering known total of over 2,375 multi-agency partnerships, action zones, action teams, and cross-sectoral committees and bodies at local level in England. – for example, on education, regeneration, neighbourhood renewal, community safety, older people, crime, town centre management, health, cultural activities, etc. Another 400 local strategic partnerships are being set up to play a key role in local governance, bringing together local councils, local agencies, police and health authorities, and voluntary and community bodies, to pursue central government's priorities. Some of central government's local initiatives involve locally elected boards of residents. But partnerships are usually appointed and self-appointing; and they are baited with additional, usually temporary funds that local authorities seeking to participate must bid for. These bodies may be companies limited by guarantee, co-operatives, or exist solely on the basis of a memorandum of understanding.

In partnerships directly promoted by government departments, it is ministers and government officials rather than local authorities who are the crucial decision-makers for a given area or function; they set the agenda, manage the criteria, decide the performance indicators, determine funding and monitor the projects. Accountability, openness and participation become divided responsibilities, especially as the government's actors stay behind the scenes. But most partnership schemes are essentially unaccountable, even to the local authorities which may have initiated or organised them, will usually be involved in them, and may even service them. Even local authority links are not sufficient to underpin their accountability, openness or public access, nor even their democratic legitimacy. Board members are not even technically accountable to their nominating bodies (though they may very well act directly in those bodies' interests).

Central government demands that partnerships undertake consultation exercises, but it is very difficult for local people to become involved within the complex institutional frameworks and time-frames that government imposes. In most cases members of the public have no say over who is appointed to a partnership, or what they do once they are appointed. Overall, the narrow 'plurality' of organisations and groups represented on partnership boards are not sufficient to overcome the absence of direct representation of the public, accountability and openness.

Joined-up local governance

Part of local government's new remit is to co-ordinate the complex institutional web of local public activity – the police, social landlords, further education colleges, hospital and social care, other quangos, partnerships, zones, etc. Local authorities also share their new 'leadership' mission with regional government officials, regional development agencies and the major strategic quangos, like the Housing Corporation and Learning and Skills Council. The Housing Corporation, and its regional offices, for example, make policy in social housing, direct some 2,000 local social landlords and control their resources. Overall, local authorities do not have sufficient powers or resources to take on the gargantuan task of co-ordination, let alone run their partnerships or consult their own publics effectively. The government has to simplify the whole local state.

1   We describe AMS at Table 5.1 above (pages 97-8). Under STV, people choose several candidates usually in large constituencies (though NI uses the Westminster constituencies). Voters are not bound by party priorities on their lists. The results are generally proportional and pluralistic. The Supplementary Vote is a simplified version of the Alternative Vote, also described in Section 5 (page XX). On expert advice, officials recommended using SV rather than FPTP for the mayoralty elections because a crowded FPTP election would probably have produced a winner on far less than a simple majority of the vote. Thus the legitimacy of a new mayor would have been compromised from the start. A cabinet committee under Lord Irvine then insisted on FPTP, but Blair personally intervened to reinstate the Supplementary Vote.

2   We prefer the word 'pluralist' to the more usual term 'hung', to describe an elected body in which no single party has an overall majority of seats. The term 'hung', taken from the idea of a hung jury, conveys the erroneous impression of a body that is so divided that it is unable to reach a decision. Its near universal use is a sign of the unconscious prejudice in favour of single-party rule that pervades political debate in this country.

Section four: democracy beyond the state

Fourteen: the international dimensions of democracy

Britain's place in the world

Does Britain promote democracy and human rights abroad? Is the UK free from

external subordination?

Our actions are guided by a more subtle blend of mutual self-interest and moral purpose . . . in the end, values and interests merge
Tony Blair, 1999

Introduction

If the core idea of democracy is that of self-government, of control by the people of the decisions that affect their collective lives, then a democratic audit cannot ignore the ways in which those decisions may be determined by institutions or forces outside the state. A country might have the most perfect democracy internally, but enjoy little real self-government if most of the decisions that mattered for the life of its citizens were taken beyond its borders. Such a situation has been called the 'hollowing out' of democracy. At the same time the quality of a country's democratic life is also to be gauged by how it treats other countries and their citizens. Does it observe the international rule of law? How far do its policies support democracy and human rights abroad?

In this section we consider first how far, if at all, UK policy is determined from outside in ways that are beyond its control; then the nature of the UK's power and influence in international bodies; its respect for international treaties and international law; its treatment of asylum seekers; and the consistency of its support for human rights and democracy abroad.

14.1 How free is the UK government from subordination to external economic, cultural or political agencies?

The UK wields more widespread political and economic power and influence around the world than its size of population alone would justify. Much of its influence is exerted through its memberships of international organisations, especially the European Union and NATO, and its historic place on the UN Security Council. Its sovereignty is qualified by the decisions taken in multi-lateral bodies, but this position does not make the UK 'subordinate' since the UK joined these bodies as an independent and sovereign state on at least an equal footing with other member states and has a voice (and often a vote) on all decisions that they take.

However, the paramount influence of the United States in the political, economic, military and cultural spheres constrains the freedom of action of the UK, and especially so in the light of Britain's subordinate role in the so-called 'special relationship' and continuing membership of NATO which is dominated by the USA. Further, the increasing use of majority voting in the European Council of Ministers and the move towards supra-national law in the European Union will over time emphasise the loss of sovereignty that EU membership entails (see below; and Section 7.6). The European Union has a close and dominant effect on British life that greatly concerns most British citizens.

Britain's role in the world economy

Within the global economy the United Kingdom is arguably vulnerable to subordination through the threat of capital flight from large multinational companies and international finance houses. The UK runs a liberal foreign exchange market and capital transfers are not regulated. Government indecision or policy proposals that alarm the financial sector can lead to serious currency and share crises, like for example, 'Black Wednesday' in September 1992 when the world markets forced the government's withdrawal from the European monetary system despite huge expenditures seeking to uphold the valuation of sterling. However, all states are weak in this respect, and the UK far less than most. Britain is one of the four of trillion-dollar economies of western Europe; its vulnerability to such systemic shocks is also cushioned by a reducing national debt and adequate exchange reserves. The probably systemic deficit in the balance of trade is offset by a surplus in financial transfers.

The reach of British multinational companies is larger than those of any other EU state. According to the Office of National Statistics, profits from these companies grew from £71.6 billion in 1990 to £116.1 billion in 1999 (a 6 per cent annual average growth rate, at current prices). UK companies were the most profitable in the world until a fall in corporate profitability in 1999 reduced them to fifth place overall (Walton, 2000). This implies a net resource flow to the UK from other countries.

The trade agreement on intellectual property rights during the 1990s Uruguay Round negotiations within the General Agreement on Tariffs and Trade (GATT; see below) has increased the earning potential of older and larger companies, like many British multinationals. Their assets now include intangibles such as patents, copyrights, franchises, leases and other transferable contracts, goodwill as well as tangible goods such as land and sub-soil assets. The balance on such 'non-produced and non-financial assets' rose from £14 million in 1996 (the first year in which they were counted separately from trade in services) to £215 million in 2000 (ONS, Balance of Payments, series FNTS); and the balance on trade in royalties and license fees, recorded as services, rose to £816 million. The combined total for earnings of this type was £3,087 million in 2000. Far from holding a subordinate position in the world market, the UK benefits disproportionately from the human stock of ideas, inventions, licenses and copyrighted materials. It may seem that this is a just reward for past enterprise. But as the conflict between the South African government and western pharmaceutical companies over Aids drugs suggests, the intellectual property regime protects established privilege and inequalities in power and resources and denies nations of the south access to essential goods at prices their peoples can afford.

Europe
The UK formally entered the (then) EEC in January 1973 and the referendum in June 1975 endorsed membership by a two-thirds majority. However, the public has never been enthusiastic about being part of the European community. Membership has become increasingly contentious since the British government's acceptance of 'qualified majority voting' (QMV). Tory (and other) opponents argue that the EU's increasing decision-making powers and the spread of EU law represents a loss of British sovereignty and, by implication, subordination to the whim of 'Brussels'. Pro-Europeans argue that sovereignty is shared rather than diminished; and that Britain's EU place secures security, stability and economic growth.

Britain's place in Europe is quite different in character from its other international links (see also Section 7.6). In most intergovernmental organisations, decisions are made by consensus and states retain a right either of veto or non-participation. Membership or ratification can be revoked or rescinded. But in the EU, majority voting, or more accurately, the weighted majority voting in effect on an increasing range of issues, rules out the power of veto. Dissenting states must accept a collective decision. The extension of majority voting to a particular issue will be irreversible, or at least extremely difficult to review. Instead of a consensual pooling of sovereignty, member states will lose some powers and control over significant aspects of public policy. The impact of majority voting has recently been tempered by making decisions taken by a majority subject to 'co-decision', meaning that decisions cannot become law unless approved by the European Parliament.

There is a countervailing initiative on 'subsidiarity' – a recent rule that holds that in all areas outside its exclusive competence, the EU can take action only if the objectives of a policy proposal cannot be achieved by member states themselves. But this initiative is not enough to address the underlying 'democratic deficit' in the EU. The European Parliament has inadequate powers of scrutiny over the secretive duopoly of the Council of Ministers and European Commission (recently criticised by the UK Public Accounts Committee as having imprecise and dangerously corruption-prone accounting and management systems; HC 690, 1999). The European Parliament has only a blunt instrument of control at hand – the dismissal of the entire European Commission. National parliaments, on the other hand, do not have sufficient time or information to scrutinise legislation agreed in Brussels (see Section 7.6).

United States

The power of the United States both within the 'special relationship' and the NATO alliance raises concerns. Britain has a subordinate role in its relations with the USA; and even Prime Ministers, like Mrs Thatcher and Tony Blair, who have established a 'strong' domestic image, have played a secondary role in US military actions such as the bombings of Libya, Iraq and Sudan, and, most recently, the war in Afghanistan. Blair, for example, against FCO advice, backed the US strike on the al-Shifa pharmaceutical factory in Sudan in 1998 in revenge for terrorist bombings of the US embassies in Nairobi and Dar es Salaam. The factory was alleged to be part owned by Osama bin Laden and to be producing nerve gas. But US intelligence was wrong and was not, as US ambassador to Sudan at the time has acknowledged, enough to justify an act of war (*Guardian*, 2 October 2001). US President Bush seems intent, as we write, upon war against Iraq to achieve 'regime change'. He looks to the UK as his principal ally.

The US government is currently intent on establishing its nuclear shield, the National Missile Defense (NMD) system, which will rely not only on British political support, but also practically on radar installations sited in the UK at Menwith Hill and Fylingdales. The NMD proposal has raised major concerns throughout Europe, as it could potentially create dangerous tensions between the USA and China and Russia, de-stabilise international relations generally, undermine arms limitation agreements and encourage nuclear proliferation. British compliance could undermine international treaty commitments and jeopardise relations with Europe, China and Russia. But can the British government withhold its co-operation? Formally the government states that it has not received a US request to use the bases for NMD, but answers to parliamentary questions indicate that ministers have sanctioned the installation of ground-based systems for the USA at RAF Menwith Hill (*Independent on Sunday*, 21 November 1999). The Campaign for Nuclear Disarmament had demanded more transparency, warning that 'By the time a formal request is made, it will probably be too late to reject it'. Meanwhile, the government argues that the UK plays a pivotal 'honest broker' role between the US and EU.

Within NATO, the USA dominates political and military strategy not only because it is a super-power but because it provides most of NATO's fire power. NATO's dilemmas over Kosovo illustrated the tensions between American dominance and European influence. The authors of an Italian democratic audit remark:

> During operations in Kosovo the US provided 80 per cent of air power and this offers a primary explanation for American leverage within NATO. At European level there is widespread feeling that no real sharing of responsibilities between Europe and the US is possible as long as the disparity in the means toward action continues to grow (Beetham et al, 2001).

Joint UK-US electronic surveillance and espionage is part of the special relationship and has contributed in part to the closed world of UK security and intelligence arrangements (see Sections 3.2). But concern goes further than the effect on civil liberties in the UK. There are suspicions throughout Europe that the UK/US electronic eavesdropping capabilities of GCHQ and other intelligence-gathering activities are being used to 'spy' on EU states, and even to carry out economic espionage on behalf of US companies – as is alleged to have occurred in the US aircraft deal with Saudi Arabia in 2000 that was contested by the European Airbus consortium (*Guardian*, 25 April 2001). The European

Parliament set up a temporary committee, opposed by the UK, to investigate the accountability of intelligence systems, and particularly Echelon, a network of listening posts in America, Britain, Canada, Australia and New Zealand which intercept telephone, fax and email messages. Echelon may also be used to invade the privacy of individual citizens.

14.2 How far are the British government's relations with international organisations based on principles of partnership and transparency?

The UK is an active member of all the major international organisations, including the UN. It also occupies a distinctive position in the Commonwealth of Nations as the former imperial power. Of its 54 members, 14 besides the UK still have the Queen as head of state, with the formal right of appointing the governor. In practice, the UK enjoys a persuasive power at most in the councils of the Commonwealth, as demonstrated most recently when it had to defer to African members over the imposition of sanctions on President Mugabe. Formally its position is that of one among equals, with all members having an equal voice.

However, in other international organisations, the UK has a guaranteed position which is at odds with the principles of equal partnership. This is particularly evident in four of the most significant global forums: the UN Security Council, the World Bank, the International Monetary Fund and the World Trade Organisation (WTO). One way of calculating this favoured position is to measure the UK's actual voting power in these organisations against that which it would possess on the basis of its population. This would be the most democratic criterion, though a substantial discrepancy would still be evident if a different principle such as one state: one vote were applied. Table 1 shows its voting power in relation to population for each of the four organisations mentioned.

1. The UK's place in the big four global bodies

Organisation

The United Nations (189 members) and the UN Security Council

Governing arrangements

15 members of the governing Security Council each have one vote. Ten are elected by the UN General Assembly for two-year terms; five (including the UK) are permanent members.

UK representative

Ambassadors and British Permanent Representatives, Sir Jeremy Greenstock, Political Director, FCO (in New York); and S W J Fuller (in Geneva)

Power of UK influence

The UK's veto power is worth 1,228.5bn people.

Organisation

World Trade Organisation (140 members)

Governing arrangements

Decisions are by consensus. Agreements are ratified in parliaments. The Dispute Settlement Body rules by adopting the findings of a panel of experts or an appeal report.

UK representative

The UK Trade and Industry Secretary 'speaks for' the UK in the formation of EU policy, which the EU Commissioner represents in the WTO

Power of UK influence

Delegates in Seattle: United Kingdom, 42 delegates (ratio of 1: 14m people); India, 41 (ratio of 1: 24.4m people)

Organisation

World Bank Group (182 members)

Governing arrangements

Below a full formal Board of Governors, the Board of 24 Executive Directors holds *de facto* power; five members (including the UK) are automatically members, 19 are elected by members

UK representative

Governor at the IBRD* and IFC*, Clare Short (Minister of Overseas Development); Alternate, Gordon Brown. Executive Director, Tom Scholar (Treasury official)

Power of UK influence

4.43% of total votes (USA, 14.9%). UK share worth 256m people in global population

Organisation

International Monetary Fund (183 members)

Governing arrangements

Below a formal Board of Governors, the Board of 24 Executive Directors holds *de facto* power; eight are single country representatives, 16 elected. Significant decisions require a 85% majority, giving the USA with 17% of the vote) a power of veto.

UK representative

Governor, Gordon Brown; Alternate, Sir Eddie George (Governor of Bank of England). Executive Director, Stephen Pickford (Treasury official)

Power of UK influence

5.02% of total votes (USA, 17.35%). UK share worth 122.3m people

* The IBRD is the International Bank for Reconstruction and Development; the IFC is the International Finance Corporation

The Security Council is dominant within the UN, and cannot be mandated by the General Assembly or its committees. Of the Council's 15 members, ten are elected for two-year terms by the General Assembly, while the other five, including the UK, are permanent members. Any major decision requires nine votes, with all the five permanent members agreeing. This rule of 'great power unanimity' gives each of the five a power of veto, and thus the ability to determine or frustrate collective action at the international level, according to their own national interests and alliances. The UK owes its privileged position to its past as a former great power rather than to its current standing or population. In the WTO, binding decisions are taken by consensus, but the figures for delegates at the Seattle conference in Table 1 indicate the dominance of northern countries, including the UK. The WTO claims that its consensual arrangements make it a 'democratic' facilitating forum; it is up to the members what they bring to the negotiating table and what they mutually agree. Yet the outcomes demonstrate the limited leverage which developing countries have to secure concessions from the richer trade blocs. They are required to open up their own markets to foreign companies while at the same time facing continued protectionism and subsidies in the EU, US and elsewhere, which undermine their own agriculture and industry. Oxfam has calculated that high tariffs and subsidies cost poor countries £70 billion a year – twice as much as they receive in foreign aid (Oxfam, 2002a).

Nations participate in the World Bank as shareholders. Their relative power is determined *de facto* by the size of the shares they hold. Formally each country appoints a governor, usually a finance minister; and governors meet annually. In practice, an executive board takes the decisions. The five largest share-holders – France, Germany, Japan, the UK and USA – each appoints an executive director, while the rest of the world shares 19 between them. Each director has votes according to the size of the share-holding represented. Thus the US has nearly 15 per cent of the vote and the UK 5 per cent, while the group of 21 African states has 6 per cent and shares one executive director. Similar arrangements pertain in the International Monetary Fund, where directorships and their voting power are determined by the size of the quota each country or group of countries contributes.

In both the World Bank and the IMF, the Blair government has argued strongly for debt reduction and poverty alleviation, and it has taken unilateral initiatives of its own to cancel debt owed by the most impoverished countries to the UK government. Yet these international institutions are after all banks, driven by orthodox banking criteria, which determine the conditions imposed on debtor countries, while at the same time producing interest and profits for the rich countries that are their major shareholders and contributors.

Most decision-making in these international institutions is opaque, and only becomes transparent when exposed to investigation by non-governmental organisations. Britain's role in them is a matter for ministers using their royal prerogative powers, which are typically then delegated to the diplomats and civil servants who act as the country's representatives. Parliamentary oversight of their activities is virtually non-existent. The most that Parliament can expect is a statement in the chamber. As Baroness Williams complained in the House of Lords:

> We do not discuss the World Trade Organisation; we do not have the pleasure of looking at the agenda for the G8; and we do not have an opportunity to talk at great length about the global environment convention. However, we all recognise that those treaties are now shaping our world and producing decisions that affect our citizens, while we are virtually voiceless in them (HL Deb, 18 July 2001).

Britain's own international agencies

The UK also operates its own agencies with an international reach. These bodies are a legacy of the country's imperial past, but remain active today, often in a semi-privatised form that removes them from public accountability, even though they continue to enjoy public funding. Of these, the Crown Agents, the Commonwealth Development Corporation (CDC) and the Export Credit Guarantee Department (ECGD) are the most significant. The Crown Agents work in 130 countries, managing logistics and supply for multilateral and bilateral donors on projects worth an estimated annual value of £4 billion. The CDC and ECGD both disburse development finance and export credits larger than the sums managed by the Department for International Development – formally, the UK's lead department for development issues, and their most public face (see 14.5 below).[1]

Of these organisations, the ECGD has been repeatedly controversial. Its role is to underwrite with publicly financed export credits those business projects by UK firms overseas which are subject to 'country risk'. Since 1997 it has supported arms sales with potential use against civilians to a number of countries; the environmentally and socially problematic Ilisu dam in Turkey; the sale of an expensive and unsuitable air traffic control system to Tanzania; and exports by a number of companies which have involved substantial bribery. Public money lent for these projects is not subject to any systematic social or environmental impact assessment, or to effective parliamentary scrutiny; and it can readily run counter to publicly declared international development policy.

14.3 How far does the government support UN human rights treaties and respect international law?

The Labour government's incorporation into domestic legislation of the European Convention on Human Rights (see Section 2) is evidence of its commitment to take human rights treaties seriously. It played a lead role in international negotiations to agree a statute for the International Criminal Court, with the power to try cases of genocide, war crimes and crimes against humanity. It supported the international criminal tribunals for Rwanda and the former Yugoslavia and an independent special court for Sierra Leone. The detention for extradition of the former Chilean dictator, Pinochet, which was upheld by the House of Lords, proved a landmark case in confirming the right of any state party to the UN Convention on Torture to bring former heads of state accused of torture to trial on their own territory.

The UK has signed and ratified:

- the major international human rights treaties, including the UN covenants on civil and political, and economic, social and cultural rights, and on the elimination of all forms of racial discrimination;
- the eight key international treaties identified in the Millennium Declaration as core documents that all nations should ratify. These are:
    - the UN Convention on the Elimination of All Forms of Discrimination against Women
    - the UN Convention on the Rights of the Child
    - Rome Statute of the International Criminal Court
    - Anti-Personnel Mine Convention
    - Protocol II of the Convention on Certain Conventional Weapons
    - Kyoto Protocol to the UN Framework Convention on Climate Change
    - Convention on Biological Diversity
    - Convention to Combat Desertification; and
- the major conventions of the International Labour Organisation (as identified by Social Watch, the international social development monitor), including conventions on minimum wages, equal pay, forced labour, collective bargaining and child labour.

The Blair government carried out a full review of its policy on international human rights, covering non-ratifications, derogations and reservations, between 1997-99. Following the review, the government signed two UN protocols on the Rights of the Child, and passed legislation enabling the UK to sign European and UN protocols abolishing the death penalty. In 1998, the government ratified the Council of Europe Framework Convention for the Protection of National Minorities.

How effectively are all these conventions implemented in practice? Sections 3 and 4 of the Audit have dealt in detail with the UK's record in respect of the main human rights treaties. Of the others, the government's ability to meet the targets set by environmental treaties arouses considerable concern. For example, the UK is committed to reduce greenhouse gas emissions by 12.5 per cent below 1990 levels by 2008-2012, and carbon dioxide emissions by 20 per cent below 1990 levels by 2010. A review of these commitments undertaken in 2000 by the House of Commons environment select committee expressed serious doubts about whether they could be met (HC194 and 441, 2000).

Respect for international law

The evidence given above demonstrates that the UK under Blair has shown a clear commitment to the international rule of law. Yet its position as chief ally to the US has also led it into military actions abroad whose legality has been dubious. This pattern was already set before 11 September by a number of actions: the repeated bombing of Iraq after December 1998 to enforce the 'no-fly' zones; the raids against alleged terrorists in Sudan and Afghanistan in August 1998; the intensive bombing campaigns over Kosovo and Serbia in 2000. The latter campaign in particular, to protect the Albanian population of Kosovo from further ethnic cleansing, led to the enunciation of a new doctrine: the international law against military intervention in other states should be qualified by the higher moral duty of powerful countries to act as unilateral enforcers of UN resolutions, in the absence of explicit Security Council authorisation. Blair justified the new doctrine in a speech in South Africa in the following terms:

> The international community has a responsibility to act. Sometimes, if collective action cannot be agreed or taken in time, [this will be] through countries with a sense of global responsibility taking on the burden. People say you can't be self-appointed guardians of what's right and wrong. True, but when the international community agrees certain objectives and then fails to implement them, those who can act must.

The new doctrine was further extended after 11 September to cover military intervention against terrorism, not just the prevention of genocide. Although the UN Security Council resolutions of 12 and 28 September 2001 condemned terrorism, and called on all states to act together to 'prevent and suppress, in their territories through all lawful means, the financing and preparation of any acts of terrorism', the Council did not explicitly authorise the invasion of Afghanistan, which was initially justified by the US in terms of its own 'self-defence'. Further, the war aims soon widened to embrace the removal of the Taliban regime as a whole, in the cause of democracy and human rights, especially of women. These are crucially important values, to be sure, but their promotion at the international level is fraught with difficulty, as Section 14.5 explores. This is especially true if the action involved is military, which inevitably involves the denial of rights to life, health and shelter of many innocent civilians.

In the case of Afghanistan, the war caused thousands of civilian deaths, some of which were caused by heavy indiscriminate bombing that was bound to produce civilian casualties, in part at least to save US and coalition lives. For example, an officer on board the US aircraft carrier Carl Vinson describing the use of cluster bombs dropped by B-52 bombers from the Diego Garcia air base, held by the USA under lease from the UK, said, 'A 2,000lb bomb, no matter where you drop it, is a significant emotional event for anyone within a square mile' (*Guardian*, 2 November 2000). Less directly, the interruption of aid and a return to war lordism brought about further deaths. Whether the balance sheet counts as a success for the new doctrine of unilateral military intervention is a matter of legitimate debate. But there is a clear danger that the doctrine has now been widened to include justifiable attack on any state which comes under President Bush's definition of the 'axis of evil'. Whether public opinion in Britain will support this re-writing of international law will be seriously put to the test if the UK commits forces to support a possible US invasion of Iraq.

Territorial disputes

The UK is involved in a variety of international quarrels over territory, most of them hang-overs from its imperial past, as follows:

- tension with Spain over Britain's continuing rule in Gibraltar;
- Mauritius claims the island of Diego Garcia in British Indian Ocean Territory and Seychelles claims the Chagos Archipelago;
- Argentina continues to claim sovereignty over the Falkland Islands (Islas Malvinas), South Georgia and the South Sandwich Islands (following the Argentinian invasion and war in 1982);
- the British Antarctic Territory is subject to dispute; and
- the Rockall continental shelf dispute has involved the UK in disputes with Denmark, Iceland and Ireland (though Ireland and the UK have signed a boundary agreement).

The UK's case in most of these quarrels is dubious. Diego Garcia houses a military base, leased to the USA under a 50-year lease agreed in 1966. The Americans use it as a base for aircraft (from which they flew sorties against Iraq during the 1990s and against the Taliban in Afghanistan) and nuclear submarines. British ownership is widely seen in Mauritius as colonial expropriation and the High Court in London found in 2000 that the then government acted unlawfully in evicting the original inhabitants of the Chagos archipelago (65 islands, of which Diego Garcia is but one) to clear the island for US occupation. The court ruled that the original inhabitants were now free to return and the government did not contest the ruling.

Britain justifies its sovereignty in the Falklands/Malvinas (and other islands) and Gibraltar on the grounds that the inhabitants do not want to be ruled by Argentina or Spain. But the islands also bring important mining and economic rights on the continental shelf and contribute to the weight of the British claim to the British Antarctic Territory; and Gibraltar also serves as a military base. For years the UK ignored appeals by the UN General Assembly for a negotiated solution between Britain and Argentina, who finally met in Madrid in 1990 and agreed a compromise settlement of conflicting claims to fishing rights. The seven-year rupture in diplomatic relations also came to an end and negotiations are underway on the proceeds of a prospective oil industry. The Blair government is also seeking a compromise agreement with Spain over Gibraltar.

14.4 How far does the government respect its international obligations in its treatment of refugees and asylum seekers, and how free from arbitrary discrimination is its immigration policy?

The asylum system in the UK has been in disarray for more than ten years. A complex and inefficient bureaucracy has struggled to cope with up to 80,000 individuals a year fleeing civil war, international conflict or regimes whose human rights abuses are well-documented. There have been four major attempts to reform asylum law and policy in that period. The latest attempt – the Nationality Immigration and Asylum Bill- is being debated in Parliament at the time of writing.

One of the main obstacles to a fair and workable asylum process has been the failure of successive governments to reconcile the conflicting political pressures they have faced. The UK is obliged by its international commitments to allow persecuted individuals to seek asylum in the UK and must protect their human rights. On the other hand, government policy has been dominated by the need to appease the popular pressure for restricting asylum laws that stems from the widespread fear, fed by sensational and largely inaccurate tabloid reporting, that large numbers of 'bogus asylum seekers' are 'swamping' the UK (see Press Myths, www.refugeecouncil.org.uk).

The UK's international obligations

The United Kingdom has signed up to several international and European human rights instruments that have a bearing on the rights of asylum-seekers. The most important is the Geneva Refugee Convention 1951 that defines who is a refugee and provides that a state cannot return a person to a country where they will be persecuted. The European Convention also stipulates that a refugee cannot be returned to a country where he or she faces a real risk of torture, inhuman or degrading treatment (Soering v UK, 1989, 11 EHRR 439; Cruz Varas v Sweden,1991, 14 EHRR 1). At a European level, the EU now has the power to pass community legislation in the fields of immigration and asylum. However, the UK (along with Ireland and Denmark) has negotiated an 'opt in opt out' protocol.

The UK asylum system

Current UK legislation incorporates some aspects of the Refugee Convention. The Asylum and Immigration Appeals Act 1993 provides that the Refugee Convention has primacy over the immigration rules which control the entry of non-nationals into the UK. An asylum seeker who is to be removed from the UK can appeal on the basis that their removal would breach the Refugee Convention. The Nationality Immigration and Asylum Bill provides a similar right of appeal. Under the Human Rights Act 1998, public authorities (including, for example, immigration officers) have a duty to act compatibly with European Convention rights. In the context of asylum, this means that the fundamental rights of asylum seekers and refugees must not be breached (but see below). The Immigration and Asylum Act 1999 gives a right of appeal to an asylum seeker or refugee whose Convention rights have been breached (and the new Bill retains that right of appeal).

Thus, someone who wishes to claim asylum in the UK may do so when they arrive at the port, or in-country. If their claim is refused they can usually appeal to an adjudicator. There may be a further right of appeal to the Immigration Appeal Tribunal, and in some cases, to the Court of Appeal or the Court of Session in Scotland. Judicial review may be available. Under the current law, an individual cannot be removed from the UK until all available appeals have been decided, subject to some exceptions. Legal funding for advice and representation is available in most asylum cases. The Nationality Immigration and Asylum Bill will maintain the general structure for immigration appeals, but introduces substantial new restrictions (see below).

On the face of it, the UK's asylum laws and procedures appear to respect the UK's international obligations under the Refugee Convention and the ECHR. A closer examination, however, uncovers real obstacles that deny individuals the protection of the international agreements.

Limitations of the system

A fundamental problem with the asylum system is that initial decisions are frequently of a poor quality. Many genuine refugees have their claims wrongly rejected. The process is inefficient and long drawn-out. Asylum seekers are left in an uncertain position for months, or even years. Rules to restrict the ability of some individuals to claim asylum are built into the asylum procedure. The 'safe third country' concept allows immigration authorities to refuse asylum point blank to someone who has passed through a 'safe' country on his or her way to the UK, without any consideration as to whether he or she is a genuine refugee. Instead, the asylum seeker is returned to the third country. The new Bill further restricts the limited appeal rights of a 'third country' asylum seeker, giving the Home Secretary power to certify that the person can be removed to a third country where their rights under the European and Refugee Conventions won't be breached. That person will have no right of appeal until after he or she has left the UK. The right of appeal from abroad has been criticised as valueless.

The Home Secretary already possesses the power to 'certify' other asylum cases on a wide variety of grounds under the Immigration and Asylum Act 1999. For example, a claim may be certified as 'manifestly unfounded.' Under the existing legislation, the certificate broadly confines the right of appeal to the adjudicator alone. Under the new Bill, an asylum seeker whose claim is certified as 'clearly unfounded' has no right of appeal until after he or she has been returned to their country of origin. Judicial review will be available only in a few cases. The government's argument is that it has no obligation to consider claims under either Convention if they are wholly without merit. The problem arises from the fact that the initial decision-making is of such poor quality. Genuine claims are often wrongly determined as 'unfounded'(see the Refugee Legal Centre briefing at www.refugee-legal-centre.org.uk/). The risk is that genuine asylum seekers will be returned to their country of origin, where they face persecution, torture and death. It is extremely unlikely that a person who is returned to his or her home country will be able to pursue an appeal. Without the protection of an appeal before removal, the rights under the Refugee and European Conventions become meaningless.

Finally, one restriction of note was passed in the aftermath of the bombing of the US World Trade Centre on 11 September 2002. In response to the attacks, legislation was passed to deny suspected terrorists the right to seek asylum.

Non-arrival policies

The government also maintains policies which make it almost impossible for people to travel to the UK to seek asylum. The UK imposes visa requirements for countries which produce large numbers of asylum seekers. In practice, it is not possible to obtain a visa for the purposes of seeking asylum, and refugees are left with no legitimate way of escaping from persecution. Airline Liaison Officers are posted abroad to intercept travellers without visas and prevent them from coming to the UK.

Airlines and other carriers also face heavy fines if they bring in stowaways. The Court of Appeal held recently that the penalties violate the right to a fair hearing under the European Convention and the Nationality Immigration and Asylum Bill now contains provisions designed to make carriers' penalties compatible. The new Bill introduces further measures to prevent refugees coming to the UK and will extend the offence of assisting unlawful immigration.

As a result of these barriers, many individuals turn to smugglers, in spite of the dangers involved. Others fall into the hands of traffickers, and are subject to sexual or other forms of exploitation. The express incorporation of the Refugee and European Conventions into UK law and procedure is undermined if, in reality, refugees simply cannot get to the UK to seek protection. The government has gone some way to recognising this problem. UK refugee organisations have welcomed provisions in the new Bill to set up 're-settlement programmes' that allow asylum seekers to have their claim determined before they leave their country of origin. Those in need of asylum will receive assistance to travel and settle in the UK.

Deterrence

Several other mechanisms exist to deter individuals from seeking refuge in the UK. Immigration officers increasingly detain asylum seekers upon arrival using broad powers to detain anyone whose application to enter the UK is being examined. Detainees may be kept in prisons as well as in detention centres, despite the government's intention to house asylum seekers in dedicated centres only. There are no time limits. People are often detained for over six months and in some cases for well over a year. Certain nationalities and ethnic groups are much more likely to be detained than others.

The UK's detention record has been heavily criticised by the UN Working Group on Arbitrary Detention, the UNHCR and others. It is doubtful whether the detention regime complies with the European Convention; and the detention of families with children is contrary to the UN Convention on the Rights of the Child. There is no right to bail under the current system (unlike in criminal law), although applications for bail may be made in certain circumstances. In practice, many asylum seekers are often refused bail because they do not know two people who are able to stand as financial surety for them. Provisions for an automatic system of bail hearings to safeguard an individual's right to liberty have never been implemented and will be repealed by the Nationality Immigration and Asylum Bill.

Oakington Reception Centre remains a key element within the government's asylum strategy. Oakington is a detention centre where claims deemed to be without merit are processed in seven to ten days. During this period, asylum seekers are detained. This is effectively for the administrative convenience of the immigration service, irrespective of whether the detainees are likely to abscond. The lawfulness of detention at Oakington was challenged in the Administrative Court in 2001. The court at first instance ruled that the detention was unlawful because it violated the right to liberty protected by Article 5. However, the Court of Appeal overturned the judgment and the case has gone to the House of Lords.

Refugees are also deterred from seeking asylum in the UK by the limited official support they receive while their claims are being determined; and dispersal policies that send them outside London, often to areas of extreme social deprivation where they suffer racial abuse. They are not allowed to work for six months after they arrive. Destitute asylum seekers receive support from the National Asylum Support

Service (NASS) – an organisation which has been heavily criticised for its administrative incompetence. The discredited voucher system has been abolished, but many asylum seekers continue to live in poverty (Oxfam and the Refugee Council, 2002). The new Bill proposes to house some asylum seekers in purpose-built accommodation centres in isolated rural areas; and to educate their children in the centres, separate from mainstream schools. This practice of segregation is potentially discriminatory and contrary to the UN Convention on the Rights of the Child.

Discrimination in immigration policy

All immigration law and policy, by necessity, discriminates. Nationals are entitled to be admitted into their home state, while the entry and residence of non-nationals is subject to immigration control. This analysis assumes that a basic distinction between nationals and non-nationals is here to stay, and considers how immigration policy discriminates beyond this minimum distinction, and in so doing, treats different groups unfairly.

Measures in both international and domestic law exist to protect people against discrimination. Under the Human Rights Act 1998, all public authorities have been under a duty not to discriminate. The Race Relations (Amendment) Act 2000 extended the Race Relations Act 1976 by imposing a duty on public authorities not to discriminate on racial grounds (see Section 3). But while immigration officials are prohibited from discriminating on the grounds of race or colour, they may be expressly authorised to discriminate on the grounds of nationality, ethnic origin or national origins (for example, against Kurds or Afghans on grounds of their country of origin).

The supposed distinction between race and colour, versus national and ethnic origins, is a false one (see Dummett, 2001). The concepts of race and nationality overlap to the extent that the definition of racial discrimination in the UN Convention on the Elimination of Discrimination includes discrimination based on ethnic or national origins. Secondly, while immigration law inevitably imposes different controls on nationals and non-nationals, the 2000 Act gives public authorities carte blanche to discriminate across the wide variety of decisions concerning immigration and nationality – for example, in the areas of visa policy, detention, the NASS scheme, dispersal and in nationality decisions amongst others. Yet, what rational and defensible basis exists for treating some asylum seekers differently because of their nationality? Or for discriminating in the grant of British citizenship according to nationality or ethnic origin?

The government has beat a partial retreat. Under the new Bill, public authorities carrying out nationality functions will no longer be permitted to discriminate on the basis of national or ethnic origins. Discrimination where immigration functions are being exercised is still permitted. Further, while the government offers protection, such as it is, against racial discrimination, neither women nor other minority groups are given specific statutory protection from discrimination in immigration and nationality decisions, apart from the general provisions of the Human Rights Act.

In the meantime, UK immigration policy is riddled by arbitrary discrimination. Some of the most noteworthy examples are considered below. Certain nationalities receive very different treatment under the asylum system. There is a disproportionate use of detention for particular groups, including Roma, young single males, and nationalities from which a large number of asylum applications come. Visa regimes have been imposed selectively on certain countries to control immigration at the point of departure, rather than arrival. Countries such as the USA and Australia are not visa countries; countries such as India and Iraq are. Thus the ability of visa-nationals to come to the UK to visit or to settle is restricted.

Discrimination is particularly apparent in immigration policies concerning family reunion. Family members from another country have no right to visit or join relatives settled in the UK. The rules that govern entry are neutral on their face, but in practice have a disproportionate impact on ethnic minority communities and women. For example, a means test tends to restrict the ability of those from ethnic minorities, women, or the disabled from seeing their families. The rules also fail to take account of cultural and religious differences in the way that families and marriages operate.

14.5 How consistent is the government in its support for human rights and democracy abroad?

The Labour Government came into power in 1997 promising that its foreign policy would have a new 'ethical dimension'. The then Foreign Secretary, Robin Cook, explained that this would involve an emphasis on human rights; tougher control of arms exports; greater environmental protection; and the concentration of development aid on tackling poverty. The government also committed itself to a bigger role in peace-keeping operations than any other UN Security Council member (*The Times*, 25 September 1999).

Of these aims, the expansion of Britain's overseas aid programme and its direction towards poverty alleviation has been the most significant achievement, due to the efforts of Clare Short as Minister for International Development and her alliance with the Chancellor, Gordon Brown. The aid budget has been increased substantially in each year, and is due to move from 0.26 per cent of GDP in 1997 to 0.4 per cent (£4.9 billion a year) by the end of the present administration. This still leaves it well short of the UN target of 0.7 per cent of GDP, but the move is strongly in that direction. At the same time the government has cancelled £5 billion of bilateral debt owed to the UK by Highly Indebted Poor Countries, provided that the money saved is used for social priorities. And Blair himself has taken the lead in promoting a new international settlement for Africa, which will help countries tackle the most serious obstacles to their economic and social development. The linking of aid to progress in democracy and human rights, begun under the Conservatives, has contributed to consolidating an international climate of opinion, from which democratising forces in many countries have benefited.

These are significant achievements, as are the government's initiatives in the human rights field already discussed (see Section 14.3). However, its commitment to human rights and democracy abroad has also been compromised when they have come into conflict with the interest of maintaining relations with powerful countries, such as China, or with the commercial interests of British firms overseas. Such compromises have created the impression of hypocrisy and double standards, which have tended to discredit the whole idea of an ethical foreign policy.

Control of arms sales
The most repeatedly controversial aspect of Labour's 'ethical' foreign policy has been the sale of arms to countries where they could be used for external aggression or internal repression. The UK is the world's second largest arms exporter, with overseas sales worth £5 billion a year. Government is

involved in two ways: first, in setting and policing the system of licences for arms exports; and secondly in providing public finance through the ECGD to support sales in case of default. Over half of the ECGD portfolio currently goes to provide cover for arms exporters.

The 1996 Scott report on arms sales to Iraq and Iran had shown how public embargoes on sales to both regimes had been subverted with the connivance of MOD and DTI ministers and officials who saw their job as promoting British exports. Labour pledged to tighten controls, and to allow some measure of parliamentary oversight. The government has introduced an annual report on arms control and has since 2001 allowed parliamentary scrutiny by select committees of arms export licences granted to countries subject to UK, UN or European embargoes. These measures have not, however, removed the issue from public controversy. Licences for a number of arms exports, typically aircraft or their spare parts, have been bitterly contested, both within government and outside, such as:

- to Indonesia in 1997, an authoritarian regime involved in military repression in East Timor. A subsequent embargo was lifted after the change of regime, but concern still continues about the use of British weapons against independence movements in Aceh and elsewhere;
- to Zimbabwe while it was militarily involved in the Congolese civil war;
- to Morocco in respect of repression of the independence movement in Western Sahara;
- to Pakistan after the military coup, and to both India and Pakistan after the flare-up of fighting in Kashmir and the two nations' military confrontation; and
- to Israel for possible use against Palestinian civilians.

Because of its size, the UK's arms industry is a powerful lobby within government through the MOD and DTI, and Blair has also shown himself ready to support the interests of British industry wherever possible.

Links with mercenaries
Early in the first Labour administration the embarrassing 'Sandline affair" surfaced. In contravention of a UN embargo, Sandline, a British security firm, had been supplying arms, mercenaries and equipment to the forces of the deposed elected government of Sierra Leone with the complicity of the UK High Commissioner. The elected government was restored. 'What's the problem?' asked Tony Blair, 'the good guys won.' The official Legg inquiry into the affair came to much the same pragmatic conclusion, saying that the High Commissioner had acted without authority but in good faith. However, the incident raises wider issues about the ongoing involvement of British security and military supply companies in wars and disorders overseas. Mostly they operate within the terms of UK law, and the companies themselves argue that they provide an essential service, filling vacuums of insecurity for legitimate governments. Yet often they do so in return for major mineral or energy concessions, which they are able to secure on highly favourable terms. They can also compromise the principles of sovereignty and self-determination in the countries where they operate. In 1999, the UN Commission on Human Rights Special Rapporteur, Enrique Ballesteros, concluded that the recruitment, financing and use of mercenaries by private companies was unacceptable under any circumstances, 'even when the aim is claimed to be the restoration of a constitutional regime overthrown by a coup d'etat'.

Overseas territories and Crown fiefdoms

The UK is currently responsible for some 16 overseas polities, including 11 colonies and three Crown fiefdoms in the Channel Islands and the Isle of Man. In general, overseas territories have governments dominated by the executive, while the fiefdoms are under the direct jurisdiction of the sovereign. The democratic and human rights arrangements in almost all of them are imperfect, and the Human Rights Act does not extend to their territories.

1   The CDC portfolio consists of US$2.5bn (on a portfolio valuation which under-estimates working funds) directly invested in over 400 businesses, and US$230m third party funds under management . The ECGD issued 167 guarantees to a value of over £3.7bn during 1998-99 while total ECGD exposure was £23.4bn at the end of 1998-99 (HC52, 2000, xii). DFID disbursed a total of £2.37bn in 1998-99.

Findings

Section 1

Is there public agreement on a common citizenship without discrimination?

- There is no clear legal statement of the rights and duties of citizenship, apart from the right to reside in and return to the UK, which is also enjoyed by other EU citizens.
- Decisions on immigration, settlement and naturalisation are at the discretion of the Home Office. Its officials can in practice discriminate systematically on grounds of ethnicity or national origin, and also in decisions whether to allow spouses and families of British citizens to join them from abroad.
- The Race Relations (Amendment) Act 2000 put obligations on all public authorities in the UK (apart from immigration authorities) to eliminate unlawful discrimination – both direct and indirect – and to provide equality of opportunity and good race relations.
- However, the UK has no single comprehensive equality statute. Disproportionately high levels of economic and social exclusion among national, ethnic and religious minorities provide evidence of continuing discrimination, and have led to communal violence in several urban areas.
- The establishment of a Disability Rights Commission has strengthened the rights of the disabled, though their protection remains patchy, as is that afforded by legislation to other minorities, such as gays and lesbians, older workers and travellers.
- Longstanding disputes over the state's territorial boundaries have been moderated in Northern Ireland by the Belfast Agreement and in Scotland and Wales by devolution.

● The absence of a written constitution leaves it to the government's discretion whether to call a popular referendum on constitutional change, and also the form of its wording, though the Political Parties, Elections and Referendum Act 2000 has introduced regulations on the conduct of referendum campaigns.

Section 2

Are state and society consistently subject to the law?

● Formally, everyone in the UK enjoys equal treatment under the law and equal access to justice. Yet there is understandable concern about how fair and effective the criminal justice system is, as a result of a number of incompetent investigations and unlawful convictions. This concern is especially strong among racial and ethnic minorities who experience discrimination at the hands of both police and courts.

● Public pressure to be 'tough on crime' has led the government to limit or threaten basic rights to due legal process, such as the right to silence, the right to jury trial and the freedom from double jeopardy. Access to the law has been denied altogether to certain categories of detainee under anti-terrorist legislation.

● New civil procedure rules have made access to the civil law simpler and quicker for smaller claims, but the limitations on legal aid continue to disadvantage all but the wealthy.

● Longstanding inadequacies in the legal accountability of ministers and public officials have been addressed through the extension of judicial review and the Human Rights Act, which makes all public authorities accountable for rights violations.

● The principle of judicial independence from the executive continues to be compromised by the multiple roles of the Lord Chancellor and his power over judicial appointments, which remain highly unrepresentative of the pluralism of society.

● Exemptions to the comprehensive reach of the law include the continued activity of paramilitary groups in Northern Ireland, the collusion of the security forces with loyalist paramilitary killers, gang warfare in British cities, parallel economies including the drugs trade, and systematic tax avoidance by wealthy individuals and companies.

Section 3

Are civil and political rights guaranteed equally for all?

● The Human Rights Act, 1998, which incorporates the European Convention on Human Rights into UK law, has gone a long way to remedying the systematic inadequacies of civil and political rights protection identified in our first Audit. The inclusion of a human rights component in the new compulsory citizenship education programme reflects an emerging rights culture in the UK.

● In Northern Ireland the shift away from organised violence coupled with the accompanying reduction in state security and reform of the police service have contributed to a safer society. However the level of sectarian violence and intimidation remains unacceptably high.

- The high incidence of deaths in prisons and police custody, including suicide, reveal an inadequacy in the duty of care towards detainees. The UK has the highest imprisonment rate in the European Union after Portugal with severe overcrowding, unsanitary conditions and curtailed rehabilitation programmes as a consequence.
- Freedom of expression is circumscribed by the 90 year old Official Secrets Act and ancient common laws of defamation, blasphemy and sedition. Defamation in particular enables the wealthy and powerful to protect themselves from adverse criticism, and there is inadequate protection for 'whistleblowers'.
- Under anti-terrorism legislation passed since 1997 protesters risk being branded as terrorists where serious damage to property occurs or is even threatened.
- The Human Rights Act has transformed the law on privacy which hitherto was not recognised as a general right. At the same time privacy is also threatened by the actions of covert state surveillance agencies and the accumulation by public bodies of personal information obtained from private institutions and service providers.

Section 4

Are economic and social rights equally guaranteed for all ?

- Poverty and inequality run deeper in the UK than in any comparable EU country, with nearly a quarter of the population living below the official poverty level (60 per cent of median income) and unable to afford two of the basic necessities of life as defined by their fellow citizens. This includes one third of all children.
- The frequent concentration of poor households in neglected neighbourhoods has left millions without access to basic facilities such as shops, banks and public transport. This deprivation is usually accompanied by higher unemployment, mortality and crime rates.
- Homelessness, overcrowding or inadequate heating affect substantial minorities of the population.
- The correlation between poverty and ill health remains strong, with the former causing an estimated 10,000 premature deaths each year.
- Parental class and ethnic origin constitute significant determinants of children's educational achievement and future employment prospects.
- The Labour government has sought to address this accumulated legacy of deprivation through a series of measures, including: Full employment policies, including a New Deal scheme to move unemployed young people into employment; legislation on a minimum wage; increases in child benefit; substantial increases in health and education spending; reversing the decline in social housing; the establishment of a Social Exclusion Unit in the Cabinet Office. Given the starting point most of these measures will take years to show significant results.
- EU directives have led to improved guarantees for workers' rights, but the UK lags behind the rest of the EU in trade-union rights, limitation on hours worked, maternity provision, equal pay for women

and other employment practices. Trade unionists do not have a basic right to strike safe from reprisals.

- The rules on corporate governance are framed to protect the rights of shareholders and other companies rather than the general public, and the powers of regulatory bodies are insufficient for them to act as effective watchdogs on corporate wrongdoing.

Section 5

Do elections give the people control over governments and their policies ?

- The composition of the lower chamber of Parliament, and thereby the selection of the governing party, is determined by periodic secret ballot. Despite attempts at reform, the upper chamber remains wholly unelected, and thus eludes popular accountability.
- The Representation of the People Act 2000 makes procedures for registration and voting easier and more inclusive, though electoral turnout remains comparatively low by European standards.
- Supervision of ballot registration and voting is independent of government and party control, and the establishment of the Electoral Commission should ensure that future changes to constituency boundaries are also fully independent.
- Opportunities for free broadcasting and mailing by political parties at election time help create a more level playing field between them. However, the governing party still enjoys an unfair advantage through prior use of official government advertising, and the Prime Minister's power to decide on the timing of a general election.
- The Labour government's readiness to introduce more proportional forms of electoral system for the devolved assemblies and the European Parliament has not been matched by change to the plurality – rule system for Westminster elections, which continue to produce excessively disproportionate results between the national vote for parties and their share of parliamentary seats, and to safeguard the dominance of Labour and the Conservatives at Westminster. Since 1979 there has only been one change in the governing party at Westminster.
- The House of Commons is socially unrepresentative of the population, being dominated by white middle-aged, middle-class men. The efforts of the Labour Party produced a dramatic improvement in the number of women elected in 1997, but their proportion (18 per cent) is still low by European standards. Ethnic minority representation is also low.

Section 6

Does the party system assist the working of democracy?

- Legislation in 1998 ended the unregulated status of political parties, which now have to register with the Electoral Commission and conform to strict rules on finance and expenditure. These include a requirement to publish all donations over £5,000, and a complete ban on overseas donations.
- The dominance of the two main parties under the plurality electoral system is formidably efficient

at forming and sustaining governments in office. Yet the loss of credibility of opposition parties as alternative governments in waiting since 1979 has deprived them of an effective parliamentary role.

- Rebellions from the party line in Parliament are discouraged by the threat to promotion prospects and various parliamentary 'perks'. However, there is no sanction on MPs switching their party allegiance altogether, as they are not required to seek a fresh mandate in their own constituency.

- UK political parties are small by European standards, and their memberships have halved over the past 20 years. Formal improvements in internal democracy have obscured increasing central control over policy making and selection of candidates for election. Many local branches are virtually defunct.

- Given the decline in their membership, and in support from trade unions and corporate sponsors, the two main parties increasingly rely on donations from wealthy individuals to meet their expensive election costs. This dependency fuels the suspicion that large donors exercise an improper influence over policy, or gain other advantages for themselves.

- Most political parties appeal across the main societal divisions, with the exception of those in Northern Ireland, which align themselves along the sectarian divide. The decision of the mainland parties thus far not to campaign in elections in the province denies its electors the opportunity of voting for a governing party at Westminster.

Section 7

Is government accountable to the people and their representatives?

- Labour has further concentrated their power of decision in the hands of the Prime Minister and the Chancellor of the Exchequer and accelerated the decline in cabinet government. Their aim is to produce effective government, but there are doubts about their 'control and command' strategy and the continuing combination of inadequate checks and balances in the policy process and a weakened civil service still produces policy fiascos such as the Millenium Dome and the handling of the foot-and-mouth crisis.

- Reforms to the select committee system and the management of business in the House of Commons have not remedied its inadequacy in scrutinising legislation and holding government to account, due to the government's continuing single-party dominance of the chamber and its committees.

- The House of Lords continues to offer a more independent check on government than the Commons, but it lacks democratic legitimacy and accountability to the public. Reform to the composition of the second chamber is currently stalled.

- The public accountability of the multitude of executive agencies and quangos, whether via the relevant minister or to the public directly, is patchy at best. The doctrine of strict ministerial responsibility is a fiction.

- In the absence of any developed system of administrative law, codes of conduct for ministers and civil servants are largely informal. Sanctions are a matter of political judgement following scandal or loss of confidence, rather than of legal accountability.

- The government has passed a Freedom of Information Act, establishing a general 'right to know' on the part of the public. However, the large number of class exemptions from disclosure, and the executive's power to override decisions by the independent Information Commissioner, indicate that the traditional habit of secrecy on issues the government considers sensitive will continue

- The elevation of Alistair Campbell, a political appointee, to command the government's communications, the presence of 'spin doctors' among special advisers, and the new 'hard-sell' orthodoxy in the government's information service compromise the integrity of government information.

Section 8

Are the military and police under civil control?

- The military in the UK is formally under civilian control, and parliamentary consent must be continually sought for the maintenance of the armed forces in peacetime. The three heads of the armed forces exercise influence over decisions on military matters through the Ministry of Defence and through the right of direct access to the Prime Minister.
- Military involvement in civilian affairs is normally confined to assisting the civilian emergency services. The exception has been their controversial role in Northern Ireland, including evidence of a 'shoot to kill' policy at one stage and of collusion with loyalist terrorists. These covert operations eluded ministerial control.
- Policing has historically been locally accountable. In 1994, the Conservative government began the process of taking control centrally and introduced Home Office appointees to re-constituted local police authorities. The Police Act 2002 further consolidates the trend of increased control of policing at the centre.
- Following long standing concerns about the lack of openness and independence of the police complaints system, a new Independent Police Complaints Commission is due to replace the existing Police Complaints Authority in April 2003. Northern Ireland already enjoys a more robust complaints system following the establishment of a Police Ombudsman in November 2000.
- Although all the intelligence and security agencies are nominally accountable to Parliament, the main security body, the Intelligence and Security Select Committee, is not independent, reporting directly to the Prime Minister and only through him to Parliament. The Regulation of Investigatory Powers Act 2000 has partially reformed state surveillance of citizens.
- The armed forces and police continue to be unrepresentative of British society despite genuine efforts to recruit more widely. Recruitment from ethnic minorities is hampered by continuing evidence of institutional racism within the services. Although recruitment to the new police service in Northern Ireland is now on a 50:50 basis from the two communities, it will take years to overcome the 90 per cent Protestant dominance.

Section 9

Are elected representatives and public officials free from corruption ?

- Following increasing evidence of 'sleaze' under the Major government, there was a marked drop in public confidence in the integrity of ministers and MPs. Since then significant progress has been made in developing codes of conduct for all national and local politicians and public officials, together with stronger enforcement mechanisms.

- However, the appointment of the first Commissioner for Parliamentary Standards, Elizabeth Filkin, was compromised by deliberate obstruction of her inquiries into a number of high-profile cases, and by the withdrawal of confidence by MPs, to whom she was formally accountable. This experience exposed the limits of parliamentary self-regulation.
- Public sector corruption remains a rarity. However, concern arises over the degree of business influence over public policy. This is not only a matter of party donations which secure privileged access and influence, but also of the increasing numbers of business employees seconded to government, and the relaxed rules for civil servants and ministers taking on lucrative posts in the private sector after leaving office. The government's insistence on public-private partnerships has further confused the distinction between the public and the private interest.
- The relatively high expectations of the British public of the probity of their politicians, combined with a low tolerance of their failings, has now led to Labour being perceived as a sleazy and disreputable party alongside the Conservatives.

Section 10

Do the media operate in a way that sustains democratic values ?

- The British media are broadly representative of a diversity of interests and opinions. However, ownership of both broadcasting and the press is becoming less pluralist reflecting similar trends across the developed world. The cross-ownership of Rupert Murdock's News International group typifies this corporate hegemony.
- Labour's proposed Communications Bill will accelerate the process of monopolisation by removing all restrictions on foreign ownership, and permitting single ownership of ITV and the acquisition of Channel 5. The government has brushed aside criticism from a parliamentary scrutiny committee to the effect that such a dramatic change will be achieved at the expense of creativity and pluralism.
- A new regulatory body, Ofcom, will have significant powers, but may find it impossible to reconcile the government's twin aims of more competition and greater pluralism of content. Its compatibility with the independence guaranteed to the BBC through its governing body is also a source of concern.
- A combination of de-regulation and intensified competition has squeezed out a great deal of quality drama, news and investigative journalism from television in favour of lightweight entertainment, a process that is also mirrored in the broadsheet press. Both media collude in a trivialisation of politics, concentrating on personalities and splits rather than policy issues.
- Labour's relationship with the media since coming to power has been fraught with difficulties. Determined to control the news agenda, Blair and his press secretary, Alistair Campbell, have scaled new heights in media manipulation, including bullying of journalists.

Section 11

Is there full citizen participation in public life ?

- The decline in party political membership is not indicative of civic participation as a whole. Britain's strong civic activist tradition embraces a plethora of different organisations, categorised variously as charities, voluntary organisations, pressure groups, protest and direct action movements.
- Voluntary work, in some form, is undertaken by nearly half the adult population, with those who are older and higher up the social ladder predominating. Women and men have generally comparable levels of activity, while ethnic minorities tend to be more involved in their own community organisations.
- In the main, voluntary associations are independent of the state. However, the huge amount of public money they receive (totalling nearly £5 billion per annum, or one third of their income), combined with their increasing involvement in service delivery, carries the risk of compromising this independence.
- Associations connected to productive activity are a significant element of public life. Despite their decline under successive Conservative governments, trade unions still account for 6.8 million workers, whilst 691 trade associations represent over 670,000 companies.
- Both central and local government rely on at least 500,000 unpaid members of the public, to deliver various statutory services. These include sitting on juries, quangos, local councils, school governing bodies and community health councils, as well as acting as special constables and JPs.
- The historic discrimination and disadvantage experienced by women in access to paid public office persists. Both Houses of Parliament, local government in England and Wales, the English and Welsh judiciary, QCs and the senior civil service all have significant gender imbalances. Similarly, ethnic minorities are under-represented in Parliament, the judiciary, the senior bar and higher civil service.

Section 12

Is government responsive to the concerns of its citizens ?

- Government procedures for public consultation on policy and legislation were extensively reformed in November 2000 with a Code of Conduct on Written Consultation, providing for simpler documentation, minimum periods of consultation and more comprehensive feedback. Doubts remain about the seriousness of the government's commitment to consultation on controversial issues, especially given its preference for secret polling and focus groups as methods of testing public opinion.
- Public inquiries into matters of widespread concern have generally provided those affected with genuine opportunities to air their grievances. Government proposals to curtail the timetable and procedures for planning inquiries have aroused criticism that they would enable ministers to bulldoze through controversial projects.
- In general, business has much readier access to government than other interests, and is over-repre-

sented on the government's 300 or so task forces to review policy. Access by the public to their MP is patchy, and usually only effective on individual matters. Public protest is a more effective last resort for groups who feel their voices are excluded from the policy process.

- The Audit Commission has severely criticised the lack of consultation across the public services, including the police, NHS trusts and councils, though inadequacies in the last of these have been substantially addressed by the government's local government legislation. All public authorities experience particular difficulties in consulting the views of the socially excluded.
- A survey conducted in 2002 showed that four out of five people believe that they lack any real influence over government policy between elections, and think they should have more. The level of overall confidence in the way we are governed is not high.

Section 13

Are decisions taken at the lowest practicable level of government for the people most affected ?

- The introduction of devolved government in Scotland, Wales and Northern Ireland, confirmed by popular referendum, signals a major constitutional change. Although Westminster retains formal sovereignty and the Treasury control of the overall budgetary allocation, including social security and most taxation, the devolved administrations have the power to determine their own policies within these limits. Constitutional conflicts with the centre have yet to be tested, though the Northern Ireland Secretary's decision to suspend the province's Assembly within its first 18 months shows where power ultimately lies in the event of a breakdown in the Belfast Agreement.
- All the devolved governments constitute a marked break with the Westminster system of government, including more proportional electoral systems and coalition government (in Northern Ireland a formal power-sharing executive). Scotland has a better freedom of information regime and a more effective system of consultation. Scotland and Wales have much higher proportions of elected women members than Westminster.
- This constitutional settlement leaves England, where the vast majority of the UK population lives, without any law-making body of its own, or any comparable regional government, except for London. Plans for elected regional assemblies will be dependent on local demand.
- The example of the London authority, which has had a highly unpopular PFI system for the Tube's redevelopment imposed from the centre despite its statutory responsibility for transport, does not encourage any optimism about the degree of autonomy English regional government will enjoy.
- Local government in England is tightly controlled from the centre, lacking any financial independence and having suffered almost continuous reorganisation and upheaval by successive governments over a quarter of a century. Unelected quangos have supplanted local councils in many areas of governance and service delivery.
- Labour has made genuine moves to reinvigorate local government by promoting service quality, public consultation and partnership with the voluntary and private sectors, but ministers continue to intervene heavily in local council affairs. It is hardly surprising that formal citizen participation as voters and candidates for election has continued to decline as a consequence.

Section 14

Are the country's external relations conducted in accordance with democratic norms, and is it itself free from external subordination ?

- The UK's external political and economic power and influence on other countries far outweighs any countervailing inward forces. Its voting power on important global bodies, including the UN Security Council, WTO, IMF and World Bank, is out of all proportion to the size of its population. Decisions by the UK's representatives on these bodies are not subject to parliamentary scrutiny.
- It is difficult to determine how far the UK's subordination to the US in aspects of foreign and military policy is freely chosen and how far a consequence of military dependence and the terms of intelligence cooperation. Such subordination is of particular concern under the unilateralist administration of President Bush.
- The extension of majority voting in the EU and the underlying democratic deficit in its institutions have served to erode its level of support among the UK population. Given that Brussels legislation takes precedence over the laws of member states, the terms of the proposed future constitutional settlement for the EU will have considerable significance for the quality of democracy in them all.
- The UK has a good record of supporting the development of international human rights standards and institutions. In addition, it has signed and ratified all of the major international and regional treaties, following a major review of its obligations. However, its involvement in US-led military actions, such as in Kosovo and Afghanistan, has been of dubious validity under international law, and has served to weaken further the authority of the UN.
- Labour's proclaimed ethical foreign policy, emphasising human rights, arms control, environmental protection and development aid, has had a mixed record. Britain has increased its aid budget and unilaterally cancelled £5 billion of bilateral debt to assist the poorest countries. But such efforts are offset, however, by the protectionist and subsidy regimes operated by all western governments, which undermine production in developing countries.
- Continued arms sales to governments which might use them for aggression or to control civilian populations constitute the worse stain on Labour's ethical credentials.
- The repeated overhaul of the asylum system (four times in ten years) reflects the disarray that it has fallen into. One of the prime causes is the failure of successive governments to reconcile international obligations with a hostile domestic press and public opinion. Deterrents to entry to the country for asylum seekers are compounded by delays, arbitrary detention, dispersal to inappropriate locations and inadequate support.

Conclusions

Jekyll and Hyde government

Reform! Reform! Aren't things bad enough already?
Sir John Astbury, judge and Liberal MP (1860-1939)

The most significant developments since our first democratic audit of the UK have been the huge constitutional changes undertaken by the Blair administrations to date. The full list of measures set out in the panel (below) indicates how extensive the government's agenda has been. At the launch conference for our first audit of Britain's political institutions in 1998, the then Home Secretary, Jack Straw, remarked that the figure of 12 constitutional bills then in progress was unprecedented; his officials had advised that just two in one session of Parliament would be ambitious.

This then is a reforming government. The purpose of these conclusions is to set its constitutional changes in a wider context – historical, constitutional and international – and to assess them against the democratic criteria used throughout the volume.

Usually a country only undertakes constitutional changes of this magnitude at the end of a war or revolution. How are we to explain them in a UK suffering neither of these calamities? An accumulation of factors was responsible. One was the experience of a long period of government under Mrs Thatcher, who ignored an unwritten convention of self-restraint in the exercise of office by centralising and concentrating power to an unusual degree in the hands of the executive, and systematically demobilising alternative centres of power in government and civil society that might frustrate her programme. The resulting decline in legitimacy of Westminster institutions was felt most acutely in Scotland, where the governing Tory party was perceived to have no electoral mandate.

Constitutional change under Blair government since 1997

- The Human Rights Act 1998 introduces the European Convention on Human Rights into British law and for the first time provides systematic legal underpinning of civil and political rights in the UK
- A Joint Committee on Human Rights is set up in Parliament to examine all Bills for compliance with the Human Rights Act and to review progress on the Act's objectives
- The government passes new legislation in 2001 requiring almost all public bodies to draw up plans to eradicate institutional racism from their operations and to promote good race relations
- Power is devolved to new administrations in Scotland, Wales and Northern Ireland after referendums. The elections to the Scottish Parliament and both assemblies use proportional systems
- The Peace Agreement in Northern Ireland inaugurates a new human rights regime (with a Human Rights Commission), cautious police reforms and a strong new Ombudsman for police complaints
- Regional development agencies and regional chambers established in English regions; a white paper proposes elected assemblies in English regions
- The government signs the Council of Europe Charter for Local Self-Government and introduces new governing arrangements and constitutions into local government. Local people are given the chance to opt for mayor in a referendum
- The government agrees to the EU Amsterdam Treaty (under European Communities (Amendment) Act 1998)
- The 1998 elections to the European Parliament are held using a closed List proportional representation system
- The new London mayoralty and assembly are set up after a referendum. The mayoral vote is conducted under the Supplementary Vote and assembly elections under the proportional AMS system
- Most hereditary peers are removed from House of Lords and the Wakeham Commission is established to chart further reform. A Joint Committee of both Houses is now charged with considering further reform, especially the balance between appointed and elected members
- A Select Committee on the Constitution is to keep constitutional change under review and to examine the constitutional implications of all public Bills
- A Modernisation Committee is set up under the Leader of the House in the Commons to initiate reforms in the House's conduct of business and in practice to facilitate the progress of government legislation
- The House of Commons agrees a reform package to strengthen the role of select committees, but rejects a proposal for a new committee of senior MPs to take responsibility for selecting their members away from the whips

- The Freedom of Information Act 2000 establishes a statutory right of access to official information which is yet to come into force
- The Electoral Commission is established in 2000 to register political parties, oversee a new transparent regime for donations, to control election spending and to oversee and review the conduct of elections and referendums. New limits are set for party and 'third party' spending on election campaigns and referendum campaigns
- An official commission under Lord Jenkins proposes a new 'mixed' electoral system for Westminster elections, but the promised referendum on reform has not yet been held
- A reform of the law gives political parties leave to adopt measures of positive discrimination to raise the proportion of women in Parliament
- Reforms to registration and voting procedures and experiments with postal and electronic voting, etc, are introduced to facilitate wider registration and participation in voting. Homeless people and other excluded groups are given an effective right to vote
- Significant 'healing' inquiries are set up into the Bloody Sunday deaths in Derry, the outbreak of BSE among humans, the murder of the black teenager Stephen Lawrence and the deaths of children from heart operations in a Bristol hospital

By the time Labour was on the threshold of office in the mid 1990s, the momentum behind Scottish devolution was unstoppable. At the same time wider circles within the British political elite had concluded from the Thatcher experience that Parliament had proved powerless to check the executive, either in defence of basic citizen rights or to prevent a series of policy fiascos; and that reforms wider than devolution were also needed. The case for a linked series of reforms and the introduction of a written constitution was made and orchestrated by a newly-created pressure group, Charter 88, which won an impressive range of signatories. The Labour Party under the late John Smith responded to these concerns and Smith particularly committed his party to a Bill of Rights and Scottish devolution.

After 1990 the Major governments added significant developments, both positive and negative. On the positive side were Major's efforts with support of the Irish government to convene all-party talks in Northern Ireland, which eventually led to the historic Belfast Agreement under Blair in April 1998. 'Sleaze', the catch-all media term for a variety of abuses and misconduct in government, was among the negative features. Sleaze brought about a widespread loss of confidence in the integrity of MPs and ministers; it was felt to infect not just the Conservative Party but the governing class as a whole, and to bring Parliament itself into disrepute.

Dealing with this accumulated legacy proved initially attractive to a Labour government which had committed itself to the self-denying ordinance of Tory spending limits: constitutional reform did not cost huge sums of money. But Labour was also driven by distinctive tendencies of its own. One continuity of Labour in office, despite being branded 'New' Labour, has been that it has seen itself as a modernising party, with a mission to modernise Britain's antiquated institutions. Under Harold Wilson in the 1960s the aim was to modernise industry through the 'white heat' of the technological revolution. Under Tony Blair in the 1990s the self-appointed mission has been to modernise the institutions of government to adapt them to the 21st century, and to a redefined conception of Britain's role in the world. The theme of 'modernisation' has linked what otherwise have been a very disparate and piecemeal set of constitutional reforms. 'New Labour was elected with a mandate to modernise,' Blair wrote in his introductions to the constitutional white papers. 'The government are pledged to clean up and modernise British politics.' Thus the white papers all bear the same brand: the white paper on partial reform of the House of Lords is entitles *Modernising Parliament*; that on local government *Modern Local Government*; and so on.

The problem with modernisation as a theme is that it can be made to cover whatever changes the government deems desirable; and these are not necessarily driven by democratic principles or a coherent democratising agenda. Take the proposals for House of Lords reform, for example. Getting rid of the hereditary peers, or most of them, clearly counts as 'modernisation'. But to see nothing wrong with having a chamber of the legislature appointed by the executive, or by a committee chosen by account-ants, is to expose the limits of modernisation as a guiding constitutional principle. Indeed, from the very beginning, Tony Blair and his closest associates have always wanted to have an appointed second chamber, and all the better if it were wholly appointed. The inquiries of the Wakeham Royal Commission on the future of the Lords, carefully chosen to favour appointment, showed that some measure of election was required to satisfy public and elite opinion. Even now the government's white paper on the next stage of House of Lords reform presents the choice between nomination and election as a purely technical matter, with the balance of advantage clearly favouring the former.

If the fiasco over reform of the second chamber reveals most openly the less than fully democratic impetus behind the government's constitutional programme, so too does its attitude in practice to its own reforms. The Blair government's attitude betrays a curious Jekyll and Hyde quality. Thus on the one hand we have substantial devolutionary measures, decentralising power to national and regional assemblies; while on the other hand Blair has tried to control the leaderships and agendas of these assemblies from the centre. Similarly across the whole range of public service delivery, local councils are being given a new leadership role and the promise of more autonomy, but their outputs are more tightly controlled from the centre through a series of targets, league tables, incentives and special schemes. The progressive achievement of the Human Rights Act has gone hand in hand with a number of illiberal measures from the Home Office, which run counter to the spirit and almost certainly the letter of the Act. New and more proportional electoral systems have been designed for the national and regional assemblies and the European Parliament, while reform of the plurality-rule system at Westminster which gave Blair a majority of 165 seats on just 40 per cent of the popular vote, has been kicked into touch.

The government strongly supported the appointment of a Commissioner for Parliamentary Standards, but she soon proved too independent in her investigations into MPs' and ministers' conduct. Ministers themselves sought to obstruct her inquiries into their affairs and the government finally colluded in the dismissal of the incumbent. The government reluctantly legislated on its pledge to give the public a statutory right of access to official information in the Freedom of Information Act 2000. But it has not yet brought the Act into force; it is unnecessarily and damagingly full of restrictions on access; and the government retains a power of veto on any disclosure. At the same time the government exercises unprecedented control over the content and timing of information through its spin machine.

The list could go on. Some of these contradictions can be argued to be intrinsic to the business of democratic government, where the pressure to deliver on electoral expectations leads governments to be impatient of constitutional impediments and the spotlight of potentially hostile exposure. In addition, there is the tension between human rights standards and less liberal sections of public opinion that are electorally significant. Much is also due to the personal style of Tony Blair and the New Labour tendency to 'control freakery' (a phenomenon not unknown under 'old' Labour).

There is, however, we think a more profound explanation for much of the government's Jekyll and Hyde tendencies. We should first pay more tribute to the Jekyll tendency in government thinking, evident for example in the attempts to end social exclusion and child poverty or to promote gender and racial equality, as well as in its constitutional reforms. But in the Hyde tendency in the government's conduct we perceive the timeless influence of 'the Thing' – William Cobbett's word for the dominant and illiberal political executive of his time. This influence runs through the contradictions we have listed above. The fact is that Blair, ministers and senior civil servants are broadly, if variously, determined to hold onto the traditional powers held at the centre and to delay or frustrate constitutional changes that would check or make transparent their exercise of those powers.

At its heart the government has clung to the doctrine of parliamentary sovereignty – the seat of the central executive's political and administrative power. So the cabinet refused to yield power in the Human Rights Act over its legislation to the courts on issues of civil and political rights. Both the cabinet and Labour party protect the plurality-rule electoral system for Westminster election which promises them the 'winner-takes-all' power at the centre for at least another seven years. The new Home Secretary hardly bothers to conceal his contempt for the idea that he or the government should be subjected to the rule of law and for 'airy-fairy' notions that political freedoms matter. The retreat from an open Freedom of Information regime; the retention of ultimate political and financial power over devolved authorities; the refusal to grant the second chamber the legitimacy of election for fear that it will obstruct the government's will; the unwillingness to improve the ability of the House of Commons to make ministers more accountable; the denial of European standards of constitutional and operational independence to local authorities – these are all signs of the longevity of 'the Thing'. The traditional habits of the British governing class are being reasserted within New Labour, with its protection of executive prerogative and distrust of those in the public sector outside the charmed circle of Whitehall. In these aspects of government conduct, we are far from a modernising and Blair's 'sharing' politics. An old political world is desperately fending off the demands of the new.

The evident distrust of the public contrasts markedly with the deference Blair has displayed towards the private sector. Here concern has focused on the privileged and sometimes purchasable access to and influence over government enjoyed by business. This influence has also brought contradictory results, as when the strictness of Treasury control over public finance has been compromised by Inland Revenue connivance in tax avoidance by large companies, or by PFI schemes which allow private companies to hold taxpayers to ransom over the terms of delivery of key public services; or when such influence has been allowed to undermine more principled aspects of foreign and international aid policy. The history of the past few years indicates that the private sector needs firmer, not weaker regulation, as business is constantly demanding from government.

How, then, should the balance sheet be drawn up from a democratic point of view? The major constitutional innovations, in particular the devolved assemblies and the Human Rights Act, are in practice irreversible, and will therefore survive the particular tendencies of the present government and its individual ministers. Over time these innovations can be expected to moderate the concentration of power in the hands of the central executive, and to encourage a style of government in England as well as the other nations which is more in keeping with the pluralist society Britain has become. The effect of EU membership has also worked in this direction, and will continue to do so.

However there is an urgent need to address the now historic imbalance between the power of the central executive and Parliament's ability to make it accountable and thoroughly to check its legislation. This imbalance is partially recognised by the prevalence of the idea that Tony Blair is President in all but name. But the imbalance goes wider and deeper than the powers in the hands of the Prime Minister, so much so that many influential commentators are already proposing a full separation of powers between the executive and Parliament. Such a profound change may yet be required to save parliamentary democracy in this country. But for the time being we believe that the adoption of proportional representation for elections to the House of Commons and a second chamber in which the great majority of members are elected, would be sufficient to redress the imbalance and create a more pluralist executive at the centre.

Proportional representation would bring to an end the damaging consequences of single-party rule on a minority of the popular vote and the executive's unmediated dominance over Parliament. The House of Commons could then begin to exercise in practice the powers to scrutinise the executive and check its legislation that it possesses only in theory; and the power to block constitutional change that belongs to single-party government in the interests of both executive and party will be removed.

A democratic reform agenda

- Introduce proportional representation for elections to the House of Commons
- Create a second chamber elected by proportional representation
- Free select committees from the control of party whips
- Give MPs the right to ask for the recall of Parliament
- Establish a Petitions Committee on the Scottish model in Parliament
- Pass a Civil Service Act with clear legal rules for executive conduct
- Pass a fully comprehensive equality law
  Make a reality of Freedom of Information
- Abolish the Lord Chancellor's judicial authority
- Set up a Human Rights Commission
- Entrench economic and social rights in British law
- Examine in public the case for and against state funding for political parties
- Make policing locally accountable
- Institute independent regulation of standards in both Houses of Parliament
- Extend affirmative action for gender equality in the political parties and public sector
- Remedy the bias towards business interests in public participation
- Review the Barnett formula for funding devolved administrations, give the Welsh Assembly primary legislation powers, and bring forward serious proposals for elected regional authorities in England and London
- Make local government more independent on the European model
- Raise aid spending to the UN target and abolish protection and subsidy regimes
- Consult the public widely on drafting a written constitution for the UK

We set out a brief agenda of other reforms in the panel. Most of these reforms are implicit in the audit that precedes these conclusions. In the last analysis, however, the test of democratic reforms is not just a matter of the structures of government, or the confidence citizens have in it, but how far they feel more empowered in their daily lives. Our audit has identified a number of measures taken by the Labour government which have a bearing on deepening democracy in this way. There are the attempts to forge partnerships with citizen groups at every level of government. There is the encouragement of voluntary action and self-help. There is the attempt to address the systematic inequalities – of class, gender, ethnicity, religion – that continue to disfigure British society. For millions of citizens the most significant developments since our first audit have been Labour's initiatives on the economic front, such as the minimum wage, the New Deal, increased child and family support, improvements in health and education, and the incorporation of EU directives on workers' rights. As we have argued, the protection of economic and social rights encourages more confident and engaged citizens. Progress here has been slow, given the appalling levels of poverty and lack of public investment when Labour came to power; but policies are moving in the right direction.

In many respects, then, the condition of the country's democracy shows a clear improvement on our first audit undertaken at the end of the long period of Conservative rule. How far this improvement is reflected in people's sense of control over their own lives and confidence in their system of government, however, must remain an open question.

Notes on contributors

Contributors

Anthony Barker is a Fellow and former Reader in the Government department, University of Essex, specialising in modern British government and politics

Steven Barnett is Professor of Communications at the University of Westminster. He writes frequently on broadcasting and has a column in the *Observer*. He is the author of several books on the media.

Sarah Bracking is lecturer in Politics and Development at the Institute for Development Policy and Management, at the University of Manchester. She is currently conducting research on the politics of poverty.

Ruth Brander is a legal research officer at JUSTICE

Tufyal Choudhury lecturers in law at the University of Durham and is a co-author of Equality – A New Framework: The Report of the Independent Review of the Enforcement of UK Anti-discrimination Legislation.

Robin Clarke is Senior Research Fellow in the public involvement team at IPPR and recently wrote New Democratic Processes.

Darren Darcy is a researcher in the Department of European Studies, University of Bradford.

Judith De Bueno Mesquita is a researcher at the Human Rights Centre, University of Essex.

Alison Gerry is human rights co-ordinator at Doughty Street Chambers.

Brigid Hadfield is a Professor of Law at the University of Essex. Her areas of expertise are constitutional law, devolution, and human rights.

Graham Hobbs is a PhD student in Social Policy at the London School of Economics and a member of the Centre for Analysis of Social Exclusion (CASE). He has previously worked in both Tanzania and Namibia.

Ben Jackson is completing a doctorate at Nuffield College, Oxford. He is conducting research on the internal democracy of British political parties for Democratic Audit, and is a research associate of Catalyst.

Chris Lord is professor of European Politics at the University of Leeds and is currently engaged on a democratic audit of the European Union. Previous books include works on Democracy, Legitimacy and the EU.

Joni Lovenduski is Anniversary Professor of Politics at Birkbeck College, London,. She is author of various books on women's political representation in Britain and Europe, candidate selection and equality policy.

Helen Margetts is the Director of the School of Public Policy at University College, London and is a Professor of Political Science. She is an expert on electoral systems and has acted as a consultant on the design of alternative electoral systems to the Jenkins Commission on Voting Reform, the government office for London, the Royal Commission on the House of Lords and Lewisham Council.

Colin Mellors is Professor of Political Science at the University of Bradford. He has written widely on British politics, including The British MP.

Gay Moon is discrimination legal officer at JUSTICE and co-author of The Discrimination Handbook.

Anisa Niaz is a legal research officer at JUSTICE.

Richard Norton-Taylor is a *Guardian* journalist and author of various books on British government and the intelligence services.

Ellie Palmer lectures in Law at the University of Essex and is a member of the Public Law and Human Rights team.

Roisin Pillay is Senior Legal Officer at JUSTICE and works on the implementation of the Human Rights Act and of international human rights standards in UK law.

Madeleine Shaw is a barrister at Ami Feder's Chambers, Lamb Building, and was previously a specialist in immigration and asylum at the House of Commons Library

Chris Skelcher is Professor of Local Government Studies at INLOGOV, at the University of Birmingham. He has recently been closely involved in developing new council constitutions in the UK.

Robin Wilson is the director and founder of Democratic Dialogue. Previously he was editor of Fortnight, the current affairs review in Northern Ireland.

Mitchell Woolf is a solicitor specialising in human rights law and, in particular, the rights of the child. He is a researcher at Doughty Street Chambers.

Authors

David Beetham is a former Professor at the University of Leeds and he has written widely on issues of democracy and human rights. He has been involved with Democratic Audit since its inauguration, and has also directed international programmes of comparative democracy assessments.

Iain Byrne is Commonwealth Law Officer at Interights. He was formerly research officer at Democratic Audit and is a Fellow of the Human Rights Centre, University of Essex. He has written on the human rights of street children and is co-author of UK Human Rights Digest.

Pauline Ngan is research officer to Dr Tony Wright MP. Previously she was part-time research officer at the Democratic Audit. Originally from New Zealand she worked at Victoria University and the Ministry of Justice.

Stuart Weir is Director of Democratic Audit. He is Visiting Professor and Senior Research Fellow at the University of Essex and was previously editor of the *New Statesman*. In 1988 he founded Charter88.

References

References are divided into a section for published books and chapters, a section for government and parliamentary reports and a final section for reports from non-governmental organisations. The division between individual and NGO publications is not watertight and it will sometimes be necessary to check both sections for a particular work. Parliamentary debates and media references are cited in the text. HC Deb and HL Deb are references to the Hansard for the debate shown; WA indicates entries in the relevant Written Answer section of Hansard. Among governmental reports, TSO stands for The Stationery Office.

Books and chapters

Anwar, M, 1994, *Race and Elections: Participation of Ethnic Minorities in Politics*, Centre for Research in Ethnic Relations, Warwick University

Arter, D, 1996, 'The Folketing and Denmark's European Policy: the Case of an Authorising Assembly' in Norton, P (ed.), *National Parliaments and the European Union*, Frank Cass

Ashdown, P, 2001, *The Ashdown Diaries, Volume Two 1997 – 1999*, Allen Lane, The Penguin Press

Barker, A, 1998, 'Public Policy Inquiry and Advice as an Aspect of Constitutional Reform', in *Journal of Legislative Studies*, vol 4, No. 2 (summer)

Barker, A, 1999, *Ruling by Task Force: The Politico's Guide to Labour's New Elite*, Politico's

Barnett, S, and Curry, A, 1994, *The Battle for the BBC: a British Broadcasting Conspiracy?*, Aurum Press

Barnett, S, and Seymour, E, 1999, *A shrinking iceberg travelling south...Changing Trends in British Television*, University of Westminster, London

Beetham, D, Bracking, S, Kearton, I, and Weir, S, 2002a, *International IDEA Handbook on Democracy Assessment*, Kluwer Law International, The Hague, Netherlands

Beetham, D, Bracking, S, Kearton, I, Vittal, N, and Weir, S, (eds), 2002b, *The State of Democracy: Democracy Assessment in Eight Nations Around the World*, Kluwer Law International, The Hague, Netherlands

Bell, D, and Christie, A, 2001, 'Finance-The Barnett Formula: Nobody's Child?', in Trench, A (ed), *The State of the Nations 2001: The Second Year of Devolution*, Constitution Unit/Academic Imprint

Blackburn, R, 1995, *The Electoral System in Britain*, Macmillan

Bower, T, 2001, *The Paymaster*, Pocket Books

Boyd, C, 1997, 'Parliaments and Courts: Powers and Dispute Resolution', in Bates, T StJ N, (ed,), *Devolution to Scotland: The Legal Aspects*, T & T Clark, Edinburgh

Bradshaw, J, 2000, *Civic involvement*, Poverty and Social Exclusion Survey

Branson, N, 1985, History of the Communist Party of Great Britain 1927-41, Lawrence and Wishart

Burch, M, and Holliday, I, 1999, 'An executive office in all but name; The Prime Minister's and cabinet offices in the UK', *Parliamentary Affairs*, vol 52, No. 2, April

Burchardt, T, 2000, *Enduring Economic Exclusion: disabled people, income and work* Joseph Rowntree Foundation/York Publishing Services

Burchardt, T, Le Grand, J, and Piachaud, D, (forthcoming), 'Degrees of Exclusion: Developing a Dynamic, Multi-Dimensional Measure,' in Hills, J, Le Grand, J, Piachaud, D, (eds), *Understanding Social Exclusion*, Oxford University Press

Butler, D, Adonis, A, and Travers, T, 1994, *Failure in British Government: the politics of the Poll Tax*, Oxford University Press

Byrne, I, 1997, *The Roots of Democratic Exclusion*, Democratic Audit/Human Rights Centre, University of Essex, Colchester

Burrows, N, 2000, *Devolution*, Sweet and Maxwell, (cited in Osmond, J, 2001)

Campbell, A, 1999, *Beyond Spin: Government and the Media*, in Tony Hall et al, *Broadcasting Politics*, Fabian Society

Clarke, A F N, 1983, *Contact*, Secker and Warburg

Clarke, R, 2002, *New Democratic Processes: better decisions, stronger democracy*, Institute for Public Policy Research

Cowley, P, Darcy, D, Mellors, C, Neal, J, and Stuart, M, 2000, 'Mr. Blair's Loyal Opposition? The Liberal Democrats in Parliament', *British Elections & Parties Review*, vol.10, Frank Cass

Cowley, P, and Stuart, M, 2001, 'Parliament: Mostly Continuity', in UK 2001, *Parliamentary Affairs*, vol. 55, No. 2

Cowley, P, 2002, *Revolts and Rebellions: Parliamentary Voting Under Blair*, Politico's

Coxall, B, 2001, *Pressure Groups in British Politics*, Pearson Education, Harlow

Curtice, J, and Steed, M, 2002, 'Appendix 2: An Analysis of the Results', in Butler, D, and Kavanah, D, *The British General Election of 2001*, Palgrave

Dahrendorf, R, 2001, Arnold Goodman Lecture 2001, quoted in *Guardian Society*, 18 July 2001

Daintith, T, and Page, A, 1999, *The Executive in the Constitution: Structure, Autonomy and Internal Control*, Oxford University Press

Davis Smith, J, 1997, *The 1997 National Survey of Volunteering*, Institute for Volunteering Research

Deakin, N, and Parry, R, 2000, *The Treasury and Social Policy?*, Economic and Social Research Council/Macmillan, Basingstoke

De Smith S, A, and Brazier, R, 1998, *Constitutional and Administrative Law*, Eighth Edition, Penguin

Doig, A, 2001, 'Sleaze: Picking Up the Threads or 'Back to Basics' Scandals?', *Parliamentary Affairs*, vol. 54, No. 2

Dunleavy, P, 1995, 'Policy Disasters: explaining the UK's record', *Public Policy and Administration* 10 (2)

Dunleavy, P, Margetts, H, and Weir, S, 1996, *The Other National Lottery: Misrepresentation and Malapportionment in British Elections*. Charter88/Human Rights Centre, University of Essex,

Dunleavy, P, Margetts, H, O'Duffy, B, and Weir, S, 1997, *Making Votes Count: replaying the 1990s general elections under alternative election systems*, Democratic Audit Paper 12, Human Rights Centre, University of Essex, Colchester

Dunleavy, P, Margetts, H, and Weir, S, 1998, *The Politico's Guide to Electoral Reform in Britain*, Politico's

Dunleavy, P, Margetts, H, Smith, T, and Weir, S, 2001, *Voices of the People: Popular Attitudes to Democratic Renewal in Britain*, Politico's

Dummett, A, 2001, 'Ministerial Statements, the immigration exception in the Race Relations (Amendment Act 2002), at www.ilpa.org.uk

Edmonds, T, 2001, *The Barnett Formula*, House of Commons Library

Flinders, M and McConnel, H, 1998, 'Maybe Minister: Quangoes and Accountability' in Flinders,M, and Smith, M J, (eds) *Quangos, Accountability and Reform: The Politics of Quasi-Government*, Macmillan, Basingstoke

Flynn, P, 1999, *Dragons Led By Poodles: The Inside Story of a New Labour Stitch-up*, Politico's

Gannon, M, 2000, *The Human Resources of the Top 200 Income-generating Charities: Report on a Survey*, Institute for Volunteering Research

Gardiner, K, Hills, J, Falkingham, J, Lechene, V, and Sutherland, H, 1995, *The Effects of Differences in Housing and Health Care Systems on International Comparisons of Income Distribution*, London School of Economics

Gaskin, K, and Davis Smith, J, 1997, *A New Civil Europe? A Study of the Extent and Role of Volunteering*, The National Volunteering Centre, London

Genn, H, 1999, *Paths to Justice: what do people do and think about going to law*, Hart Publishing, Oxford/Portland Oregon

Giddings, P, and Drewry, G, 1996, *Westminster and Europe: The Impact of the European Union on the Westminster Parliament.* Macmillan, Basingstoke

Glover, J (ed), 2001, *The Guardian Companion to the 2001 General Election*, Atlantic Books

Gordon, D, et al, 2000, *Poverty and social exclusion in Britain*, Joseph Rowntree Foundation, York

Gregg, P, Harkness, S, and Machin, S, 1999, *Child Development and Family Income*, York Publishing Services/Joseph Rowntree Foundation

Hadfield,B, 2002, (forthcoming) 'Towards an English Constitution', *Current Legal Problems*, Oxford University Press

Harris, R, 1994, *The Media Trilogy*, Faber and Faber (originally Harris, R, 1990, *Good and Faithful Servant*, Faber and Faber)

Hayes-Renshaw, F, and Wallace, H, 1997, *The Council of Ministers*, Macmillan, Basingstoke

Hepple, B, Coussey, M, Choudhury, T, 2000, *Equality: A New Framework, Report of the Independent Review of the Enforcement of UK Anti-Discrimination Law*, Hart Publishing, Oxford

Hird, C, 1993, 'Rupert Murdoch', in *Index on Censorship*, vol. 23

Hogg, S, and Hill, J, 1995, *Too Close to Call: power and politics – John Major in No. 10*, Warner

Holliday, I, 2000, 'Executives and Administrations', in Dunleavy et al, *Developments in British Politics*, Macmillan, Basingstoke

Howard, C, Kenway, P, Palmer, G, and Street, C, 1998, *Monitoring poverty and social exclusion : Labour's inheritance*, New Policy Institute

Jones, N, 1995, *Soundbites and Spin Doctors*, Cassell

Jones, N, 1999, *Sultans of Spin: the media and the New Labour government*, Gollancz

Jones, N, 2001, *The Control Freaks*, Politico's

Jordan, G, and Maloney, W, 1997, *The Protest Business?*, Manchester University Press

Jordan, G, 1998, 'Politics without Parties', *Parliamentary Affairs*

King, A, 2001, *Does the United Kingdom still have a constitution?*, (the Hamlyn Lectures), Sweet & Maxwell

Kitson, F, 1971, 'Low intensity operations: Subversion, insurgency, peace-keeping' Faber & Faber

Klug, F, Starmer, K, and Weir, S, 1996, *The Three Pillars of Liberty: political rights and freedoms in the United Kingdom*, Routledge

Leach, S, and Game, G, 2000, *Hung Authorities*, York Publishing Services (for the Joseph Rowntree Foundation)

Leather, P, et al, 2000, *The state of UK housing*' (Second Edition), (factfile on housing conditions and housing renewal policies), Policy Press/Joseph Rowntree Foundation

Lester, A, and Bindman, G, 1972, *Race and Law*, Penguin Education

Lovenduski, J, 2001, 'Women and Politics: Minority Representation or Critical Mass', in Norris, P, (ed), *Britain Votes 2001*, Oxford University Press

Lovenduski, J, 2002, 'Feminising Politics', inaugural professorial lecture, Birkbeck College

McFadyean, M, and Rowland, D, 2002, *PFI, vs Democracy? The Case of Birmingham's Hospitals*, Menard Press.

McLean, I, 2000, 'A Fiscal Constitution for the UK', in Chen, S, and Wright, T (eds), *The English Question*, Fabian Society

McLeod, M, et al, 2001, *Black and Minority Ethnic Voluntary and Community Organisations*, Policy Studies Institute for Joseph Rowntree Foundation

Mair, P, 1997, *Party System Change: Approaches and Interpretations*, Clarendon Press, Oxford

Mair, P, 2000, 'Partyless Democracy: Solving the Paradox of New Labour' in *New Left Review*, No.2

Marr, A, 1995, *The Battle for Scotland*, Penguin

Marr, A, 1995, *Ruling Britannia*, Michael Joseph

Marshall, J N, Lewis, P, Belt, V, Richardson, R, and Parkinson, A, 2001, 'The impact of organisational and technological change on women's employment in the civil service', *The Service Industries Journal*, vol. 21, No. 2

Masterman, R, and Mitchell, J, 2001, 'Devolution and the Centre' in Trench, A, *The State of the Nations 2001*, Imprint Academic

Matthews, H., et al, 1999, 'Young people's participation and representation in society', *Geoforum 30*, 135-144

Minkin, L, 1978, *The Labour Party Conference*, Allen Lane, The Penguin Press

Minkin, L, 1991, *The Contentious Alliance – Trade Unions and the Labour Party*, Edinburgh University Press, Edinburgh

Modood, T, and Berthoud, R, 1997, *Ethnic Minorities in Britain, Diversity and Disadvantage*, Policy Studies Institute

Monbiot, G, 2000, *Captive State: The Corporate Takeover of Britain*, Macmillan, Basingstoke

Moodie, G C, 1964, *The Government of Great Britain*, Thomas Crowell, New York

Moravcsik, A, 1998, *The Choice for Europe*, University College London Press

Morison, J, 2000, 'The government-voluntary sector compacts', *Journal of Law and Society*, vol 27, No. 1

Morrison, J, 2002, *Reforming Britain: New Labour, New Constitution*, Reuters

Nairn, T, 2002, *Pariah: Misfortunes of the British Kingdom*, Verso

Newton, K, 1997, 'Politics and the news media', in Jowell, J, et al (eds), *British Social Attitudes: the 14th report*, Ashgate/Social and Community Planning Research, Aldershot

Norton, P, 1975, *Dissension in the House of Commons: Intra-Party Dissent in the House of Commons Division Lobbies 1945-74*, Macmillan, Basingstoke

Norton, P, 1978, *Conservative Dissidents: Dissent Within the Parliament Conservative Party 1970-74*, Temple-Smith

Norton, P, 1980, *Dissension in the House of Commons 1974-79*, Oxford University Press, Oxford

Norton, P, 1993, *Does Parliament Matter?*, Harvester Wheatsheaf, Hemel Hempstead

Norton, P, 1994, 'The parties in parliament' in Robins, L, Blackmore, H, and Pyper, R, (eds), *Britain's Changing Party System*, Leicester University Press

Norton, P, 1996, 'The United Kingdom : Political Conflict, Parliamentary Scrutiny' in Norton, P, (ed), *National Parliaments and the European Union*, Frank Cass

Norton-Taylor, R, Lloyd, M, and Cook, S, 1996, *Knee Deep in Dishonour: the Scott Report and its Aftermath*, Gollancz

Oborne, P, 1999, *Alastair Campbell: New Labour and the Rise of the Media Class*, Atrium Press

Osmond, J, 2001, 'In Search of Stability: Coalition Politics in Wales', in Trench, A (ed), *The State of the Nations 2001: The Second Year of Devolution*, Constitution Unit/Academic Imprint

Palast, G, 2002, *The Best Democracy Money Can Buy*, Pluto Press

Parry, G, et al, 1992, *Political Participation and Democracy in Britain*, Cambridge University Press, Cambridge

Parekh, B, 2000, *The Future of Multi Ethnic Britain* (the Parekh Report), Profile Books

Passey, A, et al, 2000, *The UK Voluntary Sector Almanac 2000*, National Council for Volunteers Overseas Publications

Peele, G, 1998, 'Towards 'new Conservatives'? Organisational reform and the Tory party', *Political Quarterly*, vol.69

Pinto-Duschinsky, M, 2001, *Handbook on Funding of Parties and Election Campaigns: Overview*, International IDEA, Stockholm

Prosser, T, 1983, *Test Cases for the Poor*, Poverty Pamphlet 60, Child Poverty Action Group

Rao, N, and Young, K, 1999, 'Revitalising Local Democracy', in *British Social Attitudes* (sixteenth Report), Ashgate, Aldershot

Rawnsley, A, 2000, *Servants of the People*, Hamish Hamilton

Rhodes, R, and Dunleavy, P, 1995, *The Prime Minister, Cabinet and Core Executive*, Macmillan, Basingstoke

Riddell, P, 1999, 'A shift of power – and influence,' *British Journalism Review*, vol. 10, No. 3

Richards, P, 2000, *Is the Party Over? New Labour and the Politics of Participation*, , Fabian Pamphlet 594, Fabian Society

Robertson, G, and Nichol, A, 1992, *Media Law*, Penguin

Saggar, S, 2001, 'The General Election and Beyond', *Connections*, Commission for Racial Equality

Sampson, A, 1997, 'The crisis at the heart of our media', *British Journalism Review*, vol 7, No. 3

Sanders, P, 1998, 'Tackling Racial Discrimination' in Blackstone, T, Parekh, B, and Sanders P, *Race Relations in Britain: a Developing Agenda*, Routledge

Seeley, A, 2001, *Taxation of Charities*, Research Paper 01/46, House of Commons

Seyd, P, and Whiteley, P, 1992, *Labour's Grassroots*, Clarendon Press, Oxford

Seyd, P, 1999, 'New parties/new politics: a case study of the British Labour party' in *Party Politics*, vol 5

Shell, D, 1993, 'Conclusion' in Shell, D, and Beamish, D (eds), *The House of Lords at Work*, Clarendon Press, Oxford

Skelcher, C , and Davis, H, 1996, 'Understanding the new magistracy: a study of characteristics and attitudes', *Local Government Studies*, Summer

Smith, M, 1999, *The Core Executive in Britain*, Macmillan

Tarling, R, 2000, 'Editorial statistics on the voluntary sector in the UK', Journal of the Royal Statistical Society, vol.163, No.3

Taylor, R, 2001, 'Employment Relations Policy', in Seldon, A (ed), *The Blair Effect*, Little, Brown and Company

Timmins, N, 2001, *The Five Giants: A Biography of the Welfare State*, HarperCollins

Turner, J, W, C, 1964, *Russell on Crime*, Twelfth edition, Stevens & Sons

Watson, M, 2001, *Year Zero: an inside view of the Scottish Parliament*, Polygon, Edinburgh

Webb, P, 2000, *The Modern British Party System*, Sage

Weir, S, 1994, *Bad Timing*, Violation Paper 23, Charter 88

Weir, S, and Beetham, D, 1999, *Political Power and Democratic Control in Britain*, Routledge

Whiteley, P, Richardson, J, and Seyd, P, 1994, *True Blues*, Oxford University Press, Oxford

Willetts, D, 1998, 'Conservative Renewal' in *Political Quarterly*, vol 69

Wilkinson, P, et al, 2001, *Cold Comfort: the social and environmental determinants of excess winter deaths in England, 1986-96*, Policy Press, University of Bristol (from Marston Book Services, Abingdon)

Wilford, R, and Wilson, R, 2001, *Democratic Design: The Political Style of the Northern Ireland Assembly*, Constitution Unit

Winter, G, 1981, *Inside BOSS*, Allen Lane

Woodhouse, D, 1994, *Ministers and Parliament: accountability in theory and practice*, Clarendon Press, Oxford

Wright, T, 1994, *Citizens and Subjects*, Routledge

Wright, T, 2002, *The British Political Process: An Introduction*, Routledge

Wring, D, Baker, D, and Seawright, D, 2000, 'Panelism in action: Labour's 1999 European Parliamentary Candidate Selections', *Political Quarterly*, vol 71, No.2

Government and parliamentary reports

Cabinet Office, 1994, *Equal Opportunities for Women in the Civil Service: 10 Years Progress Report, 1984-94*, Cabinet Office

Cabinet Office, 2001, *Report of the Quinquennial Review of the Committee on Standards in Public Life*, Cabinet Office

Cabinet Office and DTLR, 2002, *Your Region, Your Choice: Revitalising the English Regions*, Cm 5511, TSO

Committee on Standards in Public Life (Nolan Committee), 1995, *Standards in Public Life*, Cm 2850, May, HMSO

Committee on Standards in Public Life, 1996, *Local Public Spending Bodies*, Cm 3270, May, HMSO

Committee on Standards in Public Life, 1997, *Misuse of Public Office: A New Offence?*, TSO

Committee on Standards in Public Life, 1997, *Review of Standards of Conduct in Executive NDPBs, NHS Trusts and Local Public Spending Bodies*, November, TSO

Committee on Standards in Public Life (Neill Committee), 2000a, *Reinforcing Standards: Review of the First Report of the Committee on Standards in Public Life*, Cm 4557, TSO

Committee on Standards in Public Life, 2000b, *Standards of Conduct in the House of Lords*, Cm 4903, November, TSO

Crowther-Hunt (Lord) and Peacock, A T, 1973, 'Memorandum of Dissent', the Kilbrandon Report, vol ii

Department of Social Security (DSS), 2000, *Income Research Centre, Estimates of Take-ups 1998/99*, DSS Electoral Commission, 2001, *Election 2001*, Politico's

Hammond, A, 2001, *Review of the Circumstances Surrounding an Application for Naturalisation by Mr S P Hinduja in 1998,* HC 287, March, TSO

Home Affairs Committee, 1999, *Accountability of the Security Service*, HC 291, TSO

Home Office, 2000a, *Statistics on Race and the Criminal Justice System: A Home Office publication under section 95 of the Criminal Justice Act 1991*, Home Office

Home Office, 2000b, *Ethnic differences in decisions on young defendants dealt with by the Crown Prosecution Service* – Section 95 Findings No. 1 by Barclay, G, and Mulanga, B, Home Office

Independent Commission on the Voting System (the Jenkins report), 1998, *Report of the Independent Commission on the Voting System*, Cm 4090, TSO

Jenkins report, 1998, see Independent Commission on the Voting System above

Joint Committee on Human Rights, 2001, *Anti-Terrorism, Crime and Security Bill*, HC 372 (second report) and HC 420 (fifth report), TSO

Joint Committee on Parliamentary Privilege, 1999, *Report and Proceedings of the Committee*, HC 214/HL 43, 30 March, TSO

Kershaw, C, et al, 2000, *The 2000 British Crime Survey: England and Wales*, Home Office

Kilbrandon report, 1973, *Report of the Royal Commission on the Constitution 1969-1973*, Cmnd 5460, HMSO

Law Commission, 1998, *Legislating the Criminal Code: Corruption*, LC 248, Law Commission

Leggatt report, 2001, *Tribunals for Users: One System, One Service*, Lord Chancellor's Department, TSO

Liaison Committee, 2000, *Shifting the Balance: Select Committees and the Executive*, HC 300, TSO

Liaison Committee, 2000, *Independence or Control? The government's reply*, HC 748, TSO

Liaison Committee, 2001, *Shifting the Balance: Unfinished Business*, HC 321, TSO

Liaison Committee, 2002, *The Prime Minister: Minutes of Evidence*, HC 1095, TSO

Macpherson, W, 1999, *The Stephen Lawrence Inquiry: Report of an inquiry by Sir William Macpherson of Cluny*, TSO

Morgan, R, and Russell, N, 2000, *The Judiciary in the Magistrates' Courts*, Home Office/Lord Chancellor's Office

Northern Ireland Human Rights Commission, 2001, *Making a Bill of Rights for Northern Ireland: a consultation paper*, NIHRC

Public Accounts Committee, 1999, *Financial Management and Control in the EU*, HC 960, TSO

Public Administration Select Committee, (PASC), 1998, *The Government Information and Communication Service*, HC 770, 29 July, TSO

PASC, 1999, *Freedom of Information Draft Bill*, HC 570, 28 July, TSO

PASC, 2001a, *Ministerial Accountability and Parliamentary Questions*, HC 61, TSO

PASC, 2001b, *The Ministerial Code: Improving the Rule Book*, HC 235, TSO

PASC, 2001c, *Special Advisers: Boon or Bane?*, HC 293, TSO

PASC, 2001d, *Mapping the Quango State*, HC 367, TSO

PASC, 2001e, *Public Participation: Issues and Innovations* (the government's response to the Committee's Sixth Report of Session 2000-01), HC 334, TSO

PASC, 2001f, *Making Government Work: The Emerging Issues*, HC 94, TSO

PASC, 2002a, *Government Information and Communication, Minutes of Evidence for Thursday 28 February 2002*, HC 303-i, 28 February, TSO

PASC, 2002b, *The Ministerial Code: Improving the Rule Book: The Government Response to the Committee's Third Report of Session 2000-01*, HC 439, TSO

PASC, 2002c, *Special Advisers: Boon or Bane: The Government Response to the Committee's Fourth Report of Session 2000-01*, HC 463, TSO

PASC, 2002d, *Ministerial Accountability and Parliamentary Questions: The Government Response to the Committee's Second Report of Session 2000-01*, HC 464, TSO

PASC, 2002e, *The Second Chamber: Continuing the Reform*, HC 494, TSO

PASC, 2002f, *The Second Chamber: Continuing the Reform: The Government Response to the Committee's Fifth Report*, HC 794), TSO

PASC, 2002g, *'These Unfortunate Events': Lessons of Recent Events at the former Department of Transport, Local Government and the Regions*, HC 303, TSO

Public Service Committee, 1996, *Ministerial Accountability and Responsibility*, HC 313, HMSO

Royal Commission on the Reform of the House of Lords (the Wakeham report), 2000, *A House for the Future*, Cm 4534, TSO

Social Exclusion Unit, 2000, *National Strategy for Neighbourhood Renewal: a Framework for Consultation*, Cabinet Office, TSO

Stephen Lawrence Inquiry, 1999, *The Stephen Lawrence Inquiry: Report of an Inquiry by Sir William Macpherson of Cluny*, Cm 4262, TSO

Treasury, 1999, *Persistent Poverty and Lifetime Inequality: The Evidence* (the UK's Fifteenth Periodic Report to the UN Committee on the Elimination of all forms of Racial Discrimination) Occasional Paper No. 10, Treasury

UN Human Rights Committee, 2001, *Concluding Observations: United Kingdom of Great Britain and Northern Ireland*, CCPR/CO/3/UK; CCPR/CO/73/UKOT, Geneva

Wanless, D, 2001, *Securing our Future Health: Taking a Long-Term View (Interim Report)*, November, HM Treasury

Walton, R, 2000, Office for National Statistics, *International comparisons of company profitability*, *Economic Trends*, No. 565 December, HMSO

Weller, P, Feldman, A, and Purdam, K, 2001, Religious Discrimination in England and Wales – Home Office Research Study 220, Home Office

Non-governmental reports

Brewer, M, Clark, T, and Goodman, A, 2002, *The government's child poverty target: how much progress has been made?*, Institute of Fiscal Studies

Bridges, L, Choong, S, and McConville, M, 1997, *Ethnic Minority Defendants and the Right to Elect Jury Trial: An Examination of Data drawn from ESRC Study of Decision Making of Ethnic Minority Defendants in the Criminal Justice System*, Economic and Social Research Council

Charity Commission, 1998a, *The Review of the Register of Charities*, Charity Commission

Charity Commission, 1998b, *The Independence of Charities from the State*, Charity Commission

Citizens Advice Bureau Service, 2000, *Review of Tribunals Consultation Paper: A Response by the Citizens Advice Bureau Service*, CABS

Council of Civil Service Unions, 1996, Second Among Equals: Women's Experience of Employment in the Civil Service, How Much Progress, Council of Civil Service Unions

Democratic Audit, 2002, *House of Lords Reform: The case for a modern and responsible Second Chamber* (Evidence to the Lord Chancellor's Department in response to the White Paper on House of Lords Reform), Human Rights Centre,University of Essex

Gordon, D, Townsend, P, Levitas, R, Pantasis, C, Payne, S, Patsios, D, et al, 2000, *Poverty and Social Exclusion in Britain*, Joseph Rowntree foundation, York

Green, A, and Philo, J, 2000, *Concerns of the National Association of Citizen's Advice Bureaux on the operation of the Community Legal Service*, The Legal Executive Journal, ILEX Publishing and Advertising Services Ltd

Hansard Society, 1993, *Making the Law: The Report of the Hansard Society Commission on the Legislative Process*, Hansard Society

Hansard Society Commission on Parliamentary Scrutiny, 2001, *The Challenge for Parliament: Making Government Accountable*, Vacher Dod

Hutton Commission, 2000, (for the Association of Community Health Council for England and Wales), *New Life for Health*, Vintage Original

Inquest 2000–01, press releases, 20 and 24 Novemebr 2000, 17 January and 18 May, 2001

Law Society, 2000a, *Review of Tribunals – Law Society Response*,
http://www.lawsoc.org.uk/dcs/third_tier.asp?section_id=3868

Nathan, M, 2000, *In Search of Work : Employment strategies for a risky world*, Industrial Society

National Council for Black Volunteering, 2000, *Noticeable by their Absence*, National Council for Black Volunteering

Nazroo, J Y, 1997, *The Health of Britain's Ethnic Minorities*, Policy Studies Institute

Oxfam, 2002a, *Rigged Rules and Double Standards*, Oxfam, Oxford

Oxfam and the Refugee Council, 2002b, *Poverty and Asylum in the UK*, Oxfam, and the Refugee Council
Peak, S, and Fisher, P (eds), 2001, *The Guardian Media Guide*, Atlantic Books

Poverty and Social Exclusion Survey, 2000, *Poverty and Social Exclusion in Britain*, Joseph Rowntree Foundation, York

Royal United Services Institute (RUSI), 1988, *The Outcome of the Strategic Defence Review: summary of the RUSI Seminar*, RUSI

The Runnymede Trust, 2000, *The Future of Multi Ethnic Britain – The Parekh Report*, Profile Books

Index